Pastplay

DIGITAL HUMANITIES

The Digital Humanities series provides a forum for ground-breaking and benchmark work in digital humanities, lying at the intersections of computers and the disciplines of arts and humanities, library and information science, media and communications studies, and cultural studies.

Series Editors:
Julie Thompson Klein, Wayne State University
Tara McPherson, University of Southern California
Paul Conway, University of Michigan

Teaching History in the Digital Age
T. Mills Kelly

Hacking the Academy: New Approaches to Scholarship and Teaching from Digital Humanities
Daniel J. Cohen and Tom Scheinfeldt, Editors

Writing History in the Digital Age
Jack Dougherty and Kristen Nawrotzki, Editors

Pastplay: Teaching and Learning History with Technology
Kevin Kee, Editor

DIGITALCULTUREBOOKS, an imprint of the University of Michigan Press, is dedicated to publishing work in new media studies and the emerging field of digital humanities.

Pastplay

Teaching and Learning History with Technology

Kevin Kee, *Editor*

The University of Michigan Press
Ann Arbor

Published in the United States of America by
The University of Michigan Press
Manufactured in the United States of America
♾ Printed on acid-free paper

2017   2016   2015   2014   4   3   2   1

A CIP catalog record for this book is available from the British Library.

DOI: http://dx.doi.org/10.3998/dh.12544152.0001.001
ISBN 978-0-472-11937-0 (cloth: alk paper)
ISBN 978-0-472-03595-3 (paper: alk paper)
ISBN 978-0-472-12048-2 (e-book)

This book has been published with the financial support of the Canada
Research Chairs program, and the Social Sciences and Humanities Research
Council of Canada Strategic Knowledge Clusters Grants program.

Social Sciences and Humanities   Conseil de recherches en
Research Council of Canada   sciences humaines du Canada   Canada

This volume is the second major publication of The History Education
Network/Histoire et éducation en réseau (THEN/HiER).

the history education network
THEN HiER
histoire et éducation en réseau

Contents

WITH TECHNOLOGY

BY BUILDING

Acknowledgments

"Community, relationship, play." The April 2010 symposium from which this book emerged was a testament to the words with which contributor Stephen Ramsay closes his chapter. Written before we met, his maxim became the catchphrase of our meeting in Niagara-on-the-Lake, Canada. Credit for that spirit is due to the symposium participants, who became (along with their co-authors) the contributors to this volume. Thanks to Timothy Compeau, Patrick Dunae, Devon Elliott, Sean Gouglas, Shawn Graham, T. Mills Kelly, Stéphane Lévesque, Richard Levy, John Sutton Lutz, Robert MacDougall, Jeremiah McCall, Bethany Nowviskie, Stephen Ramsay, Geoffrey Rockwell, Ruth Sandwell, Brenda Trofanenko, and William J. Turkel. The two days we spent together were one of the most rewarding experiences of my academic career.

I am especially indebted to William J. Turkel, who helped me conceive of the *Pastplay* project, and then pushed it beyond its initial scope. This book is broader and deeper as a result of his imagination and wisdom. Matthew Kirschenbaum, who was unable to attend the symposium, later added an important dimension to our collection with his chapter on history and board games. Several months after the meeting, Geoffrey Rockwell and I met to conceptualize the introduction. He was characteristically insightful and generous, and our fruitful collaboration was a fitting coda to the project.

The gifted graduate students with whom I have had the pleasure of working with played an important role from beginning to end. Tom Mitrovic helped organize the initial gathering; as the symposium drew to a close, he received the thanks he deserved. "It was," he was told on several occasions, "the best meeting that I've ever attended." Nicki Darbyson, Emily Nolan, and Spencer Roberts supported the editing; and Spencer organized the index, with some playful technology and a lot of elbow grease. Thanks as well to the anonymous reviewers whose careful appraisal underscored the need for this book, and led to the improvement of its contents.

The University of Michigan Press, and specifically the "digitalculturebooks" imprint, was the ideal destination for our book. Many thanks to then-Editor-in-Chief Thomas Dwyer, who agreed to publish *Pastlpay*; and Editorial Assistant Christopher Dreyer, who shepherded it to completion. At BookComp, Nicholle Lutz expertly guided me through the final editorial process.

Pastplay would not have been possible without the financial support of The History Education Network/Histoire et éducation en réseau (THEN/HiER). Led by Penney Clark at the University of British Columbia, THEN/HiER is the first pan-Canadian organization devoted to promoting and improving history teaching and learning by bringing together the multiple and varied constituencies involved in history education. Penney and my fellow THEN/HiER board members have been enthusiastic supporters of the project from the beginning, and I am honored that *Pastplay* is THEN/HiER's second major publication. Along with Penney, I gratefully acknowledge the financial support of the Social Sciences and Humanities Research Council of Canada and its Strategic Knowledge Clusters Program which has funded THEN/HiER, and sub-projects such as this book. I also appreciate the support of the Canada Research Chairs program, and Brock University, both of which provided me with the time and funds to bring Pastplay to completion.

At home, Anne-Marie, Jacob, and Kathleen personify playfulness. They do not share my interest in its research, they simply make it happen. Finally this book is dedicated to the community of researchers, educators, practitioners, and students who are exploring imaginative, engaging ways to use new tools and environments to analyze and express history. I look forward to what emerges next from our sandbox.

Introduction

Kevin Kee

"I think you've missed your audience." The speaker was a digital humanities colleague, and an amiable guy. His intent was to broker a peace, and perhaps save me from myself. I had been invited to present to a group of scholars and graduate students. All were humanists, some historians, and all for the most part interested in digital technology. The conference had been impeccably organized, the graduate students passionate and interested, and the host a paragon of hospitality. Following dinner with the organizers the night before, I had phoned home to say that it had been one of the most enjoyable social evenings I had spent with a group of strangers. But in the minutes following my presentation, that collegiality seemed to be evaporating.

My talk had outlined a new vision for the use of technology in history teaching and research, inspired by the scholars whose chapters can be found in the pages that follow. When my presentation ended, the room erupted. On one side were those who welcomed my call for a change in how we conceptualize and practice our work—as historians in particular, and as humanists in general. On the other were those who saw this call as an attack on the core of our discipline.

"I think you've missed your audience."

The speaker pointed out that those in the room who found my call misguided (if not offensive) traded in text: the core currency of the humanities. What I had referred to as "playing with technology" seemed to imply substituting cold computer code for that which they most treasured, which would require a level of expertise they did not possess. It was fine for me to follow this track, but few people in the room could manipulate (never mind master) the tools required. The presentation that I had given was not wrong; I had just chosen the wrong audience. Let's get back to what we were doing, my colleague suggested—you in your sandbox, and we in ours.

But the researchers and teachers in that room were *exactly* my audience. "Playing with technology" does not demand that we turn our backs on the substance or practices of our disciplines; indeed, the pillars of the humanities lend themselves to playful engagement. And expertise in sophisticated computer programming skills is not a prerequisite. All that is required is a commitment to, as contributor Stephen Ramsay observes in chapter 5 of this book, "community, relationship, and play."

At the same time, I understood my colleague's perspective. His response is not uncommon among humanists. In the second decade of the twenty-first century, we find ourselves in a research and teaching environment characterized by declining financial support and increasing use of technologies that were designed for business. A playful approach to teaching and learning with technology can seem like the worst of all possible worlds: the coupling of strategies developed for entertainment with tools created for commerce.

The contributors to this book have found themselves in situations similar to the one that I encountered at my presentation. We share our "non-digital" colleagues' concern about losing practices centuries in the making, and their anxiety that the use of computing technology requires skill sets that they do not possess. The contributors to this volume came together to craft a response to those concerns at a symposium held in Niagara-on-the-Lake, Canada, in the spring of 2010. Funded by The History Education Network / Histoire et Éducation en Réseau and the Social Sciences and Humanities Research Council of Canada,[1] the gathering brought together academic historians, public historians, digital humanists, history educators, graduate students, and practicing teachers.

We recognized that our work forms part of a larger conversation about the future of the humanities. In his introduction to *Switching Codes: Thinking Through Digital Technology in the Humanities and the Arts* (an influential anthology of conversations among scholars, artists, and information technology specialists) editor Thomas Bartscherer observes:

> To understand how digital technology is transforming thought and practice in the humanities and the arts, it is necessary to cultivate cross-cultural communication, to establish points of reference, and to develop a shared vocabulary. Given the globalized and decentralized nature of digital culture, this cannot be mandated from the top down, as it were, but must be cobbled together from the bottom up and on the fly. The intention here is not to compile an authoritative survey—truly a quixotic endeavour in such a rapidly changing landscape—but to model and catalyze a conversation.[2]

This is our aim too, with a focus on history in particular. We wrote *Pastplay* to create and sustain a conversation among historians and history educators across the spectrum of computational expertise. One of our core messages is that "you too can do this—and perhaps better—let's explore this together." Therefore, the chapters that follow are not for "techies": we are all learning how to use emerging technologies in our disciplines. And we do not believe that we have to choose between new technologies and the time-honored practices of our discipline. In fact, we show that computing can be a way to enhance those practices.

We tread carefully because we recognize that technology has ostensibly come to the rescue of learning on several occasions. We also appreciate that this is not the first time that subjects such as history have been apparently liberated by play—the 1960s, for instance, saw the widespread introduction of play and games across curricula. In the latest turn of this circle, recent years have seen a focus on computer games, the most interactive computer environments yet created. The "edutainment" of the 1990s was repackaged as "serious games," and educators were told that if students were allowed to play, the challenges of teaching history and other subjects could be over-come.[3] Similar claims are now being made for "gamification," the appli-cation of gameplay mechanics to non-game situations or domains such as education.[4]

Proponents of gamification sometimes appear to operate from the prem-ise that life is boring and must be invigorated with gaming strategies.[5] Appar-ently, we need to be tricked into performing tasks we would otherwise avoid. In the case of education, the central assumption is that learning is dull. The irony is that gamification proponents make this argument, then spend hours exploring the contexts of their favorite games in the hope of finding information that they can use to win (a practice that is strikingly similar to the "dull" research they want to avoid). They create forums (which bear resemblance to the best features of online courses) where they share games they have modified. They then analyze and critique each other's insights and demonstrations in long, carefully crafted forum posts (which are often constructed like essays).

The notion that learning is boring is also belied by our personal experi-ence: from cafeteria gossip to insights on the origin of the universe, we love learning. At the dawn of our Western cultural tradition, Aristotle observed that "all men by nature desire to know."[6] We are essentially curious, and once we begin to learn it is difficult to stop. As several of the contributors to this book illustrate in their chapters, give students a little bit of history and they are hooked.

The easy assumptions of those who breezily promote technology as edu-cation's salvation might also be challenged by more experience in the envi-ronments they seek to save. Many of these proponents appear not to have visited a school or university in years. If they had, they would have seen the many ways in which students engage with subjects like history. Others are perhaps too highly motivated by the windfall that may come with access to a coveted market of young consumers.[7]

Our book takes a different approach to playing with the past. We are past the play moment, roughly the first decade of the century, when the challenges of teaching history could ostensibly be solved with a new technology or game. To put it simply, these are not a panacea. What is needed, and what this book seeks to provide, is a consideration of the ways in which technology can and cannot help us interact with the *content* and *practices* of the discipline. This point bears repeating: in our case, we are not concerned with history the *subject* so much as history the *discipline*. And we do not address teaching in terms of classroom exercises but as research practices and discourses that we use alongside our students. In this book, we are preaching what we practice every day as researcher-teachers.

Why should we play with technology in history? Because doing so can help us think about the past in new ways. We expand on our thesis in four parts. In the first section of the book, "Teaching and Learning History," the contributors focus on the content and practices of the discipline, and show that playful technologies can help students better understand the way historians and storytellers create history. In the second part, "Playfully," the contributors turn their focus to the roots of our craft, and show that a ludic sensibility lies at the heart of how we research, how we teach, and how we express ideas with computers. In the third part, "With Technology," the authors illustrate how communicating ideas with computers forces us to model our thoughts, and the development and use of these models can provide us with new insights into the subjects they represent. The contributors to the fourth part, "By Building," show that, through the act of creating technologies, we can build our understanding of the past.

Teaching and Learning History

We begin by focusing on what history is all about: an encounter with the content of the past, and the manner in which historical narratives are created. This brings us to the most fundamental question: what is history? The answer has been highly contested for the last three decades. In the 1980s, this question became a hot-button political issue after evidence emerged that students had surprisingly little knowledge of the past. The timing was not accidental: the end of the Cold War and the increasingly globalized economy created anxiety among some cultural commentators. Would their countries have a future if their young people could not remember the past?

The problem was politicized, blame assigned, and sides taken in what was called the "history wars." In the United States and Canada (as well as in Great Britain, Australia, and several other Western countries, although events there lie outside the scope of this introduction) one side contended that the historical profession was to blame: historians' obsession with issues of race, class, and gender had diluted a narrative of progress that should be instilled in the young. Students did not know their country's past because they could not see through the fog of political correctness.[8] On the other side, researchers contended that this apparent problem was in fact the solution. The new historical emphases on race, class, and gender had been the result of demographic changes within universities (especially the hiring into the professoriate of women and ethnic minorities). New histories were being told, providing a fuller picture of the past that was resonating with young people from a variety of backgrounds. The problems that had been identified in history teaching, according to these researchers, lay not with this new content, but with the manner in which it was taught.

Should history be a single chronological narrative meant to provide young people with a common understanding and cohesive social purpose, or a way to evaluate diverse accounts of the past? Researchers and educators chose the latter option, and pushed it further still. They agreed that the content of history—the names and dates—were important, but they concluded that students needed to move beyond this to an understanding, and indeed use of, the skills of historical practice: generating, corroborating, representing, and assessing interpretations of the past. History educators increasingly gave attention to the concepts, methods, and vocabulary required to do history, and underscored to students the challenge of knowing the past[9] in an approach that has come to be called "historical thinking."[10]

They followed the lead of science educators who had earlier championed a shift from the absorption of scientific facts (for example, the memorization of the periodic table of elements) to the acquisition of skills of scientific practice (such as familiarity with the tools of chemistry, or a command of the language with which chemistry is discussed). History educators began to explore ways to bring students into the historical "community of inquiry," most often by encouraging them to work with the evidence—primary documents—which historians use.

In "Teaching and Learning History," the contributors address the ways that playful technologies can help us better understand how history is created, and how to think historically. "What Has Mystery Got to Do with It?" by Ruth Sandwell and John Lutz provides a cogent summary of the historical thinking literature, and especially the research on the use of primary source documents. Sandwell and Lutz also outline how theoretical and methodological developments within the discipline of history have informed the research on the teaching and learning of history in schools. They show that the conclusions of the historical thinking research are encouraging for those who develop playful history quest environments, pointing to their *Great Unsolved Mysteries in Canadian History* project as an example of what can be accomplished. In the various micro-histories that together make up the project, students must examine primary source documents (in a manner similar to that of historians) to solve a mystery. Sandwell and Lutz show how playing with technology supports the development of the skills of historical practice, such as the assessment of primary documents with contradictory information. In the *Mysteries* project historical knowledge comes not from knowing facts so much as understanding processes.

In "'Why can't you just tell us?' Learning Canadian History with the Virtual Historian," Stéphane Lévesque highlights the ways in which the historical thinking scholarship informed the development of another online environment—in this case his *Virtual Historian* website. In contrast to Sandwell and Lutz, Lévesque sounds a cautionary note: his empirical assessment of the teaching tool has yielded ambiguous conclusions about its effectiveness. In these two chapters we hear variations on two shared themes: optimism for the potential of playful technologies, and recognition that all the data are not yet in. Lévesque's *Virtual Historian* provided students with access to online documents, and asked them to solve a mystery. In the end, the students treated these sources more like infallible fact sheets than primary documents requiring careful assessment. "What is at stake for virtual history," Lévesque notes in his conclusion, "is the assumption that the rich volume of multiple-perspective sources available [online] favors historical reasoning. This cannot be accomplished with primary sources alone." The web supports almost unlimited access to digitized resources, providing opportunities for student analysis, but many students do not have the skills to do that research in the manner of historians.

Perhaps the problem is that they do not want to. Sandwell and Lutz mine the rich literature that shows that students, even in elementary school, are able to think like professional historians. But they also expose another vein, noting the conclusions of leading educational researchers that the problem of using primary sources to teach students the process of critical inquiry is not to be found simply in students' ability to engage critically with the materials, but also in their reluctance to do so.

These students do not lack the ability, but the interest. They may be passionate, however, about World War II submarines, or the ancient traditions of their ancestors. In this way, they are not unlike their professors and teachers, who majored in history primarily because they enjoyed it.

Pulitzer–prize winning author and historian David McCullough observed that "To me, history ought to be a source of pleasure. It isn't just part of our civic responsibility. To me, it's an enlargement of the experience of being alive, just the way literature or art or music is."[11] This point should not be lost on historians and history educators.

We need to remember, as Richard Levy and Peter Dawson remind us in "Interactive Worlds as Educational Tools for Understanding Arctic Life," that we are drawn to history for many reasons beyond a desire to think historically. Levy and Dawson describe the ways in which they use computer-aided design (CAD) technologies for architecture to painstakingly reconstruct ancient dwellings using archaeological evidence. In their labs, patterns of stones and whalebones are turned into 3D models that can be examined and explored. Developing digital reconstructions of ancient dwellings, like a Thule whalebone house, has enabled Levy, Dawson, and their students to explore new ideas and theories about how ancient peoples perceived and interacted with their environments. (They propose, for instance, that the Thule might have developed a more acute sense of touch to compensate for the near darkness in which they carved and sewed.) At the same time, these models have also provided opportunities for some of Canada's aboriginal peoples to connect with the lost landscapes of their past, as Levy and Dawson relate in a moving account of a visit to their lab by several Inuit Elders. Exploring the inside of the whalebone house gave these aboriginal people insight into the origins of some of their most treasured legends.

The Inuit Elders gained knowledge not just through an observation of, but also an engagement with, the digitally reconstructed dwellings of their ancestors. Timothy Compeau and Robert MacDougall push this participation further in "Tecumseh Lies Here: Goals and Challenges for a Pervasive History Game in Progress." In the final chapter in this part, they also testify to the power of lived and lost history and the potential for communicating it to adults. The difference, in this case, is the authors' focus on what they call "pervasive games," which are media agnostic, and "can spread across the entire ecology of electronic and traditional media and into public spaces like streets, museums, and schools." Rather than bringing history to life in a game environment, surrounding the user with replicas or re-creations, Compeau and MacDougall equip users with historical methods and then encourage them to discover the history that surrounds them. They share the challenges they are facing as they develop and launch a pervasive game that employs both electronic and traditional media in public spaces to engage people with the history of the War of 1812. In the end they make a case for "playful historical thinking" as a "healthy, productive, and even responsible way for citizens of the twenty-first century to relate to the past."[12]

Playfully

The notion of "playful historical thinking" may strike some as a new idea. But as the authors in this part suggest, we should play with history because it is a central component of research and teaching, and a central aesthetic of computing. These authors also address concepts central to this volume: "play," "games," and "learning." As they point out, there is significant overlap here, and separating them is a difficult task indeed. These distinctions did not exist among the ancient Romans, for whom *ludus* described both a toddler's play and a gladiator's training.[13]

Play is part of the Western philosophical tradition from which the humanities, as we know them today, have emerged. The origins of this tradition go back to Socrates, whose insights were passed on by Plato in playful dialogues.[14] Plato chose to communicate ideas as debates between Socrates and an interlocutor with an opposing viewpoint. By an iterative process of elimination, hypotheses were tested and discarded until truth was revealed. Along the way, Socrates frequently toyed with his opponent, asking leading questions that would force an adversary to contradict himself.[15] At the beginning of our present philosophical moment, often summed up by the term "post-structuralism," playfulness again emerges as a central component. In Jacques Derrida's 1966 lecture, "Structure, Sign and Play in the Discourse of the Human Sciences," which for many theorists marks the birth of post-structuralism, Derrida heralded an intellectual "event" or "rupture" that signified a break from past ways of thinking.[16] In the emerging universe nothing was fixed—all we had was "free play."[17] Derrida and the early post-structuralists saw this acceptance of ambiguities as liberating; we needed to find courage to enter this new world defined by its lack of absolutes.[18]

That is not to say that "play" requires a complete disregard for boundaries. Indeed, determining the borders of play—what is in and what is out—has been a central preoccupation of game theorists. First among these was the Dutch cultural historian Johan Huizinga, who saw play as central to cultural development. His graduate work had focused on the role of the jester in Indian drama, and several decades later he returned to some of these themes in an attempt to define play. In *Homo Ludens* Huizinga described play as a "free activity standing quite consciously outside 'ordinary' life," which nevertheless "absorb[ed] the player intensely and utterly." It was "connected with no material interest, and no profit [could] be gained from it."[19] A few years later, Roger Caillois, who found Huizinga's definition too limiting, sought to expand on it. His ultimate contribution, however, was to define what a "game" is, highlighting six specific attributes: games were not-obligatory, separate from everyday life, without a predetermined outcome, not connected to a material interest, governed by rules, and make-believe.[20]

This etymology may seem to leave little room for an incorporation of play into learning, yet psychology has underscored what the ancient Romans recognized: that "play," "games," and "learning" can be difficult to differentiate. The psychologist Mihaly Csikszentmihalyi and his colleagues have conducted experiments over the course of decades to determine the attributes of what they have coined "flow," a state in which we are totally immersed in what we are doing. To be in "flow" is to be "in the groove," a feeling of complete involvement in an activity for its own sake. We lose all sense of time, becoming absorbed in the task at hand. In this space, that which is play and that which is work, or learning, are one and the same.[21] Each of us knows this feeling of flow, and each of us knows what it is to play. For some of us, childhood memories supply the experience that provides the definition. Professional historians and history teachers can learn something from young people, which completes the loop: while we teach students history, they can help us remember play.

If play is central to the origins of the Western tradition, and to the present cultural moment, it has occasionally been lost when the computer has been applied to our resource base—the archives—where the work of historians and their students begins. Significant resources have been invested in digitizing documents and entire collections, extending access, and providing new opportunities for analysis. Additional effort has gone into building sophisticated tools that will parse the data, such as the Google Ngram Viewer, which displays the results of word string searches of the massive Google Books database.[22] As Stephen Ramsay notes in "The Hermeneutics of Screwing Around; or What You Do with a Million Books," these databases allow us to quickly answer our research questions, but real insight emerges when we browse, make unanticipated associations, and ask new questions. He dares us to approach the archives in this manner—essentially to "screw around." "There are so many books," Ramsay observes. "There is so little time. Your ethical obligation is neither to read them all nor to pretend that you have read them all, but to understand each path through the vast archive as an important moment in the world's duration—as an invitation to community, relationship, and play."[23]

Just as a playful ethic should guide our research—our encounter with, and expression of, our sources—so too should it guide the way we teach students. In "Abort, Retry, Pass, Fail: Games as Teaching Tools," Sean Gouglas and his coauthors address the ongoing debate over the definitions of "play," "games," and "learning": scholars have spent the last decade attempting to define what play and games are, and also what they are not, in the hope of being able to identify moments of genuine "learning" (which they consider a separate concept).[24] As Gouglas et al. show, separating these concepts has proven especially difficult in the case of history computer games: claims for the educational effectiveness of in-game learning have not been adequately demonstrated. Significant resources have been invested in developing interactive media tools, especially games, for our students. But are students learning? And if so, what? The authors point out that hard conclusions are few and far between, but that this should not stop our use of games. Echoing Ramsay, Gouglas and his colleagues encourage us to press on nonetheless, and suggest that separating "learning" from "play" seems impossible anyway. Gouglas and his colleagues encourage us to instead focus on building open environments. They see more potential for learning in the development of games, which encourages students to share their knowledge with one another, and then collaboratively assemble these mental models.

Bethany Nowviskie focuses specific attention on exactly *how* we should build with technology. If playfulness is central to our research practices and our teaching, Nowviskie shows that it is also a central component of our interaction with computing. Increasingly, historians and teachers are building digital tools for students and members of the public to use; but the underlying functions of these tools are often hidden from the user. In "Ludic Algorithms," Nowviskie addresses this issue by turning our focus to the origins of digital humanities and digital history, and specifically to thirteenth-century philosopher Ramon Llull and his Ars Magna. According to Nowviskie, the genius of Llull's invention and method—several inscribed, layered, rotating wheels that essentially asked questions of the user—lay in its accessibility: it revealed the decisions inherent to the creation and interpretation of its algorithms, allowing users to play with these components. Like all problem-solving devices, algorithms—the building blocks of computing—are formulated out of interpretive decisions. Humanists in general, and historians in particular, must ensure that users can view, analyze, and test—to put it another way, "play with"—our algorithms, and indeed formulate new algorithms that yield new interpretations of humanistic data.

With Technology

In the process of teaching and learning through play, technology provides an opportunity to model knowledge so that our assumptions can be demonstrated and tested. Indeed, the creation of representations alluded to by

Gouglas and Nowviskie may be one of the secret ingredients of effective learning. As Willard McCarty has shown, creating models requires us to formalize our thinking, and helps us better understand both our questions and our answers. In the building of these representations, that which may be assumed or elided when presented in textual form must be formalized and made explicit in a manner accessible to others.[25]

As McCarty points out, inherent to modeling is the notion of manipulating the model, and in the process deriving new knowledge about it, and the source material on which it is based. A model must be playable: you must be able to turn the crank and see what happens. If it breaks, you can attempt to fix the problem by opening the hood, making adjustments, or inserting or removing components, or you can throw it out and start over. In this way, the representations of digital historians, and digital humanists in general, are much more than "tools"—notwithstanding the popular terminology. As Nowviskie points out, a tool is "a self-contained and inviolable object." The models, games, and simulations that digital historians and our students build, in contrast, should be more akin to "instruments" or "environments," inhabitable spaces that can be analyzed, adjusted, and played as well as used.[26]

In "With Technology," the contributors are equally optimistic and cautious about the use of models, whether simple or complex. They encourage us to appreciate the full spectrum of "technology," using whatever is most appropriate to the task. We are reminded that the last decade has seen the application of sophisticated software (such as complicated computer games that require a significant investment of time to understand, let alone master) to questions that might have been better analyzed with pen and paper.

Innovative technologies are not always made of silicon microchips: plastic and wood best suited the purposes of William J. Turkel and Devon Elliott. In "Making and Playing with Models: Using Rapid Prototyping to Explore the History and Technology of Stage Magic," they present a case study on the history of levitation and vanishing, "two icons of performance" in the nineteenth century. Combining insights from science and technology studies and the hands-on critical making movement, and expanding on the practices of the nineteenth-century founders of archaeology (who reproduced artifacts as a way of understanding how the originals were created and used), they ask, "Where is the experimental history to match this practice in archaeology?" They show what this new approach to research and teaching might look like, and how it provides opportunities for building in addition to reading and writing. And what is the result of their development and use of replicas and representations? They see things that would otherwise have remained hidden. They point out that this kind of modeling is especially useful as pedagogy: students acquire tacit knowledge through making and playing with artifacts, gaining insight that could not be drawn from discourse alone.

Matthew Kirschenbaum makes a similar pitch for the use of a simple model, in his case in the context of games. In "Contests for Meaning: Playing King Philip's War in the Twenty-First Century" he uses the example of a board game about the King Philip's War (a brief but brutal episode in American colonial history). As is often the case when gaming and history intersect, some members of the public were outraged that a tragic event in Native American history might be "simplified" and "debased" by play. Kirschenbaum tackles this reaction head-on, and asks why playing the past evokes attitudes different from consuming it in traditional media such as film or books. But he goes beyond the public response, and engages another question: what is the educational potential for these kinds of tabletop history games? Echoing Nowviskie, but with a focus on games in particular, he points out that while computer games have been a hit in the marketplace, board games may work best for education. Tabletop games, in contrast to computer games, expose their mechanisms: the systems and processes that constitute the rules of the game are obvious. As a result, they are open to analysis by students, and this openness makes tabletop games conducive to learning.

Kirschenbaum's suggestion that board games may do a better job of teaching than computer games would not come as a surprise to Shawn Graham. In "Rolling Your Own: On Modding Commercial Games for Educational Goals," Graham explains how computer games such as Sid Meyer's *Civilization* series can act as models with which to analyze, express, and test historical interpretations. Graham was impressed by the sophisticated discussions that he read in self-organized modding communities such as the *CiviFanatics* forums, where players would meet to analyze the game and its expression of history. He hoped that using the game in his classroom would result in a similar sense of self-motivation in his students, and a similar modeling of knowledge. Yet when Graham attempted to use the game in an educational setting, his students resisted. His conclusion is instructive: in our rush to bring new technologies into education, we must remember that many of the models and practices that make these successful in the "outside world" may not necessarily carry over to the classroom or lecture hall.

In "Simulation Games and the Study of the Past: Classroom Guidelines," Jeremiah McCall addresses this problem directly, referencing a sister game to *Civilization* called *CivCity Rome*. He encourages educators to be mindful of both the educational requirements of history and the exigencies of implementing video games in contemporary schools. A high school teacher with extensive experience in the use of history computer games, McCall is keenly aware of the demands of elementary and secondary classrooms, and provides practical steps to structure, implement, and assess learning activities with computer games. Recognizing that students are there to learn, he never asks them if they are "having fun," and knows that at times he may have to "coerce" them into using these environments, in the same way that he may oblige them to read a textbook. What is important, and what he suggests games do especially well, is provide a model that structures a student's performance of the authentic skills of a historian.

By Building

As Graham and McCall note, students sometimes feel constrained because they know they need to play by the educational institution's rules, and typically those rules limit creativity. The authors in the final section of *Pastplay* show that playing with technology encourages creativity by providing opportunities to build our understanding of the past in new ways. The concept is old, but the tools are new, and they open up opportunities previously unavailable.

In the early twentieth century John Dewey showed that the use of objects—not just words—is an essential component of learning.[27] Jean Piaget, for his part, argued that knowledge is not deposited into the student, what Paolo Freire termed "banking,"[28] but rather constructed in the mind of the learner.[29] He coined the term "constructivism" to describe the manner in which students should be supported as they build knowledge. For Piaget's student, Seymour Papert, "building" was not a metaphor to describe processes in the brain, but a literal description of a physical activity. From his post at the Massachusetts Institute of Technology—an institution with the motto "Mens et Manus" (mind and hands)—Papert insisted that students build the instruments by which they learn, in a process he called "constructionism."[30] Illustrating his theory, Papert developed a simple computer programming language called Logo with which young people could build their own software programs and bring robots to life. (See Gouglas et al.'s chapter in this volume for a more complete explanation of learning theory.) The Dewey-Piaget-Papert lineage has become a de facto starting point for many developers of educational technology. Each of the authors in "By Building" connects to this lineage, in chapters that address constructivism in museums and classrooms, and test the use of websites, multimedia mash-ups, 3D environments, and computer games.

Brenda Trofanenko reminds us that the use of technology in teaching and learning does not guarantee a constructivist or constructionist approach.

Her chapter, "Playing into the Past: Reconsidering the Educational Promise of Public History Exhibits," shows that technology can just as easily end up "banking" as "building." Trofanenko wants to answer the question, "How should museums best take up the challenge of engaging history with computer technologies?" Museums are increasingly employing technology, especially multimedia, to engage young people with the past, but the new toys are sometimes proving to be unsuitable for communicating a singular view of history. At the National Museum of American History, in Washington, D.C., an exhibit that used multimedia to frame history as fixed and serious failed to engage or teach. But when the museum provided opportunities for high school students to use technology on their own terms within the exhibit space, the engagement and learning increased exponentially. How should museums best use technology? By letting students create multimedia mash-ups of museum content, for one. It turns out that mash-ups are not just playful; they are also a way for students to rethink what they know about the past, and how they know it.

Kevin Kee and Shawn Graham reach a related conclusion in "Teaching History in an Age of Pervasive Computing: The Case for Games in the High School and Undergraduate Classroom." In their chapter, however, the focus is games in the university and high school classroom. Over the last decade, the results here have been disappointing. The problem, according to the authors, is that we have fundamentally misunderstood how games communicate. We presume that a game that claims to be about ancient Rome will support student learning in a course about ancient Rome. Ignore the promotional material, the authors direct; focus instead on the argument the game's computer code promotes. To this end, Kee and Graham propose a new typology for history games. They also see the greatest opportunity for teaching history with computer games in "meta-gaming," an outside-looking-in awareness of game mechanics. In this "gaming of the game," students move beyond playing games, or studying games as artifacts, to modifying and even building them for themselves, developing their own representations in computer code.

Patrick Dunae and John Sutton Lutz propose a different kind of making in "Victorian SimCities: Playful Technology on *Google Earth*." They believe that students learn best when they can literally *see* the past. They describe an undergraduate course in which students were tasked with virtually reconstructing buildings using fire insurance maps (used by insurance companies to determine the dimensions and structures of buildings in case of their destruction by fire). Combining history (the development of historical skills) with play (puzzle solving), students used the maps and old photographs and lithographic views to reconstruct the urban landscape of nineteenth-century Victoria, British Columbia. The authors carefully outline the different stages of the project, and how students used *Google SketchUp* and *Google Earth* to bring the results of their research into view. In the end, the students were able to draw conclusions that challenged the historical orthodoxy on immigrant settlement patterns at a key moment in the city's history.

T. Mills Kelly takes a different approach to developing historical thinking through building. "What happens when you teach students to lie?" he asks. The answer: "they learn how to be historians." In "True Facts or False Facts—Which Are More Authentic?" Kelly reflects on a historical methods course in which his students created a historical hoax, "the last American pirate," which they subsequently launched into the digital ether through a blog and *Wikipedia* page. Kelly eloquently expresses the motivation of many of the contributors to this volume when he observes, "I think history has just gotten a bit too boring for its own good. This course is my attempt to lighten up a little and see where it gets us." And just where did they end up? Kelly attests to the benefits of playful building; his students were uniformly enthusiastic about the course, and the process of lying on a bogus *Wikipedia* page helped them better understand the ways in which historians seek to truthfully portray the past. But he also highlights its risks: some of Mills's fellow historians were taken in by the hoax, and the ensuing controversy landed his course on the pages of the *Chronicle of Higher Education*.

Alternative Readings and Future Experimentation

Kelly may take some comfort in knowing that the work of his students has been selected as among "The 10 Biggest Hoaxes in Wikipedia's First 10 Years."[31] Receiving recognition of this kind is not the goal of most aspiring historians or teachers, but he undoubtedly considers it a badge of honor. It signals a willingness to experiment, take risks, and support student creativity. Often this experimentation goes according to plan; sometimes it brings unintended consequences. Kelly's chapter, like the others, is iterative and reflective. In contrast to some of the literature in the educational technology domain, the contributors do not declare victory, then turn the page (while retreating). We learn more from our mistakes than we do our successes, and in the chapters that follow we have tried to analyze what happened when our use of technology to communicate history went wrong, and how we can do better next time.

We have intentionally written these chapters for educators and practitioners in different educational environments. K–12 teachers will want to focus on Sandwell and Lutz's reflections on their *Mysteries* project (chapter 1), Lévesque's analysis of his *Virtual Historian* (chapter 2), and McCall's description of simulation games in the classroom (chapter 11). Instructors of undergraduate history courses, for their part, should concentrate on Compeau and MacDougall's development of augmented reality games (chapter 4), the insights of Gouglas and his colleagues on games for university history learning (chapter 6), Turkel and Elliott's use of models for history (chapter 8), Graham's experiences with game mods (chapter 10), Kee and Graham's use of mods and student-built games (chapter 13), Dunae and Lutz's development of nineteenth-century computer models using *Google SketchUp* (chapter 14), and Kelly's undergraduate course on historical hoaxes (chapter 15). Professors, thesis directors, and students at the graduate level will benefit from Ramsay's consideration of how we treat our sources (chapter 5), Nowviskie's insights into building with technology (chapter 7), and Turkel and Elliott's use of models to gain historical insights (chapter 8). Finally, public historians and museum professionals will appreciate Levy and Dawson's development of computer models and visualizations for the Glenbow Museum and the Canadian Museum of Civilization (chapter 3), Compeau and MacDougall's pervasive game for history enthusiasts (chapter 4), and Trofanenko's work with students at the National Museum of American History (chapter 12).

The contributors to this book also describe different "ways of doing" history and humanities. We can do the humanities and history by theorizing: Ramsay describes how research might be considered as serendipitous play (chapter 5), and Nowviskie suggests that the fruits of that research must be playable, that is, able to be viewed, analyzed, and tested by others (chapter 7). We can also do history through building and modeling, as described by Levy and Dawson in chapter 3, Turkel and Elliott in chapter 8, Trofanenko in chapter 12, Kee and Graham in chapter 13, Dunae and Lutz in chapter 14, and Kelly in chapter 15. The practice of history can also take place in the context of playing a game, as described by Compeau and MacDougall in chapter 4, Gouglas et al. in chapter 6, Graham in chapter 10, and McCall in chapter 11.

Finally, readers interested in building specific kinds of objects can find examples across the spectrum, from plastic models to websites to computer and pervasive games. Websites for history teaching and learning are the focus of chapters 1 (Sandwell and Lutz's *Mysteries*), chapter 2 (Lévesque's *Virtual Historian*), and chapter 15 (Kelly's historical hoaxes). Trofanenko focuses attention on the development of iMovie projects in museum contexts in chapter 12. The development and use of 3D computer models are addressed in chapter 3 (Levy and Dawson's Arctic interactive worlds), and chapter 14 (Dunae and Lutz's Victorian Victoria in *Google SketchUp*). Turkel and Elliott describe their creation and use of wood and plastic physical models in chapter 8, and Kirschenbaum focuses on the controversy created by a history board game in chapter 9. Computer games for history figure in several chapters: student and research projects in Gouglas et al.'s chapter 6, the best-seller *Civilization* in an undergraduate online course in Graham's chapter 10, *CivCity Rome* in an elementary and secondary context in McCall's chapter 11, and game mods and games built by students from scratch in Kee and Graham's chapter 13. Finally, pervasive games (which mix gaming in the real and virtual worlds, and have also been called "alternate reality games") are the focus of Compeau and MacDougall's chapter 4.

The contributors to this book hope that the objects, ways of doing history, and educational environments described here will encourage others to experiment in their own unique ways. Notwithstanding the considerable research and innovation among digital historians and teachers, some of which we have captured in these chapters, we still have work to do in exploring and communicating the potential and drawbacks of teaching history with technology. This volume is a collaborative effort at beginning the conversation.

NOTES

This introduction was organized during a two-day working session with Geoffrey Rockwell at a meeting in March 2011 at the University of Alberta. Thanks to Geoffrey, the central ethic that animates this volume, best summed up by Stephen Ramsay as "community, relationship, and play," was in abundance, notwithstanding the weather.

1. More information about The History Education Network / Histoire et Éducation en Réseau can be found at their website, accessed July 31, 2012, http://www.thenhier.ca/; more information about the Social Sciences and Humanities Research Council of Canada can be found at their website, accessed July 31, 2012, http://www.sshrc-crsh.gc.ca/.

2. Thomas Bartscherer, "Introduction," in *Switching Codes: Thinking Through Digital Technology in the Humanities and the Arts*, ed. Roderick Coover and Thomas Bartscherer (Chicago: University of Chicago Press, 2011), 3.

3. According to some commentators, these games were so effective that teachers might become redundant. In his book, *Digital Game-Based Learning* (New York: McGraw-Hill, 2001), Marc Prensky approvingly quoted, "any teacher who can be replaced by a computer, should be" (342). Prensky attributes this quotation to the anonymous "Aging Sage"; others have claimed Arthur C. Clarke, Carl Sagan, or David Thornburg.

4. The term "gamification" has recently come into vogue, promoted by theorists such as Jane McGonigal (*Reality Is Broken: Why Games Make Us Better and How They Can Change the World* [New York: Penguin, 2011]), and is especially, though not exclusively, tied to Internet-based marketing. Websites or location-based (mobile) platforms that feature achievement levels, badges, or virtual currency might all be cited as examples of gamification. Some critics point out that gamification is a new term for

long-established techniques, and in many cases a rebranding of the concepts central to "serious gaming."

5. See the critique of Heather Chaplin, "I Don't Want to be a Superhero: Ditching Reality for a Game isn't as Fun as It Sounds," *Slate*, Tuesday March 29, 2011, http://www.slate.com/id/2289302/pagenum/all/#p2, accessed July 4, 2011.

6. Aristotle, *Metaphysics*, book I, part I, accessed July 13, 2011, http://classics.mit.edu//Aristotle/metaphysics.html.

7. "Harnessing the Power of Video Games for Learning," published by the Federation of American Scientists, calls for research into the skills that games can teach, but at other times unfairly brands education as a sector that could be saved if only it followed the practices of the business community: "Many companies and industries have transformed themselves by taking advantage of advances in technology, and new management methods and models of organization. As a result, they realized substantial gains in productivity and product quality while lowering costs. No such transformation has taken part in education. Education is not part of the IT revolution" (6).

8. The most prominent critic in the United States was Lynne V. Cheney, the former chair of the National Endowment for the Humanities. In her report to the Congress in 1988, and later in *Telling the Truth: Why Our Culture and Our Country Have Stopped Making Sense and What We Can Do about It*, Cheney argued that American history had been nearly destroyed by historians' obsession with issues of identity such as race and gender (Lynne V. Cheney, *Humanities in America: A Report to the President, the Congress, and the American People* [Washington, D.C.: National Endowment for the Humanities, 1988]; idem, *Telling the Truth: Why Our Culture and Our Country Have Stopped Making Sense and What We Can Do about It* [New York: Simon & Schuster, 1995]). Much of Cheney's attack was focused on the "National History Standards." In 1992, three history professors, Gary Nash, Ross Dunn, and Charlotte Crabtree, were enlisted by the National Endowment for the Humanities to draw up standards for the teaching of history in schools in the United States. In 1994, before their standards were published, they came under attack. For the response of Nash, Dunn, and Crabtree to their critics, see Gary B. Nash, Ross E. Dunn, and Charlotte A. Crabtree, *History on Trial: Culture Wars and the Teaching of the Past* (New York: Random House, 1997). In Canada, the conservative charge was led by Jack Granatstein, who claimed that Canadian history was dead, "or perhaps on life support" (J. L. Granatstein, *Who Killed Canadian History?* [Toronto: HarperCollins, 1998], 141). The distinction mattered little to Granatstein, and less, he argued, to most Canadians. The general public, according to Granatstein, had no interest in following the work of scholars infatuated by historical minutiae. He stood by his well-publicized complaint that historians were obsessing about matters such as "the history of the housemaid's knee in Belleville in the 1890s. Really, who cares?" (quoted in Christopher Moore, "The Organized Man," *The Beaver* 71 [April–May 1991]: 59). The academics' response came from A. B. McKillop in "Who Killed Canadian History? A View from the Trenches," *Canadian Historical Review* 80, no. 2 (Summer 1999).

9. Thomas Holt, *Thinking Historically: Narrative, Imagination, and Understanding* (New York: College Entrance Examination Board, 1990); Samuel Wineburg, *Historical Thinking and Other Unnatural Acts* (Philadelphia: Temple University Press, 2001).

10. In Canada, this shift has been instantiated in the adoption by teachers, and in some cases Ministries of Education (education is a provincial jurisdiction), of the "Benchmarks of Historical Knowledge." Developed by Peter Seixas at the University

of British Columbia, the "Benchmarks" articulate "structural historical concepts" that can "guide and shape the practice of history" (Peter Seixas, *Benchmarks of Historical Thinking: A Framework for Assessment in Canada* [Vancouver: Centre for the Study of Historical Consciousness, University of British Columbia, 2006], 2). According to the "Benchmarks," students should be able to: i. determine what constitutes *historical significance*; ii. effectively use—including asking good questions of—primary source *evidence*; iii. identify *continuity and change*; iv. analyze *cause and consequence*; v. take *historical perspectives*; vi. understand the *moral dimension* of history interpretations (ibid., 3–11).

11. David McCullough, interview conducted by National Endowment of the Humanities Chairman Bruce Cole, 2002, accessed July 13, 2011, http://www.neh.gov /whoweare/mccullough/interview.html.

12. See the chapter by Compeau and MacDougall in this volume.

13. See the chapter by Gouglas et al. in this volume.

14. For a contemporary example of Socratic dialogue by one of the contributors to this volume, see Geoffrey Rockwell and Kevin Kee, "The Leisure of Serious Games," *Game Studies* 11, no. 2 (May 2011), accessed July 13, 2011, http://gamestudies.org/1102 /articles/geoffrey_rockwell_kevin_kee.

15. For notable examples of these dialogues, see Plato's *Cratylus* or *Phaedrus*, both accessed July 13, 2011, http://classics.mit.edu/Plato/cratylus.html and http://classics .mit.edu/Plato/phaedrus.html.

16. Jacques Derrida, *Writing and Difference*, trans. Alan Bass (London: Routledge, 1978), 278. Previously, man stood at the center of the universe and a historical narrative defined by progress. For Derrida and many of his contemporaries, events of the twentieth century such as the Holocaust had called into question this notion of progress; he contended that related intellectual "centers" were in retreat as a result.

17. Philosophers would be quick to point out that Derrida's notion of "play" is not what we generally think of today. For him, it referred to an acceptance of ambiguities, and in the context of using technology in history we share this willingness to reconsider previous assumptions and consider new possibilities.

18. Peter Barry, *Beginning Theory* (Manchester: Manchester University Press, 2002), 66–70.

19. Johan Huizinga, *Homo Ludens: A Study of the Play-element in Culture* (Boston: Beacon, 1950), 13.

20. Roger Caillois, *Man, Play, and Games,* trans. Meyer Barash (New York: The Free Press, 1961), 9–10.

21. Mihaly Csikszentmihalyi, *Flow: The Psychology of Optimal Experience* (New York: HarperPerennial, 1991).

22. See Google Labs, accessed July 5, 2011, http://ngrams.googlelabs.com/info.

23. See the chapter by Ramsay in this volume.

24. Jesper Juul, "Games Telling Stories?" in *Handbook of Computer Game Studies*, ed. J. Raessens and J. Goldstein (Cambridge, Mass.: MIT Press, 2005), 175–89; Celia Pearce, "Towards a Game Theory of Game," in *First Person: New Media as Story, Performance, and Game*, ed. N. Wardrip-Fruin and P. Harrigan (Cambridge, Mass.: MIT Press, 2004), 143–53; Eric Zimmerman, "Narrative, Interactivity, Play, and Games: Four Naughty Concepts in Need of Discipline," in *First Person: New Media as Story, Performance, and Game*, ed. N. Wardrip-Fruin and P. Harrigan (Cambridge, Mass.: MIT Press, 2004), 154–63.

25. Willard McCarty, *Humanities Computing* (Basingstoke: Palgrave MacMillan, 2005), see especially chapter 1.

26. See the chapter by Nowviskie in this volume.

27. John Dewey, *Democracy and Education: An Introduction to the Philosophy of Education* (New York: Macmillan, 1916).

28. Paolo Freire, *Pedagogy of the Oppressed* (New York: Herder and Herder, 1970).

29. Jean Piaget, *Genetic Epistemology*, trans. Eleanor Duckworth (New York: Norton, 1971).

30. Idit Harel and Seymour Papert, eds., *Constructionism* (Norwood, N.J.: Ablex, 1991).

31. Jon Brodkin, "The 10 Biggest Hoaxes in Wikipedia's First 10 Years," *PCWorld*, January 14, 2011, accessed July 5, 2011, http://www.pcworld.com/article/216799/the_10 _biggest_hoaxes_in_wikipedias_first_10_years.html.

Teaching and Learning History

ONE

What Has Mystery Got to Do with It?

Ruth Sandwell and John Sutton Lutz

Overview

Should history be playful? Fun to do? If it should be, at least as presented in secondary schools, it is not. Most students would be sympathetic to James Joyce, who said, "History is a nightmare from which I must awake!"[1] In our enthusiasm to cover the syllabus, to show the big picture, the vast canvas of history, we have squeezed both the fun and the fascination out. To go from "Plato to NATO" we take the flesh from the stories and deliver only the skeleton.[2] Typically, we ask students to commit this to memory and regurgitate it at exam time instead of teaching the detective work—the critical skills of the historian applied to evidence from the past. The most able teachers have shown us for centuries that we can make history engaging while we teach its most important lessons. Now, as we are able to explore the affinities between game-based learning and the goals and tools of history teaching, we have some new tools at our disposal to make history "playful."

In a 2006 article, Richard Van Eck argued that it is time that discussions about digital game-based learning (DGBL) move beyond research that has, by this point, already convincingly demonstrated its efficacy as a place for, or site of, learning.[3] We need to move on now, he argues, to create "research explaining why DGBL is engaging and effective" and to provide "practical guidance for how (when, with whom, and under what conditions) games can be integrated into the learning process to maximize their learning potential." We take up Van Eck's challenge to explain and prescribe appropriate uses for history-related games as we explore links between our DGBL history project, the *Great Unsolved Mysteries in Canadian History*, and recent

Fig 1.1: Victoria students exploring the "Death on The Kettle Valley Railway" mystery. *Great Unsolved Mysteries in Canadian History* project. Used with permission.

Fig 1.2: Original homepage of the *Great Unsolved Mysteries in Canadian History* website. *Great Unsolved Mysteries in Canadian History* project. Used with permission.

research and writing about historical thinking and knowing. (See figures 1.1 and 1.2.) More specifically, we draw on two separate academic discussions, one exploring research into the teaching and learning of history in the schools and the other relating to theoretical and methodological developments within the discipline of history itself. We suggest that the intersection, or overlap, of these two areas provides a research- and theory-based explanation for how the *Great Unsolved Mysteries in Canadian History* project works to include playful elements in the teaching of serious history. In the process, we also help to explain why this online history education project has become so widely used and so critically acclaimed as a way of teaching history.

The History Educators

Recent years have witnessed an increasing amount of research in the field of history education. Educators, long interested in how to teach students to think scientifically, have turned their attention to what constitutes historical thinking, or, in the current parlance, "historical literacy." There are a number of factors involved in this renewed interest in history education, but perhaps most often cited is the decline of the more general social studies movement in the wake of research documenting students' staggering historical ignorance about the origin and accomplishments of their own particular nation-state—this in an era of globalization with its increasing unease about the loss of national and religious identity following the end of the Cold War.[4] Notwithstanding clear evidence that nationalism and indeed patriotism have been the engines driving often-intense public discussions about the purpose of history education, responses to the recent perceived crisis of historical understanding have been varied.[5]

Conservatives have lobbied unapologetically, and sometimes successfully, for a highly partisan, nationalistic "return to basics" move within schools and museums,[6] but there has been a significant movement in quite another direction as well: history researchers and educators alike are encouraging students to do their own "document analysis"—the interpretation of original historical or archaeological evidence from the past—as an important pillar of history education.

Their motives have varied. Many teachers and public historians (in museums, heritage villages, and other historical sites and monuments) have discovered that students are simply more interested in history, and seem to remember more of it for the final exam, when they can actively engage with original historical sources; because it keeps students busy, occupied, and apparently learning, this approach is widely perceived to work as an educational strategy. As a result, compilations of primary documents along with supporting educational materials have become a major industry, particularly in the United States.[7]

Researchers in the field of history education do not deny that students can be more engaged by working with primary documents, but their strong advocacy of teaching students to use primary documents in the history classroom is not related just to the immediate appeal that working with these documents provides to students. Rather, researchers and theorists in the field of history education tend to share a conviction that, because history essentially is a dialogue among people about the interpretation of evidence left over from the past, then history education must, to be effective, at the very least introduce students to what history is by inviting them to participate actively in the process or practice of what doing history involves.[8] Like the revolutionary science educators of an earlier era, history educators are suggesting that historical knowledge, like scientific knowledge, is not about knowing facts so much as it is about understanding processes. For teachers who see science as a kind of knowledge or process of knowing rather than simply the final product or conclusion, Bunsen burners and the techniques of scientific observation overshadow the memorization of complicated nomenclatures. For teachers who see history as a kind of knowledge or process of knowing, primary documents and the techniques of inquiry-based interpretation overshadow the memorization of events, names, and dates. As Peter Seixas has argued, it is only in this way that students can become truly engaged in the "community of inquiry" that comprises the disciplinary, evidence-based critical inquiry that history is.[9] (See figure 1.3.)

Ken Osborne has pointed out that the idea that students need to "do history" in order to understand history—that is, analyze and interpret primary historical documents—is not new; the history teacher Fred Morrow Fling was actively advocating this practice more than one hundred years ago, and the idea has been an important component of progressive reform in educational circles ever since.[10] The idea may not be new, but research in the field of history education is now documenting just how difficult it is to convey this to students. One of the unanticipated consequences of the increased use of primary documents in the classroom has been research documenting that, engaging as they are, these primary sources cannot on their own be relied on to provide an increased understanding of history. In his well-known 1991 study, Samuel Wineburg asked students and historians to think aloud as they read historical texts, both primary and secondary.[11] He noted that whereas historians entered into a complex dialogue with the multiple meanings of the text, students were generally able to marshal only one question about what they were reading: is it true? With little familiarity

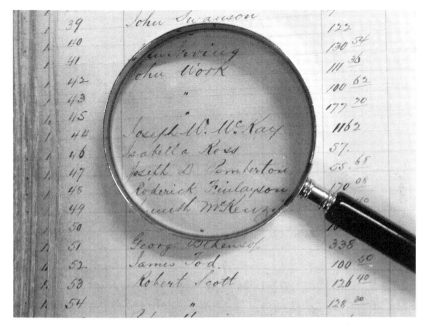

Fig 1.3: Historical research is like detective work. Image courtesy of the authors.

with primary documents, without the appropriate background knowledge, and without an understanding of the processes of critical inquiry, students were simply not able to engage in constructing historical knowledge from the documents. As Wineburg has argued since, historical thinking really is an "unnatural act" that involves thought processes that are counterintuitive to most students.[12]

Wineburg's work demonstrates that students need considerable scaffolding if they are to learn to use primary documents to construct knowledge about the past. The research of history educators such as Peter Lee, Ros Ashby, S. G. Grant, Bruce Van Sledright, Keith Barton, Linda Levstik, and Stella Winert has provided considerable evidence about how students as young as age 6 or 7 can successfully be taught the kinds of critical, evidence-based thinking they need to think historically.[13] But it turns out that, left to themselves, students are reluctant to critically engage primary sources. Andrew Milson argues that students using web-based materials regularly sought out the "path of least resistance" when looking for ways of constructing historical knowledge, rather than searching for a more complex understanding.[14] Other research has documented that rather than evaluating information from multiple sources, students using primary documents on the world wide web moved directly to search engines to find sites they thought would give them all necessary information to accomplish their task[15] as quickly as possible, and in a way that was most likely to meet the approval of the teacher.

Barton's study of fourth- and fifth-grade American students highlights the problems. His research documented students' remarkable ability to engage critically with such issues as the contingency of historical narratives and the constructed nature of historical documents. But after students had critically examined the historical documents, Barton discovered "one remarkable and unexpected problem":

> After three days of this [critical inquiry] activity, the teacher pulled students together to discuss their conclusions. . . . Each student had an opinion, and they were eager to share. *But none of the opinions had any relationship to the evidence that they had just spent three days evaluating.* Students did not use the evidence to reach conclusions; they were just making up what they thought must have happened.[16]

Barton aptly entitled his article "'I just kinda know.'" European educators have noted a similar reluctance in their students to bring critical inquiry to bear on history education in the classroom, and new research into levels of historical consciousness and differences between historical knowledge and historical belief is now underway to account for the phenomenon whereby students know about history as critical inquiry, but refuse to take it seriously.[17] Keith Barton and Linda Levstik have argued that the solution to the problem is to be found in the articulation of a coherent purpose for history education, and have found it in history's unique suitability to provide students with the kind of humanistic education they need to participate in a democratic and pluralistic society. The study of primary documents, they argue, provides an important foundation for the kind of evidence-based reasoning that members of a participatory democracy need to deliberate on, and make decisions about, their society.[18]

On a slightly different tack, Ruth Sandwell has argued that the problem is essentially epistemological: students do not engage with a critical evaluation of historical evidence because, in spite of what they learn about critical inquiry, they still believe that history really is a set of received truths that they must memorize and tell back to their teachers.[19] Conducting reasoned, educated interpretations of evidence becomes just one more example of busywork in the classroom. And why wouldn't they? After all, knowing "the facts" rather than understanding the process is what they are most often, and most rigorously, evaluated on. As Peter Lee puts it, if students do not "get" the idea that history is dialogue among people about the interpretation of meaningful evidence about the past, and believe instead that it exists only by authoritarian fiat or only through the always-flawed accounts of individual eyewitnesses, then it becomes impossible, meaningless, or both, for students to understand history.[20]

The Historians

Historians have changed a lot over the past fifty years. Since the defeat of fascism and the triumph of American modernity, historians have been increasingly rejecting the notion of a single unified narrative of history in favor of histories that are more complex and varied. They have expanded their studies beyond one class, gender, or ethnically defined group, and beyond their earlier, predominant interest in public life and formal political systems. As a result, historians' research and writing has become much more interdisciplinary, and much less the narrative of "the winners." This concern with a wider range of peoples and issues in the past has, furthermore, encouraged some historians to take (and admit to) a more active role in contemporary concerns, particularly those involving historical injustices based on gender, class, or ethnicity. They have become much more open about their concerns about contemporary, relevant issues, and the ways in which these contemporary issues have helped to shape their professional interests. As Christopher Dummitt phrased it in his article "Beyond Inclusiveness: The Future of Canadian History," "by far the largest fields that historians now claim to be affiliated with are those generally associated with inclusive history: social; women and gender; and cultural."[21]

Dummitt goes on to articulate some of the problems that the new consensus on inclusivity has created, but this is not to diminish the fact that historians have become much more cognizant of the relationship between knowledge and power than they used to be. Not only do they believe that history involves more than the single narrative about the winners in the past, but many historians argue that portraying history as a particular one-dimensional narrative only helps to maintain structures of power within today's society.[22] These changes are aspects of historians' growing awareness that their research is more a process of critical inquiry, a kind of knowledge, than it is a series of authoritarian, factual statements, let alone final judgments, about the past. The past is gone, and all historians can do is try to understand some of its meaning and complexity through ongoing discussions about how best to interpret evidence from the past that is meaningful in the present, albeit for a wide variety of reasons.[23] (See figure 1.4.)

In moving beyond the positivism that largely defined nineteenth-century historical writing, historians are openly acknowledging that history is a process

Fig 1.4: Historians solving historical mysteries at the Playing with Technology in History Unconference, 2010. Image courtesy of the authors.

of critical inquiry, a painfully meticulous process of piecing together—constructing—into a narrative, pieces of evidence about a meaningful past in the context of what other historians have written about. Acknowledging that history is an interpretive act where historians enter into an ongoing dialogue with others about fragmented, contingent evidence from the past has had an important influence not only on what historians study, but on how they present their work. Increasingly, historians are arguing that it is not enough to be more inclusive in who we consider legitimate historical subjects, or how we represent them: our history needs to articulate more clearly the dialogical nature of our work. As historian Lyle Dick has recently argued, historians have identified the need to move beyond a focus on diversity of content toward embracing a greater diversity of form. In this regard, we might consider replacing univocal narratives or harmonized syntheses relying on partial perspectives or evidence with forms incorporating a larger selection of voices and perspectives. Instead of weaving the different strands together into tight narratives, we might be trying to combine different forms, genres, and voices into looser structures. Rather than seeking resolution and coherence, we might be juxtaposing conflicting and even contradictory materials to more accurately represent the contested character of the Canadian past and the actual diversity of perspectives bearing on its interpretation.[24]

Like history educators, historians are increasingly declaring the importance of the processes of historical practice to good historical thinking. Three decades ago, the craft of conveying the complex interplay of forces was recaptured by European scholars in a method called "micro-storia" or "micro-history." Micro-history is a return to the story of real people with all the messy, fascinating, sometimes microscopic details of their lives. But the goal in exploring the details is to see the larger forces at work, forces that are invisible when the scope is much larger:

> By reducing the scale of observation, it becomes possible to document the ways that particular people work out their lives within a shifting set of patterns—beliefs, practices, relationships—in which they make sense of their own lives, adapting themselves to each other and to their environment, or by changing their environment to suit their society. It is in people's day-to-day practices that they make the "innumerable and infinitesimal transformations of and within the dominant cultural economy in order to adapt it to their own interests and their own rules." It is in these practices that microhistorians hope to see and sometimes explain variation and change in history.[25]

Micro-history is the asking of the big questions of history and looking for the answers in small places.[26]

The Great Unsolved Mysteries in Canadian History *Project*

As we have argued above, history educators and professional historians now agree that understanding history means understanding the dialogical processes involved in interpreting evidence from the past in the context of what others have thought relevant. History is a conversation about interpreting evidence. The project that John Sutton Lutz, Ruth Sandwell, and Peter Gossage established, *Great Unsolved Mysteries in Canadian History* (www.canadianmysteries.ca), is a web-based history education project that explicitly sets out to introduce students to the unnatural act of doing history. As we described the history of the project in 2009:

> When we first imagined the site, we were intrigued by the dissonance between using late 20th century technology to investigate a mid-19th century murder. What John and I had originally liked about the technology was the strange co-incidence between web based technology and late 20th century ideas about history. We felt that the lecture format and the textbook, both first developed in the 19th century

as important ways of teaching history, were used by earlier generations of history teachers because they were particularly well suited
to particular 19th century understandings of history. That is, history
is "just the facts," plain and simple; a chronicle of events told in an
epic format, with good guys and bad guys (and we mean guys) and
a strong, simple and one dimensional plot line. The world wide web,
by contrast, was, we thought, particularly well suited to late 20th
century ideas of what history is: not a linear, authoritarian declara-
tion by an eminent historian about what "really" happened, but a
broader, more inclusive discussion of varied peoples in varied places,
discussions that were sensitive to race, class, gender, sexual preference,
regional differences. History involves multiple perspectives, ambiguity and dissonance. It also involves some very particular disciplined
approaches to evaluating evidence, to building reasoned arguments,
and to making persuasive claims about the past.[27]

What we had created was, in effect, a digital game-based learning site
where visitors to the site would "do history": in interacting with the materials
on the site, they would engage in, or would at least be forced to confront,
complex forms of historical thinking as they used the primary documents
on the site to come to a reasoned interpretation of the real-life historical
mystery they were presented with in each of the twelve mysteries.

The premise of the *Great Unsolved Mysteries in Canadian History* project is simple. Take an intriguing mystery—a story that has no single, clear
resolution—put all the kinds and range of evidence you can find on the
Internet, and challenge students and others to solve the mystery. In fact,
we provide the first part of the story and the tools for students to write
the ending. The method is micro-historical so the mysteries are not random. They involve some of the big issues that concern historians: race,
gender, ethnicity, immigration, religious intolerance, terrorism, war, climate change, aboriginal–non-aboriginal relations, wrongful convictions,
and child abuse, to name a few.

Between 1997 and 2008 the project created twelve mystery websites, each
available in their entirety in French and English. Each website is a multimedia archive based on the particular mystery, with dozens and even hundreds of documents, each totaling about 100,000 words of text, along with
dozens of images; several have oral interviews, 3D re-creations, and video.
They range from some of the big questions (where was the Viking Vinland
and why did it not survive?) through the burning of Montreal in 1734, an
Indian war of the 1860s, to mysterious deaths and murders, including that of
the well-known artist Tom Thompson and the Canadian diplomat hounded
by the CIA, Herbert Norman. These are great mysteries, not because they

Fig 1.5: One of the *MysteryQuests* focused on the mysterious death of the child Aurore in rural Quebec in 1920. *Great Unsolved Mysteries in Canadian History* project. Used with permission.

are famous, but because of the amazing access they give us to the lives and issues of real people facing dramatic and often violent crises.

To provide the necessary pedagogical support for the mysteries, an educational director (Ruth Sandwell) was appointed to create materials for teachers and students interested in developing and refining the techniques of primary source document analysis. These include introductory lessons for interpreting historical evidence complete with teachers' notes and fully developed unit plans comprising several lessons and support materials for teachers and students. We also created an entire *MysteryQuests* website (www .mysteryquests.ca) that contains thirty-nine student-focused and age-specific lesson plans that pertain to the individual mysteries. Other forms of teacher and student support (see the Teachers' Corner for each of the mystery sites) make it easier to use the mysteries to teach history within elementary, secondary, and even university classrooms. (See, for example, figure 1.5.)

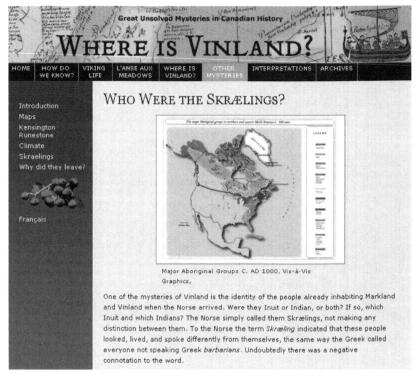

Fig 1.6: One of the webpages on the "Where was Vinland?" mystery site. *Great Unsolved Mysteries in Canadian History* project. Used with permission.

Further testing is needed to confirm exactly how and to what extent the sites work at conveying new ways of thinking about and doing history, but our preliminary studies indicate some success in providing willing viewers both the raw materials of an engaging micro-historical mystery, and the intellectual and pedagogical support to interpret them.

The mysteries take two forms. Some of them present a historical puzzle for the student to solve. Others take a crime, or a mysterious death that might have been a crime, and invite the student in as a detective-historian. In some cases, the students find themselves absolving convicted murderers they believe were wrongly convicted and hanged in a travesty of justice. In others, they identify potential murderers who have walked free. All the mysteries were chosen because there is no single "correct" solution. In all cases, students are assembling a narrative out of a diverse, unordered, and sometimes contradictory set of evidence, and having to make the case that their solution is more plausible than the alternatives.

Let us give an example of the first type, "Where was Vinland?" chronologically the first in our series. (See figure 1.6.) All of our websites were created

Fig 1.7: Inside one of the 3D reconstructions of L'Anse Aux Meadows dwelling on the Vinland site. *Great Unsolved Mysteries in Canadian History* project. Used with permission.

by leading scholars in the field who, in most cases, pitched the mysteries to the directors in a national competition. In this case, the research director, archaeologist Birgitta Wallace, had spent her entire career studying the Norse in North America and is acknowledged to be one of the world's experts. Only one Viking-era settlement site has been documented in North America at L'Anse Aux Meadows, in northern Newfoundland, and it does not seem to coincide with the description from the Viking stories, or sagas, which identifies Vinland as the "Land of Grapes." The site where Europe first met America is of global significance. Proponents locate Vinland in many places between Rhode Island and Labrador. So the website presents all the saga evidence and virtually all the archaeological evidence of Vikings in North America; extensive cultural and linguistic evidence from the Norsemen of the era so we can learn what "grapes" or wine might have been to them; and the flora and climate in eastern North America in 1000 C.E. It also examines the prominent Viking hoaxes. We know so much about the extensively excavated and documented L'Anse Aux Meadows site that we were able to create a 3D immersive environment for students to explore as well as scan many of the key artifacts in 3D and present them virtually on the website. A hint: the butternut root fragment is a significant piece of the puzzle. (See figure 1.7.)

The other type of mystery, based on a crime, offers students the chance to play the ever-popular role of detective, or crime scene investigator, which, as it turns out, is very analogous to that of the historian.[28] But where detectives are often satisfied when they have identified the immediate cause of death and the specific perpetrator, the historian is even more interested in the context that created the crime and the contributing causes. The mystery "Who Killed William Robinson? Race, Justice, and Settling the Land," which was the first one launched, is an example. When three black men were killed in 1867–68 in the small farming settlements on Salt Spring Island between Vancouver Island and Vancouver, native people were widely blamed. Only one of these murders, that of William Robinson, resulted in a conviction, and in that case an aboriginal man named Tshuanahusset was hanged. A closer look at all the cases suggests the possibility that it was easy to blame and convict a native person at that time when they could not speak the language of the courts and were widely seen as savages. The jury deliberated a full five minutes before Tshuanahusset was convicted on flimsy and conflicting circumstantial evidence, and his alibi was overlooked. When one explores motive, the case starts to point to members of the settler community who later are associated with a series of questionable activities relating to Robinson's valuable waterfront property. The case is not just a "who-dunnit?" but an opening into the whole process of settlement of British Columbia, the dispossession of aboriginal people, the role of black settlers, and the question of whether justice was possible in such a race-based society. In this case, like Vinland and the other ten cases, small mysteries open up big questions.

Playful has proven popular. Every day, on average, more than 2,000 students use the website. Last year there were more than 800,000 user sessions, primarily in Canada and the United States but also in 50 countries around the world. The project has been extensively peer-reviewed (see http://www .canadianmysteries.ca/en/reviews.php) and it has won major prizes in the field. In 2008 the series won the award for the best online teaching resource in history from the MERLOT network and the Pierre Berton award from the National History Society of Canada for exemplary work in the dissemination of history. We continue to work on the project and a new mystery on the lost Franklin expedition is due to be launched in 2015.

The success of the project stems from the convergence described above: new ideas in historical pedagogy that support the active engagement of the learner at the center; new models of how historical thinking develops, particularly through primary source evidence relating to a micro-historical problem; a new technological format that provides both the fertile ground where a rich body of evidence can be accumulated, displayed, and widely accessed and the pedagogical scaffolding that allows visitors to research and analyze the evidence within online multimedia archives. Bringing these threads together,

Fig 1.8: Artist's reconstruction of the crime scene in the William Robinson case. *Great Unsolved Mysteries in Canadian History* project. Used with permission.

the *Great Unsolved Mysteries in Canadian History* project shows that the fascinating stories from the past can be used as a window to engage students in the big questions of then and now. Much more research is needed to examine the ways in which site visitors actually use the mysteries to build their historical understanding, and to test and refine the pedagogical support available on the site. But so far, the project seems to be providing just one more example of how learning history can be serious and playful at the same time.

A Full List of the Mysteries Available on The Great Unsolved Mysteries in Canadian History *Website*

Where is Vinland?

Use archaeological, historical, climatic, and environmental clues with a new 3D reconstruction to solve one of the most intriguing mysteries in world history: where did Europe first meet America?

Torture and the Truth: Angélique and the Burning of Montreal

When Montreal caught fire in April 1734, suspicion fell on a Black slave called Marie Angélique. But did she really start the fire?

Life and Death in the Arctic:
The Mystery of the Franklin Expedition

In 1845 2 ships with 110 men, the elite of the British Navy, set off from England to find the Northwest Passage and were never seen again. [To be launched in spring 2015.]

Jerome: The Mystery Man of Baie Sainte-Marie

On September 8, 1863, a stranger was found on the beach of Sandy Cove in Nova Scotia, alive but with no legs and unable to speak. Who was this "mystery man"?

Who Killed William Robinson? Race, Justice, and Settling the Land

When three Black men were murdered in the space of eighteen months around 1868 on bucolic Salt Spring Island in British Columbia, alarm bells went off. An Aboriginal man was hanged, but was he guilty?

We Do Not Know His Name: Klatsassin and the Chilcotin War

As dawn broke on April 30, 1864, some twenty-five Tsilhqot'in men surprised the sleeping camp of a crew building a road to the Cariboo gold mines, killing fourteen. Was this war?

Heaven and Hell on Earth: The Massacre of the "Black" Donnellys

In 1880 the Donnelly farm in Ontario was burned to the ground and five family members were murdered. No one was ever found guilty of the crimes despite considerable evidence. Why?

Who Discovered Klondike Gold?

For a century, controversy has swirled around the question of who deserves credit for the discovery that set off the greatest gold rush in the history of the world. You be the judge!

The Redpath Mansion Mystery

Who killed Ada Redpath and her son in their Montreal mansion in 1901? Find out what really happened as you look into the lives of the rich and famous in their elite neighborhood.

Death on a Painted Lake: The Tom Thomson Tragedy

Investigate the mysterious 1917 death of artist Tom Thomson. Was his drowning accidental?

Aurore! The Mystery of the Martyred Child

The corpse of a young girl was found in a quiet Quebec village in 1920. What is the story behind this tragic case, and why does it still haunt the collective memory of the Québécois?

Explosion on the Kettle Valley Line: The Death of Peter Verigin

An explosion on a train killed the leader of the pacifist Doukhobor religious community in Castlegar, British Columbia, in 1924. Investigate the many theories about who did it. Accident or murder?

Death of a Diplomat: Herbert Norman and the Cold War

What would persuade the Canadian ambassador to Egypt to jump from a Cairo building in 1957?

MysteryQuests

This website consists of thirty-nine interactive, user-friendly lessons designed for use by individuals working alone or with a partner; suggestions for adapting these resources for use by an entire class are found in the teacher notes attached to each MysteryQuest.

NOTES

1. James Joyce, *Ulysses*, episode 2: Nestor, accessed July 31, 2012, http://www.online-literature.com/james_joyce/ulysses/2/.

2. Ruth Sandwell, "School History vs. the Historians," *International Journal of Social Education* 30, no. 1 (Spring 2005): 9–17.

3. Richard Van Eck, "Digital Game-Based Learning: It's Not Just the Digital Natives Who are Restless," *Educause Review* 41, no. 2 (March–April 2006): 16–30, accessed February 10, 2011, http://www.educause.edu/EDUCAUSE+Review/EDUCAUSEReviewMagazineVolume41/DigitalGameBasedLearningItsNot/158041.

4. See Margaret McMillan's *Uses and Abuses of History* (Toronto: Penguin, 2009) for a recent articulation of the relationship between the revival of interest in history

and the end of the Cold War. See also Ken Osborne, "Teaching History in Schools: A Canadian Debate," *Journal of Curriculum Studies* 35, no. 5 (2003): 585–626; and Peter Seixas, "Parallel Crises: History and the Social Studies Curriculum in the USA," *Journal of Curriculum Studies* 25 (1993): 235–50.

5. See, for example, Tony Taylor, "Disputed Territory: The Politics of Historical Consciousness in Australia," in *Theorizing Historical Consciousness*, ed. Peter Seixas (Toronto: University of Toronto Press, 2004), 217–39. For a discussion of Canadian reflections on history and history education over the past generation, see Ruth Sandwell, "'We were allowed to disagree, because we couldn't agree on anything': Seventeen Voices in the Canadian Debates over History Education," in *History Wars and the Classroom: Global Perspectives*, ed. Tony Taylor and Robert Guyver (Charlotte, N.C.: Information Age Publishing, 2012), 51–76; Anna Clark and Stuart Macintyre, *The History Wars* (Melbourne: Melbourne University Press, 2003); for comparative perspectives, see Tony Taylor and Robert Guyver, eds., *History Wars and the Classroom: Global Perspectives* (Charlotte, N.C.: Information Age Publishing, 2012); Anna Clark, "Teaching the Nation's Story: Comparing Public Debates and Classroom Perspectives of History Education in Australia and Canada," *Journal of Curriculum Studies* 41, no. 6 (2009): 745–62; and Anna Clark, *History's Children: History Wars in the Classroom* (Sydney: University of New South Wales Press, 2008).

6. For the way this was worked out in the American context, see Linda Symcox, *Whose History?: The Struggle for National Standards in American Classrooms* (New York: Teachers College Press, 2002).

7. For an overview of the practical problems and consequences of using primary documents in the classroom, see Keith Barton, "Primary Sources in History: Breaking Through the Myths," *Phi Delta Kappan* 86, no. 10 (June 2005): 745–53; Ruth Sandwell, "History is a Verb: Teaching Historical Practice to Teacher Education Students," in *New Possibilities for the Past: Shaping History Education in Canada*, ed. Penny Clark (Vancouver: UBC Press, 2011), 224–42.

8. See, for example, Peter Seixas, "A Modest Proposal for Change in Canadian History Education," *Teaching History* 137 (December 2009): 26–32; idem, "What is Historical Consciousness?" in *To the Past: History Education, Public Memory and Citizenship Education in Canada*, ed. Ruth Sandwell (Toronto: University of Toronto Press, 2006), 11–22; Ken Osborne, "Teaching History in Schools: A Canadian Debate," *Journal of Curriculum Studies* 35, no. 5 (2003): 585–626. There is a large and growing literature on this, which is perhaps best summarized in Keith Barton and Linda Levstik's *Teaching History for the Common Good* (Mahwah, N.J.: Lawrence Erlbaum Associates, 2004). These issues are expanded in the Canadian context most recently in Penney Clark, ed., *New Possibilities for the Past: Shaping History Education in Canada* (Vancouver: UBC Press, 2011).

9. Peter Seixas, "The Community of Inquiry as a Basis for Knowledge and Learning: The Case of History," *American Educational Research Journal* 30, no. 2 (1993): 305–24.

10. Ken Osborne, "Fred Morrow Fling and the Source Method of Teaching History," *Theory and Research in Social Education* 71 (2003): 466–501.

11. Samuel Wineburg, "On the Reading of Historical Texts: Notes on the Breach Between School and Academy," *American Educational Research Journal* 28, no. 3 (1991): 495–519.

12. Samuel Wineburg, "Historical Thinking and Other Unnatural Acts," *Phi Delta Kappan* 80, no. 7 (March 1999): 488–500.

13. S. G. Grant and Bruce Van Sledright, *Constructing a Powerful Approach to Teaching and Learning in Elementary Social Studies* (Boston: Houghton Mifflin, 2001); Jere E. Brophy and Bruce Van Sledright, *Teaching History in Elementary Schools* (New York: Teachers College Press, 1997); Stella Rose Weinert, "Young Children's Historical Understanding" (MA thesis, University of British Columbia, 2001); Peter Lee, "Putting Principles into Practice: Understanding History," in *How Students Learn: History in the Classroom*, ed. M. Suzanne Donovan and John D. Bransford (Washington, D.C.: National Academies Press, 2005), 29–78; Ruth Sandwell, "Reading Beyond Bias: Teaching Historical Practice to Secondary School Students," *McGill Journal of Education* 38, no. 1 (Winter 2003): 168–86; Keith C. Barton and Linda S. Levstik, "Why Don't More History Teachers Engage Students in Interpretation?" *Social Education* 67, no. 6 (2003): 358–62; Keith C. Barton and Linda S. Levstik, *Researching History Education: Theory, Method and Context* (New York: Routledge, 2008); Bruce A. Van Sledright, *The Challenge of Rethinking History Education* (New York: Routledge, 2011).

14. Andrew J. Milson, "The Internet and Inquiry Learning: Integrating Medium and Method in a Sixth Grade Social Studies Classroom," *Theory and Research in Social Education* 30 (2002): 330–53.

15. Keith C. Barton, "Inquiry and the Book of James," paper presented at the annual meeting of the College and University Faculty Assembly, National Council for the Social Studies, Phoenix, Arizona, November 2002.

16. Keith C. Barton, "'I just kinda know': Elementary Students' Ideas about Historical Evidence," in *Researching History Education: Theory, Method, and Context*, ed. Linda Levstik and Keith Barton (New York: Routledge, 2008), 209–27.

17. James V. Wertsch, "Is It Possible to Teach Beliefs, as Well as Knowledge about History?" and Peter Lee and Rosalyn Ashby, "Progression in Historical Understanding among Students Ages 7–14," in *Knowing, Teaching and Learning History: National and International Perspectives*, ed. Peter Stearns, Peter Seixas, and Sam Wineburg (New York: New York University Press, 2000).

18. Barton and Levstik, "Teacher Education and the Purposes of History," chapter 13 in *Teaching History for the Common Good* (Mahwah, N.J.: Lawrence Erlbaum Associates, 2004), 244–65.

19. Sandwell, "Reading Beyond Bias," 172–74.

20. Peter Lee, "Putting Principles into Practice: Understanding History," in *How Students Learn: History in the Classroom*, ed. Suzanne Donovan and John D. Bransford (Washington, D.C.: The National Academic Press, 2005), accessed February 10, 2011, http://www.nap.edu/openbook/0309089484/html/31.html.

21. Christopher Dummitt, "Beyond Inclusiveness: The Future of Canadian History," in *Contesting Clio's Craft: New Directions and Debates in Canadian History*, ed. Christopher Dummitt and Michael Dawson (London: Institute for the Americas, 2009), 102.

22. See, for example, Robert F. Berkhofer Jr., "The Challenge of Poetics to (Normal) Historical Practice," in *The Rhetoric of Interpretation and the Interpretation of Rhetoric*, ed. Paul Hernadi (Durham, N.C.: Duke University Press, 1989), 197.

23. This section has been adapted from Sandwell's article "School History vs. the Historians," *International Journal of Social Education* 30, no. 1 (Spring 2005): 10.

24. Lyle Dick, "Fragmentation and Synthesis from the Standpoint of Critical History," ActiveHistory, ca. April 26, 2011, http://activehistory.ca/papers/ldick/, accessed October 25, 2012.

25. Ruth W. Sandwell, "History as Experiment: Microhistory and Environmental History," in *Method and Meaning in Canadian Environmental History*, ed. Alan McEachern and William Turkel (Toronto: Thomas Nelson Publishers, 2008), 123. Quotation from Michel de Certeau, *The Practice of Everyday Life* (Berkeley: University of California Press, 1984), xiv.

26. George G. Iggers, "From Macro- to Microhistory: The History of Everyday Life," in *Historiography in the Twentieth Century: From Scientific Objectivity to the Postmodern Challenge* (Hanover: Wesleyan University Press, 1997). Two classics of the genre include Carlo Ginzburg, *The Cheese and the Worms: The Cosmos of a Sixteenth-Century Miller*, trans. John and Anne Tedeschi (Baltimore: Johns Hopkins University Press, original in Italian 1976, English translation 1980); and Natalie Zemon Davis, *The Return of Martin Guerre* (Cambridge, Mass.: Harvard University Press, 1983). In the Canadian context, see Ruth W. Sandwell "Introduction: Reading the Rural with a Microhistorical Eye," in *Contesting Rural Space: Land Policy and the Practices of Resettlement on Saltspring Island, 1859–1891* (Kingston: McGill-Queen's University Press, 2005), 3–14.

27. Ruth Sandwell, "Reflections on the Great Unsolved Mysteries in Canadian History Project: A Pedagogical Perspective," *Canadian Diversity / Diversité canadienne* 7, no. 1 (2009): 88–92.

28. For an excellent book-length examination of just how, exactly, history works when taught as mystery, see David Gerwin and Jack Zevin, *Teaching U.S. History as Mystery* (New York: Routledge, 2011).

———

TWO

"Why can't you just tell us?"

Learning Canadian History with the Virtual Historian

Stéphane Lévesque

Introduction

What do students learn from educational technology? What expertise do digital history applications develop in computer users? Surely, for most educators web entertainment and serious game skills are inadequate answers to these questions—and for sound reasons. For today's secondary school and university students, technology plays an integral part in their learning experiences.[1] Students are "digital natives" and savvy.[2] No longer does it suffice for a history teacher to present an overhead and have students take notes. No longer is it viable for a museum to count on traditional exhibits to attract new visitors. For Marc Prensky,

> Today's students have not just changed *incrementally* from those of the past, nor simply changed their slang, clothes, body adornments, or styles, as has happened between generations previously. A really big *discontinuity* has taken place. One might even call it a "singularity"—an event which changes things so fundamentally that there is absolutely no going back. This so-called "singularity" is the arrival and rapid dissemination of digital technology in the last decades of the 20th century.[3]

Twenty-first-century students are used to interacting with hypermedia, to downloading music on their cell phones, to consulting a library database on their laptops, and to beaming instant messages while watching television or playing video games. They are actively involved in social networks and have little patience for classroom lectures, content-driven textbooks, and standard literacy tests. In this period of apparent "discontinuity" with past generations, it may seem futile to have young learners read passages from authorized textbooks or to introduce them to primary sources written in a seemingly "foreign" language from historical actors so distant from their busy, technological lives. From this perspective, the question should no longer be about whether to use digital technology but rather how to use it to further the acquisition and development of expertise in domains of knowledge.

This chapter addresses some of the fundamental questions of digital technology in education from a disciplinary perspective. Using history as a domain of knowledge, it first reviews the research base related to inquiry-based learning and digital technology in history education. Then, the chapter explores the implications of using technology in the history classroom, focusing on the findings from a study with a digital history program. For the purpose of this study, "digital technology" refers to computer or network-based applications—including online learning programs supporting the teaching and learning of subject matters—whereas "virtual history" means the study and use of the past with digital technology.

Doing History . . . with Technology

History educators have long argued for more authentic forms of history teaching and learning.[4] From the nineteenth-century inquiry ideas of Leopold von Ranke through to Fred Morrow Fling's source methods, progressive historians have believed in a theory of school history anchored in teaching the discipline with inquiry. Meaningful and enduring understanding, from this perspective, is an active and continuous process of knowledge acquisition and (re)construction in light of students' prior knowledge, understanding, and engagement with the discipline.[5] In history education, several studies have documented the futility of storytelling and textbook-centered instruction on students' historical learning.[6] Instead, they have pointed to the necessity of engaging students actively in the heuristics of reading, sourcing, researching, and doing historical investigations.

Yet, as Samuel Wineburg puts it so eloquently, historical thinking is not a "natural" act.[7] It is a sophisticated form of knowledge. Novices intuitively view history as a story of the past whereas historians develop expertise in thinking critically about the past. For the former, learning history is equated to "getting the story right," usually in the form of a simplified narrative.

For the latter, however, knowing history implies a complex—and always tentative—dialogue with the past using the available evidence and tools of the discipline. Growing evidence suggests that the development of a community of inquiry can help develop expertise among novices.[8] Linda Levstik and Keith Barton indicate that the process of asking meaningful questions, finding evidence, and drawing conclusions is known as inquiry. Teachers, they argue, "can capitalize on children's natural enthusiasm for learning by making their classrooms places where students explore important and meaningful questions."[9]

Equally challenging for twenty-first-century classrooms is the use of educational technologies. I have argued elsewhere that rich technological open learning environments, such as digital history programs, can support inquiry-based learning because of the types of resources and opportunities they offer to learners.[10] With the development of the Internet and related applications, there has been a push in the last decade to infuse technology into the history curriculum. As John Saye and Thomas Brush argue, digital open learning environments (1) create more realistic, vivid engagements with history (lifelike inquiries) than what is currently available, and (2) draw on and stimulate student development of expertise in history and new technologies.[11]

While school subjects such as science, language arts, and geography have directly benefited from instructional technologies, history lags behind.[12] Particularly in Canadian education, few digital programs focus on history education beyond archival websites, virtual tours, and online texts. The recent development of the *Great Unsolved Mysteries in Canadian History* project[13] presents refreshing initiatives to Canadian educators (see the chapter by Ruth Sandwell and John Sutton Lutz in this volume). In their own unique way, such programs put users in the virtual shoes of detectives engaged in investigating past and contemporary issues of significance.

Students' Learning and the Virtual Historian

Instructional experience and the effectiveness of digital technology directly affect student learning. Empirical studies have revealed the limited pedagogical impact of storytelling and textbook reading on students' historical development and reasoning.[14] There is thus a need for a shift in students' existing habits of classroom work. The integration of digital technology in the history classroom can provide a catalyst for such a change.[15]

Yet educators must not hold unrealistic expectations. Recent findings suggest that technology alone is not a viable solution. Adam Friedman argues in his study of high school history teachers and technology that the use of online sources "depended to a greater extent on their access to computer projectors and school computing facilities."[16] In the same way, the experimental studies of Saye and Brush, the qualitative works of John Lee and Brendan Calandra and Andrew Milson on *WebQuest*, and finally the *Google* search study of Bing Pan et al. offer important recommendations to consider.[17] Affordable access to online resources, such as primary source documents, artifacts, and hypertexts, provides users with a rich base of historical information rarely available in traditional textbooks. From such sources, students can navigate more randomly and be exposed to a greater variety of source types and perspectives on a given subject, widening their horizons and responding to their inquisitive minds. Yet many students in these studies have expressed concerns with regard to the nature of the sources and the amount of information available. Online historical texts are rarely produced in a language and narrative genre familiar to students. In the same way, the large—seemingly infinite—amount of texts available at the click of a mouse can easily overwhelm students who lack the searching and skimming skills necessary to navigate multiple, and often contradictory, sources. The result, as Milson observes, is that many students adopt a "path of least resistance," scanning the material for quick and easy cut-and-paste factual answers.[18]

Available to users in both French and English, the Virtual Historian (VH) (www.virtualhistorian.ca) is an instructional technology developed to meet some of the challenges of digital history learning (see figure 2.1). Unlike textbooks, learning guides, and WebQuests, the VH provides users with nonlinear, authentic, and realistic inquiries ("missions") about key issues in Canadian history. Web-based inquiries are framed around "topical questions," which call for critical analysis, dialectical reasoning, and sophisticated understanding of key phenomena in the history curriculum.[19]

To complete their inquiries, students have access to an online tutorial and a brief synopsis of the mission with a topical question to answer. Curriculum rubrics present all the learning objectives addressed in the mission. Students are provided with conflicting primary and secondary sources on the subject, with embedded reading and sourcing questions, and with a web-based notepad to record and write answers. Students also have access to an online glossary for key words, to additional web resources, as well as to an integrated email program to communicate with their teacher or the program administrator.

Even though the VH was designed to promote digital inquiry learning, does it really work? Does it have a positive impact on students' understanding of history? To answer these questions, a quasi-experimental study was conducted with 107 Ontario high school students in 2007–8. Following the

Fig 2.1: The Virtual Historian library. The Virtual Historian.

Canadian history curriculum for grade 10 (Ontario Ministry of Education, 2005), one task was developed in the VH program: a case on "World War II and the Dieppe Raid, 1942" with four grade 10 history classes (two classroom-based and two VH) from two different English-speaking urban schools. By using the VH in Canadian classrooms, the study aimed to uncover the still unclear role and influence of such educational technology on students' historical thinking and literacy—in terms of substantive knowledge acquisition (e.g., events, actors, dates), procedural knowledge development (e.g., use of evidence, perspective, significance), and epistemological knowledge understanding (how historical knowledge is constructed). Because of the potential of modern technology, the assumption was that digital history, as built in the VH program, can "*mediate* and *support* student historical thinking."[20]

Methodological Matters

As noted above, the subject focus for this study was on Canada's participation in World War II: the Dieppe Raid of 1942. The participation of Canadians at Dieppe in 1942 is an important episode in the study of World War II. It marked the first official engagement of Canadian troops on the European front. Of the six thousand soldiers involved in the Allied raid of August 1942, five thousand were from French and English Canadian units. The Dieppe Raid was not a military success: 907 Canadians died in the battle and nearly 2,000 were captured by the German army. The outcome and impact of the raid are still debated today by historians: useless massacre to test German defense, or necessary lesson for D-Day?

The tasks included for this study first comprised a pre-instruction test that identified students' prior knowledge and understanding of World War II and the Dieppe Raid. This test was administered before students received formal teaching on the subject by the selected teachers (see following item for participating teachers). The second task focused on the experimental use of the Virtual Historian as an online teaching tool. Selected students from the VH groups received a brief introduction to the program by their respective teachers and spent three additional classes on the web-based historical investigations. During these classes, the teacher's role was to assist students in their learning of the topic from the VH. The "case" from Canada's participation in World War II developed in the Virtual Historian comprises a series of authentic, primary, and secondary source documents on the issue. The case also provided a historical map and photographs, declassified Allied and German newsreels and memoranda, a Canadian newspaper article of the time, sounds and animations, and extra resources in the form of hyperlinks to relevant official websites.

Students in the classroom groups did not use the VH but learned from one classroom lesson and an inquiry-based activity in the form of a carousel set with resources distributed to them at each station. Teachers in these classes were responsible for designing three inquiry-based lessons on the subject matter and were instructed to use the same sources on Dieppe. These included primary sources (historical photographs of the raid, paintings, and maps) and secondary sources (excerpts from three textbooks, video clips from CBC *Canada: A People's History* and *Canada at War* series, and the Canadian Encyclopedia online) that students analyzed during the activity. The lessons were submitted and reviewed before teachers engaged in the study of Dieppe with their students. Both the VH and classroom groups had to answer the same questions on the Dieppe Raid and were provided with the same report template. More specifically, the history case asked students to study the strategic importance (or "historical significance") of the Dieppe Raid for Canada, for the Allies, and ultimately for World War II. Students in all groups wrote an essay on the raid of 1942 based on the worksheets and sources at their disposal. Finally, the same questions from the pre-instruction test were used in a post-instruction test to assess students' progression in historical learning of the subject.

The participants for this study were made up of four classes of grade 10 students from two urban Ontario school districts (n = 107). The selection of participants followed a multiple-case design.[21] Two large urban schools in Ontario provided windows into two comparable grade 10 classes per district. The demographic information for the participating schools indicates that 787 students were enrolled in school #1 (174 students in grade 10), and 887 students in school #2 (170 students in grade 10). Results of the Ontario grade 10 literacy test for the schools indicate that 92 percent of participating first-time eligible students successfully completed the literacy test for school #1 and 64 percent of participating first-time eligible students for school #2 (compared to 84 percent as an average for the province). Each school had one classroom and one VH group with similar achievement means. Two different teachers (one for the VH group and one for the classroom group) were selected for each school. Selection was based on willingness to participate in the study.

Findings

Table 2.1 presents data on the VH and comparison groups concerning their understanding of the subject matter, discipline, and epistemology. For both instructional and VH groups, pre-test, post-test, and essay scores show that students increased their comprehension of the subject matter, understanding of history, and literacy skills.

Findings reveal, however, that using the VH led to the organization and writing of more sophisticated essays as evidenced by students' mean scores

TABLE 2.1. Mean scores and standard deviations for each variable by group

Variables	Instructional Groups			Virtual Historian Groups		
	Pre-Test Mean (SD)	Post-Test Mean (SD)	Essay Mean (SD)	Pre-Test Mean (SD)	Post-Test Mean (SD)	Essay Mean (SD)
Tests and essay School #1	3.51 (1.17)	10.29 (2.65)	12.26 (3.69)	3.94 (1.78)	11.51 (2.60)	15.93 (2.89)
Epistemology School #1		3.53 (1.38)			4.23 (1.59)	
Tests and essay School #2	4.11 (2.67)	9.08 (2.60)	12.55 (2.58)	3.72 (2.76)	10.57 (2.45)	12.73 (4.03)
Epistemology School #2		2.99 (1.71)			4.38 (1.58)	

(m = 15.93 vs. m = 12.26 for school #1). A t-test reveals a statistically reliable difference between the mean scores of the two groups for school #1, $t(44)$ = 3.570, p = 0.001, α = 0.05. Students in the VH group were able to construct more structured and coherent arguments than their counterparts. Their knowledge of the subject (e.g., series of events, actors, facts) was greater and their ability to think historically (present clear arguments supported by appropriate evidence, consider historical significance, and make judgments on the issue) was significantly more sophisticated than those in the classroom group. The same pattern could not be found with school #2 (m = 12.73 vs. m = 12.55), $t(45)$ = 0.172, p = 0.865, α = 0.05. Yet, when looking at students' understanding of epistemology, findings indicate that participants in the VH group for school #2 developed more advanced understanding of the nature of historical knowledge than their counterparts in the classroom (m = 4.38 vs. m = 2.99), $t(50)$ = 3.049, p = 0.004, α = 0.05.

To investigate the relationship between variables (schools, groups, instructional strategies), an analysis of variance (ANOVA) was conducted using the essay scores as the dependent variable and the strategies (instructional, VH) and groups (school #1, school #2) as factors. The results (table 2.2) confirm the main effect of the strategy and school on essay scores. The results also indicate an effect between the instructional strategy and the school.

The non-statistically reliable differences on essay scores with students in school #2 are intriguing. Although further analysis is needed at this point, it can be hypothesized from the ANOVA test that external factors related to the school influenced the performance of these students. The lower scores of students from this population on the literacy test and the greater number of students with individualized educational programs (IEPs) and also having English as an additional language (26 percent of the grade 10 population for school #2 compared to 10 percent for school #1) are factors that appear to

TABLE 2.2.   ANOVA test

Dependent variable: Essay scores

Source	Sum of Squares	df	Mean Square	F	Sig.
Corrected model	173.02	3	57.67	4.81	.004
Intercept	15920.08	1	15920.08	1327.17	.000
Strategy	82.57	1	82.57	6.88	.010
Boards	46.97	1	46.97	3.92	.051
Strategy * Schools	67.89	1	67.89	5.66	.019
Error	1067.59	89	11.99		
Total	17376.38	93			
Corrected Total	1240.62	92			

have impacted significantly on their overall performance. A section of this chapter below addresses this point.

Discussion and Conclusion

Learning to think critically about the past is a long and arduous process likely to put students and teachers at odds with popular history and standardized tests. There has been a misleading tendency in education to view knowledge as a binary "all-or-nothing" mode of acquisition. Learning outcomes in curriculum guidelines are often designed for teachers to assess whether or not students master the prescribed expectations for history. But like in any sport or apprenticeship program, history learners do not instinctively turn into experts after some limited exposure to the field. They gradually become skilled when engaged in various drills, practices, and exercises suited for their own development.[22] Even then, intuitive and common-sense ideas often remain durable after repeated learning activities and experiences. To achieve expertise, people require "ample doses of discipline in the alternative sense of the term: regular practice, with feedback, in applying those habits of mind that yield understanding."[23]

The Virtual History program was designed to provide students with *some* digital exposure to what it is like to gradually inquire and think like a historian. Students in the VH groups, particularly from school #1, developed a deeper understanding of the subject matter and the discipline than those who studied the same subject from classroom learning activities. They were able to describe more specifically the events and actors involved in the Dieppe Raid, provide more supporting evidence for their claims, and explain more thoroughly what history is and how historical interpretations are generated. In other words, they showed a more advanced progression in thinking historically about the events. For Catty, a female student from school #1, different interpretations of Dieppe are valid "so long as there is evidence to support the other interpretation" (TOE-004).[24] Virgil goes further and discusses the contingency of historians' claims by arguing that "some interpretations can be different. Like some sources today may still be available to historians that they have not investigated yet" (TOE-016). The following essay explanation from Pearce on the lessons learned from the raid illustrates very well how students from this group used the historical documents in their essay. Lessons are specific to the context of the battle, look at both sides, and are supported by references or direct quotations to the sources in question.

There were many lessons learned from the mistakes at Dieppe. The need for fire support provided itself to be one of the biggest lessons, as there was no fire support at Dieppe (Report 128). A more confirming lesson learned was one of weapons. The Allies learned that most weapons performed wonderfully with the exception of the incendiary bullet, which was virtually useless (Notes from the Theatres of War). A battleship was thought to have potentially "turned the tide in our favour" according to Capt. J. Huges-Hallet. . . . The Germans learned that any attempt to invade the town could be promptly destroyed on the beach (Hamilton Newspaper Article).

In contrast, more students from the classroom (non-VH) groups understood history intuitively and produced essays in story form without use of the evidence provided to them in class. This finding was more evident with students from school #2. Sources were largely absent or considered exclusively for the information they convey (facts, dates, events). In many ways, their essays mirrored their school textbook—in terms of both content and structure. The following excerpt from Vero is typical:

The raid at Dieppe was useful because troops learned lessons from it. It was used as a learning experience that provided the Allies important information about Germany and battle strategies. Lessons learned were used two years later in 1944 for the D. Day battle. Britain developed armoured vehicles. This allowed their engineers to perform their tasks protected by amour. These vehicles were successfully used on D. Day. (TOC-023)

Unlike the previous student's explanation, this one offers only vague statements on the lessons. It is not clear from this essay what has been learned or why "Britain developed armoured vehicles" for D-Day. In fact, no source is referenced in text, making it extremely difficult to understand the reasoning of this student and her ability to infer knowledge from sources. Information is presented in a descriptive manner, only without a coherent, evidence-based argument.

Equally interesting from the findings is the positive relationship between students' historical thinking and their ability to write essays—a correlation that has also been observed in previous studies.[25] An analysis of the relationship between essay structure (thesis, composition, citations/references) and thinking skills (argumentation, use of sources, significance of the raid) reveals a high coefficient of correlation between the two sets of scores for school #1 (Pearson $r = 0.779$, $p < 0.001$) and school #2 (Pearson $r = 0.795$,

p < 0.001). These results suggest that students who have acquired some sophisticated understandings of history as a discipline are more likely to develop well-structured and coherent historical essays. Similar results were also found in a previous study with Canadian students,[26] which established that the VH favors engagement with the subject matter and focuses students' attention on the resolution of an investigation based on historical evidence and inquiry steps. Students in the VH group did not see a disconnection between the web-based inquiry and the writing of their argumentative essays, as did students in the comparison group. More than this, they had the feeling they could personally investigate and go into greater depth in the study of a significant episode in Canadian history.

But since the direction of the correlation is not clear from this study, it can also be hypothesized that historical literacy skills have a direct impact on how students make sense of the past. Research shows that those who have successful reading comprehension strategies and writing skills tend to create more coherent historical arguments supported by appropriate evidence. "Deeper processing," as Jennifer Voss and James Wiley contend in light of their own experimental study, "is facilitated by the individual's prior knowledge, of the specific topic, related topics, and history in general and a more advanced level of general information and thinking skills, such as knowledge of essay structures."[27] Valerie, a student from school #1 who used the VH, comments on her positive research experience: "My interest in history has increased because I've learned how many sources you can get info from and to never give up when researching" (TVE-018).

This is to say, then, that students who have already acquired some ability to search and collect sources, skim through them, compare and contrast their arguments, and make a structured argument on the strategic importance of the raid are also more likely to create essays with deeper understanding of the events and actors using multiple historical sources in a critical way. Steve, the history teacher from school #1 who used the VH, recorded the following in his teacher log: "The experimental group used far better vocabulary. . . . The bottom line is the good students got a lot out of the VH, handling it with ease."

There has been a tendency in computational technology literature to blend critical research with self-advocacy. Supporters of new technologies in education tend to see the positive impact in the marketplace as an indicator of their uncontested potential for classroom improvement. These people, as Kathleen Swan and Mark Hofer argue, "appear to assume that technology is preferable to traditional modes of instruction, that it can make a good teacher better, and that it leads to more student-centered (and therefore preferable) instruction."[28] Findings from this study suggest some positive impact of the program on student achievement. As Katy, who successfully used the VH for her research, puts it: "I prefer in the computer lab because you can learn it your own way" (TVE-001). Yet the educational community will be better served in the end if researchers look at how specific technologies affect students and how digital programs support or detract from particular kinds of learning and achievement. Instead of presenting narrowly defined case studies of best practices, it may be worth analyzing both the potential for, and challenges of, integrating digital technology in history education. As a matter of fact, this study presents challenges that are critical for further use of digital history.

Sources as Fact Sheets

While students who used the program exclusively increased their overall understanding of history significantly, a majority continued to look at historical sources from a "readerly" perspective.[29] Texts—whether they are print, visual, audiovisual, or artifactual—are examined primarily for their conventional, straightforward messages, not for the subtexts and contextualized meaning they convey. Primary sources are comparable to textbooks in that they contain answers ("facts") that must be discovered. Students fail to understand the constructed nature of texts and the purpose and perspective of their authors. Charles Perfetti, Anne Britt, and Mara Georgi refer to this readerly approach as "content-based justification," indicating that students are "considering more what is in a document than the status of the document as evidence."[30] More problematic, the study reveals that many participants attribute greater importance and reliability to simplified secondary sources, such as textbooks, because they convey intelligible truths that are often concealed in primary sources. As Victoria, a student in school #2, confesses, "in class reading a textbook is better because it's very hard to find accurate info on the computer" (TOE-019). Kris, from school #1, concurs: "Being given pages and pages of facts and accounts of what happened is boring. It is easier to understand when the information is to the point" (TVE-015).

Consider, for example, this longer excerpt from Pearce (referenced above), a high-achieving student who used the VH for his assignment:

> Of the 4,963 Canadians who sailed, 56 officers and 851 other ranks were killed." There were 1,944 prisoners taken, and only 2,211 returned to Britain (Hamilton Spectator Newspaper Article). By 1:00 PM, the troops had withdrawn, and trapped soldiers had surrendered. The

results were devastating, as less than half returned home (Timeline for Dieppe Raid). There were many lessons learned from the mistakes at Dieppe. The need for fire support provided itself to be one of the biggest lessons, as there was no fire support at Dieppe (Report 128). A more confirming lesson learned was one of weapons. The Allies learned that most weapons performed wonderfully with the exception of the incendiary bullet, which was virtually useless (Notes from the Theatres of War). A battleship was thought to have potentially "turned the tide in our favour" according to Capt. J. Huges-Hallet. . . . The Germans learned that any attempt to invade the town could be promptly destroyed on the beach (Hamilton Spectator Newspaper Article).

Unlike several of his peers, this student displays a deep understanding of the events and engagement with the content. He provides many factual details about the raid (casualties, timing, weapons, etc.) as well as valuable lessons learned from the amphibious operations. Several historical sources from the VH library, such as declassified reports and a newspaper article, are referenced in support of his argument. In many ways, and for many teachers, Pearce has done exactly what we expect. Facts are correctly presented in sequence and key information from the sources strategically included in the argumentation. What poses a problem from a historical thinking point of view, however, is how the sources are used in shaping the argument. Pearce completely overlooked the nature of the sources and the meaning of the subtexts, naively assuming that documents are bearers of information from a distant past. There is no distinction between primary and secondary sources, between a simplified time line presenting key dates and a declassified report (no. 128) from the Canadian Military Headquarters. The student failed to question the provenance, context, perspective, and credibility of the documents—to employ "sourcing heuristic"[31]—by asking such questions as: Who created the source? When? From what perspective? How is the information supported or contradicted by other sources? All these questions and others were provided to Pearce in scaffolds and worksheets available directly from the VH program.

With such an engagement with the sources, it would have become possible to realize that Report 128 was produced in England by a Canadian historical officer, Colonel Stacey, two years after the raid, in light of D-Day landing. A critical reading of the sources would also allow for an interesting contrast between Stacey's retrospective observations and Report 083 from Captain Brown, an officer who participated directly in the raid, or with Report 116, a secret German intelligence report of the battle produced immediately after Dieppe and offering a very bleak picture of the Canadian operation. Yet, as long as history is understood as a quest to "get the story right," it is impossible for students to realize that knowing history is more complex and tentative than knowing how to find facts from historical sources and create a content-based justification. For Dennis Shemilt, "many pupils take knowledge about the past for granted because they have done little or no work with sources and have rarely, if ever, been asked 'How do we know?'"[32]

The use of sources as fact sheets is not particular to digital history. Students typically adopt such a naive approach to classroom resources as well.[33] What is at stake for virtual history, however, is the assumption that the rich volume of multiple-perspective sources available electronically favors historical reasoning. This cannot be accomplished with primary sources alone. Unless students know how to read texts historically, their engagement will remain simplistic.

Visuals as Illustrations

The challenge of knowing the past online is not only with historical texts. The VH case on Dieppe contains a variety of visuals, audiovisual and animations, which students also failed to analyze in their essays. There is, for example, an informative German photograph (see figure 2.2) taken minutes after the raid, revealing crucial details on the terrible slaughter that Canadians faced upon landing on the well-guarded beach of Normandy. The dead bodies lying on the shore, the brand-new Churchill tanks immobilized in the pebbles, and the smoking landing crafts hit by the German artillery are all important pieces of information in understanding the level of preparedness and firepower of the German forces. The photograph also provides a powerful empathetic window into the chaotic experiences of Canadian soldiers who landed on the beach at Dieppe.

Yet students from this study continued to see visuals as "illustrations," not as "evidence."[34] They did not view themselves as historical agents, as potential interpreters of nonverbal texts that convey particular meanings about the past. "Visual texts," as Walter Werner observes, "are more than 'things' or instructional means set before students; their meanings emerge during interactions with readers (viewers)." "To think of images independent of readers," he goes on, "is naive, for they do not speak apart from interpreters."[35] As with historical texts, analyzing visuals for historical interpretation requires a set of heuristics that will ultimately turn imagery sources into evidence for particular inferences. With this approach, the authority of

Fig 2.2: Bodies of Canadian soldiers from captured German files. Unknown photographer, photo from Dieppe (Operation "Jubilee").

visuals is shifted from the photographer to the questions and inferences that interpreters formulate about them.

Surprisingly, today's textbooks are filled with authentic photographs and colorful graphics that have replaced the seemingly dense, unintelligible content of earlier versions. Still, students are not educated in a classroom environment that encourages them to become historical interpreters of visual texts and animated objects. For Hofer and Swan, "Just as the reader must consider context, point of view, audience, and other keys to understanding textual historical documents, one must view images in much the same way. . . . Like analyzing textual documents, the strategies for reading historical and contemporary images do not necessarily develop naturally and must be explicitly taught."[36]

With the arrival of high-speed Internet and augmented reality technology, users now have instant access to visual information about the real world that becomes interactive and digitally usable. In history, such developments have led to the design of simulations and augmented reality games (ARGs) such as *Reliving the Revolution.* These "serious games" engage learners in historical challenges and encounters with authentic visuals and animated objects about the past. Findings from this study suggest that despite a high penetration of such technology in young people's lives, many students continue to employ a video game approach to visual sources in the history classroom. Instead of reading them as evidence, they view them as "cool" illustrations that enhance the reality of past times.

Digital "Natives" and "Foreign" History

Clearly, engaging students in digitally enhanced inquiries forces them to think differently about history and the subject matter. Storytelling, textbook reading, lecture notes, and heritage consumption must inevitably give way to active participation in investigating the distant, foreign past, and in generating evidence-based interpretations. For some, the progression in thinking historically is colossal and far from linear between the variables used in this study. In some instances, students can provide a sophisticated understanding of history (e.g., what history is) and in others (e.g., use of evidence) offer very naive ideas. As Peter Lee and Rosalyn Ashby observe, "it is possible that development in different conceptual areas may occur at different times."[37] For others, this digital approach to history learning represents a significant departure from their comfortable schooling "path of least resistance" and their intuitive learning outside the school. For Cassey, a student from school #2, the overall experience could be summed up in these terms: "I found your program pretty boring. I would have preferred to have teacher lecture me on it or read it in the text-book. . . . The way it was written was hard to understand. The language used in the text-book is simpler. The sound effects and animations in the program, however, were pretty successful" (TOE-024).

Cassey is far from alone. More than 60 percent of students in this study reported preferring either classroom teaching or a combination of teacher-computer to virtual history. This percentage was even higher among students from school #2. Reasons given by students range from the familiarity with the teacher's style; the unchallenging nature of classroom lectures; the difficulty of navigating and analyzing multiple texts (even with online scaffolds); deep confidence in simplified textbook stories; and finally classroom interactions with the teacher, students, and learning objects. Samuel, a student who used the VH in school #1, said, "I personally prefer learning Canadian history in class because we go through it and you don't need to look for your own information" (TVE-017). For Alex, another student who used the VH, "it's better in the lab, because it's more fun; however, it is distracting" (TOE-019).

For us in digital history, these are surprising comments. What could account for such critical remarks from students who performed relatively well with the computer program? How can digital natives, born and raised with technology, prefer classroom instruction to a computer lab activity and claim to be distracted by online learning? There is no simple answer to these startling yet fundamental questions. Despite remarkable progress in digital history over the years, we know very little from empirical studies. Results are still scarce and scattered and generalizations too problematical at this point.

Although it is difficult and tentative to provide any firm conclusion, it is possible to present certain hypotheses that may help explain the results in terms of educational practice and students' experiences.

First we must look more carefully at current education practices. Many history teachers in Ontario and elsewhere continue to rely extensively on storytelling and direct classroom instruction in the form of lectures and textbook reading. Despite successive waves of curricular reforms in the province, which emphasize active instructional strategies, authentic evaluation, and experiential learning, classroom teaching remains relatively traditional and teacher-centered in many public schools.[38] For Barton and Levstik, the pressure to conform to conservative educational cultures, to control student behaviors and classroom routines, and to cover content knowledge for examination places teachers in unworkable situations. "In one study of preservice teachers who had engaged in a document-based methods course," they argue, "participants made it clear that they were unlikely to use such approaches in the classroom."[39] Writing in the French Canadian context, Robert Martineau found that most classrooms observed were characterized by teacher lecture, reliance on the textbook, and the memorization of facts.[40] According to Ken Osborne, this finding is "consistent with other data, and with a long record of commentary on the unsatisfactory state of history teaching in Canada stretching back almost a hundred years, but we simply do not know whether the situation is different in other parts of Canada today."[41]

With this state of affairs, it is no surprise that many grade 10 students from this study have great difficulty learning about the past using an experiential, student-centered approach fundamentally different from their earlier schooling experience. As long as teachers see history as "a mere accumulation of facts or stories," Robert Bain concludes, we should not be surprised that they "transform curricular or pedagogical moves designed to promote student meaning-making back into lessons that merely transmit facts."[42] Learning to think historically necessitates a particular epistemology of the text that cannot be equated with note taking and general reading skills emphasized in school programs. The Ontario curriculum places great emphasis on literacy across subject areas. As the *Think Literacy* document of the Ministry indicates: "When a math teacher demonstrates how to skim and scan for signal words to help students solve complex math problems, these skills also prepare them to read any subject text more effectively."[43] This process of literacy homogenization, which suggests that learning to read math problems is helpful for historical learning, obscures the disciplinary challenges of learning to think like historians. Wineburg is thus correct to claim that "learning about disciplines is not simply a matter of acquiring new knowledge; it entails examining previously held beliefs."[44] Students cannot see contextualized meaning in historical (sub)texts if they do not believe they exist in the first place. Understanding what happened at Dieppe from the perspective of a Canadian or German soldier is thus more complex than retrieving and putting together a set of facts about the raid. Reading history is not simply a process of reading about the past. It is a particular way of thinking and engaging with the past. The British research experience suggests that through changes in students' conceptions of history it becomes possible to envision progression in understanding the past critically. But what is puzzling from this study is that the selected teachers were not traditional. They were history majors who believed deeply in inquiry-based learning and rarely lectured in class.

This experimental study was designed to assess the value of a digital history program on students' performance. The role of the teacher was therefore restricted significantly in the computer lab in order to limit—and ultimately control—this variable. In reality, however, classroom teachers have a greater role to play in the design, implementation, and delivery of lessons—whether or not they rely on educational technology. "It is important to remember," Bain cautiously observes, "that the computer scaffolding does not substitute for instruction, but rather supports students in developing disciplinary habits after they have had at least initial instruction in each procedure."[45]

The history teacher from school #2 who used the VH for the study clearly supports this approach to technology in light of his experience:

> Over and over, I heard the same refrain from the students, which was "why can't you just tell us?" Many students found the number of sources to read, and the amount needed to read confusing and intimidating. I think that the final task they were assigned—which was a research project resulting in an argumentative essay—required either much more teacher direction than the study allowed or much more concrete direction on what to do with each source.

Expertise in teaching history as a form of knowledge in the twenty-first century depends on access to and use of complex systems of various knowledge—including technology. Too often, however, knowledge of technology in education is considered in a vacuum, disconnected from disciplinary knowledge and pedagogy, as if an understanding of how technological affordances work translates into sound practice. Students' and teachers' familiarity with technology does not automatically turn them into disciplinary experts, as evidenced in this study. Results confirm that building a community of inquiry in the twenty-first-century classroom cannot be accomplished with educational technology alone. Even if teachers and students possess, to varying degrees, technological knowledge about software and hardware, they must be attentive to how learning in the discipline might be improved by "complex relationships between technology, content, and pedagogy, and [by] using this understanding to develop appropriate, context-specific strategies and representations."[46] In other words, using technology in educational design cannot be understood simply as an add-on component to established coursework. It must lead to a fundamental reconsideration of disciplinary content knowledge and pedagogy so as to develop a coherent educational framework that recognizes how teaching and learning can be changed as a result of technological affordances.

The pedagogical shift in approaching technology in history appears to be even more necessary with students who have learning and/or language difficulties. Although most grade 10 students in this study reported having high computer literacy skills, many struggled to engage actively with the various functionalities of the VH program (e.g., scaffolds, learning objects, and sources). This was particularly evident with students from school #2, which has a very large number of immigrant students for whom English is a second language. In the face of Prensky's grand claim, not all students are digital natives. They may be born with technology, but their relationship to it is often practical and intuitive. Their immersion in and use of interactive technological tools do not necessarily enhance their inquisitive mode of learning. In fact, recent evidence suggests that "a significant proportion of young people . . . do not have the levels of access or technology skills predicted by proponents of the digital native idea."[47] It is not clear from research that the high level of interactivity and need of multiprocessing skills so prevalent in computer games and simulations have direct correlation with history learning. Generalizations about digital natives do not take into consideration the various cognitive differences in students of different ages and cultural-linguistic backgrounds. What students do with technology outside the school may have little or no significance to the competencies needed to engage in disciplinary inquiries. As Sue Bennett, Karl Maton, and Lisa Kervin conclude: "students' everyday technology practices may not be directly applicable to academic tasks, and so education has a vitally important role in fostering information literacies that will support learning."[48]

Mark, a history teacher in this study, reflects on how best to use technology with his grade 10 students in these circumstances:

Our students have never been exposed to such a large collection of primary source materials; it is the richness of the materials that created both the most positive responses ("Cool!," "Hey have you seen this picture?!'" "I can't believe they did that") and the most negative ("There's too much to read and it all sounds the same to me," "What is the point of all these pictures?," "What are we supposed to be *doing*?!"). . . . I would have liked to be able to use the VH for a less challenging question or a more concrete and directed activity.

Technology in education is inevitable. Yet no single technology can be universally applied by teachers. Just as progressivism never entirely replaced formalism in twentieth-century education, digitally enhanced inquiry-based learning methods may never completely displace textbook-centered instruction in the classroom. Teaching is a complex human activity that cannot be reduced to a set of pre-established pedagogical steps that invariably produce positive outcomes. Saye and Brush concur: "technology is no panacea for the challenges students and teachers face when engaging in disciplined inquiry into social problems."[49] Indeed, teachers must be flexible in their use of knowledge to design successful lessons adapted to their audience with the most effective learning tools at their disposal. Digital history programs, such as the Virtual Historian, provide an additional tool to achieve inquiry-based learning in history.

Important questions remain unanswered, however. We need to know more about how teachers can design lessons and meaningful activities with technology and, perhaps more importantly, how digital programs can be used to build on students' prior knowledge and learning preferences and to develop new epistemologies and ways of thinking about the past. How can it be that digital natives, born and raised with technology, still prefer classroom instruction to a computer lab activity and claim to be distracted by online learning objects? How is it that, despite the passionate and compelling scholarly discourse in recent years relating to meaningful learning and teaching in history, students continue to ask: why can't you just tell us? We urgently need some empirical studies and practice-informed answers to these pressing questions.

NOTES

1. Gail Salaway, Judith B. Caruso, and Mark R. Nelson, *The ECAR Study of Undergraduate Students and Information Technology, 2008*, Research Study, vol. 8 (Boulder, Colo.: EDUCAUSE Center for Applied Research, 2008), accessed July 31, 2012, http://www.educause.edu/ECAR/TheECARStudyofUndergraduateStu/163283.

2. Mark Prensky, "Digital Natives, Digital Immigrants," *On the Horizon* 9, no. 5 (2001), accessed July 31, 2012, http://www.marcprensky.com/writing/Prensky%20%20 Digital%20Natives,%20Digital%20Immigrants%20-%20Part1.pdf.

3. Prensky, 1.

4. Stéphane Lévesque, *Thinking Historically: Educating Students for the 21st Century* (Toronto: University of Toronto Press, 2008).

5. Veronica Boix-Mansilla and Howard Gardner, "Of Kinds of Disciplines and Kinds of Understanding," *Phi Delta Kappan* 78, no. 5 (1997): 381–87.

6. Peter Seixas, "The Purposes of Teaching Canadian History," *Canadian Social Studies* 36, no. 2 (2002), accessed April 1, 2008, http://www.quasar.ualberta.ca/css/Css _36_2/ARpurposes_teaching_canadian_history.htm; Dennis Shemilt, "Adolescent Ideas about Evidence and Methodology," in *The History Curriculum for Teachers,* ed. Christopher Portal (London: Falmer, 1987), 39–61; Samuel Wineburg, *Historical Thinking and Other Unnatural Acts: Charting the Future of Teaching the Past* (Philadelphia: Temple University Press, 2001).

7. Wineburg, 7.

8. Linda S. Levstik and Keith C. Barton, *Doing History: Investigating with Children in Elementary and Middle Schools*, 2nd ed. (Mahwah, N.J.: Lawrence Erlbaum Associates, 2001); Peter Seixas, "The Community of Inquiry as a Basis for Knowledge and Learning: The Case of History," *American Educational Research Journal* 30, no. 2 (1993): 305–24; Bruce Van Sledright, "What Does It Mean to Think Historically . . . and How Do You Teach It?" *Social Education* 68, no. 3 (2004): 230–33.

9. Levstik and Barton, 13.

10. Stéphane Lévesque, "Learning by 'Playing': Engaging Students in Digital History," *Canadian Issues* (Fall 2006): 68–71.

11. John W. Saye and Thomas Brush, "Comparing Teachers' Strategies for Supporting Student Inquiry in a Problem-Based Multimedia-Enhanced History Unit," *Theory and Research in Social Education* 34, no. 2 (2006): 183–212.

12. Daniel J. Cohen and Roy Rosenzweig, *Digital History: A Guide to Gathering, Preserving, and Presenting the Past on the Web* (Philadelphia: University of Pennsylvania Press, 2005); John W. Saye and Thomas Brush, "Using Technology Enhanced Learning Environments to Support Problem-Based Historical Inquiry in Secondary School Classrooms," *Theory and Research in Social Education* 35, no. 2 (2007): 196–230.

13. Canadian Mysteries, accessed July 31, 2012, http://www.canadianmysteries.ca.

14. Jennifer Voss and James Wiley, "A Case Study of Developing Historical Understanding via Instruction," in *Knowing, Teaching and Learning History: National and International Perspectives*, ed. Peter N. Stearns, Peter Seixas, and Samuel S. Wineburg (New York: New York University Press, 2000), 375–89; Elizabeth Anne Yeager and Frans H. Doppen, "Teaching and Learning Multiple Perspectives on the Use of the Atomic Bomb: Historical Empathy in the Secondary Classroom," in *Historical Empathy and Perspective Taking in the Social Studies*, ed. O. L. Davis Jr., Elizabeth Anne Yeager, and Stuart J. Foster (Lanham: Rowan & Littlefield, 2001).

15. Elizabeth Alexander Ashburn, Mark Baildon, James Damico, and Shannan McNair, "Mapping the Terrain for Meaningful Learning using Technology in Social Studies," in *Meaningful Learning Using Technology: What Educators Need to Know and Do*, ed. Elizabeth Alexander Ashburn and Robert E. Floden (New York: Teachers College Press, 2006), 117–40; Robert Bain, "Seeing the Meaning 'Hidden' in History and Social Studies Teaching," in *Meaningful Learning Using Technology: What Educators Need to Know and Do*, ed. Elizabeth Alexander Ashburn and Robert E. Floden (New York: Teachers College Press, 2006), 87–116; Anne Britt, Charles Perfetti, Julie Van Dyke, and Gareth Gabrys, "The Sourcer's Apprentice: A Tool for Document-Supported Instruction," in *Knowing, Teaching and Learning History: National and*

International Perspectives, ed. Peter Stearns, Peter Seixas, and Sam Wineburg (New York: New York University Press, 2000), 437–70.

16. Adam Friedman, "World History Teachers' Use of Digital Primary Sources: The Effect of Training," *Theory and Research in Social Education* 34, no. 2 (2006): 139.

17. Thomas Brush and John Saye, "The Effects of Multimedia-Supported Problem-Based Inquiry on Student Engagement, Empathy, and Assumptions about History," *Interdisciplinary Journal of Problem-Based Learning* 2, no. 1 (2008): 21–56; John Saye and Thomas Brush, "Using Technology-Enhanced Learning Environments to Support Problem-Based Historical Inquiry in Secondary School Classrooms," *Theory and Research in Social Education* 35, no. 2 (2007): 196–230; John Lee and Brendan Calandra, "Can Embedded Annotations Help High School Students Perform Problem Solving Tasks Using a Web-Based Historical Document?" *Journal of Research on Technology in Education* 36, no. 4 (2004): 65–84; Andrew Milson, "The Internet and Inquiry Learning: Integrating Medium and Method in a Sixth Grade Social Studies Classroom," *Theory and Research in Social Education* 30, no. 3 (2002): 330–53; and Bing Pan, Helene Hembrooke, Thornsten Joachims, Lori Lorigo, Geri Gay, and Laura Granka, "In Google We Trust: Users' Decisions on Rank, Position, and Relevance," *Journal of Computer-Mediated Communication* 12 (2007): 801–23.

18. Milson, 344.

19. Grant P. Wiggins and Jay McTighe, *Understanding by Design*, 2nd ed. (Alexandria, Va.: Association for Supervision and Curriculum Development, 2005), 113.

20. Bain, 109; emphasis added.

21. Robert K. Yin, *Case Study Research: Design and Methods*, 2nd ed. (Newbury Park, CA: Sage, 1994).

22. Bruce Van Sledright, "Narratives of Nation-State, Historical Knowledge, and School History Education," *Review of Research in Education* 32 (2008): 109–46.

23. Gardner and Boix-Mansilla, 147.

24. In order to preserve the identity of participants, all the names of students and teachers have been changed to pseudonyms and research codes.

25. Pietro Boscolo and Lucia Mason, "Writing to Learn, Writing to Transfer," in *Writing as a Learning Tool: Integrating Theory and Practice*, ed. Päivi Tynjälä, Lucia Mason, and Kirsti Lonka (Dordrecht, Netherlands: Kluwer Academic, 2001), 83–104; Charles Perfetti, Anne Britt, and Mara C. Georgi, *Text-Based Learning and Reasoning: Studies in History* (Hillsdale, N.J.: Lawrence Erlbaum Associates, 1995); Bruce Van Sledright, *In Search of America's Past: Learning to Read History in Elementary School* (New York: Teachers College Press, 2002).

26. Stéphane Lévesque, "'Terrorism plus Canada in the 1960's equals hell frozen over': Learning the October Crisis with Computer Technology in the Canadian Classroom," *Canadian Journal of Learning Technology* 34, no. 2 (2008), accessed July 31, 2012, http://www.cjlt.ca/index.php/cjlt/ article/view/493/224.

27. Voss and Wiley, 386–87.

28. Kathleen O. Swan and Mark Hofer, "Technology and Social Studies," in *Handbook of Research in Social Studies Education*, ed. Linda Levstik and Cynthia Tyson (New York: Routledge, 2008), 321.

29. Wineburg, 69.

30. Perfetti, Britt, and Georgi, 180.

31. Wineburg, 76.

32. Shemilt, 44.

33. Alaric Dickinson, A. Gard, and Peter Lee, "Evidence in History and the Classroom," in *History Teaching and Historical Understanding*, ed. A. Dickinson and P. Lee (London: Heinemann, 1980), 1–20.

34. Dickinson, Gard, and Lee, 15.

35. Walter Werner, "Reading Visual Texts," *Theory and Research in Social Education* 34, no. 2 (2002): 404.

36. Mark Hofer and Kathleen O. Swan, "Digital Image Manipulation: A Compelling Means to Engage Students in Discussion of Point of View and Perspective," *Contemporary Issues in Technology and Teacher Education* (online serial), 5, nos. 3–4 (2005): 294, accessed July 31, 2012, http://www.citejournal.org/vol5/iss3/socialstudies/article1.cfm.

37. Peter Lee and Rosalyn Ashby, "Progression in Historical Understanding Among Students Ages 7–14," in *Knowing, Teaching and Learning History: National and International Perspectives*, ed. P. Stearns, P. Seixas, and S. Wineburg (New York: New York University Press, 2000), 213.

38. Bob Davis, *Whatever Happened to Secondary School History?* (Toronto: J. Lorimer, 1995).

39. Keith Barton and Linda Levstik, "Why Don't More History Teachers Engage Students in Interpretations?" *Social Education* 67, no. 6 (2003): 359.

40. Robert Martineau, *L'histoire à l'école, matière à penser* (Montreal: L'Harmattan, 1999), 296.

41. Ken Osborne, *Teaching Canadian History in Schools*, report for the Historica Foundation of Canada (2004), 24, accessed July 31, 2012, http://www.histori.ca/prodev/file.do?id=22988.

42. Bain, 104.

43. Ontario Ministry of Education, *Think Literacy: Cross-Curricular Approaches, Grades 7–12.* (Toronto, Ont.: Queen's Printer, 2003), 1.

44. Wineburg, 152.

45. Bain, 113.

46. Punya Mishra and Matthew Koehler, "Technological Pedagogical Content Knowledge: A Framework for Teacher Knowledge," *Teachers College Record* 108, no. 6 (2006): 1029.

47. Sue Bennett, Karl Maton, and Lisa Kervin, "The 'Digital Natives' Debate: A Critical Review of the Evidence," *British Journal of Educational Technology* 39, no. 5 (2008): 778–79.

48. Bennett, Maton, and Kervin, 781.

49. Saye and Brush, "Using Technology-Enhanced Learning Environments," 218.

THREE

Interactive Worlds as Educational Tools for Understanding Arctic Life

Richard Levy and Peter Dawson

Introduction

Interactive 3D worlds and computer modeling can be used to excite interest in the many unique traditional dwellings constructed by indigenous groups in the Canadian High Arctic. General cultural trends toward the use of digital media show greater acceptance by students, teachers, and the public. Beyond mere representation of past architectural forms, digital reconstructions can be used to delve into the behavior and performance of unique structures. In research and teaching, it is now possible to model and investigate the response of these structures to the extreme environmental conditions of the North. In this context, a virtual laboratory can offer teachers case studies that motivate students in their studies of history and culture, as well as math and science. Virtual worlds can also evoke emotive and effectual knowledge in indigenous users. Experiences derived from primary school and college students, and Padleirmiut Inuit Elders who experienced digital reconstructions of pre-contact Inuit dwellings in a 3D virtual theater (CAVE [computer automated visualization environment]) at the University of Calgary, suggest that virtual environments may also be useful in initiating and establishing archaeological interpretation and discourse, as well as assisting personal identity recovery.

Public Archaeology: Giving Back to the Community

In the United States and Canada, archaeological project funding often stipulates that public opportunity for engagement be provided. The level of participation can be a simple website, a museum display, or a presentation to the community of the archaeological discoveries. Digital imaging can become an essential part of this outreach effort.[1] In an effort to make the authors' research findings in Arctic archaeology more accessible to a larger audience, interactive 3D worlds and computer modeling have been included to excite interest concerning traditional dwellings constructed by indigenous groups.[2]

With the expansion of broadband into remote communities in the North, it is now possible to extend the reach of these archaeological discoveries to the desktop of a student's computer, far away from more conventional locations of museums in major and regional centers. In addition, there is the sensitive issue of repatriation of native artifacts. Virtual 3D artifact copies allow archaeologists to return sacred objects to their original communities, while keeping valuable information from the artifacts available for research and study.

Display and Interaction

Finding the appropriate venue for artifact display and interaction requires sensitivity to the object's type and physical scale. Today, accessing historic materials through the Internet demands that any representation of an object be web-compatible. By placing artifacts in surroundings with other objects, a context is constructed for understanding what life was like in the past. With artifacts that have deep cultural significance, there is also an opportunity to associate virtual objects with myths and ethnographic commentary. In addition, the growth of social media allows users in remote communities to add their comments, stories, videos, or photos to websites with accessible virtual copies of artifacts, as part of a running dialogue that can be shared with the world.

For museums, this connection between the real and virtual offers exciting possibilities of linking physical displays with virtual interactive content. With Arctic content, the authors have experimented with the web, kiosks, and 3D stereoscopic projection systems, including passive and active projection systems, autographic screens, CAVEs, and 3D theaters. These environments have been used for both teaching and museum exhibits. Now with affordable 3D TVs the opportunity to augment museum exhibits and explore whole worlds is possible.[3] Ultimately, the success of these new displays will be measured by their ability to engage students and the public in virtual worlds that promote both play and exploration.

Why Create Virtual Objects: Why Laser Scanning?

Creating virtual worlds begins with the conversion of field data and archaeo-logical and historical records into 3D computer models. Creating 3D objects usually requires some knowledge of CAD (computer-aided design). When CAD is used as a tool to create a digital object from drawings and field data, both aesthetic and practical concerns impact the final results. This is par-ticularly true when drawings are incomplete or missing critical dimensions. In this sense CAD models are representations, limited by the data, skill, and time available to a digital artist to translate historic documents into a 3D form. As developers of educational content, a high priority must be given to virtual worlds that present an accurate likeness of archaeological artifacts and their context. With greater acceptance of laser scanning over the last decade, archaeologists now have a tool for accurately creating 3D images of objects from the size of an arrowhead to the extent of a building or city. A major advantage of laser scanning is that measurements can be made off the 3D model without damaging the actual object, avoiding the impact that repeated measurements can have on fragile objects. With laser scanners it is possible to acquire point measurements on a vast scale and at high fidelity. Laser scanners can be designed to capture minute detail, with resolutions as fine as 30 micros, providing researchers with a source of data not possible to acquire with more traditional hand measurement techniques.

Virtual 3D replicas also have distinct advantages over real objects because replicas facilitate a systematic analysis of shape and form. This is particularly self-evident in the case of fragile pottery, where laser-scanning technology has been used to arrive at the shape of a vessel. In cases where only a partial vase has survived, it has been possible to reconstruct the entire pot from the remaining potsherds. In an attempt to automate this process, researchers at the University of Tiburg have developed algorithms that can take a collec-tion of potshards and reassemble the pot into its most likely shape.[4]

Long-range laser scanning technology can be used to create 3D images of a building or an entire archaeological site. By taking successive scans of a site over time it is possible to create a virtual record of the excavation. The authors' work on a Mackenzie Inuit house in the western Canadian Arctic on the shore of Richards Island, 3 kilometers south of Kuukpak (69° 20.6′N and 134° 03.3′W), demonstrates that even in remote locations it is possible to use laser scanning technology in the documentation of archaeological sites.[5] Ultimately, this record serves both the researcher's need for measure-ments and the conservationist's interests in monitoring the condition and state of a site over time. By combining the advantages of different laser scanners that capture data at different resolutions, it is now possible to

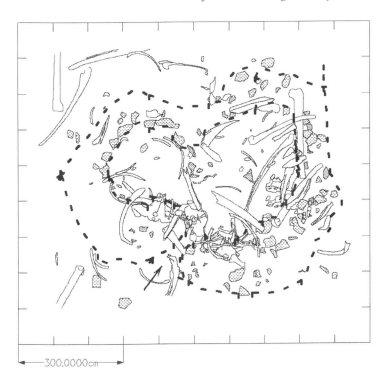

Fig 3.2: Thule whalebone house (QiLe-1) on Bathurst Island, Nunavut:
(a) computer-aided design (CAD) drawing. Image courtesy of the author.

Fig 3.3: Computer model of an Arctic Thule whalebone house from Bathurst
Island, Nunavut. Image courtesy of the author.

The Value of a Virtual Laboratory

One criticism of computer modeling in archaeology is that models are merely pretty pictures. With the availability of high performance PCs, however, a researcher can answer questions about structures from the past. Using CAD and engineering design applications, it is possible to simulate the lighting conditions inside a space or test the behaviors of structures under snow and wind loads. Structural analyses of Thule whalebone houses verified the structural stability of proposed reconstructions. Having conducted these analyses, we can state: "We are not sure what they looked like, but at least we know that the proposed construct could have withstood the environmental harshness of the North, where snow and wind would have collapsed all but the strongest of structures." In the case of the Thule whalebone architecture, the authors have also used the results of the structural analysis to answer the following questions:

- Given the challenges of working with whalebone, to what extent were Thule houses structurally sound architectural forms?
- Did the use of whalebone in a symbolic capacity affect the structural integrity of whalebone houses?
- Would weaker structures have increased the level of maintenance required to keep the dwelling habitable, or even placed the structure in danger of collapsing?

Multiframe, an application used by structural engineers, was employed to conduct the actual analysis of the structural frame of the Thule whalebone house. Like many FEM (finite element methods) applications, Multiframe has been used to understand potential modes of structural failure.[10] With laser scanning technology, accurate 3D data can serve as the basis of these analyses.[11] Rather than generalized geometric models based on historical drawings, laser scanning can provide an important snapshot of a building's current condition. This approach can consider the rate of deterioration over time and how this degradation impacts structural stability. More important with structures subjected to potential catastrophic failures from earthquake, considerable redesign efforts are needed to guarantee the integrity of a structure in the future. As an instructional tool, the approach used in this research, which incorporates cultural-based content, has potential to stimulate students to learn more about math and science. In this case study, these worlds illustrate how an intuitive understanding of structural analysis is essential in building complex architectural forms.

Light, Space, and Activity:
Modeling the Light from a Whalebone Lamp

Understanding how ancient cultures lived inside their homes requires knowledge of the lighting technology of the period. Ultimately, simulating the experience of being inside a space reconstructed from archaeological data demands the use of computer software capable of rendering 3D forms under various lighting conditions. Using a virtual world to simulate the experience of being inside a Thule whalebone house provides a case study of how 3D computer models can re-create a sense of space of architectural forms from the past. The first step in simulating light levels inside a Thule winter house was to calibrate the light produced by a whale-oil lamp. A whale-oil lamp provided light levels much lower than Western architectural standards. Inhabitants doing domestic chores in a Thule whalebone house would likely have had to make greater use of their sense of touch. In order to test this idea, replicas of *qulliq* lamps were crafted out of soapstone. A 60-watt light bulb was used as a standard. By calibrating this standard light source, it was possible to determine the illumination of a whale-oil lamp. In testing replicas of a typical *qulliq* it was discovered that they would have been capable of producing light equivalent to a 15-watt light bulb.[12] Using these data, the computer modeled the illumination in the interior of the space. These light sources are most commonly found to one side of the sleeping platform.[13] The reflection of surfaces, such as walls and floors, also influences how light is distributed inside buildings. For the purposes of this experiment, surfaces inside the whalebone house were considered to be reflective at 15 percent (though this value is probably much lower due to the amount of soot that would have been deposited on the walls and floor of the dwelling). Using the Lightscape plug-in for 3D Studio Max, a pseudocolor rendering of the interior of the house was created, mapping both luminance and illuminance. (Luminance is a measure of how bright or dark a surface is perceived, while illuminance measures how much energy has fallen on the surface. Illuminance is also a function of the distance from the light source and is, therefore, a useful measure for gauging the light available to perform domestic tasks [figure 3.4]).

Inside these small dwellings, which lacked interior partitions, the distribution of light and shadow may have been used to "zone" areas of public and private space. For example, the sleeping platforms would have appeared dark even with multiple lamps lit inside the space. Many of the activities found inside a Thule whalebone house would have required higher levels of illuminance by Western standards because individuals must be able to resolve very fine detail or small objects. Light levels close to the source (*qulliq* lamp) would

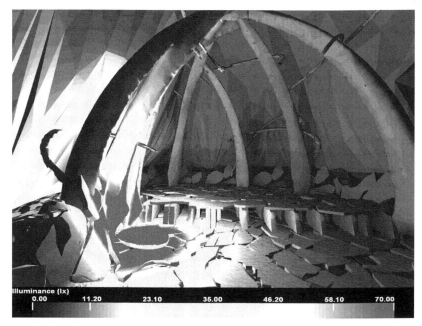

Fig 3.4: Illuminance map, interior of Thule whalebone house. Image courtesy of the author.

have provided sufficient light for activities such as cooking (46.45 cd), but not for sewing (92.9 cd).[14] The inhabitants would certainly have been able to perform household tasks under much lower levels of light. Archaeological and ethnographic data prove that Inuit and their ancestors were extremely good at carving and sewing. There are many excellent precontact examples.[15] Many everyday Inuit objects like harpoons, knives, needle cases, and children's toys have incised lines arranged in geometric patterns.[16] It seems reasonable that under these conditions of prolonged periods of darkness, household members would have compensated for the lower light levels in a manner similar to individuals who are blind or deaf, who often talk about a compensating effect, in which one or more of their remaining senses becomes more acute.[17]

The results of this study demonstrate that technologies like computer modeling and virtual reality can be used to obtain a more holistic understanding of how humans perceive and interact with the environments they inhabit. Using virtual worlds to reconstruct the sensory ecologies of past landscapes and built environments may afford researchers, teachers, and students an opportunity to explore ideas and theories more fully. Ultimately, it is the means of displaying these results that makes the results of these research findings accessible to students and teachers.

The Virtual Museum Program

With funding from the Virtual Museum Program in 2008, the researchers had the opportunity to create a virtual presence on the web to bring research on Arctic life to the public.[18] The mission was to create a site in which visitors would have the opportunity to learn about the environment surrounding Thule life. The site would focus on building materials, domestic architecture, hunting, as well as sources of food and production of clothing. The website would also be devoted to the importance of bowhead whales in Thule culture, including a section on how bowhead whales were hunted, and how various skeletal elements were used in house construction. There would also be sections on "myths" that link the whale to aspects of the "house," which may have existed as a metaphor for actual living whales.

Once inside the houses, the attention centers on the organization and atmosphere of the interior space. Issues of light, heat, and privacy are explored in relation to the shape of the structure and the whale-oil lamp, which was used to heat and light these houses. While inside the space, the online visitor learns about the tools and implements needed to exist in the Arctic landscape. Organized by men's, women's, and children's objects, animated GIFs of laser-scanned artifacts are presented, including *ulus,* needles, lamps, bow drills, knives, and toys. Explanations are provided on how they were used for daily tasks. Other aspects of the website included a time line and a section about how 3D imaging and computer modeling was used in the research.

The constructed website, though utilitarian and straightforward in its structure, was constrained by design specifications that barred the use of virtual worlds and online games. In the original proposal a series of virtual environments were suggested to explore life in the Arctic. For example, to introduce virtual visitors to the connection between light and space, a virtual walk-through of the interior was proposed. With only a whale-oil lamp to light the way, the contribution of light to a sense of community or privacy could be revealed. Navigating through the different areas of the interior, one would be introduced to virtual inhabitants who would demonstrate how to use various tools for cooking, hunting, and sewing waterproof clothing. Similarly, it would have been possible to give the web visitor a set of virtual whalebones from which to construct a house. Once completed, a virtual test could be conducted to see if a design could have stood up against the elements of snow and wind. Unfortunately, design specifications that restrict the use of plug-ins and limit performance to computers built more than a decade ago made it difficult to offer these kinds of exploratory environments as part of the web experience.

For those creating learning environments, both technical and institutional constraints are often difficult to predict at the onset of a project. Unlike video designed for consoles with known computing and rendering capability, web-based environments assume a universal audience. Issues of accessibility that come with publicly sponsored programs can place limits on the types of media that can be hosted on a site. Designed for the lowest common denominator, these websites can never be cutting edge. Though there will always be some constraints on a public website, improvements in the general level of personal computing technology should present less restrictive specifications for web designers in the future. Finally, there is always the issue of what is politically acceptable in a publicly sponsored website. For example, it would be inadvisable to show a whale hunt on a website, even though it represents an important aspect of the lives of many Northern communities.

The Kiosk: Museum of Civilization

A few years earlier, a kiosk installation was constructed at the Canadian Museum of Civilization, Ottawa. As part of a special exhibition, "Journey to Kitgaaryuk," sponsored jointly by the Canadian Museum of Civilization and the Prince of Wales Northern Heritage Centre in Yellowknife, Northwest Territories, an interactive world was developed for a stand-alone kiosk.[19] The experience first provided a tour of the outside of an Inuit sod house. The house, a traditional Mackenzie Delta Inuit winter house, was modeled using archaeological, ethnographic, and ethnohistoric data. These types of dwellings would have been constructed out of wood, sod, and caribou or muskox hide even as late as the early nineteenth century. In constructing this virtual model, the user began by exploring the outside of the structure. Once inside, the interior could be examined. Clicking on artifacts located on the sleeping platform of the dwelling activated a video that showed how the objects were used in daily life. For example, clicking on a stone *ulu* initiated a movie that showed a member of the Inuvialuit community creating a sealskin parka. Located at the center of the gallery, visitors could interact with a virtual model of a sod house while being surrounded by actual artifacts from the region. Like many virtual worlds, one tracker ball provided control over the environment. Several audio headphones were attached to the single kiosk. Curiously, having the control of the environment in the hands of a single person did not present any serious barriers for small groups. One person would naturally gravitate toward navigating the world, while other participants would offer suggestions about where to go next, or would ask questions about the virtual world. Interestingly, young children were most adept at this kind of joint decision making.[20]

Virtual Reality: At a Larger Scale

At the University of Calgary, students from classes in archaeology have the opportunity to view the whalebone house and other environments, including the skeleton of a baleen whale and an Inuit sod house, in a virtual world in the I-Centre, CAVE. The I-Centre CAVE, designed by Barco Ltd., creates an immersive environment with walls that can be rearranged to form a virtual reality theater or CAVE. A CAVE is a room-sized cube composed of four walls. In the I-Centre, the walls are right, left, center, and floor. Each screen is 8 feet high by 10 feet wide. With the VRPACK module of Virtools (www.Virtools.com), virtual worlds can be viewed in stereo using active shutter glasses. Interactive sound and atmospheric lighting all contribute to the totality of the experience.[21]

One of the central problems archaeologists face is making their research both interesting and relevant to the broader communities they work with. Archaeologists tend to focus on technical explanations of the past, such as defining the function of a tool, the optimality of diet choices, or the chronometric age of a site. In contrast, indigenous peoples and the general public often relate to the past in more personal and emotive ways. In response, archaeologists have begun to explore the use of narrative structures and conjectural histories to provide an impression of what life might have been like in the past. One of the most famous examples of this type of approach is Janet Spector's *What This Awl Means*.[22] In Spector's story, a young aboriginal woman brings recognition to her family through her prowess at sewing and beading. Although based entirely on conjecture, the awl in the story acquires special meaning because of its association with the aspirations of Spector's young aboriginal protagonist. When the awl is lost, the reader subsequently empathizes with the young woman's anguish. Its recovery by an archaeologist many centuries later further adds to the object's emotional impact. Encountering archaeological objects in this way makes them of greater interest to the broader community because the affecting, emotive qualities of the artifact are drawn out through the arc of the story.

In many instances, objects that carry great meaning are inaccessible to indigenous peoples. They may be held in museum collections or, as is the case with Thule whalebone houses, they may no longer exist. In these instances, encountering digital replicas of these objects in immersive environments may provide opportunities for indigenous peoples to explore their heritage in ways that are far more meaningful. Recent research into the use of digital images of ethnographic objects by the Maori of New Zealand suggests that some of the cultural values associated with traditional objects, such as life force, oratory, narratives, and life essence, are transferred to digital replicas of artifacts, to a greater or lesser degree, depending on circumstance.[23] This suggests that laser scans of artifacts, and computer models of archaeological features such as dwellings may provide affecting, emotive experiences that might assist in the recovery of personal and cultural identities.

In order to explore this further, three respected Inuit Elders from the community of Arviat, Nunavut, were invited to the iCORE CAVE at the University of Calgary's Schlumberger iCenter, where they toured the 3D model of a Thule whalebone house. Surrounded by the structure of whalebones and hide, they sat together and whispered among themselves in Inuktitut. "All of the stories I used to hear when I was young are coming back to me," remarked Mark Kalluak, as he navigated through the virtual dwelling. "It really makes me think about what it would have been like to live in my ancestors' home." Donald Uluadluak explained in Inuktitut that he felt like a magician: "No one has ever seen these buildings before. Now we are able to and it will help us understand who we are." The experience of being able to view the whalebone architecture of the dwelling in 3D also reminded Mark Kalluak of a traditional Inuit tale about a man who lived inside a whale. "Maybe this legend comes from when we lived in these kinds of houses," he explained.

"It's hard to imagine something if you've never seen it before and something like this makes it so much easier to imagine what life was like in the old days than just reading about it in a book," said Nunia Qanatsiaq, a member of the government of Nunavut's curriculum and school services division who accompanied the Elders to Calgary. For Mark Kalluak, exploring traditional lifeways using computer animation is exciting because it may excite interest in younger Inuit who are becoming increasingly computer literate. "A lot of young people don't seem too interested in learning about the old ways, but I think they would with something like this," he said. "It's a new way for them to learn and that is always valuable."

Comments shared with us by Inuit Elders about their experiences within the CAVE suggest that their encounters with the digital whalebone house and the objects contained within were both emotive and affecting. The Elders seemed genuinely moved by their experiences, as communicated through their awe at what their ancestors had been able to accomplish centuries ago. The Elders' immersion in this virtual world of their own past also served as a powerful mnemonic device, as seen in Mark Kalluak's recollection of a childhood story involving a man swallowed by a whale. All indications are that the Elders recognized their encounter as a simulation and therefore not an

Fig 3.5: A group of archaeology students in the CCIT Cave, University of Calgary. Photo courtesy of the author.

authentic view of their past. Nevertheless, they appreciated the experience because it moved them closer to a point of contact with their own history and identity. In this way, it would seem as though meanings and values can be transferred to digital replicas of traditional objects, especially when placed in immersive environments like the CAVE.

University, high school, and primary students have also had the opportunity to view the whalebone house and other archaeological reconstructions within the iCORE CAVE. Like the Elders, their experiences provided them with an appreciation for the geometric complexity of these dwellings, and the challenges of working with construction materials as unique as whalebone (figure 3.5). The ability to discover the connections between space, light, and culture is an advantage of virtual exploration of the space at actual human scale.

One issue in using the CAVE for these types of immersive experiences is that interaction is generally limited to a single user. Without trackers and other input devices, the experience is more like a 3D movie for most of the students. Though CAVEs are not common on most college campuses, the ability to construct multiscreen immersive environments from standard workstations and inexpensive flat panel displays will greatly expand their

Fig 3.6: (*from left*) Louis Angalik, Mark Kalluak, and Donald Uluadluak. Photo courtesy of the author.

use in research and education. In a museum environment, the real challenge is creating experiences that will open opportunities for the user to interact with the virtual world (see figure 3.6).[24]

3D Virtual Reality Theaters

In 2008, Dessault Systemes announced a competition for designing virtual world experiences for the Geode in Paris. A goal of this competition was the promotion of 3DVIA, an integrated development platform. 3DVIA (Virtools) provides tools for creating interactive worlds for display on PCs, CAVES, and 3D theaters. Ultimately, the virtual worlds resulting from this competition would be showcased in the Geode, the largest virtual reality theater in the world. Reopened in 2008 after renovation, this spherical-shaped theater is located in the Parc de la Villette at the Cité des Sciences et

Fig 3.7: La Geode is the world's largest virtual reality center.

de l'Inustrie in Paris (figure 3.7). First constructed to show movies in IMAX format, it also has the capability of presenting 3D interactive worlds.[25]

In this competition it was possible for the authors to draw on assets from worlds created over several years, including 3D computer reconstructions of a Thule Inuit whalebone house, as well as a virtual kayak simulation. In addition to these completed structures, learning objects created with long- and short-range scanners were also utilized. These objects ranged in size from a small stone *ulu* to the much larger skeleton of a North Atlantic right whale.

Using a traditional story or myth as the underlying plot for a game is a common strategy among game developers. In this project, myths and stories collected by researchers visiting the far North, including Knud Rasmussen of the Danish Fifth Thule Expedition (1921–24), provided the background for the virtual experience focused on life in the Arctic. One tale in particular, "The Raven's Story," became the underlying plotline for the virtual world.[26] Ultimately, a quest (a genre that is well understood by game makers) was used as the armature for "Exploring Arctic Cultures."

In the prologue, you are given your mission, to find your way home with the help of mythical creatures. To help guide you, whale-oil lamps, which appear suspended about the water, light your journey. At the beginning of your quest you are introduced to the Raven, whose story will be retold during your journey (figure 3.8). For the Inuit, the connection between one's life, nature, and myth would have been reaffirmed by everyday experiences.[27] To emphasize this connection, many of the mythical characters, represented by their likenesses in stone, are found in natural state swimming, dancing, or flying. The setting is also used to reinforce the sensation that you are in a

Fig 3.8: *Left*, image from the interactive world, "The Raven." *Right*, interior of the Thule whalebone house from "The Raven." Image courtesy of the author.

mythical world. Here in the world of endless dusk, both night and day exist together. Huge icebergs, mirrored by their reflection on the water, appear to be floating magically on the sea, underscoring the connection between the mythical and physical worlds.[28]

At the end of your journey, you find yourself inside a traditional Inuit house. Here, objects that have been created by laser scanning actual artifacts can be found. Each object serves as a mnemonic placeholder for accounts of everyday life.[29] In this space you find an *ulu*, harpoon, snowknife, adz, sewing needle, and thimble. Accompanied by video and animations, objects are shown in context. For example, in one video, a pick, adz, and snowknife are shown being used to create basic shelter.

Though designed for a virtual theater, the experience has been shown to fourth- and fifth-graders in the I-Centre facility. It was also made available over the Internet as a download that plays inside Internet Explorer or Mozilla Firefox. Though designed for a virtual theater, "The Raven's Story" has been shown to more than two hundred fourth- and fifth-grade classes in the I-Centre facility as part of the summer program sponsored by the University of Calgary. What has been learned from this experience in the CAVE is that even when students do not have direct control over movement within the virtual world, it is possible to create an engaging experience by using a series of questions and responses. A challenge using an interactive world in a theater setting is building into the experience a feeling of participation during the actual experience.

Discussion and Summary

Interactive 3D worlds and computer models can be used to excite interest in indigenous culture. With the growing acceptance of digital media by students, teachers, and the public, it is now possible to employ virtual worlds that can both entertain and educate. Virtual worlds and advanced multimedia that go beyond mere representation can be used to delve into the behavior and performance of unique architectural forms. In addition to motivating students to learn about cultural history, archaeology, math, and science, these virtual worlds have been used to evoke emotive and effectual knowledge in indigenous users. The experiences with primary school and college students as well as Padleirmiut Inuit Elders who experienced digital reconstructions of Inuit dwellings in a 3D virtual theater (CAVE) at the University of Calgary suggest that virtual environments may be useful in initiating and establishing archaeological interpretation and discourse as well as assisting personal identity recovery.

In creating a virtual world for teaching and public education, venue is always an important consideration. Learning can take place on a computer in a lab, in a classroom in front of a Smartboard, in a museum gallery, or in a university CAVE like the one at the University of Calgary. Each presupposes a different level of engagement. Worlds designed for the individual user must be self-contained, with careful attention paid to the design of an intuitive interface, virtual guides, and online help. Virtual worlds designed for small gatherings of individuals around a single display can create experiences that promote social interaction. In a theater where individuals sit on benches or banked rows of theater chairs, the opportunity for engagement with a virtual world only occurs with the assistance of a guide. In this setting, the use of questions and responses from the audience can provide some sense of spontaneity and exploration in the virtual world. With the growing use of audience response systems—"clickers"—it may be possible to improve engagement with larger groups. Having been used successfully at many universities, this technology could also be implemented in museum settings.

Currently, plans are being developed for a website that will build on the researchers' past experience with virtual worlds. In addition to databases of artifacts, virtual worlds, and videos, plans are being made to preload content devoted to life in the North. It is hoped that this initial content will serve as the basis of a community-based repository. By allowing members of the community to add comments, personal stories, videos, and photos to the site, it will be possible to encourage the sharing of local history. One goal of this project is to provide opportunities, through a virtual space, to share content using a repository structure that gives open access to contributors and users. Perhaps most important of all, the project is designed to support and embody the idea of constructivist learning, in which learners construct knowledge for themselves. The idea is that as they learn they are building meaning, both individually and in groups.

It is also hoped that this project will benefit the community. For example, by giving artisans and craft persons access to a virtual space to display their work, they will reach a much larger community. Though at the early stages of development, one possibility being explored is to use existing social media sites like *Facebook*, *Myspace*, and *Google Earth* as mechanisms for disseminating content and encouraging members of Northern communities to participate in this discussion. *Facebook* is commonly used by many members of the Northern communities. Having this link into *Facebook*, the researchers hope to build on the current capacity established over the last few years to link into existing collections of family stories, images, and videos that will ultimately contribute to the preservation of local history and traditional knowledge.

NOTES

1. Alonzo C. Addison, "Emerging Trends in Virtual Heritage," *IEEE Multimedia* (April–June 2000): 22–25; idem, "Virtual Heritage—Technology in the Service of Culture," *Proceedings of the 2001 Conference on Virtual Reality, Archaeology and Cultural Heritage* (November 2001): 28–30; Johannes Bauerlein, Rafael Pokorski, Stefan Maass, and Jürgen Dolner, "Visualization Project of Roman Cologne—How to Make VR Models Available for Scientific Work," *Computer Application and Quantitative Methods in Archaeology, Proceedings* (2007): 126; Marcello Carrozzino, Chiara Evangelista, A. Scucces, Franco Tecchia, G. Tennirelli, and Massimo Bergamasco, "The Virtual Museum of Sculpture," *3rd International Conference on Digital Interactive Media in Entertainment and Arts, DIMEA* (2008): 100–106.

2. Erik Champion, "Applying Game Design Theory to Virtual Heritage Environments," *Proceedings of the 1st International Conference on Computer Graphics and Interactive Techniques in Australasia and South East Asia* (2003): 273–74.

3. Kiyoshi Takenaka and Franklin Paul, "WRAPUP 2-Sony, Samsung Detail 3D TV Plans," *Reuters*, March 9, 2010, accessed July 31, 2012, http://www.reuters.com /article/idUSN0922582320100309.

4. Laurens van der Maaten and Guus Lange, "Visualization and Automatic Typology of Ceramic Profiles," *CAA Proceedings* (2009): 153–54.

5. Peter C. Dawson, Richard M. Levy, Gerald Oetelaar, Charles Arnold, and Dominic Lacroix, "Documenting Mackenzie Inuit Architecture Using 3D Laser Scanning," *Alaska Journal of Anthropology* 7 (2009): 31–44.

6. Moreau S. Maxwell, *Prehistory of the Eastern Arctic* (New York: Academic, 1985); Robert McGhee, *Canadian Arctic Prehistory* (Toronto: Van Nostrand Reinhold, 1978).

7. Wolfgang Boehler and Andreas Marbs, "3D Scanning Instruments," *Proceedings of the CIPA WG6 International Workshop on Scanning for Cultural Heritage Recording* (2002), accessed July 31, 2012, http://www.i3mainz.fh-mainz.de/publicat /korfu/p05_Boehler.pdf; M. Johansson, "Explorations into the Behavior of Three Different High-Resolution Ground-Based Laser Scanners in the Built Environment," *Proceedings of the CIPA WG International Workshop on Scanning for Cultural Heritage Recording* (2003): 33–38.

8. Peter Dawson, "Interpreting Variability in Thule Inuit Architecture: A Case Study from the Canadian High Arctic," *American Antiquity* 66 (2001): 453–70.

9. Peter C. Dawson, Richard M. Levy, and Charles Arnold, "Reconstructing Traditional Inuit House Forms Using 3 Dimensional Interactive Computer Modeling," *Visual Studies* (2004): 26–35.

10. Alberto Guarnieri, Francesco Pirotti, Marco Pontin, and Antonio Vettore, "Combined 3D Surveying Techniques for Structural Analysis Applications," *Proceedings of the ISPRS Working Group V/4 Workshop 3D-ARCH 2005* (August 2005): 22–24.

11. V. Cóias e Silva, Paulo B. Lourenço, and Luís F. Ramos, "Portugal Accounting for the 'Block Effect' in Structural Interventions in Lisbon's Old 'Pombaline' Downtown Buildings," in *Historical Constructions*, ed. P. B. Lourenço and P. Roca (Guimarães Portuguese Science and Technology Foundation [FCT], 2001), technical report, accessed July 31, 2012, http://www.civil.uminho.pt/masonry/Publications/2001_Silva_et_al.pdf.

12. Peter C. Dawson, Richard M. Levy, D. Gardner, and M. Walls, "Simulating the Behavior of Light Inside Arctic Dwelling: Implications for Assessing the Role of Visual Perception in Task Performance," *World Archaeology* 39, no. 1 (2007): 17–35.

13. Elmer Ekblaw, "The Material Response of the Polar Eskimos to Their Far Arctic Environment," *Annals of the Association of American Geographers* 17, no. 4 (1927): 147–98; D. Jenness, *Material Culture of the Copper Eskimos, Report of the Canadian Arctic Expedition, 1913–1918*, vol. 16 (Ottawa: Edmond Cloutier, King's Printer and Controller of Stationery, 1946); T. Mathiassen, *Archaeology of the Central Eskimos* (Copenhagen: Glydendalske Boghandel, 1946).

14. Wesley Woodson, Barry Tillman, and Peggy Tillman, *Human Factors Design Handbook: Information and Guidelines for the Design* (New York: McGraw-Hill, 1992).

15. Maxwell.

16. Maxwell; Mathiassen; McGhee; Peter James Whitridge, "The Construction of Difference in a Prehistoric Whaling Community" (Ph.D. dissertation, Arizona State University, 1999); idem, "Landscapes, Houses, Bodies, Things: 'Place' and the Archaeology of Inuit Imaginaries," *Journal of Archaeological Method and Theory* 11, no. 2 (2004): 213–50.

17. Constance Classen, David Howes, and Anthony Synott, *Aroma: The Cultural History of Smell* (London: Routledge, 1994).

18. Glenbow Museum, "Thule Whalebone House," Virtual Museum Program, accessed July 31, 2012, http://www.glenbow.org/thule/?lang=en&p=home (2008).

19. Richard Levy, "Interactive Multimedia Learning Program," Canadian Museum of Civilization Exhibit, Ottawa, November 6, 2003, to January 9, 2005.

20. Levy.

21. Addison, "Emerging Trends"; Erhard Berndt and Jose Carlos, "Cultural Heritage in the Mature Era of Computer Graphics," *IEEE Computer Graphics and Applications* 20, no. 1 (January–February 2000): 36–37.

22. Janet Spector, *What This Awl Means: Feminist Archaeology at the Wahpeton Dakota Village* (St. Paul: Minnesota Historical Society Press, 1993).

23. Deidre Brown, "Te Ahua Hiko: Digital Cultural Heritage and Indigenous Objects, People, and Environments," in *Theorizing Digital Cultural Heritage: A Critical Discourse*, ed. Fiona Cameron and Sarah Kenderdine (Cambridge, Mass.: MIT Press, 2007), 77–91.

24. Champion, 273–74.

25. Dessault Systemes, *Virtual Reality Competition*, 2008.

26. Knud Rasmussen, *Eskimo Folk Tales*, trans. W. Worster (London: Gylglendal, 1921).

27. Whitridge, "The Construction of Difference."

28. Elizabeth Losh, "The Palace of Memory: Virtual Tourism and Tours of Duty in Tactical Iraqi and Virtual Iraq," *Proceedings of the 2006 International Conference on Games* (2006): 77–86.

29. George Sabo III, G. Jacobs, and John D. Jacobs, "Aspects of Thule Culture Adaptations in Southern Baffin Island," *Arctic* 33, no. 3 (1980): 487–504.

FOUR

Tecumseh Lies Here

Goals and Challenges for a Pervasive History Game in Progress

Timothy Compeau and Robert MacDougall

> We live in a complex world, filled with myriad objects, tools, toys, and people. Our lives are spent in diverse interaction with this environment. Yet, for the most part, our computing takes place sitting in front of, and staring at, a single glowing screen. . . . From the isolation of our work station we try to interact with our surrounding environment, but the two worlds have little in common. How can we escape from the computer screen and bring these two worlds together?
> —Pierre Wellner et al., "Computer Augmented Environments"[1]

Imagine a game that takes as its raw material the actual record of the past, and requires its participants to explore museums, archives, and historical sites. Imagine a series of challenges where students and others perform the genuine tasks of practicing historians—collecting their own evidence, formulating their own hypotheses, and constructing their own historical narratives. Imagine a large-scale, ongoing activity that ultimately connects hundreds or thousands of players across the country and around the world in a sustained encounter with the past.

Alternate or augmented reality games (ARGs), also known as pervasive games, are an emerging genre that breaks down boundaries between the online world and the real.[2] Unlike traditional computer games or simulations, which contain gameplay inside sealed virtual environments, pervasive games can spread across the entire ecology of electronic and traditional media and into public spaces like streets, museums, and schools. Although it is difficult to generalize about such a rapidly evolving form, most ARGs to date have combined an underlying story or narrative, a series of puzzles and challenges, and a collaborative community of players. Game designers distribute story pieces, clues, and missions via websites, email, mobile messaging, and even physical objects sent through the postal system or installed in public spaces. Game players then use wikis, chat rooms, and blogs to analyze evidence, solve puzzles, and ultimately cocreate the narrative of the game.

While the first ARGs were designed as entertainment, and often as promotions for commercial media such as computer games and films, designers and players were immediately intrigued by the genre's potential for education and addressing real-world problems. MIT's educational ARG *Reliving the Revolution* (2005) turned the site of the American Revolutionary Battle of Lexington into an augmented learning environment where students learned techniques for historical inquiry, effective collaboration, and critical thinking skills. In the PBS-funded ARG *World Without Oil* (2007) more than two thousand players from twelve countries came together to manage a simulated global oil crisis, forecasting the results of the crisis and producing plausible strategies for managing a realistic future dilemma. And the World Bank's *Urgent Evoke* (2010) enlisted more than 19,000 players in an effort to empower young people, especially in Africa, to come up with creative solutions to environmental and social problems.[3]

Historians have only begun to take note of these developments and devices.[4] Yet pervasive games may have the potential to enhance and inform history education and public history outreach. We became curious about the possibilities of ARGs and pervasive games for history education through our interests in history pedagogy, game design, and the new digital humanities. Could we design a pervasive game that taught genuine historical thinking? Could we bring a large group of players into a sustained, evidence-based encounter with the history around them and so awaken them to the pervasive presence of the past? Could we engage an ad hoc, multilingual, international group of players in a parallel and distributed process of historical research? We set out to try. In this chapter we discuss our goals, our progress, and the challenges we have met along the way—challenges we believe will be relevant to anyone contemplating a project in this space.

Goals

Playful Historical Thinking

Hundreds of thousands of Americans who do not earn their living as history professionals dedicate considerable time, money, and even love to historical pursuits. They volunteer at local historical organizations, lead tours of historic houses, don uniforms for battle reenactments, repair old locomotives for the railway history society, subscribe to *American Heritage* and *American History Illustrated*, maintain the archives for their trade union or church, assemble libraries from the History Book Club, construct family genealogies, restore old houses, devise and play World War II board games, collect early twentieth-century circus memorabilia, and lobby to preserve art deco movie houses.

—Roy Rosenzweig and David Thelen, *The Presence of the Past*[5]

"Every few years," observes social studies educator Bruce Van Sledright, history teachers go through "an embarrassing national ritual." In the United States, Canada, Britain, and other countries, the ritual is much the same. Students take a standardized history test. Almost invariably, a sizeable percentage cannot identify basic events in their country's history. These results are published in the media and taken up as ammunition in a long-running battle over curriculum content. The sides in this struggle are drearily political. Conservatives blame academic historians and educational bureaucrats for moving away from a traditionally heroic, nation-building narrative. Liberals blame the very narrative that conservatives seek to preserve. Both sides bemoan the ignorance of today's students, worry that we are losing touch with our history and heritage, and indict teachers and educators for failing to make the grade. Real as these problems may be, the so-called history wars have become a predictable pantomime that sheds neither heat nor light.[6]

There is today a robust literature on history pedagogy and historical thinking that seeks to transcend this stale debate. Decades of research argue for an inquiry-oriented approach to teaching history, one built around arguing from evidence, assessing and questioning the reliability of sources, and evaluating and synthesizing competing narratives about the past. This approach arms students with the skills of historical investigation, yet aims to go beyond skills training to inculcate a way of thinking about history that is skeptical but also charitable and mature.

ARGs, or pervasive games, exhibit many features that would complement an inquiry-oriented history pedagogy. They are investigative exercises. They are collaborative and open-ended. They often involve piecing together clues, questioning sources, and assembling a narrative from incomplete or contradictory evidence. Teaching critical historical thinking does not require elaborate technology or activities of this kind, but the genre seems to contain potential it would be foolish for educators to ignore.

One possible criticism of the literature on historical thinking, especially in its first wave, is that it sometimes took as a given that the goal of history education must be to get students to think about history in the same ways that professional historians do. We agree that the thought processes and skills of professional historians are a useful model for students and teachers to emulate—but are they the only model? How do we want our students to think about history, not just while they are in class, but when they leave the classroom, become adults, and set out into the world? This is a question that cannot be answered without serious thought about what history is for.

Our modest contribution to the literature on historical thinking is to argue for the value of play. We want to make a case for playful historical thinking as a healthy, productive, and even responsible way for citizens of the twenty-first century to relate to the past. Playful historical thinking is, or can be, critical and engaged. It recognizes limits on our ability to fully know other peoples and times, yet makes the effort to know them just the same. It wears its certainties lightly and takes pleasure in the whimsy, mystery, and strangeness of the past.

Professional historians can of course be playful in their thinking. Samuel Wineburg notes the "ludic" nature of a skilled historian's engagement with her sources—right down to the way she reads certain passages in funny voices to signal distance from the text.[7] But play is also mistrusted by many professional historians, and whatever playful engagement they may have with their sources rarely trickles down into classrooms or survives translation into articles and books. For more models of playful historical thinking, we turned to a wider community of vernacular history makers, including history gamers, reenactors, and amateur history buffs. These groups engage with history in ways that are different from approaches of professional academics, but can still be valuable, rigorous, and even scholarly. We do not need to give up our professional standards to listen and learn from these communities. They have much to teach us about what makes history engaging, fascinating, or fun.

The Tecumseh Mystery

> The challenge is to find a way of illustrating critical engagement with the past in a manner that captures the imagination of a lay audience—an audience that may well be eager for dramatic narrative and impatient with ambiguity and contention. I have no clear answers for this and I would not wish to be prescriptive. Nonetheless, as a tentative suggestion as to how that might be managed I suggest that there is great potential in the model of the detective story.
> —Alexander Cook, "The Use and Abuse of Historical Reenactment"[8]

In the spring of 2009, we received a moderately sized grant to investigate the potential of ARGs and pervasive games for history and heritage education.[9] The approaching bicentennial of the War of 1812 suggested a topic for such a game. Our plan was to design and run a short prototype game in 2010, with an eye to acquiring further funding for a more elaborate game in the bicentennial year of 2012.

The War of 1812 was a messy, confusing frontier war, and today it is poorly remembered and often misunderstood. In the United States, the conflict was once touted as the Second War for American Independence, but it is almost entirely forgotten by Americans today. In Canada, the war was unpopular and only reluctantly fought, yet was later mythologized as a great nation-building victory. And for the First Peoples of the Great Lakes region and the Old Northwest, the war marked the zenith and then the end of hopes for an autonomous pan-Indian confederacy. These contradictory narratives offer rich material for a game that demands collaboration among players on both sides of the border, with different backgrounds, biases, and understandings of the war. We see our project as a kind of subversive commemoration, one that explores the murky history of the war while challenging some of the banal nationalism on display in bicentennial commemorations.

For our prototype game, we chose as our subject the death of the Shawnee war-chief Tecumseh and a century-long controversy regarding his remains. In the first few years of the nineteenth century, Tecumseh and his brother Tenskwatawa organized a large confederacy of native peoples to resist American expansion in the Old Northwest. Tecumseh's followers allied with the British in the War of 1812, and their support was pivotal in the defense of British North America. Tecumseh died at the Battle of the Thames in October 1813, but his body was never identified, giving rise to rumors that he had not died or that his body had been spirited away.

Tecumseh's fame only grew after the war, as did white fascination with the question of his remains. During the U.S. election of 1840, zealous supporters of William Henry Harrison dug up native bones that they declared to be Tecumseh's and exhibited them at rallies. Outraged Canadians, who by then remembered Tecumseh (rather dubiously) as a loyal British martyr, sought to build a monument to their fallen hero, but plans ran aground in disagreement over the true location of his bones. The natives of the region responded to this mystery with silence. But every decade or so, some native informant proved willing, for a price, to lead a gullible white man to a different hillock or thicket and declare it the great chief's secret grave.[10]

On this historical foundation, we built the framing narrative for our game, *Tecumseh Lies Here*. The game imagines a kind of underground demimonde of 1812 enthusiasts still searching for Tecumseh's remains. Players seeking to solve the mystery encounter the squabbling factions of this history underground and are drawn into their struggles over the memory and meaning of the Shawnee leader and the war. We recognize that this is a sensitive topic, potentially offensive to some (see "Professional and Ethical Questions," below, for more on this), but the admittedly morbid question of Tecumseh's final resting place is for us both an interesting hook and a metaphor. The search for Tecumseh's bones has always really been a struggle over public memory and commemoration. "Tecumseh lies here" is a dark sort of pun: nobody knows where Tecumseh lies, but lies and myths about Tecumseh are all too common. The point of our game is certainly not to locate any physical remains, but to demonstrate that Tecumseh's memory—though distorted, contested, layered with wishful thinking and myth—is nevertheless unavoidable in this region.

"History Invaders": The Problem with Educational Games

> The more one begins to think that *Civilization* is about a certain ideological interpretation of history (neoconservative, reactionary, or what have you) . . . the more one realizes that it is about the absence of history altogether, or rather, the transcoding of history into specific mathematical models. . . . So "history" in *Civilization* is precisely the opposite of history, not because the game fetishizes the imperial perspective, but because the diachronic details of lived life are replaced by the synchronic homogeneity of code pure and simple.
> —Alexander Galloway, "Allegories of Control"[11]

Those who design games with educational goals in mind face deceptively difficult challenges. One lies in the interface between a game's procedures and its subject: what you do versus what you are supposed to learn. As Alexander Galloway insists, "games are actions."[12] The deep lessons of a game come not from its ostensible subject matter but from the decisions its players make and the actions they perform. Our goal in *Tecumseh Lies Here* has been to make the skills and lessons we want to teach inextricable from the play of the game itself.

We have no interest in simply squeezing educational content into existing game genres. It is easy to imagine a game of *Space Invaders* where players shoot down historical errors instead of invading aliens. It is also easy to see why this is next to useless in pedagogical terms. Such a game's historical content is only a superficial screen between the player and the actual mechanics of the game. To master an activity like this often means ignoring that layer of surface content and focusing on the game's deep tasks. All a player or student learns from "History Invaders" is how to play *Space Invaders*—moving from side to side and shooting descending blocks.

That example is intentionally banal, but the "History Invaders" problem infects far more sophisticated game designs. Many commercial computer games, like the *Civilization* series produced by Sid Meier, purport to simulate history or at least draw heavily on historical themes and content. Scholars and educators have experimented with using such games for history education.[13] We enjoy games of this type, yet we are skeptical of such projects. Historical simulations can indeed be compelling, challenging, and fun, but it is far from clear what historical skills they teach.

Debates about suitability of simulation games for the classroom have typically centered on the ideologies they appear to endorse. Does a game like *Civilization* reward militarism and imperialist expansion? Perhaps. But, following Alexander Galloway, we argue that this question is ultimately beside the point. Getting good at most simulation games means internalizing the logic of the simulation and its algorithms. In so doing, a player learns to ignore all the things that make it a game about history and not about, say, fighting aliens. "The more one begins to think that *Civilization* is about a certain ideological interpretation of history," Galloway writes, "the more one realizes that it is about the absence of history altogether."[14] Mastering the simulation game necessarily involves a journey away from reality toward abstraction, away from history toward code. If what you learn from a game is what you do while playing it, then what complex simulation games teach is how to interact with a complex computer model. That may indeed be a useful skill, but is it history? Is it the kind of historical thinking most educators wish to instill and inspire?

For a game to work as meaningful pedagogy, its lessons must be embedded in its very mechanics and procedures, in the stuff players manipulate and the actions they perform. If we as public historians and history educators are serious about teaching history with games, we have to inject ourselves deep into the game development process. We need to articulate what we think history and historical thinking are good for in the first place. Then we have to build outward from the kinds of historical thinking we want to inculcate, creating games and activities whose procedures are historical procedures, whose moving parts are historical ideas.

Our goal in designing *Tecumseh Lies Here* was to unite mechanics and subject, procedure and context, what players do and what we hope they will learn. We wanted our game to demand multiple kinds of historical thinking: first, the sorts of activities performed by professional historians; second, more vernacular kinds of history making performed by amateur history communities and affinity groups; and finally, some kinds of collective collaboration across a distributed community of players.

Tecumseh Lies Here: The Game

[The] idea was that we would tell a story that was not bound by communication platform: it would come at you over the web, by email, via fax
and phone and billboard and TV and newspaper, SMS and skywriting
and smoke signals too if we could figure out how. The story would be
fundamentally interactive, made of little bits that players, like detectives
or archaeologists, would discover and fit together. We would use political
pamphlets, business brochures, answering phone messages, surveillance
camera video, stolen diary pages. . . . In short, instead of telling a story,
we would present the evidence of that story, and let the players tell it to
themselves.

　　　　　　　　　　　　　　—Sean Stewart, "Alternate Reality Games"[15]

Because ARGs remain unfamiliar to many, it makes sense at this point
to offer some description of *Tecumseh Lies Here*. Yet it is surprisingly difficult to describe a game of this kind in definitive terms. Pervasive games
are by their very nature open-ended. This is a key pedagogical feature of the
genre. Designers cannot predict what decisions players will make or how a
narrative will unfold. As one student of the form has observed, "audience
participation"—if one can even speak of an "audience" for ARGs—is "not a
byproduct, but rather an essential and formative component of the text."[16]
Each iteration of *Tecumseh Lies Here* has turned out very differently. So what
follows is only a loose description of the game's first run.[17]

Tecumseh Lies Here begins, as many ARGs do, with a plea for help on
the Internet. A man has awoken in a field near the village of Thamesville,
Ontario, cold and wet, with no memory of how he got there or why. He
wears a Napoleonic-era uniform. Is he a time traveler? A refugee from some
alternate history? Or just an 1812 re-enactor recovering from a lost weekend?
He does not know. The man finds the name "Captain Smith" on a label
sewed into his uniform, but this sounds like an alias. Not only does "Smith"
not know his real identity, he has no knowledge of any historical events from
the last two hundred years. Naturally, he starts a weblog.

To solve this fictional mystery and cure Smith's amnesia, players must
delve into the real mystery of Tecumseh's remains, and confront a much
broader case of historical amnesia surrounding native history, national memory, and the War of 1812. Players interact with Smith through his website,
commenting on his blog posts, sending him email, and receiving responses
from him in return. Smith is portrayed in these interactions by a member
of the game design team, who follows a loose script but also improvises to
respond to player choices and actions.

Some of the game's first puzzles concern the clues on Smith's person. He tells and shows visitors to his blog that when he first awoke without his memory, he was wearing some kind of military uniform. By looking at the images Smith posts on his website, asking the right questions, and researching Napoleonic-era facings and insignia, players can discover that Smith's uniform is a replica of those worn by the Independent Company of Foreigners, a fairly notorious regiment of French prisoners who fought for the British in the War of 1812. Googling the Independent Company of Foreigners brings players to the website of a (fictional) group of war gamers and 1812 reenactors who have adopted that regiment's name.

At first glance, the Independent Company's website displays only the charming earnestness common to its breed, but players who explore the site find odd phrases and anomalies, guarded talk of shadowy adversaries, and references to "anachronists" and historical "de-enactment." The implication seems to be that the Independent Company reenacts the past for a purpose—to ensure that history itself does not get altered or erased. And the Foreigners are themselves investigating a mystery—the death of Tecumseh and the fate of his remains.

Another puzzle concerns strings of text in an unfamiliar language that active players begin receiving by email, *Twitter*, and other means. The text is transliterated Shawnee. Translated, it forms only strings of letters and numbers—a code within a code. These are in fact library call numbers, page numbers, and individual library identifiers. Players who figure this out, go to their local library, and locate the right books and pages find they all refer in different ways to Tecumseh and the War of 1812. Players who go to the specific libraries identified by the library codes—libraries scattered around Ontario, Quebec, Michigan, Indiana, Ohio, and New York—find additional rewards: slipped between the leaves of the books are pages torn from Smith's own notebooks, each one bearing further clues.

And so the plot thickens. As in any mystery story—just as in historical research—every discovery leads to further questions. Each layer of the onion is peeled back to reveal another layer that casts the existing facts in a new light. As game designers, we direct the players' attention to a series of historical documents. We lead them, through the Shawnee call numbers and other clues, to gather a sheaf of pages from secondary and primary sources. But we do not tell them what to make of all these fragments; we leave them to reconstruct the past together and debate what it might mean. "Instead of telling a story," says author and ARG designer Sean Stewart, "we . . . present the evidence of that story, and let the players tell it to themselves." Elsewhere, Stewart has called this process "storytelling as archaeology—or possibly, the other way around."[18] What Stewart describes, of course, is very close to the process of real historical research.

Thus, playing *Tecumseh Lies Here* is very much like doing real historical research. Players visit libraries and archives. They gather evidence. They interpret, analyze, and debate the evidence they have found. Some of our fictional characters are not above misusing history by forging or fabricating documents, so players must also learn to question their evidence and consider its source. Historical content is not layered on top of a game activity; historical research *is* the game.

Heritage and historical sites become part of the game too, through puzzles that can only be solved by visiting real locations. Riddles refer to museum exhibits. Objects are hidden in parks and battlegrounds. The patter of costumed interpreters occasionally includes statements with in-game as well as historical significance. New puzzles lead players to scour the Internet but also to visit libraries, archives, and commemorative sites in a widening circle around the Great Lakes region and beyond. One lesson of the game is that the past is everywhere. A pervasive game trains its players to look for game-like clues and patterns in nongame places. Even a forgotten war leaves its mark in place names, political boundaries, and local mythologies. *Tecumseh Lies Here* aims to open eyes to the pervasive presence of the past.

As players work their way through our game, they encounter allies and adversaries in the squabbling factions of the history demimonde. Each fictional group has its own interpretation of history, a point of view that is valid in some respects and lacking in others. These groups set open-ended tasks for players, asking them to find and tag places and buildings named after Tecumseh, to locate and document errors and mistruths in history textbooks and other secondary sources, or to perform re-enactment activities like starting a fire without matches (as Tecumseh's brother Tenskwatawa required his followers to do).

At a deeper level, each of these factions represents a different kind of historical thinking that we hope players will learn from but also critique. Thus, Smith's cadre of 1812 reenactors embodies a black-and-white "just the facts" approach to history. Partial to old-fashioned "drum and bugle" history and deeply suspicious of revisionism, they are admirable in their passion for the past but hidebound in their thinking. Meanwhile, a cabal of pedigreed academics believe themselves the heirs to a two-hundred-year-old secret society called the American Incognitum, who meddle in the historical record to further nefarious ends. This group represents the lure of conspiracy theory and the paranoid style in popular history. A third group affects a cynical disdain for all flavors of history, and a punk or nihilist impulse to smash the "lies" perpetrated by all the other groups. Completing the game involves learning from each point of view, but ultimately requires synthesizing or transcending the perspectives and disputes of all the rival factions.

If these puzzles and activities sound challenging, that is because they are meant to be. ARG players typically work together, connecting in online forums and tackling puzzles as a group. Does someone read French? How about Shawnee? Is there someone who can visit an archive in Chicago? Sault St. Marie? Ghent? Does anyone know how to decrypt an eighteenth-century cipher? Interpret an aerial photo? Track an animal in the wild? The short history of this genre suggests that large, determined groups of players will quickly crack almost every puzzle put before them. Once player groups reach a certain size, they become "alarmingly efficient," combining a range of competencies and skills.[19] ARG puzzles must have the character of a "trap-door function" in cryptography: easy to create but difficult or impossible to solve without large-scale effort and cooperation. The collective nature of most ARG-play contains its own fundamental lesson, one we are happy to endorse: that the strength of a network lies in the diversity of its members.

Problems and Challenges

Several of our playtesters said, "Where are the monsters?" A good question to ask of any serious games initiative.
—Edward Castronova, on his "failed" educational MMORPG *Arden*[20]

We began work on *Tecumseh Lies Here* in the summer of 2009 with high hopes and enthusiasm. A small team of history graduate students spent the summer doing research for the game, gathering archival and secondary sources, mapping and photographing historical sites, and brainstorming possible puzzles. Timothy Compeau and Robert MacDougall began actively designing the game, constructing activities, writing its fictional framing narrative, and plotting the direction of play.

Soon, however, we encountered challenges and problems. Some of these were specific to our circumstances and are probably extrinsic to the project of designing a pervasive game, or ARG, for history education. Others, however, may be intrinsic to the genre as currently understood. It seems worthwhile to describe these difficulties, both to help others working on similar projects and to qualify some of the exuberance in this current cycle of enthusiasm (hardly the first) for educational games.

Time and Cost

One of the most difficult tasks people can perform, however much others may despise it, is the invention of good games.
—Carl Jung[21]

The first difficulty we encountered was predictable yet profound. Designing, mounting, and running a successful ARG is, very simply, an immense undertaking. Though we sought this challenge out, and still welcome it, we now admit we were not prepared for the size of the task, and particularly for the way the dynamic, open-ended nature of an ARG constantly multiplies the time and effort involved.

Budget issues concerned us too, but never as much as time. We have no illusions about the ability of educators or public history sites to compete with the cost and production values of commercial video games.[22] ARGs and pervasive games, by contrast, may offer a more level playing field. There certainly have been slick, expensive ARGs, such as Levi Strauss's *Go Forth* (2009), which used the poetry of Walt Whitman to advertise jeans, or McDonald's and the International Olympic Committee's *The Lost Ring* (2008), tied to the 2008 Olympics in Beijing. Yet there have been at least as many highly successful low-budget games. Pervasive games do not require sophisticated graphics or software. Indeed, a "lo-fi" aesthetic and underground sensibility is often part of their appeal.

The real barrier we faced—and it will be a critical one for almost any teacher, professor, or public-sector educator—was the time involved. Designing an open-ended, multithreaded narrative for a large group of players means juggling the tasks of a programmer, a novelist, a screenwriter, and a game designer, plus a researcher and a teacher if the game has educational goals. It involves anticipating and planning for innumerable contingencies, and generating large amounts of content for a wide variety of media channels such as websites, email, video or audio, and physical clues. Much of the content for *Tecumseh Lies Here* came from the actual historical record and did not need to be written from scratch. Yet our historical sources still had to be identified, gathered, and organized, and our fictional framing story built around them.

And all this describes only the design and production stage of a dynamic game. As many ARG designers have reported, and as we learned directly when beta testing *Tecumseh Lies Here* in the fall of 2011, running a pervasive game is an extremely demanding experience. Game mastering during runtime was a round-the-clock blend of writing, troubleshooting, improvisational theater, and community and crisis management. Even modest games can generate hundreds of emails, text messages, and the like, and any game, if designed correctly, will go in directions its designers have not planned.

Some game designers have responded to these challenges by relinquishing narrative control of their games and moving toward almost entirely player-generated content. This trajectory, from what Jesper Juul calls "games of progression" toward "games of emergence," can be seen in the work of well-known game designer Jane McGonigal.[23] Her first major game, *I Love Bees* (2004), was a traditional ARG—indeed, it is one of the archetypal ARGs—with a story line and puzzles crafted by writer Sean Stewart and others. McGonigal was the game's community lead, working to guide, motivate, and organize the emergent community that came together to play the game. McGonigal's more recent games, such as *World Without Oil* (2007), *Superstruct* (2008), and *Urgent Evoke* (2010), had no predetermined solutions or narrative line. Almost all the content of these games was created by their many players—an ARG 2.0 model, if you will.[24]

In planning *Tecumseh Lies Here*, we tried to compromise between designer- and player-authored content, mixing prewritten puzzles and story lines with open-ended activities and tasks. Shifting from prewritten to player-generated content relieves, but hardly removes, the challenges of designing and running an ambitious game. Instead, it shifts the work of the game runners from content creation toward community management, and from the design and production stages of a game's development toward the run-time stage. *Urgent Evoke* boasted a large paid staff and an even larger team of volunteers, yet its game runners reported being seriously overwhelmed by the success of the game and the volume of player-generated material they had to quickly process and respond to.[25]

We report all these difficulties not to make excuses for ourselves but because we wonder whether they are intrinsic to ARGs and pervasive games as currently conceived. Our intent was always to limit the scope of our own game. Perhaps naively, we originally imagined *Tecumseh Lies Here* as the limited prototype for a more ambitious game to be designed and run during the two-hundredth anniversary of the War of 1812. But there is something in the narrative architecture of pervasive games that encourages them to grow.

Markus Montola writes that the imperative strategy for "visceral" and "unforgettable" experiences in pervasive game design is to set and then surpass player expectations.[26] The most effective, memorable moments in pervasive game play are often those moments when players discover the game to be bigger or more ambitious than they had originally imagined: a clue on one website leads to another, far more extensive set of sites; a game that heretofore took place online suddenly manifests in the offline world. This is arguably the whole point of pervasive play, but it creates a kind of arms race between game designer and player expectations. Players in *The Beast* (2001) became used to calling phone numbers and hearing cryptic answering machine messages; midway through the game they were stunned when the phone was answered by a live actor. Eight years later, players in *The Jejune Institute* (2009) were amused when San Francisco pay phones rang and voices on the other end ordered them to dance. But they were surprised and delighted when a man in a gorilla suit and a 1980s-style b-boy with a boom box emerged from a nearby alley to dance with them.

At its best moments, historical research has similar qualities, minus perhaps the gorilla suit. A good source leads to more sources, a good question leads to further questions, and the most satisfying discoveries are often those that suddenly connect previously minor details to much larger things. Our own experience of such moments and our desire to share that feeling form much of our motivation for writing a pervasive game about historical research. Designing for that experience, however, means a constant and powerful tendency toward structural inflation and narrative sprawl.[27]

Specific personal and professional circumstances certainly exacerbated the challenges described above and slowed our progress on *Tecumseh Lies Here*. At the time we designed and beta tested the game, Timothy Compeau was a PhD student completing his dissertation; Robert MacDougall was an untenured faculty member with small children. But what educator's working life does not involve pressures and interruptions? In January 2010, we decided to postpone the running of *Tecumseh Lies Here*. We eventually ran a beta test involving two dozen players in the fall of 2011—one year behind schedule. After this test, we redesigned the game for a younger and broader audience, partnering with the organizers of the Battle of the Thames Bicentennial in Chatham-Kent, Ontario, to run a new version of *Tecumseh Lies Here* for more than one hundred elementary school students in the fall of 2013. We have been happy with our results. But the larger question can hardly be evaded. Is this kind of sprawling, immersive game a practical model for cash- and time-strapped educators? Can public-sector labor practices accommodate the demands of ARG production? Is the work involved in designing and running a game of this sort really feasible for university professors, K–12 history teachers, graduate students, or museum staff?

Audience, Community, and Impact

> ARGs have the economics of films and the audiences of novels. They require a deep level of engagement. That's great for some audiences, but . . . they lose their way. One of the things about mystery series: they have to get weirder. . . . So the audience gets smaller and weirder. And it's harder to join that audience. You can't reboot the complexity.
> —Cory Doctorow on ARGs[28]

A second set of challenges involved questions about our game's audience or community, its impact, and its replayability.

It is very difficult to predict how many players a pervasive game, or ARG, will attract. As with many online activities, only a small fraction of those who encounter a game of this sort typically become active players. And only a smaller fraction of active players will leave their computers to perform more demanding real-world tasks. More than 19,000 players registered for *Urgent Evoke*. Fewer than two hundred completed the game's final mission. While developing *Tecumseh Lies Here*, we have worried at different times about handling too many players and about reaching too few.

We have also wrestled with defining our intended audience. Should *Tecumseh Lies Here* be designed to appeal to the small but dedicated community of experienced ARG players or to a larger, more casual public audience? Our working answer has been to shoot for something in the middle— to design a game that celebrates, and hopefully appeals to, the world of amateur history buffs, history gamers, reenactors, and similar vernacular history communities. But this is a difficult needle to thread. The challenges necessary to engage expert ARGers can quickly discourage less experienced players. But new and casual players cannot be counted on to perform the kinds of tasks or cultivate the collective community that sustains an ambitious or challenging game.

Augmented reality games are said to build community, and for a time, most do. But once an effective player community has been established, its need for new members and the opportunity for new arrivals to usefully contribute rapidly decline. Jeff Watson argues that "elite players with available time, an appropriate range of competencies, and relevant social capital will gather, process, and analyze data faster and more thoroughly than a non-integrated outsider ever could."[29] This tendency must temper hopes for ARGs as inclusive, community-forming experiences.

Game designer Greg Costikyan observes:

In fact, game design is not merely difficult; it is impossible. That is, it is impossible, or virtually impossible, to spec a game at the beginning of a project, and have it work beautifully, wonderfully, superbly, from the moment a playable prototype is available. There's just too much going on here, too many ways for it to fail. Game design is ultimately a process of iterative refinement, continuous adjustment during testing, until, budget and schedule and management willing, we have a polished product that does indeed work.[30]

Related to these concerns is the question of replayability. Most ARGs are designed to be played only once. They have been described as "rock concerts": large, one-time events that are powerful and engaging for those present, but not reproducible for those who are not.[31] This is understandable given the demands of running a dynamic game, but it makes iterative design difficult and seriously limits the impact and accessibility of the form.

Some games do leave static elements behind, with activities that can be performed by late arrivals without the active participation of game runners or designers. *Ghosts of a Chance* was an ARG hosted by the Smithsonian American Art Museum in 2008. The ARG invited gamers to create objects and mail them to the museum for an exhibition "curated" by two fictional game characters, while simultaneously uncovering clues to a narrative about these objects. The game culminated with a series of six scavenger hunts at the museum. While the bulk of the game cannot now be replayed, the scavenger hunts remain for museum visitors to enjoy. *Ghosts of a Chance* was certainly a successful ARG and we have kept its model in mind. But some Smithsonian staff reported disappointment that the game did not reach a larger audience beyond the existing ARG community, and that more of the game's experience could not be repeated or replayed by the general public.[32]

As with our concerns about the time and cost of mounting a successful game, the larger question here is whether these worries are simply cold feet at the midpoint of a demanding project, or whether they point to something intrinsic about the genre. Two motifs that often appear in pervasive games are hidden conspiracies and secret worlds hidden behind the one we know. This is no coincidence. Part of the fun of such games is the appeal of being "illuminated," of perceiving an alternate reality (the world of the game) that leaves others (nonparticipants) in the dark. Thus, ARGs are exclusive and irreproducible experiences almost by design. Alexander Galloway has argued that simulation games are always "allegories of control," whatever surface ideologies they may project.[33] In a similar way, ARGs and pervasive games may inevitably enact allegories of conspiracy, of the unknowing masses and the illuminated few. Such tropes have an appeal that it would be naive to deny, but they are not an appealing model, practically or philosophically, for most educators.

Participating in a successful pervasive game is undoubtedly a powerful and lasting experience. Players of *The Beast*, *I Love Bees*, and other seminal ARGs still gather years later to talk about these games. Our beta testers reported the same intense engagement. But this intensity is predicated, at least in part, on the exclusivity and irreproducibility of the games. Is it in fact necessary to bewilder or exclude a large group of people so that a much smaller few can enjoy a powerful, unrepeatable experience? At least one researcher has argued that making ARGs more accessible would "remove important triggers to hard-core player production and enjoyment."[34] Like many intense group activities, pervasive games described after the fact have a strong "you had to be there" quality. Maybe these experiences would not be so powerful, and the communities around completed games would not be so tightly knit, if the games were easier to join and play and understand. We have struggled to split the difference, to imagine a play experience that combines intensity with accessibility. It is not obvious whether this can be done.

Professional and Ethical Questions

Are computer games necessarily and inherently countercultural and escapist? Is what makes them engaging, like rock and roll (and frankly, like poetry), their protest, desperation, and defiance? Or, like comic books and movies, their ability to transport one to a different and irrelevant place?

—Clark Aldrich, *Learning By Doing*[35]

A final set of challenges involved dealing responsibly with sensitive historical topics, and also with professional and ethical questions surrounding history and play.

Certainly, the history surrounding the death and burial of Tecumseh remains sensitive to some. In particular, many native Canadians and Americans are leery of the subject, in light of the long history of white misrepresentation of the native past and white desecration of native remains. (See chapter 9 for a similar situation involving aboriginal people's concerns about a game [in this case a board game] that addresses their history.) We are mindful that our game may seem to perpetuate the same morbid fascination with Tecumseh's remains that it ostensibly critiques.

We can only confess: it is in part the very unpleasantness of this story that intrigued us and appealed to us as a way to explore and critique the official memory of this strange and poorly remembered war. Again, *Tecumseh Lies Here* aspires to be a subversive commemoration. The complexities of the War of 1812 have not been well served by the nationalist myths that later grew up around it. Honoring Tecumseh's memory, we argue, requires challenging outdated historiography on both sides of the border. Our aim is certainly not to offend. But popular history has always contained a fascination with war, death, and crime. And we cannot see how to make an engaging game with multiple characters and input from diverse players that could not possibly offend anyone. Instead, we have tried to make our own misgivings part of the game itself. The different factions in our game constantly criticize each other; we hope our players will critique our use of Tecumseh's memory too.

Constance Steinkuehler writes:

As a Pew Internet and American Life Report on the digital disconnect between children and their schools details with excruciating clarity, what students do with online technologies *outside* the classroom is not only markedly different from what they do with them in schools . . . it is *also* more goal driven, complex, sophisticated, and engaged. If we care to understand the current and potential capacities of technology for cognition, learning, literacy, and education, than we must look to contexts *outside* our current formal education system rather than those within.[36]

We intended from the start that *Tecumseh Lies Here* would engage and critique certain "misuses" of history. Our game therefore includes fake and forged historical documents, conspiracy theories, and counterfactuals. We considered even more fantastical elements, such as time travel and alternate history. Professional historians are extremely wary of such pseudohistorical tropes, yet they are familiar and beloved by many amateur history makers and enthusiasts. They are basic elements of much historical play.

We were inspired by educational projects like *The Lost Museum* and the *Great Unsolved Mysteries in Canadian History* (see chapter 1), which manage to be playful yet remain eminently respectable in their historical practice. Still, we believed there was room for something edgier, less sober, and more playful than these examples. We hoped to produce something that might capture the imagination of gamers and playful history subcultures. We wanted a game that did not look or feel like it was designed for a classroom. We wanted, frankly, to play with toys that historians are not supposed to play with. James Paul Gee has asserted that video games, and perhaps all games, require an element of social transgression.[37] All games have rules, but play is not truly play until some rules are broken. This did not mean that we abdicated our responsibility to think and talk about the ethical and professional questions posed by pseudohistorical play. Instead, it meant that we talked about these questions all the time.

We took some guidance from our subjects and desired audience in both gaming and vernacular history communities. Many hobby subcultures, especially those that are in any way transgressive, develop their own codes of ethical practice and self-regulation.[38] ARG players debate codes and practices about privacy, trespassing, interacting with nonparticipants, and so on. Historical reenactors care devoutly about authenticity and respect for the past. And history gamers place a high priority on historical realism even or especially when their scenarios diverge wildly from actual history. These codes are not the same as the codes of the classroom or the professional historian—nor should they be. But respecting these communities, we felt, meant at least listening to, and trying on, alternate ways of interfacing with the past.

We developed our own set of internal rules for *Tecumseh Lies Here* to follow. For instance, all fictional events in the game take place in the present day. The players must decide for themselves, based on the real historical record, what really happened in the past. All our forged documents are considered to have been created by in-game characters and are exposed as fakes in the course of the game. And while our fictional characters spout all manner of pseudohistorical theorizing—most of it competing and conflicting with one another—the game as a whole never endorses their positions.

Issues of scale and replayability come up again here. Can these ethical and professional questions be worked out only once? Or do they have to be renegotiated every time by every educator who contemplates this sort of activity? What is at stake in these questions, and who is ultimately accountable for the answers we choose? We may be willing to flirt with sensitive topics and pseudohistorical tropes for the sake of a one-time experiment. But is this a model one can recommend to other educators? We do not know.

Conclusion

> The best games make you more suspicious of, more attentive to, the world around you. They make you seek out the pieces of something you're already a part of. But first they must make you a part of it.
> —Elan Lee, ARG designer[39]

The potential promise of this investigation seems clear. Our 2011 beta test and our larger public launch in 2013 were fun, engaging, and educational. Playful historical thinking—an attitude toward the past that is at once playful, critical, and alert—seems to us a worthy goal for history educators and a great gift to pass on to the citizens of the twenty-first century. Public historians, educators, and others have long dreamed of an immersive historical environment. Yet perhaps the best way to immerse someone in history is not to surround them with replicas and re-creations, but to arm them with historical methods and have them discover the history that is all around them. Pervasive games and activities seem tailor-made for this kind of teaching and learning.

Yet the challenges of pervasive gaming are significant and remain unsolved. Playing in the "real world" means accommodating real-world constraints on budget and time. A pedagogical idea that cannot be employed in actual educational institutions, by individual teachers and professors, by small museums and heritage sites, by people on the front lines of history education, is unlikely to take root. A prototype game that cannot be reproduced is more of a curiosity than a true innovation.

So we close with questions rather than answers. Must play equal games? Can we imagine inquiry-based historical play without a sprawling, highly designed game experience? Could a historical narrative be fractured into many discrete episodes without losing its immersive power? Could there be quick pervasive games, easy to deploy and repeat? Can we imagine more casual historical games? Or historical toys? Or ambient location-centered historical experiences that borrow certain ARG techniques but are not dependent on collective problem solving or time-sensitive events? We hope that by playing with history in *Tecumseh Lies Here*, we can approach more definitive conclusions. These questions, fittingly, demand both critical thought and creative play.

NOTES

1. Pierre Wellner et al., "Computer-Augmented Environments: Back to the Real World," *Communications of the ACM* 36, no. 7 (1993): 24–26.

2. Dave Szulborski, *This Is Not a Game: A Guide to Alternate Reality Gaming* (Macungie, Pa.: New Fiction, 2005); Jane McGonigal, "This Might Be a Game: Ubiquitous Play and Performance at the Turn of the Twenty-First Century" (Ph.D. dissertation, University of California, Berkeley, 2006); Markus Montola et al., *Pervasive Games: Theory and Design* (Amsterdam: Elsevier, 2009).

3. The number of fully active players is generally much smaller—by one estimate, fewer than a tenth of *World Without Oil*'s players submitted more than one piece of content.

4. Karen L. Schrier, "Revolutionizing History Education: Using Augmented Reality Games to Teach Histories" (master's thesis, Massachusetts Institute of Technology, 2005).

5. Roy Rosenzweig and David Thelen, *The Presence of the Past: Popular Uses of History in American Life* (New York: Columbia University Press, 1998), 34.

6. Bruce Van Sledright, *The Challenge of Rethinking History Education: On Practices, Theories, and Policy* (New York: Routledge, 2011); Samuel Wineburg, *Historical Thinking and Other Unnatural Acts: Charting the Future of Teaching the Past* (Philadelphia: Temple University Press, 2001).

7. Wineburg, 72.

8. Alexander Cook, "The Use and Abuse of Historical Reenactment," *Criticism* 46, no. 3 (2004): 495.

9. The grant was an Image, Text, Sound, & Technology (ITST) Grant from the Social Sciences and Humanities Research Council of Canada (SSHRC). Robert MacDougall was principal investigator, with Kevin Kee and William Turkel listed as co-investigators, Shawn Graham as a collaborator, and Timothy Compeau as project manager. Since 2010, *Tecumseh Lies Here* has been supported by the Ontario Augmented Reality Network. This article was originally written in 2011, before *Tecumseh*

Lies Here was completed. In preparing this chapter for publication, we have revised only lightly, in order to preserve and present a snapshot of our thinking while originally designing this game. We will discuss our experiences actually running *Tecumseh Lies Here* in forthcoming work.

10. Guy St-Denis, *Tecumseh's Bones* (Montreal: McGill-Queen's University Press, 2005).

11. Alexander Galloway, *Gaming: Essays on Algorithmic Culture* (Minneapolis: University of Minneapolis Press, 2006), 103.

12. Galloway, 2. See also Ian Bogost, *Persuasive Games: The Expressive Power of Videogames* (Cambridge, Mass.: MIT Press, 2007).

13. See, for example, Kurt Squire, "Open-ended Video Games: A Model for Developing Learning for the Interactive Age," in *The Ecology of Games: Connecting Youth, Games, and Learning*, ed. K. Salen (Cambridge, Mass.: MIT Press, 2008), 167–98.

14. Galloway, 103. See also Bogost, 103–9, 242; Kevin Kee et al., "Towards a Theory of Good History Through Gaming," *Canadian Historical Review* 90, no. 2 (June 2009).

15. Sean Stewart, "Alternate Reality Games," June 11, 2006, accessed July 31, 2012, http://www.seanstewart.org/interactive/args/.

16. Jeff Watson, "ARG 2.0," July 7 and July 9, 2010, accessed July 31, 2012, http://henryjenkins.org/2010/07/arg_20_1.html.

17. Many early ARGs took great pains to disguise the circumstances of their creation, even the fact that they were games. Today, it is less common to go to these lengths. As the conventions of the genre take shape, players are more and more willing to suspend their disbelief, and absolute verisimilitude is no longer required.

18. Stewart; Jim Hanas, "The Story Doesn't Care: An Interview with Sean Stewart," January 25, 2006, accessed July 31, 2012, http://www.hanasiana.com/archives/001117.html.

19. Watson; Jane McGonigal, "Why I Love Bees: A Case Study in Collective Intelligence Gaming," in Salen, ed., *The Ecology of Games*, 199–228.

20. Edward Castronova, "Two Releases," November 27, 2007, accessed August 1, 2012, http://terranova.blogs.com/terra_nova/2007/11/two-releases-ar.html.

21. Quoted in Greg Costikyan, "I Have No Words and I Must Design: Toward a Critical Vocabulary for Games," in *Proceedings of Computer Games and Digital Cultures Conference*, ed. Frans Mäyrä (Tampere, Finland: Tampere University Press, 2002), 32.

22. The production and launch budget for a recent game industry blockbuster, *Call of Duty: Modern Warfare 2*, was in the vicinity of $200 million. Ben Fritz, "Video Game Borrows Page from Hollywood Playbook," *Los Angeles Times*, November 18, 2009.

23. Jesper Juul, *Half-Real: Video Games Between Real Rules and Fictional Worlds* (Cambridge, Mass.: MIT Press, 2005); Jane McGonigal, *Reality Is Broken: Why Games Make Us Happy and How They Can Change the World* (New York: Penguin, 2011).

24. Watson.

25. Our source here is an off-the-record conversation with game runners, but see also Jane McGonigal, "What Went Right, What Went Wrong: Lessons from Season 1 of EVOKE," *Evoke Blog*, July 26, 2010, accessed July 31, 2012, http://blog.urgentevoke.net/2010/07/26/what-went-right-what-went-wrong-lessons-from-season-1-evoke1/.

26. Montola et al., 137–38.

27. See also Neil Dansey on designing for "apophenia," the perception of meaning or pattern in events that are actually accidental. Neil Dansey, "Facilitating Apophenia

to Augment the Experience of Pervasive Games," paper presented at the "Breaking the Magic Circle" seminar, University of Tampere, Finland, April 2008, www.determined software.co.uk.

28. Annalee Newitz, "Cory Doctorow Talks About the Future of the Novel, Including His Own," *io9* (September 30, 2009), accessed August 1, 2012, http://io9.com /5371362/cory-doctorow-talks-about-the-future-of-the-novel-including-his-own.

29. Watson.

30. Costikyan, 25.

31. "Events, Not ARGs: Interview with the Founders of 4th Wall," *Variety*, May 4, 2009, accessed August 1, 2012, http://weblogs.variety.com/technotainment/2009/05 /events.html.

32. Our source here is an off-the-record conversation with Smithsonian staff, but see also Georgina Bath, "Ghosts of a Chance Alternate Reality Game Final Report," *Smithsonian American Art Museum*, November 6, 2008, 17, accessed July 31, 2012, http://ghostsofachance.com, 17.

33. Montola et al., 59; Galloway, 85–106.

34. Christy Dena, "Emerging Participatory Culture Practices: Player-Created Tiers in Alternate Reality Games," *Convergence* 14, no. 1 (2008): 41–57.

35. Clark Aldrich, *Learning By Doing: A Comprehensive to Simulations, Computer Games, and Pedagogy in e-Learning and Other Educational Experiences* (San Francisco: Pfeiffer, 2005), 159.

36. Constance Steinkuehler, "Cognition and Literacy in Massively Multiplayer Online Games," in *Handbook of Research on New Literacies*, ed. Julie Coiro et al. (New York: Lawrence Erlbaum Associates, 2008), 612. Emphasis in original.

37. James Paul Gee, *What Video Games Have To Teach Us About Learning and Literacy* (New York: Palgrave Macmillan, 2004).

38. Montola et al., 198; Henry Jenkins, *Fans, Bloggers, and Gamers: Exploring Participatory Culture* (New York: New York University Press, 2006).

39. Quoted in Jane McGonigal, "A Real Little Game: The Performance of Belief in Pervasive Play," Digital Games Research Association, "Level Up" conference proceedings, November 2003.

Playfully

FIVE

The Hermeneutics of Screwing Around; or What You Do with a Million Books

Stephen Ramsay

According to the world wide web, the phrase "So many books, so little time" originates with Frank Zappa. I do not believe it, myself. If I had had to guess, I would have said maybe Erasmus or Trithemius. But even if I am right, I am probably wrong. This is one of civilization's oldest laments—one that, in spirit, predates the book itself. There has never been a time when philosophers—lovers of wisdom broadly understood—have not exhibited profound regret over the impedance of mismatch between time and truth. For surely, there are more books, more ideas, more experiences, and more relationships worth having than there are hours in a day (or days in a lifetime).

What everyone wants—what everyone from Sargon to Zappa has wanted—is some coherent, authoritative path through what is known. That is the idea behind "Dr. Elliot's Five Foot Shelf," Mortimer Adler's *Great Books of the Western World*, Modern Library's *100 Best Books*, and all other similar attempts to condense knowledge into some ordered list of things the educated should know. It is also the idea behind every syllabus, every curriculum, and most of the nonfiction books that have ever been written. The world is vast. Art is long. What else can we do but *survey* the field, *introduce* a topic, plant a *seed* (with, what else, a *seminar*). Amazon.com has a feature that allows users to create reading guides focused on a particular topic. They call it, appropriately, "Listmania."

While the anxiety of not knowing the path is constant, moments of cultural modernity provide especially fertile ground for the creation of epitomes, summae, canons, and bibles (as well as new schools, new curricula, and new ways of organizing knowledge). It is, after all, at the end of history that one undertakes summation of "the best that has been thought and said in the world."[1] The aforementioned "great books" lists all belong to the early decades of the twentieth century, when U.S. cultural anxiety—especially concerning its relationship to Europe—could be leavened with a bold act of cultural confidence. Thomas Jefferson had said something similar at a time closer to the founding of the country, when he noted that "All that is necessary for a student is access to a library, and directions in what order the books are to be read."[2] But the same phenomenon—the same play of anxiety and confidence—was at work in the writing of the Torah, the *Summa*, Will Durant's *Story of Civilization*, and all efforts of similar grandeur. All three of those works were written during moments, not just of rapid cultural change, but during periods of anxiety about change. "These words YHWH spoke to your entire assembly at the mountain from the midst of the fire, the cloud, and the fog (with) a great voice, adding no more";[3] "We purpose in this book to treat of whatever belongs to the Christian religion, in such a way as may tend to the instruction of beginners";[4] "I wish to tell as much as I can, in as little space as I can, of the contributions that genius and labor have made to the cultural heritage of mankind."[5] This essay will not aim quite so high.

Even in the very early days of the web, one felt the soul-crushing lack of order. One of the first pages I ever visited was *Jerry and David's Guide to the World Wide Web*, which endeavored to, what else, guide you through what seemed an already impossibly vast expanse of information.[6] *Google* might seem something else entirely, but it shares the basic premise of those quaint guides of yore, and of all guides to knowledge. The point is not to return to the more than three million pages that relate in some way to Frank Zappa. The point is to say, "Relax. Here is where you start. Look at this. Then look at this."

We might say that all such systems rely on an act of faith, but it is not so much trust in the search engine (or the book, or the professor) as it is willingness to suspend disbelief about the yellow wood after having taken a particular road. Literary historian Franco Moretti states the situation starkly:

> We've just started rediscovering what Margaret Cohen calls the "great unread." "I work on West European narrative, etc." Not really, I work on its canonical fraction, which is not even one per cent of published literature. And again, some people have read more, but the point is that there are thirty thousand nineteenth-century British novels out there, forty, fifty, sixty thousand—no one really knows, no one has read them, no one ever will. And then there are French novels, Chinese, Argentinian, American.[7]

Debates about canonicity have been raging in my field (literary studies) for as long as the field has been around. Who is in? Who is out? How do we decide? Moretti reminds us of the dispiriting fact that this problem has no practical solution. It is not just that someone or something will be left off; it is that our most inclusive, most enlightened choices will fail against even the most generous requirements for statistical significance. The syllabus represents the merest fraction of the professor's knowledge, and the professor's knowledge is, in the scheme of things, embarrassingly slight.

Gregory Crane, who held a series of symposia on the general question, "What Do You Do With A Million Books?" a few years ago, rightly identifies it as an ancient calculus:

> The Greek historian Herodotus has the Athenian sage Solon estimate the lifetime of a human being at c. 26,250 days (Herodotus, *The Histories*, 1.32). If we could read a book on each of those days, it would take almost forty lifetimes to work through every volume in a single million book library. The continuous tradition of written European literature that began with the Iliad and Odyssey in the eighth century BCE is itself little more than a million days old. While libraries that contain more than one million items are not unusual, print libraries never possessed a million books of use to any one reader.[8]

Way too many books, *way* too little time.

But again, the real anxiety is not that the Library of Congress contains more than five hundred human lifetimes worth of reading material (I am using the highly generous Solon-Crane metric, which assumes you read a book every day from the day you are born until the day you die). The problem is that that much information probably exceeds our ability to create reliable guides to it. It is one thing to worry that your canon is not sufficiently inclusive, or broad, or representative. It is another thing when your canon has no better chance of being these things than a random selection. When we get up into the fourteen-million-book range, books that are known by more than two living people are already "popular." A book like *Hamlet* has overcome enormous mathematical odds that ruthlessly favor obscurity; the fact that millions of people have read it might become a compelling argument for why you should read it too. But in the end, arguments from the standpoint of popularity satisfy neither the canoniclast nor the historian. The dark fear is that no one can really say what is "representative" because no one has any basis for making such a claim.

Several solutions have been proposed, including proud ownership of our ignorance and dilettantism. A few years ago, Pierre Bayard famously—and with only the barest sheen of satire—exposed our condition by writing a book entitled *How to Talk About Books You Haven't Read*. In it, intellectual facility is presented as a kind of trick: "For knowing how to speak with finesse about something with which we are unacquainted has value far beyond the realm of books."[9] It is a lesson thoroughly absorbed by anyone who stands on the right side of a Ph.D. oral exam. But amazingly, even Bayard sees this as a means toward guiding people through knowledge. "[Students] see culture as a huge wall, as a terrifying specter of 'knowledge.' But we intellectuals, who are avid readers, know there are many ways of reading a book. You can skim it, you can start and not finish it, you can look at the index. You learn to live with a book. . . . I want to help people organize their own paths through culture."[10]

At some level, there is no difference at all between Pierre Bayard and, say, Mortimer Adler. Both believe in culture. Both believe that one can find an ordered path through culture. Bayard just thinks there are faster ways to do it than starting with volume 1 of *Great Books of the Western World*. Indeed, Adler himself almost seemed to agree; books 2 and 3 of *Great Books* presented what he called a "Synopticon." What could such a thing be but the *Cliff's Notes* to the main ideas of Western civilization? There also is not much of a difference between Bayard on the one hand and Crane and Moretti on the other. All three would like us to dispense with the silly notion that we can read everything, so that we can get on with the task of organizing our own paths through culture. It is true that the latter—as well as digital humanists generally—propose that we use computers, but I would like to argue that that difference is not as crucial as it seems.

There have always been two ways to deal with a library. The first is the one we are most used to thinking about. I am doing research on the influence of French composer Edgard Varèse on the early work of Frank Zappa. I go to the library and conduct an investigation, which might include the catalogue, a bibliography or two, the good people at the reference desk, or any one of a dozen different methods and tools. This is search. I know what I am looking for, and I have various strategies for locating it. I cannot read everything on this subject. I cannot even locate everything on this subject. But I have faith in the idea that I can walk out of the library (this afternoon, or after ten years of focused research, depending on my situation) being able to speak intelligently and convincingly on this topic.

The second way goes like this: I walk into the library and wander around in a state of insouciant boredom. I like music, so I head over to the music section. I pick up a book on American rock music and start flipping through it (because it is purple and big). There is an interesting bit on Frank Zappa, and it mentions that Zappa was way into this guy named Edgard Varèse. I have no idea who that is, so I start looking around for some Varèse. One look at the cover of his biography—Varèse with that mad-scientist look and the crazy hair—and I am already a fan. And so off I go. I check out some records and discover Varèse.

This is called browsing, and it is a completely different activity. Here, I do not know what I am looking for, really. I just have a bundle of "interests" and proclivities. I am not really trying to find "a path through culture." I am really just screwing around. This is more or less how Zappa discovered Varèse. He had read an article in *LOOK* magazine in which the owner of the Sam Goody record chain was bragging about his ability to sell obscure records like *The Complete Works of Edgard Varèse, Vol. 1.*[11] The article described Varèse's music as, "a weird jumble of drums and other unpleasant sounds."[12] The rest is history (of the sort that you can search for, if you are so inclined).

We think of the computer as a device that has revolutionized search—"information retrieval," to use the formal term—and that is of course true. Until recently, no one was able to search the content of all the books in the library. There was no way to ask, "Which of these books contains the phrase 'Frank Zappa'?" The fact that we can now do that changes everything, but it does not change the nature of the thing. When we ask that question—or any question, for that matter—we are still searching. We are still asking a question and availing ourselves of various technologies in pursuit of the answer.

Browsing, though, is a different matter. Once you have programmatic access to the content of the library, screwing around potentially becomes a far more illuminating and useful activity. That is, presumably, why we called the navigational framework one used to poke around the world wide web a "browser," as opposed to, say, a "searcher." From the very start, the web outstripped our ability to say what is actually there. Jerry and David could not say it then and *Google* cannot say it even now. "Can I help you?" "No, I'm just browsing." Translation: "I just got here! How can you help me find what I'm looking for when (a) I don't know what's here and (b) I don't know what I'm looking for?" The sales clerk, of course, does not need a translation. He understands perfectly that you are just screwing around. Our irritation arises not because the question is premature or impertinent, but because we are being encouraged to have a purposive experience when we are perfectly happy having a serendipitous one.

And that is absolutely not what the people who are thinking about the brave new world of large-scale digital corpora (*Google Books*, or the web itself) want to talk about. Consider Martin Mueller's notion of "not reading"—an idea he puts forth during a consideration of the power of the digital surrogate:

A book sits in a network of transactions that involve a reader, his interlocutors, and a "collective library" of things one knows or is supposed to know. Felicitous reading—I adapt the term from John Austin's definition of felicitous speech acts—is the art of locating with sufficient precision the place a given book occupies in that network at a given moment. Your skill as a reader, then, is measured by the speed and accuracy with which you can do that. Ideally you should do it in "no time at all." Once you have oriented a book in the right place of its network, you can stop reading. In fact, you should stop reading.[13]

Perhaps this is not "search," classically understood, but it is about as far from screwing around as the average game theory symposium is from poker night. You go to the archive to set things right—to increase the likelihood that your network of associations corresponds to the actual one (or, as seems more likely, the culturally dominant one). That technology could assist you in this august task—the task of a lifetime for most of us—should not obscure the fundamental conservatism of this vision. The vast digital library is there to help you answer the question with which you began.

Gregory Crane imagines a library in which the books talk to each other—each one embedded in a swirl of data mining and machine learning algorithms. What do we do with a million books? His answer is boldly visionary: "Extract from the stored record of humanity useful information in an actionable format for any given human being of any culture at any time and in any place."[14] He notes that this "will not emerge quickly," but one might legitimately question whether, strictly speaking, such a thing is logically possible for the class of problems traditionally held within the province of screwing around. What "useful information" was Zappa looking for (in, of all places, *LOOK*)? He did not really know and could not say. Zappa would have loved the idea of "actionable formats," however. As it turns out, it took him more than a year to find a copy of a Varèse record, and when he finally did, he did not have the money to buy it. He ended up having to convince the salesman to part with it at a discount. Lucky for us, the salesman's "network of transactions" was flawed.

How would Zappa's adventure have played out today? *LOOK Online* mentions Varèse, and the "actionable format" is (at best) a click away, and at worst, over at *Pirate Bay*. And it is better than that. *Amazon* says that if you like Varèse, you might also like Messiaen's *Quartet for the End of Time*, which Messiaen actually wrote in a prison camp during World War II, the fifth movement of which (the piece, not the war) is based on an earlier piece that uses six Ondes Martinot, which is not only one of the first electronic instruments, but possibly the most beautiful sound you have ever heard.

And I do not believe this. There is a guy in Seattle who is trying to build an Ondes, and he has already rigged a ring controller to a Q125 Signal Processor. And he has got video.

This is browsing. And it is one of the most venerable techniques in the life of the mind. Ian F. McFeely and Lisa Wolverton make the point forcefully in their book, *Reinventing Knowledge*:

> The categorization of knowledge, whether in tables, trees, or Dewey decimals, has exerted a fascination among modern-day scholars far disproportionate to its actual importance. Classification schemes are arbitrary conveniences. What matters is not whether history is grouped with poetry or with politics and what that says about the ancient mind, but simply whether such schemes make books readily and rapidly accessible to roaming encyclopedic intellects.[15]

It is sometimes forgotten that a search engine does not need information to be organized in a way that is at all meaningful to human beings. In fact, a fully automated library—one that uses, say, search engines and robots to retrieve books—would surely not organize things according to subject. Search engines are designed so that the time it takes to locate a text string is as close to constant as possible. Linear ordering is more often a liability in such frameworks, and if we are using robots, it might make more sense to order the physical books by color or size than by subject area.

Libraries today try to facilitate both forms of engagement. The physical card catalogue (another technology designed to facilitate serendipitous browsing) has been almost universally replaced with the search engine, and yet the stacks themselves continue to privilege the roaming intellect. It is a sensible compromise, even if we (and more importantly, our students) are more likely to forego browsing the stacks in favor of searching. *Google Books*, ironically, tries to do the same thing. Its search engine undoubtedly conceives of the book as a bounded collection of strings within an enormous hash table. Yet on the sidebar, there is a list of subjects and a link labeled "Browse Books." Clicking the latter will take you to an apparently random selection of books within "Classics," "Magazines," "Gardening," "Performing Arts," and others. It will even show you, in a manner vaguely reminiscent of Vannevar Bush's ideas about paths in "As We May Think," "Trending Topics" (books located by other users' search queries).

As a search tool, *Google* is hard to beat. By providing lookup access to the contents of the books, it provides a facility that no library has ever been able to offer in the history of the world. Yet as a browsing tool—as a tool for serendipitous engagement—it falls far behind even the most rudimentary library. It can successfully present books on gardening, but because all categorization within *Google Books* is ultimately a function of search, it has a hard time getting you from gardening to creation myths, from creation myths to Wagner, and from Wagner to Zappa. It may sound perverse to say it, but *Google Books* (and indeed, most things like it) are simply terrible at browsing. The thing they manage to get right (search) is, regrettably, the one thing that is least likely to turn up something not already prescribed by your existing network of associations. In the end, you are left with a landscape in which the wheel ruts of your roaming intellect are increasingly deepened by habit, training, and preconception. Seek and you shall find. Unfortunately, you probably will not find much else.

What is needed, then, is a full-text archive on the scale of *Google Books* that is like the vast hypertextual network that surrounds it (and from which it is curiously disconnected). Hand tagging at this scale is neither possible nor desirable; ironically, only algorithmic methods can free us from the tunnel vision that search potentially induces. Without this, the full text archive becomes something far less than the traditional library.

There are concerns, of course. A humanist scholar—of whatever discipline, and however postmodern—is by definition a believer in shared culture. If everyone is screwing around, one might legitimately wonder whether we can achieve a shared experience of culture sufficient to the tasks we have traditionally set for education—especially matters such as participation in the public square. A media landscape completely devoid of guides and standards is surely as lethal to the life of the mind as one so ramified as to drown out any voice not like one's own. But these concerns are no sooner raised than reimagined by the recent history of the world wide web. Today, the dominant format of the web is not the "web page," but the protean, "modded" forum: *Slashdot, Reddit, Digg, Boing Boing*, and countless others. They are guides of a sort, but they describe themselves vaguely as containing "stuff that matters," or, "a directory of wonderful things." These sites are at once the product of screwing around and the social network that invariably results when people screw with each other.

As usual, they order this matter better in France. Years ago, Roland Barthes made the provocative distinction between the "readerly text" (where one is mostly a passive consumer) and the "writerly text," where, as he put it, the reader, "before the infinite play of the world (the world as function) is traversed, intersected, stopped, plasticized by some singular system (Ideology, Genus, Criticism) which reduces the plurality of entrances, the opening of networks, the infinity of languages."[16] Many have commented on the ways such thoughts appear to anticipate the hypertext, the mashup, and the web. But Barthes himself doubted whether "the pleasure of the text"—the writerly text—could ever penetrate the institutions in which readerly paths through culture are enshrined. He wrote:

> What relation can there be between the pleasure of the text and the institutions of the text? Very slight. The theory of the text postu-lates bliss, but it has little institutional future: what it establishes, its precise accomplishment, its assumption, is a practice (that of the writer), not a science, a method, a research, a pedagogy; on these very principles, this theory can produce only theoreticians or practitio-ners, not specialists (critics, researchers, professors, students). It is not only the inevitably metalinguistic nature of all institutional research which hampers the writing of textual pleasure, it is also that we are today incapable of conceiving a true science of becoming (which alone might assemble our pleasure without garnishing it with a moral tutelage).[17]

Somewhere in there lies a manifesto for how digital humanities might reform certain academic orthodoxies that work against the hermeneutics of screwing around. Have we not already begun to call ourselves "a community of practice," in preference to "a science, a method, a research, a pedagogy"?

But the real message of our technology is, as usual, something entirely unexpected—a writerly, anarchic text that is more useful than the readerly, institutional text. Useful and practical, not in spite of its anarchic nature, but as a natural consequence of the speed and scale that inhere in all anar-chic systems. This is, if you like, the basis of the Screwmeneutical Impera-tive. There are so many books. There is so little time. Your ethical obligation is neither to read them all nor to pretend that you have read them all, but to understand each path through the vast archive as an important moment in the world's duration—as an invitation to community, relationship, and play.

NOTES

1. Matthew Arnold, *"Culture and Anarchy" and Other Writings*, ed. Stefan Collini (Cambridge: Cambridge University Press, 1993), 190.

2. Thomas Jefferson, "To John Garland Jefferson, 11 June 1790," in *The Works*, vol. 6 (New York: Putnam, 1905), 71.

3. Deuteronomy 5:19, in *The Five Books of Moses*, trans. Everett Fox (New York: Schocken, 1995), 877.

4. Thomas Aquinas, *Summa Theologiae*, vol. 1 (Scotts Valley, Calif.: NovAntiqua, 2008), 1.

5. Will Durant, *Our Oriental Heritage, Story of Civilization 1* (New York: Simon and Schuster, 1963), vii.

6. The site would go on to become *Yahoo!*—which would go on to achieve a market capitalization of more than $55 billion within ten years.

7. Franco Moretti, "Conjectures on World Literature," *New Left Review* 1 (2000): 55.

8. Gregory Crane, "What Do You Do with a Million Books?" *D-Lib Magazine* 12, no. 3 (2006).

9. Pierre Bayard, *How to Talk About Books You Haven't Read* (London: Granta, 2007), 184.

10. Alan Riding, "Read It? No, But You Can Skim a Few Pages and Fake It," *The New York Times,* February 24, 2007.

11. Peter Occhiogrosso, *The Real Frank Zappa Book* (New York: Picador, 1990), 31.

12. Frank Zappa, "Edgard Varèse: The Idol of My Youth," *Zappa Wiki Jawaka,* accessed February 26, 2011, http://en.wikipedia.org/wiki/Frank_Zappa#cite_note -Varese-14.

13. Martin Mueller, "Digital Shakespeare or Toward a Literary Informatics," *Shakespeare* 4, no. 3 (2008): 284–301.

14. Crane.

15. Ian F. McNeely and Lisa Wolverton, *Reinventing Knowledge: From Alexandria to the Internet* (New York: Norton, 2009), 20–21.

16. Roland Barthes, *S/Z: An Essay* (New York: Farrar-Hill, 1974), 5.

17. Roland Barthes, *The Pleasure of the Text* (New York: Farrar-Hill, 1975), 60.

SIX

Abort, Retry, Pass, Fail

Games as Teaching Tools

Sean Gouglas, Mihaela Ilovan,
Shannon Lucky, and Silvia Russell

Games and play have always served an educational function. Computer games are only the latest incarnation in a vast history of playful learning environments and educational game tools. Three particular threads interweave in this general introduction. First, play and games are ancient elements of human learning. The former instills basic social cues that facilitate human interaction and group cohesions, while the latter improve complex skill acquisition, abstract thinking, and peer cohesion. Johan Huizinga, who described play as an essential (although not sufficient) element to cultural development, paid tribute to this dual nature by titling his book *Homo Ludens*, or "Man the Player."[1] His oft-quoted opening line is worth citing again: "Play is older than culture, for culture, however inadequately defined, always presupposes human society, and animals have not waited for man to teach them their playing."[2]

Second, a simple dichotomy between "play" and "game" belies the complexity that exists between them. Roger Caillois places the tension between play and game on a spectrum with *paidia* at one end of the axis, reflecting unstructured, spontaneous play, and *ludus* at the other, reflecting rule-based, explicit games.[3] The ancient Romans understood the spectrum between play and game. The Latin word *ludus* meant both play and sport, but also training, as the word was used to describe primary schools for boys and girls. And, reflecting the seriousness with which some games were taken, *ludus* also described gladiatorial schools. Generally, humanity tends to formalize play into games, at both the individual level as children become adults, and at the cultural level as cultures become increasingly complex and economically developed. As seen in the differences between children kicking stones on a playground and professionals earning a living on the soccer pitch, this spectrum reflects instantiations of cultural formation. Indeed, the tendency to translate the *paidic* into the *ludic*, from the organic to the planned and structured, may reflect the very essence of cultural development.

Third, the spectrum between play and game in terms of definition mirrors the playfulness in which people participate in games. Players can "game" a system by adapting, bending, or breaking the rules, resulting in a completely satisfying gaming experience for them that readily thwarts the intentions of the designer or instructor.[4] With respect to education, this playfulness means, in part, that the prescribed educational message may be completely ignored or subverted by the student game-player. The medium may not effectively impart the desired message. A parallel to television may help. Some of the earliest critics of television, for example, saw it as a tool of cultural and industrial domination as the viewers passively absorbed the privileged message of capitalistic giants.[5] Television, like games, however, is a heavily mediated environment with complex modes and messages that are actively constructed by an active audience.[6] It is a demanding ephemeral medium requiring conscious construction of meaning but does so through a series of images and conventions that are deeply familiar—close, but not quite, like reality. Games are similar. What is learned from playing a game may not reflect the desired outcome of the game designer.

This chapter surveys the history of games and how they have been used in teaching, especially teaching the liberal arts. While there is a long history of games and research into the history of gaming, there is less research into how serious games can enhance learning. We are at an experimental stage where games are being designed, often without much educational theory behind them. We propose that one promising area, especially in history, is to teach through game design where students do not just play games, but have to design games and through the design of games, learn about the subject matter being simulated.

Doll Houses

Although recent trends in educational philosophy have highlighted the importance of creating play spaces for creative development, these efforts are not new. Miniaturized domestic settings have been found in Egyptian tombs of children and adults dating back four thousand years. By the seventeenth century, doll houses became common play spaces for little girls and young (and older) women.[7] These miniature settings implied "a space specifically designated for play, often by adults who intend that children play nowhere else."[8] Often large and heavy, doll houses created spaces relatively free of interference where complex games could be set up and played out over a long period of time. To the designers and the purchasers, these spaces provided training for moral instruction, a point made clear in early modern literary references to tidiness, order, and domestic roles. Certainly much of the play that took place within the minds of the children reflected common domestic routines, even if adults did not structure the play along these lines, although some extant narratives may have encouraged such activity. The affordances offered by these ludic spaces, however, permitted significant interpretive play outside intended moral lessons: "It seems quite clear that most girls were able to regard doll houses as their own ludic spaces, places dedicated to their own play, rather than as sites for training in compliance."[9] Unsupervised, children often engaged in transgressive play, giving the dolls more interesting lives than their roles intended, moving them into spaces they should not have occupied, and exploring anxieties experienced during the daily domestic routine.[10]

Card Playing

In eighteenth-century Europe a rage for card play developed throughout all levels of society, even though most historical academic attention has been placed on aristocratic play. Popular card games such as Whist, Faro, and Pope Joan promoted not only a common framework for understanding gameplay mechanics, but also a common set of social norms associated with hosting and attending a night of cards. These card games created a common framework underpinning not only the mechanics of play, but also gentility and hospitality, which evolved from a learned habit to a seemingly natural state. This change was particularly important for merchants, most of whom maintained financial dealings with the aristocrats. Social commentators remarked on "the increasingly genteel manners of the middling sort, especially those in the hospitality, retail and commercial sectors, and credited their frequent contacts with aristocratic customers with the change."[11] An understanding of polite society and commercial affability paved the way for better financial relationships and allowed those in the middle classes to move more self-assuredly among the social circles of their customers. Card games helped solidify a growing set of social rules that defined the emerging middle class. Carding was a part of this learning to fit in.[12]

Such lessons were not restricted to adults; children were encouraged to play as well. Games such as "commerce," which involved small pots of money, introduced children to accepted norms of social interaction at first with family members, then later with guests and friends. As children matured and expanded their social networks, "they joined more advanced adult players at more involved games, absorbing lessons in risk management as they dropped their pocket money into the pool."[13] The games framed social conventions that reinforced a comfortable system of expected behaviors and developing cultural norms for the middle class, essentially a blend of gentility with moderation and restraint.

War Games

Games in military training are perhaps the most studied aspect of games as teaching tools. The visualization of hunting and battlefield situations is an effective form of tactical communication and has served humanity in one form or another for millennia. Some scholars assert that military leaders in Asia used icons (colored stones, etc.) more than five thousand years ago. Certainly, convincing evidence exists that generals of the Roman Republic abstracted the chaotic nature of battlefield movements with sand tables and figures.[14] This military tool allowed competing strategies to be played out in advance of battle, and later, to provide training exercises for generals and their staff.[15] Games, as such, appear to have gone hand in hand with such developments. Three games in particular appear to be either descendants of, or antecedents to, battlefield visualizations.

Wei Hai, meaning "encirclement," is dated to approximately 2500 B.C.E. and, in some sources, is attributed to Sun Tzu, the author of *The Art of War*. It features players' use of colored stones to represent large army units. The game appears to have been an early predecessor to *Go*, and the goal of encircling one's opponent has obvious military and hunting parallels. *Petteia*, meaning "pebbles," is an ancient Greek game that may have had an older Egyptian origin. It is played with black and white stones and the goal is to surround your opponent's piece between two of yours. Pots and vases, which appear to be contemporary with the Trojan War, depict soldiers and heroes playing the game. Polybius, commenting on the Carthaginian general Hamilcar's battlefield prowess, compared his considerable tactical talent to that of a skilled *Petteia* player.[16] And *Chaturanga*, probably meaning "army," was developed in India in the sixth century and is often considered a precursor to chess. Here, game pieces represented specific military formations and resources, such as elephants and chariots.[17]

Although different in rules and form, all three games share the same abstractions of landscape and pieces, which permit the development and refinement of strategic thinking. These lessons included military parallels in addition to flanking and encirclement mentioned before: removing pieces from play, controlling resources, slowing battles of attrition, and controlling space.[18] Furthermore, depending on skill level, players and observers may deduce the "game state," determining what had recently come to pass and what would likely happen in the future, simply by looking at the current position of the pieces on the board.

Such advances led to the development of more realistic warfare games, the first of which, most scholars agree, was Christopher Weikhmann's *King's Game* (*Koenigspiel* in German). The game was more realistic in the sense that the board was larger and included more playing pieces representing a broader array of military figures with more diverse movement options; these included a "king, his marshal, a pair of chaplains, chancellors, heralds, couriers, lieutenants, adjutants, bodyguards, halberdiers, and a set of eight private soldiers, which were given sixteen different powers of movement on the board."[19] *Koenigspiel* was more visually realistic than its predecessors, and certainly contained more complicated gameplay elements. The game functioned more like an enhanced version of chess, however, and did not possess realistic technical details about unit strength and ability—essentially lacking a sense of procedural realism meaning that a paradigm for simulating gameplay processes with an emphasis on conceptual realism was noticeably absent.[20]

The inclusion of such elements in war games appeared rather quickly, with new games and their various iterations appearing between the late eighteenth and early nineteenth centuries. These games introduced a number of realistic game innovations, including real topographical and terrain maps with an overlying grid as a game board, realistic movement limits that were affected by the terrain, the representation of multiple units with one figure, supply and support logistics (bridges, bakeries, and wagon convoys), and the inclusion of an umpire to mediate disputes over game rules.[21] In 1811, all these features appeared in Baron von Reisswitz's *Kriegsspiel* (War Game), which was presented to the Prussian king, Friedrich Wilhelm III. The king was soon "contesting his friend the Czarevich Nicholas in their diplomatic trips between Moscow and Berlin, the two young royals acting out little conflicts just as their elders had ordered men of flesh and blood into battle."[22] Reisswitz's son published an updated version of the game that came with a sixty-page manual entitled *Rules for a New Wargame for the Use of Military Schools*. The most significant aspect of this update was that the game attempted to "codify actual military experience and introduced the details of real-life military operations lacking in his father's game. In particular, he quantified the effects of combat so that results of engagements were *calculated* rather than discussed."[23] Later versions even included dice to mimic the random, often chaotic occurrences that can tip a battle.

The increasingly realistic nature of war games, while suitable for battle-field planning, training, and re-enactments, had lost its "playful" nature in the complexity. As such, the later nineteenth century saw the split of war games along two equally popular tracts: rigid *Kriegspiel*, which focused on formal rules and realism, and free *Kriegspiel*, which focused on playability and symbolic play.[24] Both versions worked their way into training academies in Britain and the United States, and then into the hands of enthusiasts and hobbyists the world over, as pointed out by Milton Weiner in 1959:

> The free play game has received support because of its versatility in dealing with complex problems of tactics and strategy and because of the ease with which it can be adapted to various training, planning and evaluation ends. The rigid play game has received support because of the consistency and detail of its rule structure and its computational rigor.[25]

These two streams codified the various game elements and mechanics that would influence game design over the next century and a half. The inclusion of computing technologies would add several others.

As early as 1960, computers were introduced to enhance the procedural realism of tabletop war games.[26] While the initial efforts of computation focused on speeding up gaming mechanics, computers began to enhance the realism and utility of the game in a number of significant ways: the concurrent evaluation of hypothetical game decisions prior to action, the modeling of the complex interactions of multiple players, the simulation of multiple views of the same game state, and the ability to play against the computer rather than another human. As computers became more and more powerful, these games and simulations found a home not only in military academies around the world, but also in the homes of civilians. That the U.S. military developed *America's Army* as both a training and recruitment tool reflects this ready transition.

Games and Education Theory

The manner in which instructors use computer games in the classroom, particularly at the university level, necessitates an examination of educational theory because, in this case, theory drives practice. On the whole, efforts to include gaming in the classroom, particularly at the university level, rely

on intuitive leaps by faculty attempting to bridge the gap between dissemination and uptake, often without due consideration or even awareness of
the efforts by educational theorists to assess the efficacy of using games in
the classroom. These often-inspired efforts may remain isolated from similar
efforts elsewhere, falling by the wayside when the professor teaches a different course or takes a research leave.[27]

When considered from a broader theoretical perspective, the motivation
to use games (technologically enhanced games in particular) as teaching
tools falls into two broad pedagogical paradigms. The first relates to student
engagement, often invoking some aspect of active or experiential learning
as a pedagogical approach, even if that term is more intuitively understood
than precisely defined. This is particularly true with respect to learning hierarchies, such as Benjamin Bloom's taxonomy, where instructors instinctively
prompt students to move from passive recipients of knowledge to active
participants in the synthesis and evaluation of information and argument.
Theoretical frameworks, however, do exist. Within the larger frame of Jean
Piaget's constructivism, which argues that education is not a transfer process
but a process in which students construct their own knowledge through
observation of the surrounding reality, Seymour Papert takes the leap from
the contemplative to the action driven. He argues that learning occurs especially when students are required to construct the tools of their own learning experience.[28] His constructionism is not the only pragmatic view on
learning, but it is one of the most radical. David Kolb's experiential learning
cycle, for example, posits two elements to effective learning: a prehension
element, where students take hold of an event through concrete experience;
and a transformation element, where internal reflection and active manipulation reconsider and apply the event.[29] The key here is that experiential
learning occurs "only after experiences or events have been transformed by
either reflection or action, or preferably both."[30]

The second incorporates variations of Fred Davis's technological acceptance model, which evaluates the likelihood of individuals and groups
adopting a particular technology. This well-validated model has technologically focused variables (specifically, perceived usefulness and perceived ease
of use) as well as more common metrics used to evaluate the likelihood of
acceptance of information technology.[31] Its effective use can correct or at
least mitigate assumptions that students generally familiar with technology
(so-called digital natives) will prefer and benefit from digital game-based
learning. Even a brief consideration of this assumption should raise flags
in the minds of researchers. Students need to learn the affordances of video
games in the same way that traditional classroom mechanics, such as note
taking during lectures, are learned. To ensure the effective adoption of

gaming technologies, educators need not only assess the perceived effectiveness of the game as a pedagogical tool, but also the video game literacy of
the students (essentially, the perceived ease of use by students with disparate
gaming experience) and the learning opportunities as an effect of its utility.[32]

In a study that implicitly reflects these two theoretical perspectives, Henry
Jenkins, a leading light in the design and study of computer games, and Kurt
Squire conducted important preliminary work on the use of video games in
the classroom. They tested five different games (ranging from commercially
available software to games developed at the MIT Media Lab) as teaching
tools at various education levels.[33] Under certain circumstances, they argued,
games can model complex scientific, social, and economic processes, thus
increasing the students' understanding of such complex subject matters.

- *Civilization III*—a real-time strategy game employed to teach high
  school disadvantaged students about large-scale, long-term historical
  change and the ways various aspects of a civilization are interconnected.[34]
- *Revolution*—a multiplayer historical role-playing game developed at
  MIT, used to teach the impact of short-term events, and the potential
  for and limitations of individual activity within these constraints.[35]
- *Prospero's Island*—a single-player game based in the complex world of
  Shakespeare's *Tempest*, aimed to increase the players' understanding of
  the play; the story is not retold, but reinvented in this environment
  and the player is given freedom of choice.[36]
- *Environmental Detectives*—an augmented reality game (ARG) with
  an ecological theme, played in teams with personal digital assistants
  (PDAs); the game emphasized win-loss strategies employed during
  imagined contamination scenarios.[37]
- *Biohazard: Hot Zone*—a training simulation game designed by MIT,
  which helped students learn introductory biology and environmental
  science.[38]

The experiments described show that game-based learning is often a holistic, immersive experience that encouraged a type of critical learning beneficial
to the intellectual development of the students. Such efforts appear, at least
on the surface, to improve cognitive learning outcomes among students. In a
large meta-analysis of studies publishing results of game-enhanced teaching,
Jennifer Vogel et al. synthesized the conclusions of 32 studies (from a list of
248 potential studies) that compared traditional teaching methods to teaching that included games and simulations.[39] The authors concluded the following: "significantly higher cognitive gains were observed in subjects utilizing interactive simulations or games versus traditional teaching methods."[40]

These authors, and other critics, argue that these conclusions are tentative at best. The Vogel study, for example, contains a number of secondary conclusions that speak to the topic's complexity. First, there appears to be a significant gender difference, with male students preferring traditional teaching approaches while female students prefer games and simulation—a perhaps counterintuitive assertion given common, albeit incorrect, perceptions of the average gamer.[41] Second, they suggest that user control over the environment is an important indicator of cognitive gain. The more freedom the student has to navigate the environment, the better the result.[42] Third, factors often considered important to engagement, such as graphic realism, do not seem to have a significant impact on cognitive learning.[43] Perhaps most significantly, most of the studies included in the meta-analysis focused on teaching engineering, science, or the health sciences.

Proponents of the inclusion of video games in the science curriculum have explicitly championed it as a form of active learning—exploring problems within the constraints and affordances of software. These participatory simulations and experiences "immerse players in complex systems, allowing them to learn the points of view of those systems and perhaps even develop identities within the systems."[44] In addition, the very nature of computer games allows students to learn at their own pace, receive immediate and often continuous feedback, and review through replay elements that were misunderstood. These features have shown increased learning outcomes over traditional lecture approaches for students in science, technology, engineering, and mathematics.[45] University students who played the game *Virtual Cell* as part of the biology curriculum, for example, obtained a 40 percent increase in learning outcomes over students who attended lectures instead.[46] Other studies report similar improvements in the quality of learning outcomes in computing science education studies.[47] Here, the potential for video games seems enormous.

Take, for instance, the demand for educational reform in the medical profession, where the lack of appropriate skill acquisition has dramatically increased the use of simulation and role-playing environments.[48] Human patient simulators, virtual emergency rooms and intensive care units, and role-playing environments employ many of the gameplay mechanics established over the past century.[49]

Liberal Arts

The application of video games in the liberal arts seems, on the face of it, a more risky proposition. The paucity of good "serious games" at the university level in the humanities and social sciences speaks to this difficulty. In addition, despite popular perception, university-level history courses are not litanies of facts and dates. Good history courses evaluate and synthesize the interpretations of historians about why something happened, not just what happened. This sort of scholarly debate does not readily lend itself to a gripping game mechanic. In addition, when such games are attempted, they frequently focus on either entertainment, which oversimplifies the content, or on education, which detracts from the gameplay.[50] As games may only adhere to the "broader strokes of history," [51] as one game commenter claims, they are not suitable as a digital textbook. Too often designers sacrifice the education content of the game to improve game mechanics, graphic detail, or production values. This dumbing down or "sweetening" of the content is clearly a poor pedagogical choice.[52] Such games make poor substitutes for traditional teaching techniques. There are exceptions, such as games like *Power Politics III*, which places the player in the role of a campaign manager of current and historic presidential candidates.[53] Released in 2005 by Kellog Creek Software, the game has been used with some success in political science classes at American universities.[54]

Combining university-level learning outcomes with entertainment is the principal challenge facing postsecondary serious games. Overcoming this challenge requires attention to a number of factors: active involvement and stimulation of all players, sufficient realism to convey the essential truths of the simulation, clarity of consequences and their causes in both rules and gameplay, and the repeatability of the entire process.[55] Educational and domain experts must, therefore, be included at all levels of the game design process, and not simply viewed as content creators. In particular, agreement on and iterative assessment of three elements of the game design process will reduce the likelihood of the educational content being lost: the purpose of the game (acquiring skills or knowledge), the affordances of the gameplay (improved social interaction, for example), and the effects of gameplay (learning outcomes, enjoyment, etc.).[56] Without proper consideration to these elements throughout the design process, it is unlikely that specific learning outcomes would be achieved. This is a significant challenge considering that there is little empirical evidence that games are even capable of teaching what the educators think they can. This challenge is due in part to the *paidia-ludus* tension inherent in gameplay (the game may increase cognitive output, but may not in any way affect a teacher's specific education outcomes).[57] There is reason to doubt that assigning a competitive game in a class so that it is now mandatory is an effective teaching tool; as Charles Bailey states, mandatory games do not necessarily "build character."[58]

One popular approach to overcoming this difficulty is to create learning environments that improve students' campus experience. Given the popularity of massively multiplayer online role-playing games (MMORGs), educators have sought to leverage the open-ended nature of these environments for learning purposes. Virtual worlds are not necessarily games; however, they do mimic many game-like elements. *Second Life*, perhaps the most well-known manifestation of this technology, extended previous technologies such as multiuser dungeons (MUDs) and the somewhat recursive MUD object orienteds (MOOs). In *Second Life* many universities have created models of their campuses (often for promotional purposes). There is also a university-focused space called *Campus*, which adds additional tools restricted to postsecondary institutions. *Campus* serves as an interesting middle ground between MMORGs and virtual worlds, essentially adding curriculum creation tools to a large, digitally populated campus environment. Players may "game" the system, however, subverting the intent of the game's designer and transforming the instructional intent in ways not intended. Like many technologies that once seemed cutting edge, *Second Life* may already have seen its glory days. *Second Life* now seems a research environment where academics use other academics (rather than students) as subjects in experiments on teaching effectiveness and engagement.[59]

Still, researchers have published significant research on the potential of virtual worlds. Andrea De Lucia et al., for example, describe the establishment of a virtual campus for e-learning courses.[60] The virtual campus consists of four virtual spaces—a common student campus, collaborative zones, lecture rooms, and recreational areas—bound together with a Moodle plug-in to allow the integration of multimedia content. Similarly, Marcus Childress and Ray Braswell describe in detail the effectiveness of *Campus* at a small Midwest university.[61] Their project sought to increase student participation within the university community and curriculum, particularly for those uncomfortable with lack of visual feedback associated with chat rooms and email. The authors of both studies conclude that when compared to less immersive environments, MMORGs create a stronger sensation of presence; this arises from an increased awareness of others within the setting and to enhanced communication resulting from avatar gestures and expressions. On the downside, users describe particular difficulties with navigation and the use of the 3D interface.[62] On the whole, the authors concluded that virtual environments support synchronous communication and social interaction, and increase the participants' level of motivation, although discipline-specific efforts remain understudied. Similarly, Yolanda Rankin et al. found that by facilitating interactions with native speakers in MMORPGs (*Everquest II*), English-as-a-second-language (ESL) students improved significantly more in second-language acquisition than students learning through more traditional methods.[63]

Using these games as objects of study for the depiction of particular instantiations of historic events is another matter altogether. José Lopez and Myriam Caceres, for example, theorized that many popular commercial games can be classified not by their genre or technical features, but by their subject matter as defined by the liberal arts: war and conflict, urbanism and territorial management, democracy and citizenship, economy and trade, and the environment. [64] As objects of study thematically defined, games become a sociocultural resource readily mined by humanists and social scientists in terms with which they are more familiar.

Learning through Game Design

A constructionist, rather than an instructionist, approach to video games provides students with the means to build their own games, rather than simply play someone else's.[65] In order to design a game, not only do students need to develop and consider the content of the game (synthesizing and evaluating the most pertinent elements of the topic), they must also consider how to convey that information in a meaningful manner that makes sense to someone with less domain expertise.

Teaching meaningful communication through game design is a double-edged sword. On the one hand, video games specialize in the development of knowledge transfer and skill acquisition, which may provide important pedagogical lessons:

- Good games make information available to the player at the moment and place where said information is needed, seamlessly integrating this information into the game world.
- Good games push the player's competence by being both doable and challenging, a pleasant frustration with the task at hand.
- Good games are customizable, placing the player in the role of co-creator of the game world.
- Good games introduce skills gradually, usually through a tutorial section that is integrated into the game's story, building on "a cycle of expertise,"[66] in which the player integrates old skills with newly acquired ones.
- Good multiplayer games are highly collaborative, allowing the players to pool and share both knowledge and skills.[67]

On the other hand, the skill passed down to the player may be only suitable for improving the playing of video games. Neil Postman's caution regarding educational television seems an obvious parallel, where the skills acquired watching *Sesame Street*, for example, only better prepare children to absorb and decode the signs and symbols associated with television. According to Postman, the skills are not transferable.[68] It could be that teaching through game design teaches primarily about game design, leaving little time for the student to learn the target subject matter.[69] The complexity of game-authoring environments could distract from what the course is supposed to be about even if there is some learning in game design.

That said, a constructionist approach in the liberal arts could also ameliorate the disconnect between what a teacher thinks a game is teaching and what the students are actually learning. As students must develop sufficient domain expertise prior to (or concomitant with) the creation of the game, cognitive learning outcomes desired by the instructor are more likely, particularly if the game is embedded in an authentic context.[70] An added benefit of creating such games themselves is that students gain additional skills not normally associated with traditional liberal arts courses. Technical fluency, such as that acquired using the game toolsets, such as Aurora for Bioware's *Neverwinter Nights*, will introduce students to computer scripting, databases, flow control, variables, and basic logic structures. Positive results in this area have been documented at multiple education levels.[71] More ambitiously, educators have created game design engines to create specific games for specific pedagogical purposes. Pablo Moreno-Ger et al. designed and described a toolset for the creation of adventure games that can readily be adapted for use by students, particularly those working in interdisciplinary teams with some facility in document markup.[72] At the University of Alberta we have developed an alternative–augmented reality gaming platform with which students may design games rather than just play them.

Closing Thoughts

Although there are historical precedents and many experimental projects to examine, the application of gaming technologies to teaching in the humanities and social sciences remains an understudied area. Games may promote discovery and exploration in a manner that traditional teaching techniques do not—skills which when acquired may, through proper reflection and mentorship, be transferred to disparate situations.[73] What remains sorely lacking is comprehensive testing of the efficacy of such games in improving learning outcomes at the university level in the liberal arts.[74] In the Humanities Computing program at the University of Alberta, we caution students about rose-colored views of technology. The application of computing technologies to the complicated, nuanced arguments made by liberal arts scholars is full of potential and risk. It will always cost more money than expected. It will always take longer than expected. But, if done carefully, with considered, measured steps, it will almost be as good as the way you were doing it before.

NOTES

1. Clearly, the title served as a play on the Pleistocene species *homo habilis* (the "handy man"), as well as *homo faber* ("Man the Maker"), described by Henri-Louis Bergson in the *L'Evolution créatice* (1907). As Huizinga places his anthropological work within an evolutionary structure, his title seems quite cleverly chosen.

2. Johan Huizinga, *Homo Ludens: A Study of Play-element in Culture* (London: Routledge and Kegan Paul, 1949), 1.

3. Roger Caillois, *Man, Play, and Games*, trans. Meyer Barash (Urbana: University of Illinois Press, 2001), 13.

4. See, for example, J. Barton Bowyer, *Cheating: Deception in War & Magic, Games & Sport, Sex & Religion, Business & Con Games, Politics & Espionage, Art & Science* (New York: St. Martin's, 1992), and Mia Consalvo, *Cheating: Gaining Advantage in Video Games* (Cambridge Mass.: MIT Press, 2007).

5. See, for example, the strident views of the Frankfurt School, such as Theodor Adorno and Max Horkheimer, "The Culture Industry: Enlightenment as Mass Deception," in *Dialectic of Enlightenment: Philosophical Fragments*, ed. Gunzelin Schmid Noerr and trans. Edmund Jephcott (Stanford: Stanford University Press, 2002), 94–136; and Walter Benjamin, *The Work of Art in the Age of Mechanical Reproduction*, 1936, transcribed by Andy Blunden 1998, accessed July 31, 2012, http://www.marxists.org/reference/subject/philosophy/works/ge/benjamin.htm.

6. See, for example, John Fiske and John Hartley's *Reading Television*, 2nd ed. (New York: Routledge, 2003), and Ien Ang, *Living Room Wars: Rethinking Media Audiences for a Postmodern World* (London: Routledge, 1996).

7. Frances Armstrong, "The Dollhouse as Ludic Space, 1690–1920," *Children's Literature* 24 (1996): 23–54.

8. Armstrong, 27.

9. Armstrong, 24.

10. Armstrong, 36. Alternately, see the second chapter of Mary Flanagan's excellent *Critical Play: Radical Game Design* (Cambridge, Mass.: MIT Press, 2009).

11. Janet E. Mullin, "'We Had Carding': Hospitable Card Play and Polite Domestic Sociability Among the Middling Sort in Eighteenth-Century England," *Journal of Social History* 42, no. 4 (Summer 2009): 991.

12. Mullin, 989–1008.

13. Mullin, 994.

14. See Milton G. Weiner, "An Introduction to Wargames," P-1773, The RAND Corporation, August 17, 1959; Peter Perla, *The Art of Wargaming: A Guide for Professionals and Hobbyists* (Annapolis: Naval Institute Press, 1990); and Roger Smith, "The

Long History of Gaming in Military Training," *Simulation & Gaming* 41, no. 1 (February 2010): 6–19.

15. Smith, 7. See also Perla.

16. In English translation: "Like a good draught-player, by isolating and surrounding them, he [Hamilcar] destroyed large numbers in detail without coming to a general engagement at all"; Polybius, *Histories* 1, no. 84, in Perseus Digital Library, edited by Gregory Crane, accessed July 31, 2012, http://www.perseus.tufts.edu/hopper/text?doc =Perseus%3Atext%3A1999.01.0234%3Abook%3D1%3Achapter%3D84. The game in the original version of the text is *Petteia*.

17. Smith, 7.

18. Mariana Paredes-Olea, "Procedural Realism in Computer Strategy Games" (MA thesis, University of Alberta, 2009), 73.

19. Ed Halter, *From Sun Tzu to XBox: War and Video Games* (New York: Thunder's Mouth, 2006), 36.

20. Perla 17; see also Ian Bogost, *Unit Operations: An Approach to Videogame Criticism* (Cambridge, Mass.: MIT Press, 2006), 9.

21. Perla, 18; Halter, 37; Paredes, 78. See also Kalman J. Cohen and Eric Rhenman, "The Role of Management Games in Education and Research," *Management Science* 7, no. 2 (January 1961): 132.

22. Halter, 41.

23. Perla, 25; emphasis added.

24. Cohen and Rhenman, 134.

25. Weiner, 9.

26. Weiner, 9.

27. Although Carolin Kreber focuses on case studies instead of games, her criticisms of why active and experiential learning approaches fail is worth considering. See Carolin Kreber, "Learning Experientially Through Case Studies? A Conceptual Analysis," *Teaching in Higher Education* 6, no. 2 (2001): 217–28.

28. Seymour Papert, "Situating Constructionism," in *Constructionism: Research Reports and Essays, 1985–1990*, ed. Idit Harel and Seymour Papert (Norwood, N.J.: Ablex, 1991).

29. See David Kolb, *Experiential Learning: Experience as the Source of Learning and Development* (Englewood Cliffs, N.J.: Prentice-Hall, 1984), and Kreber, 218.

30. Kreber, 220. See also Brent D. Ruben, "Simulations, Games, and Experience-based Learning: The Quest for a New Paradigm for Teaching and Learning," *Simulation Gaming* 30 (1999): 498.

31. Fred D. Davies, "Perceived Usefulness, Perceived Ease of Use, and User Acceptance of Information Technology," *MIS Quarterly* 13, no. 3 (1989): 319–39; Fred D. Davis, Richard P. Bagozzi, and Paul R. Warshaw, "User Acceptance of Computer Technology: A Comparison of Two Theoretical Models," *Management Science* 35, no. 8 (1989): 982–1003. This model has been extended and enhanced by a number of researchers. See, for example, Yogesh Malhotra and Dennis F. Galletta, "Extending the Technology Acceptance Model to Account for Social Influence: Theoretical Bases and Empirical Validation," *Proceedings of the 32nd Hawaii International Conference on System Sciences* (1999), 1–14.

32. Jeroen Bourgonjon et al., "Students' Perceptions about the Use of Video Games in the Classroom," *Computers & Education* 54, no. 4 (May 2010): 1145–56. The authors came to their conclusions based on descriptive statistics applied to a survey questionnaire given to 858 Flemish secondary school students.

33. Kurt Squire and Henry Jenkins, "Harnessing the Power of Games in Education," *InSight* 3, no. 1 (2003): 8. For a similar view, see David Williamson Shaffer, Kurt R. Squire, Richard Halverston, and James P. Gee, "Video Games and the Future of Learning," *The Phi Delta Kappan* 87, no. 2 (October 2005): 104–11.

34. Squire and Jenkins, 11.

35. Squire and Jenkins, 15. Although the article does not state it, the screenshot on p. 16 suggests that the games were developed using Bioware's *Aurora* toolset for *Neverwinter Nights*.

36. Squire and Jenkins, 19.

37. Squire and Jenkins, 23.

38. Squire and Jenkins, 26.

39. Jennifer J. Vogel et al., "Computer Gaming and Interactive Simulations for Learning: A Meta-analysis," *Journal of Educational Computing Research* 34, no. 3 (2006): 229–43. To qualify for the meta-analysis, the study needed to include statistical assessments of teaching and had to specifically focus on cognitive gains or attitudinal changes. See also Harold O'Neil, Richard Wainess, and Eva L. Baker, "Classification of Learning Outcomes: Evidence from the Computer Games Literature," *Curriculum Journal* 16, no. 4 (2005): 455–74.

40. Vogel et al., 233.

41. Vogel et al., 234.

42. Vogel et al., 234.

43. Vogel et al., 235.

44. Kurt Squire, "From Content to Context: Videogames as Designed Experience," *Educational Researcher* 35, no. 8 (2006): 27. See also Kurt D. Squire, "Video Games in Education," *International Journal of Intelligent Simulations and Gaming* 2, no.1 (2003): 49–62; and Kurt D. Squire, "Replaying History: Learning World History through Playing *Civilization III*" (PhD dissertation, University of Indiana, 2004).

45. Merrilea J. Mayo, "Video Games: A Route to Large-Scale STEM Education?" *Science* 323, no. 2 (2009): 79–82.

46. Mayo, 81.

47. See, for example, Marina Papastergiou, "Digital Game-Based Learning in High School Computer Science Education: Impact on Educational Effectiveness and Student Motivation," *Computers & Education* 52, no. 1 (2009): 1–12. For a particularly positive view of the potential of games, see Rosemary Garris, Robert Ahlers, and James E. Driskell, "Games, Motivation, and Learning: A Research and Practice Model," *Simulation Gaming* 33 (2002): 441–67.

48. J. Lindsey Lane, Stuart Slavin, and Amitai Ziv, "Simulation in Medical Education: A Review," *Simulation & Gaming* 32, no. 3 (September 2001): 297–314.

49. These efforts are distinct from treating patients with video game technologies, such as the improvements documented in visual coordination in patients with several forms of visual impairment or the improvement in cognitive processing in patients with mental impairments. See, for example, M. Nieto, *Ambliopía: Introducción de videojuegos en su tratamiento* (Madrid: Centro de Optometría Internacional, 2008); C. Shawn Green and Daphne Bavelier, "Action Video Game Modifies Visual Selective Attention," *Nature* 423 (2003): 534–37; P. J. Standen, Francesca Rees, and David J. Brown, "Effect of Playing Computer Games on Decision Making in People with Intellectual Disabilities," *Journal of Assistive Technologies* 3, no. 2 (2009): 4–12.

50. Pablo Moreno-Ger et al., "Educational Game Design for Online Education," *Computers in Human Behavior* 24, no. 6 (2008): 2530–40.

51. "The Ten Commandments of Assassin's Creed: Brotherhood," http://xbox360 .ign.com/articles/112/1125500p1.html. For example, the visual re-creation of Renaissance Italy in *Assassin's Creed: Brotherhood* is remarkable. The historic accuracy of people and events (outside of the fantasy elements) is less so. The game designers approached historical accuracy quite practically. According to the mission director Gaelec Simard: "if you can find the information within 30 seconds on the net, then it should be accurate in our game."

52. Yasmin B. Kafai, "Playing and Making Games for Learning: Instructionist and Constructionist Perspectives for Game Studies," *Games and Culture* 1, no. 1 (2006): 36–40.

53. *Power Politics III* was released in 2005 by Kellog Creek Software. The complexity of the game can be varied depending on the skill level of the player, and deals with topics like dirty tricks, electoral crises, and disputed results.

54. David Michael, *Serious Games: Games That Educate, Train and Inform* (Boston: Thomson Course Technology, 2006).

55. Clark C. Abt, *Serious Games* (Lanham, Md.: University Press of America, 1987); see also Michael.

56. Yolanda A. Rankin, McKenzie McNeal, Marcus W. Shute, and Bruce Gooch, "User Centered Game Design: Evaluating Massive Multiplayer Online Role Playing Games for Second Language Acquisition," in *Sandbox '08: Proceedings of the 2008 ACM SIGGRAPH Symposium on Video Games* (2008), 43–49.

57. Sara I. de Freitas, "Using Games and Simulations for Supporting Learning," *Learning, Media & Technology* 31, no. 4 (2006): 346.

58. Charles Bailey, "Games, Winning and Education," *Cambridge Journal of Education* 5, no. 1 (1975): 41.

59. Lowell Cremorne, "Why Second Life is Already Second-Best for Education," accessed August 1, 2012, http://www.metaversejournal.com/2010/10/06/why-second -life-is-already-second-best-for-education/.

60. Andrea De Lucia, Rita Francese, Ignazio Passero, and Genoveffa Tortora, "Development and Evaluation of a Virtual Campus on Second Life: The Case of SecondDMI," *Computers & Education* 52, no. 1 (2009): 222.

61. Marcus Childress and Ray Braswell, "Using Massively Multiplayer Online Role-Playing Games for Online Learning," *Distance Education* 27, no. 2 (2006): 187–96.

62. De Lucia et al., 231.

63. Rankin et al., 46.

64. José M. Cuenca Lopez and Myriam J. Martin Caceres, "Virtual Games in Social Science Education," *Computers & Education* 55, no. 3 (2010): 1336–45.

65. Kafai, 37–38. The terms come from Seymour Papert, *The Children's Machine: Rethinking School in the Age of the Computer* (New York: Basic, 1993), chapter 1.

66. Carl Bereiter and Marlene Scardamalia, "Intentional Learning as a Goal of Instruction," in *Knowing, Learning, and Instruction: Essays in Honor of Robert Glaser*, ed. Robert Glaser and Lauren B. Resnick (Hillsdale: Lawrence Erlbaum Associates, 1989), 361–92.

67. James Paul Gee, *What Video Games Have to Teach Us about Learning and Literacy* (New York: Palgrave Macmillan, 2003); and James Paul Gee, "What Video Games

have to Teach Us about Learning and Literacy," *ACM Computers in Entertainment* 1, no. 1 (October 2003): 1–3.

68. Neil Postman, *Amusing Ourselves to Death: Public Discourse in the Age of Show Business* (New York: Penguin, 1985), 143.

69. Kevin Kee and John Bachynski, for example, suggest this difficulty in "Outbreak: Lessons Learned from Developing a 'History Game,'" *Loading* . . . (The Canadian Game Studies Association) 3, no. 4 (2009).

70. David H. Jonassen, "Toward a Design Theory of Problem Solving," *Educational Technology Research and Development* 48, no. 4 (2000): 64. An additional, though dated piece addressing the same topic can be found in Lloyd P. Reiber, "Seriously Considering Play: Designing Interactive Learning Environments Based on the Blending of Microworlds, Simulations, and Games," *Educational Technology Research and Development* 44, no. 2 (1996): 43–58.

71. For university-level education, see Nathan Sturtevant, Sean Gouglas, H. James Hoover, Jonathan Schaeffer, and Michael Bowling, "Multidisciplinary Students and Instructors: A Second-Year Games Course," *SIGCSE 2008: Technical Symposium on Computer Science Education* (Portland, Ore., 2008); for elementary education, see Judy Robertson and Cathrin Howells, "Computer Game Design: Opportunities for Successful Learning," *Computers & Education* 50, no. 2 (February 2008): 559–78.

72. Pablo Moreno-Ger, José Luis Sierra, Iván Martínez-Ortiz, and Baltasar Fernández-Manjón, "A Documental Approach to Adventure Game Development," *Science of Computer Programming* 67, no. 1 (2007): 31.

73. de Freitas, 344.

74. Michael, 74–75.

SEVEN

Ludic Algorithms

Bethany Nowviskie

Llull's Great Art

"Calculemus!"

Jonathan Swift's Gulliver, on the aerial leg of his *Travels*, finds himself in the lofty scholastic community of Laputa. There he encounters a professor with a strange device. The mechanism consists of a series of rotating blocks on which are inscribed words in the Laputian language and which, in use, resemble nothing so much as a mystical foosball table (figure 7.1). A few vigorous turns of the crank (for which the professor employs a team of undergraduates) produce what Robert de Beaugrande might call a "combinatoric explosion" of information: words combine randomly to produce sense and nonsense, the finest fragments of which are diligently recorded as the "wisdom" of Laputa. In this manner, Swift tells us, "the most ignorant person at a reasonable charge, and with a little bodily labour, may write books in philosophy, poetry, politics, law, mathematics, and theology, without the least assistance from genius or study."[1]

The Laputian device, a "Project for improving speculative Knowledge by practical and mechanical means," and Swift's unflattering description of the professor who invented it, are sometimes thought to satirize Gottfried Wilhelm Leibniz, whose 1666 *Dissertatio de Arte Combinatoria* made far-reaching claims for the ability of mathematical and mechanical languages to generate wisdom and solve conflict.[2] Leibniz went so far as to suggest that, in the future, every misunderstanding or disagreement "should be nothing more than a miscalculation . . . easily corrected." Disputing philosophers could take up their abaci and settle even delicate theological arguments mechanically, saying "Calculemus!"—"Let us compute!" (Leibniz).

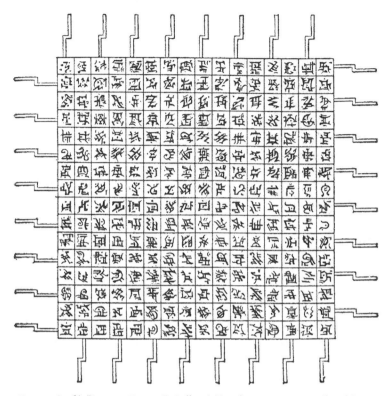

Fig 7.1: Swift's "Literary Engine." *Gulliver's Travels*, 1892 George Bell and Sons edition. Project Gutenberg.

In fact, a better-supported candidate for Swift's vitriol is Leibniz's acknowledged predecessor in the combinatoric arts, a colorful medieval polymath and sometime poet, rake, and martyr named Raimundus Lullus, or Ramon Llull (ca. 1232–1316). Llull's chief invention was a so-called Ars Magna of inscripted, inter-rotating wheels developed in the latter decades of the thirteenth century and articulated in a treatise titled *Ars Generalis Ultima*. Its purpose was at once generative, analytical, and interpretive, and while its primary subject matter was theological, Llull was careful to demonstrate the applicability of the Ars Magna to broader philosophical and practical problems of the day. In other words, Llull's wheels constituted a user-extensible mechanical aid to hermeneutics and interpretive problem solving (figure 7.2). Properly understood, Llull and his Great Art can take their place, not in the soaring halls of Laputian "speculators" and pseudoscientists, but among a cadre of humanists with fresh ideas about the relation of mechanism to interpretation.

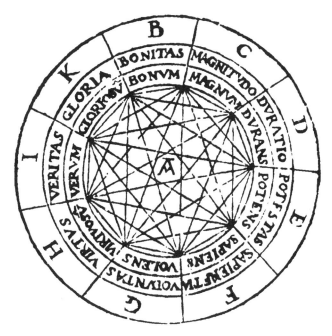

Fig 7.2: Lullian Wheel. Wikimedia Commons.

A review and description of Llull's tool, with attention to its structure and function and to past misunderstandings as to its purpose, will help situate instrumental issues that many digital humanities projects must address today. Among these are problems involved in establishing scholarly primitives and developing the rules or algorithms by which they can be manipulated in creative and revelatory ways.[3] Llull also provides a framework in which to examine the relationship between algorithmic and combinatorial methods and subjective hermeneutic practices, and to demonstrate the utility of performative instruments or environments that share in his design model. This is a model for mechanisms that are generative, emergent, and oriented toward what we would now call humanities interpretation.

Llull's intriguing device is widely recognized as a precursor both to computer science—in its emphasis on a mechanical calculus—and to the philosophy of language, in its use of symbols and semantic fields.[4] After early popularity in the universities of Renaissance Europe, however, it met with sharp and lasting criticism.[5] François Rabelais's Gargantua warns Pantagruel against "Lullianism" in the same breath as "divinatory astrology"; it is "nothing else but plain abuses and vanity."[6] And Francis Bacon describes the Ars Magna as "a method of imposture . . . being nothing but a mass and heap of the terms of all arts, to the end that they who are ready with the terms may be thought to understand the arts themselves." Such collections, Bacon observes, "are like a fripper's or broker's shop, that has the ends of everything, but nothing of worth."[7]

Modern critics also deride Llull. Even Martin Gardner, whose 1958 *Logic Machines and Diagrams* views the Ars Magna as foundational to the history of visual and mechanical thinking—Llull is Chapter One!—suggests that the best uses for his once-influential combinatoric system are (in Gardner's words) "frivolous": for example, to generate possible names for a baby, to work anagram puzzles, or to compare and combine colors for application in design and interior decorating.[8]

Gardner holds that any more sophisticated or scholarly use of Llull's device—particularly in fields like history and poetics—is wholly inappropriate. The spinning wheels, when applied to humanistic subject matter lacking in native "analytic structure" and for which there is "not even agreement on what to regard as the most primitive, 'self-evident' principles," generate only circular proofs. "It was Lull's particular distinction," Gardner writes, "to base this type of reasoning on such an artificial, mechanical technique that it amounted virtually to a satire of scholasticism, a sort of hilarious caricature of medieval argumentation."[9] We may not wish to go so far (like his great proponents Peter Bexte and Werner Künzel) as to claim Llull as "der erste Hacker in den himmlischen Datenbanken" (the first hacker of the heavenly databases!), but it seems clear that the most scathing criticisms of the Ars Magna stem from a fundamental misunderstanding of the uses to which Llull meant his device to be put.[10]

Künzel is right, in *The Birth of the Machine*, to describe Llull's system of interlocking, inter-rotating wheels as an ancestor of the Turing machine, a logic device, "producing results, statements—output of data in general—by a clearly defined mechanical algorithm."[11] However, we would be wrong to assume, as Bacon and Gardner did, that we are to interpret as truth the statements generated through this algorithm (that is, by Llull's proscribed procedure of marking and spinning wheels and diagramming their results). In fact, the linguistic combinations that Llull's wheels produce are only meant to be interpreted. That is, Llull invented a device for putting new ideas into the world out of the fragments of old ideas and constraining rule sets, but left the (inherently subjective) evaluation and explication of these emergent concepts up to a human user—a person explicitly figured in his writing as an *artista*. Llull's machine generates "truthful" formulations equally with falsehood, and makes no claim about or evaluation of its own output: "naturally, only the artist using the machine is able to decide which statement is true and which is false. The machine independently produces both: the universe of truth and the universe of the false, step by step."[12]

"Right Round, Baby, Right Round"

In building the Ars Magna, Llull began by establishing a manipulable alphabet of discrete, primary concepts or primitives on which his algorithmic and mechanical procedures could operate. The most commonly accepted (and least complex) version of this art associates nine letters of the Latin alphabet, *B* through *K*, with fundamental aspects of divinity: goodness, greatness, eternity or duration, power, wisdom, will, virtue, truth, and glory. The letter *A* stands in for the Divine, and is placed at the center of a circular diagram (figure 7.3), which in itself becomes a hypothetical definition of God.[13] When lines are drawn to connect each of the nine letter-coded aspects (showing in binaries, for example, that God's goodness is great [*BC*], God's virtue lies in truth [*HI*], etc.), Llull expresses the basic relational character not only of divinity, but also of his very notion of an *ars combinatoria*. Combinatoric elements are not simply reordered, as with Swift's Laputian machine; here they are placed for careful consideration in conjunction.

Resultant graphs—which, as we will later see, Llull considered to be dynamic rather than static—form the simplest interpretive tool of the Ars Generalis Ultima. The art is properly thought of as interpretive rather than explicatory, because the conjoined components of the definition of God that it expressed were not meant to be accepted flatly by its audience, but rather contemplated, analyzed, and above all contrasted against the opposites implied by the structural workings of the diagram—the qualities of fallen mankind. Rich rhetorical expression in these combinations comes into focus through the user's own faculties of comparison and analogy as generated structures suggest, for example, that the power of human rulers (letter *E*)—unlike that of the defined divinity—is not always commensurate with their wisdom (letter *F*).

As a next step, Llull's binary relationships are complicated by the application of a separate assemblage of meanings attached to his established alphabet, and a further series of diagrams. The concept of "an ending" in these elaborations, for example, may be interpreted as it relates geometrically to labeled notions of privation, termination, or perfection. Therefore, even the graphic organization of Llullian concepts participates in an expression of the enabling constraints under which his concepts are meant to function and through which they are enlivened.

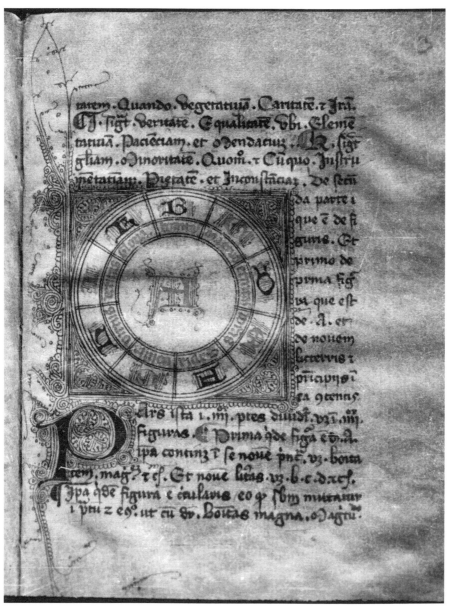

Fig 7.3: Llull's Figure A. Ars Brevis, Biblioteca El Escorial, Madrid Ms. f.IV.12 folio 3r. Digital reproduction, Raimundus-Lullus-Institut, Freiburg.

Llull's embodied relations permit the generation—for further analysis—of a phrase like "goodness has great difference and concordance." An elevated pronouncement, indeed, but steps are taken to constrain output that could otherwise provoke an overly general discussion, through a generative process involving the insertion (via separate diagrams, figures 7.4 and 7.5) of a set of specific sense-perceptive and intellectual relations. A statement like "goodness has great difference and concordance," then, is presented by Llull's circles not as an eternal truth, but rather in order that it be interpreted within a specified context—that of sensual and intellectual differences—and in all the embedded relations among those fundamental domains.

For all its complexity and utility in generating relational assertions, thus far the Great Art limits itself to binary structures, and to interpretations based on fundamentally invariable graphs and matrices. With the introduction of a novel fourth figure, however, Llull expands his system from binary into ternary relationships, and moves from abstract algorithm and diagrammatic reasoning into the realm of mechanically aided hermeneutic practice (figure 7.6). He does this first by adding to the semantic weight of the primary alphabet a set of interrogatives (who, what, why, etc.) or—as he puts it—interpretive prompts. The prompts become part of a functioning rule set for procedure and elucidation when they are inscribed, along with Llull's other encoded alphabets, on *volvelles*—exquisite, manipulable, inter-rotating wheels.

While versions of Llull's wheels have been fashioned from a variety of media (including, most interestingly, the copper "covers" of a portable Italian Renaissance sundial masquerading as a book), they typically took the form of paper circles secured within incunabula and manuscripts by small lengths of string (John Dalton). The compartments, or *camerae*, of an outer circle would be inscribed on the page, while two inner circles were fastened on top of it in such a way as to permit them to rotate independently, mechanically generating interpretive problems based on ternary combinations of the alphabetic ciphers inscribed on them.

Llull's wheels appear deceptively simple, but for the basic combination of two letters alone, they are capable of posing thirty-six issues to their human interpreters: twelve propositions (such as "goodness is great") and twenty-four questions or philosophical problems (like "what is great goodness?" and "whether goodness is great") multiplied down the succession of associations between, for example, goodness and difference, goodness and concordance, and so on. When three rather than two primary elements are combined with their associated questions or interpretive rules, as is enabled by the embedded, rotating wheels, even more complex problems can present

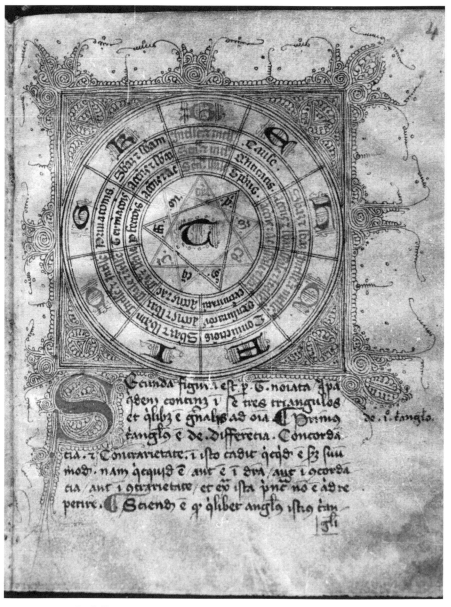

Fig 7.4: Llull's Figure T. Ars Brevis, Biblioteca El Escorial, Madrid Ms. f.IV.12 folio 4r. Digital reproduction, Raimundus-Lullus-Institut, Freiburg.

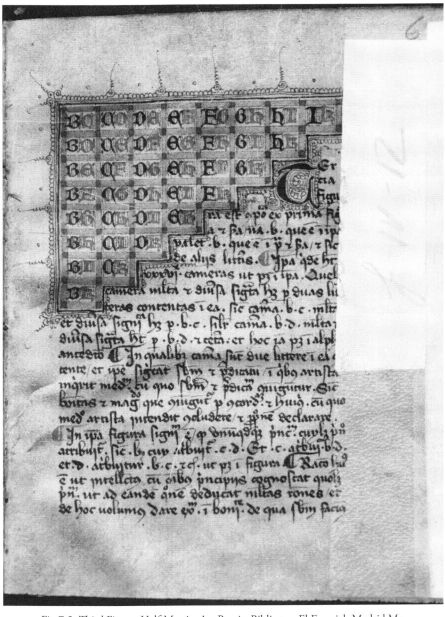

Fig 7.5: Third Figure, Half Matrix. Ars Brevis, Biblioteca El Escorial, Madrid Ms. f.IV.12 folio 6r. Digital reproduction, Raimundus-Lullus-Institut, Freiburg.

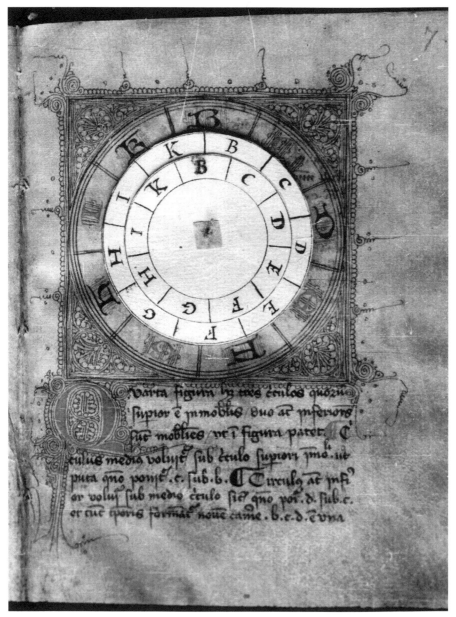

Fig 7.6: Llull's Fourth Figure, The Volvelle. Ars Brevis, Biblioteca El Escorial, Madrid Ms. f.IV.12 folio 7r. Digital reproduction, Raimundus-Lullus-Institut, Freiburg.

themselves: for example, "whether goodness contains within itself difference and contrariety."[14]

Llull works out the results of his generative machine in tables similar to the half matrix used to express the simple relations of his first circular figure. In the Ars Brevis of 1308, a simplified version of his Great Art, the corresponding table has seven columns—but Llull's Ars Generalis Ultima presents the relations that emerge from expanded iterations of the rotating wheel concept in a table with no less than eighty-four long columns. Each alphabetic expression in these tables has been algorithmically, logically, and mechanically generated for rhetorical and hermeneutic purposes, in service to what Stephen Ramsay has called "humane computation."[15] The cumulative effect is of an "extraordinary network of systems systematizing systems,"[16] and yet the Llullian apparatus exists in service of interpretive subjectivity.

Llull is thought to represent the "earliest attempt in the history of formal logic to employ geometrical diagrams for the purpose of discovering non-mathematical truths, and the first attempt to use a mechanical device—a kind of primitive logic machine—to facilitate the operation of a logic system."[17] Llull's wheels can be thought of as the "hardware" of this system, with the interpretive method he advocates for their use serving as software, expressed, along with output from the devices, in user manuals like the Ars Generalis Ultima.

It is important to remember, however, that most of the diagrammatic figures generated by Llull's wheels do not explore "truths" at all, but instead pose interesting queries and hypothetical situations for their users: for example, "when it might be prudent to become angry" or "when lust is the result of slothfulness." Llull also uses the wheels to help puzzle out such "typical medieval problems" as "If a child is slain in the womb of a martyred mother, will it be saved by a baptism of blood? . . . Can God make matter without form? Can He damn Peter and save Judas?" Llull's *Book of the Ascent and Descent of the Intellect* moves beyond the theological sphere to apply his method to eight categories of natural philosophy, in order to pose and suggest possible answers to scientific problems like "Where does the flame go when a candle is put out?" or "Why does rue strengthen the eyes [while] onions weaken them?"[18]

In the books accompanying his charts and diagrams, Llull sometimes offers full arguments and commentaries on such questions, sometimes outlines the combinatorial processes by which the questions could be addressed using his wheels, and sometimes simply demonstrates diagrammatically that such sophisticated questioning can be generated by means of the Ars Magna. At no point does Llull imply that his machine can produce "truth" independently from its human user, no matter how scientific his alphabetic abstractions appear. Instead, he himself tells us that the system employs "an alphabet in this art so that it can be used to make figures as well as to mix principles and rules for the purpose of investigating the truth."[19] That is, the mechanism enables interpretation through visualization, by making the core elements it operates on and the rules by which it plays explicit. The flat generation of combinations is not the point of his Great Art: that is not hard to do. In addition to the requisite hardware, Llull provides his users with a clearly specified method for analyzing both process and output outside of the generative system—and more importantly, for refining that system iteratively, based on subjective human assessment of its mechanical output. Interpretation is the real activity of the Ars Magna, not the spinning of wheels.

Despite their hermeneutic teleology, Llull's devices participate closely in two traditions that exhibit a vexed relationship with humanistic interpretation. Any "step-by-step" production of what Künzel terms interpretive "universes" is by nature an algorithmic production, and the mixing of principles and rules on which Llull's work depends is a nice elaboration of the notion of an *ars combinatoria*. An appreciation of both of these traditions and the methods that support them is critical to our understanding, not only of Llull and his interpretive devices, but also of the promise of digital tools and environments—that they might augment our methodologies and offer greater latitude to humanities scholarship.

Performance and Interpretation

Fitting Four Elephants in a Volkswagen

Llull is often listed among the first philosophers "compelled to delineate clearly a general method" for deriving conclusions.[20] Frances Yates goes so far as to assert that the "European search for method . . . began with Llull."[21] We now commonly accept that "logical reasoning is, in a sense, computation" and that it "can be formalized and validated by controllable means,"[22] but Llull's clear and materially embodied articulation of this concept has been seen as an advance in Western philosophy, constituting the first major formal extension of traditional mnemonics, a "now-forgotten integral part of medieval education: the complex set of elaborated techniques for reminding and structuring things in human memory in a printless age."[23] Perhaps more important, Llull's devices also implemented, for the first time in Western Europe, the newly translated rule-based work of the Arabian mathematician al-Khwarizmi, from whose name the word "algorithm" stems.

The relationship between algorithmic operation (as both a concrete and an abstract methodology) and the design and use of interpretive toolsets like the Ars Magna is underappreciated and perhaps easily misconstrued by humanities arts scholars outside of the tight community involved in building, making accessible, and computationally manipulating the modern digital archive. Algorithms, when thought of as remote, inflexible mathematical structures underlying computer programming and the more deterministic branches of science and engineering, can seem irrelevant or even antithetical to the work of scholarship. Practitioners of the digital humanities face the skepticism of colleagues: by building algorithmic text analysis tools, do we unthinkingly imply that the craft of scholarship can be mechanized? Are we tacitly putting constraints-based process forth as substitute for contemplation and insight? Or (a far more insidious assumption) are scripts and software, as the quiet servants delivering us the "content" of an archive, simply beneath our notice? In fact, algorithms—like various hermeneutic methods and historical schools of thought accepted by humanities scholars—can be understood as problem solving and (with a slight methodological recasting I will suggest in a discussion of the "ludic algorithm") as open, participatory, explorative devices.

The algorithm is formally defined as a finite sequence of instructions, rules, or linear steps which, if followed, guarantees that its practitioner—whether a human or machine agent—will reach some particular, predefined goal or establish incontrovertibly that the goal is unreachable. The "guarantee" part of this description is important, as it differentiates algorithms from heuristics, or what are generally called "rules of thumb." Like algorithms, heuristics can function iteratively to solve a problem and can be responsive to human input. Computer programs that modify themselves in response to their users, such as word processing spell-checkers, are sometimes—despite their algorithmic basis—termed heuristic. The heuristic process, however, is fundamentally one of informal trial and error rather than constrained activity according to a set of predefined rules.

Almost any everyday problem can be solved heuristically or algorithmically. For example: I have lost my car keys. Ordinarily, a harried new mother faced with this situation will proceed by heuristics: "I look in my purse. I look in my purse again. I brave the cluttered diaper bag. I check the front door because I have developed a bad habit of leaving them dangling there. I go to the last place I remember holding them in my hand. I ask my partner to help me find them. I wish the baby could talk." In formal, graph-based problem solving, heuristics are sometimes used to guide the search for solutions by identifying the most promising branches of a search tree for further exploration, or even by cutting out unpromising branches altogether. The weak point of the heuristic method becomes evident when its user needs to shift gears. I am not finding my keys in the usual places. Should I retrace my steps next? Is it worth considering that I may have locked them inside the car? The basic "problem with heuristics"—in some cases a crippling problem, which could lead to the inadvertent elimination of the entire branch of a desired outcome branch from the search tree—"is how to decide half-way what would be an appropriate next action, i.e. how to design heuristic rules that lead to good solutions instead of bad ones" (Krista Lagus). Tellingly, we often attribute decisions in successful heuristic processes to intuition and those that result in undesirable outcomes to confusion and bad luck.

If the heuristic process fails or seems too unsystematic for comfort, a desperate searcher can always resort to a true algorithm:

> For each room in the house; and
> For each item in the room;
> Pick up and examine the item.
> If the item appears by objective criteria to be the missing object, terminate the search.
> If not, put down the item and continue this loop until all items have been tested.

Eventually, if this little program is executed perfectly, I will either find my keys or determine conclusively that they are not in the house. There's a kind of predestination or special providence about an algorithm, formally defined. That is to say, I know to expect one of two prescribed outcomes before even undertaking the search process. And—as its strict definition requires—the algorithm is almost wholly generalizable. If I suspect I have left my keys at your house, I can run the process there. If the misplaced object is a watch, or a hat, the algorithm is equally applicable. (Of course, it is not a very efficient algorithm because it requires me, for example, to pick up and examine the house-cat—and to do so every time it saunters into a new room—but we can easily imagine more elegant versions of this basic method.)

Some common refinements to the concept of the algorithm are particularly relevant to interpretive or hermeneutic activity, which, by virtue of its realm of application, is generally predicated on ambiguity and flux. Algorithms are expected to be both perfectly precise and entirely implementable. An old bubblegum wrapper joke helps to make this point: how do you fit four elephants into a Volkswagen? The algorithmic answer is that you simply put two in the front seat and two in the back. Although those steps are clearly unambiguous, they are impossible to implement. In contrast is a commonplace algorithm for finishing one's dissertation:

Step 1: Write the next paragraph.
Step 2: Repeat Step 1 until dissertation is complete.

This procedure is clearly implementable—graduate students perform it with great fortitude all the time—but it is far too ambiguous to be a "textbook," or even a useful, algorithm. How exactly does one write a paragraph? What criteria indicate that the thing is "complete"? What is a "paragraph," anyway? How does the algorithm know that you are writing a dissertation and not a thesis, or a novel, or a comic book? (How do you know? That is to say, how determinable from the point of view of the algorithm's designer are the elements in this—in any—interpretive field?) And so the algorithm, originally applied to mathematical operations and associated almost inextricably in the contemporary mind with computer science, emerges as a step-by-step, linear, precise, finite, and generalizable process that produces definitive, anticipated results by constraining the actions of the agent who performs the process.

Almost as quickly as the application of algorithmic methodology to modern mechanical and computational apparatus became a fundamental aspect of design (with Charles Babbage's 1837 Analytical Engine), algorithms themselves fell under fire as analytical or investigative devices. Babbage's colleague, Augusta Ada Byron King, Countess of Lovelace—the daughter of Lord Byron who is celebrated as the first computer programmer for her elaborations of the Jacquard loom-like cards on which the engine operated—famously critiqued the algorithm:

> The Analytical Engine [and, by extension, the algorithmic method on which it is based] has no pretensions whatever to originate anything. It can do whatever we know how to order it to perform. It can follow analysis; but it has no power of anticipating any analytical relations or truths. Its province is to assist us in making available what we are already acquainted with. [24]

Lovelace's objection hinges on the reasonable idea that an algorithm can yield nothing more than its designer knew to ask it for in the first place. Algorithms are not fundamentally creative or revelatory. They merely perform predefined transformations and produce requested—and therefore anticipated or even presumed and therefore potentially flawed—results. We could see this quality, by way of example, in a purely mechanical performance of our car-key algorithm. The procedure's outcome (confirmation or disconfirmation of the presence of car keys) could be in no way unexpected; it is in fact built inextricably into the process. Algorithms are certainly applicable to problem solving, but Lovelace suggests that they only (perversely) solve problems whose answers are projected, which is to say pre-known.

The Lovelace objection and its descendant Turing machine critiques bear a striking resemblance to Martin Gardner's derisive description of Llull's Ars Magna as a means built toward inappropriate ends, and for the manipulation of intractable objects.[25] In such a case, any application of the algorithmic process to subjects for which, in Jerome McGann's formulation, "imagining what you don't know" is a desirable outcome, seems misguided at best. At worst, the use of algorithmic process in an interpretive or humanistic context could be seen as self-delusion justified through pseudoscientific formalism. (Critiques of "frivolous" combinatorial and deformative text manipulations and dire warnings against AI optimism in our ability to apply computational methods to text analysis participate in this limited acceptance of the uses to which algorithms might be put.)

Algorithms admittedly define and constrain a field of activity, even as they enable certain preordained interactions and solutions. Still, this is not to say that the results of algorithms—and even more, algorithmic methodology as subjective (most likely human) agents could actively and iteratively employ it—cannot paradoxically expand our thinking rather than atomize it, or limit it to presumptive outcomes. The precision a true algorithm requires of its elements and processes assumes a certain determinability and fixity of identity that is difficult if not impossible to maintain in interpretive fields. But to attempt, in data modeling or in performative criticism, an algorithmically enforced specificity is to experience and exploit a productive brand of what William Morris might have called "resistance in the materials" of humanities scholarship. Real challenges and opportunities arise for expanding our understanding of interpretive fields (including, at the most deceptively basic level, graphic and textual book artifacts) in the rigorous and thoughtful application of algorithmic method to our analysis and manipulation of indeterminate objects and ideas.

Lovelace gets at these consequences of algorithmic method in a neglected passage immediately following her well-known "objection." She explains that the Analytical Engine's facility in following rules and orders, producing expected results, and "making available what we are already acquainted with" is effected

primarily and chiefly of course, through its executive faculties; but it is likely to exert an indirect and reciprocal influence on science itself in another manner. For, in so distributing and combining the truths and the formulae of analysis, that they may become most easily and rapidly amenable to the mechanical combinations of the engine, the relations and the nature of many subjects in that science are necessarily thrown into new lights, and more profoundly investigated. This is a decidedly indirect, and a somewhat speculative, consequence of such an invention.[26]

Here Lovelace takes up, in the context of combinatorial mathematics, that product of algorithmic, diagrammatic, deformative, and mechanical method I will cite under the broad rubric of "aesthetic provocation."[27]

The Gift of Screws

After-the-fact (after, that is, data-marking or -modeling) applications of aesthetic provocation are the principal manner in which information visualization enters the broader picture of humanities computing. This is in part because the digital humanities have long orbited the double stars of corpus linguistics and database construction and mining. An intense emphasis on the encoding and analysis of primarily textual human artifacts—coupled with institutional and disciplinary devaluation of methodological training and a sore lack of publication venues for image-intensive work—have contrived to make visualization, from the end-user's perspective, generally a product to be received rather than a process in which to participate. Nonetheless, algorithmically or combinatorially generated aesthetic provocation, generally thought of as information visualization, has both rhetorical and revelatory power.

Visionary computer scientist Alan Turing, in a noted critique of the Lovelace objection, examines these revelations—the tendency of algorithmic mechanisms to provoke or surprise their users—and ultimately offers us a socialized, humanized view of algorithmic methodology. He begins the discussion with an attempt to reframe Lovelace:

A variant of Lady Lovelace's objection states that a machine can "never do anything really new." This may be parried for a moment with the saw, "There is nothing new under the sun." Who can be certain that "original work" that he has done was not simply the growth of the seed planted in him by teaching, or the effect of following well-known general principles?[28]

These "well-known general principles" are perhaps commonly thought of by humanists as the informal, heuristic methods transferred to us over the course of a rich and varied education. (One would generally rather take this stance than that; when writing on this subject, one must avoid that quagmire; etc.) But what if Turing means us to understand our day-to-day practices in "following" these principles as little more than the playing-out of socially acquired algorithmic procedures, the output of which in a human context feels like originality, invention? In other words, might we not follow formal, specific (and wholly ingrained) rules even—or perhaps most of all—when we engage in our most creative and supposedly inventive work? What is it, precisely, that inspires us?

There is no question that algorithmic method as performed by humans or machines can produce unexpected (even if, as Lovelace points out, fundamentally predictable) and illuminative results. The religious traditions of gematria and Kabbalah, the conceptual art of Sol LeWitt, John Cage's aleatory musical compositions, OuLiPian literary production, and the procedural experiments of Ron Silliman, Jackson Mac Low, and others (for example, Lisa Samuels's poetic deformations) are primary examples of the inventive application of algorithmic method in the "analog" world. The inspirational power of constraining systems and algorithmic methodology is everywhere evident; it is the reason we have highly articulated poetic forms like the sestina. In a practical, humanities computing context, computational algorithmic processes have been employed to perform revealing and sometimes startling graphical and statistical transformations under the rubric of text analysis. Jerome McGann's Photoshop deformations of Rossetti paintings in the 1990s participated in this tradition. And digital information artists like Ben Fry work through strict systems of constraint in works that fruitfully blur the boundaries between creative and critical production.[29]

The contributions of cognitive science to the humanities over the past few decades have (for better or worse) participated in what Colin Symes terms a "progressive demystification" of fundamental assumptions, long held in some quarters of the academy, about interpretive and artistic creativity. A Romantic vision of the artist unbound, as liberated in thought (a vision perhaps too easily countered with reference to the empowering constraints that drive even Romantic poetic practice), has given way among cognitive scientists to a growing "emphasis on the importance of a structured imagination."[30] According to this understanding, a top-down model of cognition that builds on Marvin Minsky's notion that mental framing devices both structure and filter our thought processes, creativity functions almost wholly through elaborate systems of constraint. The idea that, as Jon Elster posits, "artists tend to maximize their options through minimizing their choices" may strike some as counterintuitive, but creative work in any number of disciplines bears this theory out, and it remains useful despite more contemporary critique.[31]

Perhaps equally peculiar is the suggestion that Minsky's framing system, which is structured hierarchically, could foster the subjective, nonhierarchical, out-of-the-box thinking we associate with interpretive and artistic production. According to this model of cognition, information filters progressively through top-level framing structures into lower-level "terminals." Minsky's primary interest is in the mechanisms of simple perception, but his concept of cognitive frames is equally applicable to more complex linguistic and creative processes. Uppermost frames in this case constitute a "range of primordial scripts" and "default grammars that control the structures of language."[32] There are, however, secondary constraining grammars. Margaret Boden terms these mental constraining systems, which structure critical and artistic thought and production within specific genres, forms, or disciplines, "computational spaces." According to this theory, nonhierarchical cognition is fostered through supporting structures "whose computational spaces or frameworks are derived from particular epistemological and aesthetic domains." These specialized spaces function both within and beyond the primary framing system that hosts them, generating, for instance, "forms of linguistic organization which transgress and even transcend those governing natural language."[33]

Poetic composition provides a clear example of the use of meta-grammars both to organize and to provoke subjective response. This distinction between organization and provocation is an important one because cognitive systems of constraint act simultaneously as matrices in which the fundamental units of language are placed, and as generative processes or algorithms. That is to say, a poet perceives the sophisticated metrical and rhythmic constraints of a sestina not simply as structures, but as a performative or procedural imperative. The linguistic patterns such constraints make impossible are as crucial to the composition of a poem as those they privilege and enforce. In this understanding of subjective response to algorithmic imperatives, poetry is shaped by what it cannot be, and poets by what their chosen forms will not let them do.

Some evidence exists that such genre- and form-specific shaping may become a physical or neurological condition of the performer. Cognitive scientist K. I. Foster has identified in the brain, with repeated linguistic use, a restructuring of the neural circuits or "connectionist pathways that excite mutually consistent arrays of language." Interestingly, these pathways "at the same time inhibit those that are inconsistent with the exigencies of the constraint."[34] For the poet, the development of self-organizing mental systems results in a greater facility, over time, within his most familiar computational spaces and in the production of his chosen forms. And for this reason, writers exercise their faculties by engaging in rhetorical and metrical exercises and linguistic games, such as acrostics, bouts-rimés, or complex forms like hendecasyllabics. (Gerard Manley Hopkins, who constructed poetic matrices of ever-increasing complexity, maintained in his journals—or perhaps sought to reassure himself—that "freedom is compatible with necessity." Likewise, Emily Dickinson's "Attar from the rose" is "not expressed by Suns—alone— / It is the Gift of Screws.") In fact, scientific investigation of the processes underlying poiesis suggests that artistic freedom may only be embodied—artifactually and physiologically—through the necessities of constraining, algorithmic systems.[35]

Experimental and synthetic work in analyzing literary expertise also tends to support a constraints-based reading of the poetic and interpretive process. Cognitive research by Marlene Scaramalia and Carl Bereiter indicates that the presence of strict constraining systems promotes greater linguistic fluency in writers, by lending "form and direction to the more localized decision-making" involved in word choice within a particular genre or format.[36] In effect, as Jon Elster demonstrates, this concentrates creative energies by economizing on the number of aesthetic and subjective choices available to the artist at any one time.[37] Robert De Beaugrande explains the futility of any attempt at artistic composition unfettered by localized systems of constraint in terms of the "combinatoric explosion" that would occur should the range of choices become "unmanageable."[38]

Regardless of our acceptance of the theoretical assertions of cognitive science, the dual operation of computational spaces as structured matrices and generative algorithms functioning both within and beyond Minsky's top-down, framing filters becomes usefully, provocatively evident in our attempts at modeling and encoding the artworks these spaces engender. Poetic conventions generate linguistic artifacts that, despite the regularity their constraining patterns enforce, are essentially nonhierarchical. This fact is attested to by the infelicity of common text markup systems at capturing poetic (as opposed to informational) organization hierarchically.[39] We should also note that constraint does not operate at the same, uniform scale throughout a creative or interpretive procedure, but rather shifts in specificity depending on choices made and exigencies encountered. And all these notions are complicated by a necessarily performative slant to any algorithmic or constraints-based methodology.

The Ludic Algorithm

What may look inaccessibly, mechanistically algorithmic in (for instance) the OuLiPian project might be better understood as a ludic algorithm, which I posit as a constrained, generative design situation, opening itself up—through performance by a subjective, interpretive agent—to participation, dialogue, inquiry, and play within its prescribed and proscriptive "computational spaces." This work may embed within itself a proposed method, but does not see its ultimate product as simply the output of a specified calculation or chance operation. In fact, the desired outcome of a ludic algorithm is the sheer, performative, and constructive enactment of the hermeneutic circle, the iterative "designerly" process we go through in triumphing over interpretive or creative problems we pose ourselves.[40] In undertaking such activity, we are more than Jacques Bens's "rats qui ont à construire le labyrinth dont ils se proposent de sortir."[41]

Turing touches on this brand of dialogue in his contemplation of the relationship between a machine (the very embodiment of algorithmic process) and its fallible, creative human interlocutor:

A better variant of the [Lovelace] objection says that a machine can never "take us by surprise." This statement is a more direct challenge and can be met directly. Machines take me by surprise with great frequency. This is largely because I do not do sufficient calculation to decide what to expect them to do, or rather because, although I do a calculation, I do it in a hurried, slipshod fashion, taking risks. Perhaps I say to myself, "I suppose the Voltage here ought to be the same as there: anyway let's assume it is." Naturally I am often wrong, and the result is a surprise for me for by the time the experiment is done these assumptions have been forgotten. These admissions lay me open to lectures on the subject of my vicious ways, but do not throw any doubt on my credibility when I testify to the surprises I experience.

The view that machines cannot give rise to surprises is due, I believe, to a fallacy to which philosophers and mathematicians are particularly subject. This is the assumption that as soon as a fact is presented to a mind all consequences of that fact spring into the mind simultaneously with it. It is a very useful assumption under many circumstances, but one too easily forgets that it is false. A natural consequence of doing so is that one then assumes that there is no virtue in the mere working out of consequences from data and general principles.[42]

If its performative and cooperative components are not appreciated, Turing's notion of algorithmic surprise could lead to justification of a grossly limited vision of the interpretive activity possible in digital environments, an idea of algorithm that restricts its application to after-the-fact "aesthetic provocation." In fact, the real "surprise" involved here is less a matter of the algorithm working to its inevitable result on a set of data (as in a conventional information visualization) than of what that action, under observation, reveals about human thought processes. Turing is not a passive recipient of algorithmic output, but rather a predictive, constructive participant in its fashioning and reception. He makes assumptions, holds expectations, and awaits algorithmic response as just another part of a feedback loop. He is, in this, a reader of algorithms and their output, just as we are all readers of the machine of the book. Still, despite the cumulative (socializing and humanizing) effect of Turing's assessment, as Ramsay reminds us, "to speak of an algorithm is usually to speak of unerring processes and irrefragable answers"—not of the participatory and iterative work of humanities interpretation.

Turing's vision of the imperfect, risk-taking, intuitive human in conversation with a precise, calculating, fundamentally surprising machine partner is now familiar to us not only from science fiction and technological speculation but from our daily lives. We experience this brand of surprise perhaps most often as frustration in our interaction with algorithmic mechanisms (like telephone voice-response systems and the purgatory of the Department of Motor Vehicles)—interaction that can make us feel more like passive victims than active participants. We must realize, however, that Turing is documenting a fresh brand of dialectic, and by casting their facility in the "mere working out of consequences from data and general principles" as an anthropomorphized virtue machines can model for and perhaps teach us, he effectively rehabilitates computer-mediated algorithmic method as a creative and critical mode of performance. Recognition of the value of "working out . . . consequences" is as tangible a benefit, and perhaps as great a "surprise," as the mechanically generated results of any imaginable algorithm. Performance (including human performance of algorithmic action) is valued here over passive reception. Turing's surprises are provocations to further action, not those unpragmatic, theory-ridden "answers to enigmas in which we can rest" decried by William James. That is, we are sure from his description and subsequent proposals (indeed from the whole character of his project) that Turing means to take these dialogues further.

My own desire for an enhancement of the typical aesthetic provocation paradigm hinges—like Turing's observation and like OuLiPian practice generally—on the methodological uses of algorithmic constraint and calls for a new, more ludic and performative application of the notion of "aesthetic provocation."[43] The problem with a visualization (or any other last-step provocation to interpretation) generated algorithmically from previously encoded data is that pre-encoded data is pre-interpreted data. And programmed algorithms that are flatly, "automagically" applied to a data set, not opening themselves up to examination and modification by a user, filter the object of interpretation even further. The user of such a system is not properly figured as a user at all, but rather becomes an audience to statements being made by the designers of the system's content model and visualization or other representational algorithms.

While these statements can constitute—in all fairness—remarkable critical moves on their own part, the culminant effect of an unbalanced use of this approach is to reinforce a mistaken notion that digitization (and the concomitant application of algorithmic process of any sort) is a pre-critical activity, the work of a service industry providing so-called content to scholars. As an interpreter of algorithmic statements, a scholar (the end-user) is of course enfranchised to respond critically or creatively in conventional ways: by writing, speaking, teaching, or even by answering visualizations in kind, responding with new images. All of these responses, however, typically take place outside the system that provokes them, and to date (despite the early promise of projects like *NINES* and the *Ivanhoe Game*), few scholarly systems have created meaningful opportunities for critical engagement on the part of users. Sadly, the scholar's interpretive act plays a distant second to the primary interpretation or algorithmic performance encoded by the creators of most allegedly "interactive" digital environments.

A more fruitful interest in algorithms and algorithmic processes—as first embodied in Llull's combinatoric wheels—lies in their design and our subjective experience in using them, rather than in their (oddly, at once) objective and Delphic output. A suggestion that digital humanists move beyond the conventional application of "aesthetic provocation" is by no means a denigration of the measured use of traditional information visualization—of the algorithmic "product." My own work, however, is much more invested in digitally or mechanically assisted algorithmic methodology as an interpretive strategy.[44] How are such provocative statements as those made by Fry's *Valence* produced? Can we insinuate ourselves (our subjective responses, interpretations, participatory acts) more deeply into their production? We may find that the greater understanding of algorithmic process we gain in dialogue and co-creation with our Turing machines leads to a deeper appreciation of the self-replicant, recombinant documentary world in which humanities scholars live and move and have their being. For even the most pedestrian algorithmic construct opens itself up as an interpretive field in productive ways. Our simple car-key algorithm, for example, could easily, in performance, become a synthetic, interpretive, and creative ludic exercise—a game.[45]

Even at its most basic level—setting aside the intimate manipulations of a designer or programmer—algorithmic performance by subjective agents is revelatory. Imagine actually going through the prescribed physical process of picking up every item in your house, individually, and examining it for car-key-ness or not-car-key-ness. You might well find your keys by the end of the algorithm—but, by that time, the "success" of the operation would certainly seem beside the point. Undertaking this structured, constraints-based activity as a thinking human being, either practically or imaginatively, means more than performing it mechanically with one end in sight (confirmation or disconfirmation of the presence of car keys). Instead, you would be prompted continually to interpret and reinterpret your environment, your goal, your scope of activity, and your very actions, simply because a constraining system was compelling you to think algorithmically. You would, in performance, act on and reinterpret the objects of your rule set and the rule set alike.

Repositioning closed, mechanical, or computational operations as participatory, ludic algorithms requires acknowledgment of a primary definition, derived from the studies of the game theorist Martin Shubik, a figure sadly neglected in literary or new media game studies. He concludes a powerful survey of "the scope of gaming" with the simple statement that "all games call for an explicit consideration of the role of the rules."[46] Shubik means us to understand this "consideration" not only as adherence by players to a set of constraints, but also as appreciation of the impact of rules on the whole scope of play. The rule set or constraining algorithm in any ludic system becomes another player in the process and, as expert gamers often testify, can seem to open itself to interpretation and subjective response—in some cases, to real, iterative (which in this case is to say, turn-based) modification.[47] In our "consideration of the role of the rules" we must follow C. S. Peirce, and understand algorithmic rule sets "in the sense in which we speak of the 'rules' of algebra; that is, as a permission under strictly defined conditions."[48] The permission granted here is not only to perform but also to reimagine and reconfigure.

Llull in Application

"The Farmer and the Cowman Should Be Friends"

Algorithmic and ludic operations, however fundamental to artistic and scholarly activity, remain exotic concepts to most humanities researchers. Ramon Llull, our benchmark designer of the participatory, ludic algorithm, is more generally appreciated by academics in the historical context of *ars combinatoria,* a practice described by the installation artist Janet Zweig and others as rooted in mysticism and divination and leading up to the aleatory experimentation of the modern conceptual artists, musical composers, and mathematically inspired writers. *Ars combinatoria* have been called "the software of the baroque," with an output as rich as Bach's fugues, at once mechanical and occult.[49]

Anthony Bonner, in tracing the evolution of Llull's mechanical design from early forms more dependent on prose description, reference tables, and static figures, draws attention to the shift to *ars combinatoria* proper brought about with the introduction of the inter-rotating wheel:

> Initially it appears as a device to compensate for the loss of basic principles that formerly constituted the building blocks of the Art; but soon one sees that it is in fact the replacement of a vast sprawling structure, whose parts are loosely and often only implicitly (or analogically) interrelated, by a far more compact structure, whose parts are tightly and much more explicitly and mechanically interrelated.[50]

Not only does the device, first embodied as the Fourth Figure of the Ars Brevis, serve that work's aim of making plain the complexities of Llull's Ars Magna, it also demonstrates that the essence of a "vast sprawling" and analogical structure can be usefully condensed into a set of combinatorial relations—so long as the concretization and precision implied by the new form can be matched by flexibility in an open, interpretive rule set.

Unfortunately, the association of Llull's Great Art with *ars combinatoria* implies for some a focus that is either mystical (almost alchemical) or inextricably linked to an allegedly uncritical or precritical artistic value on "pure process and play."[51] What relevance can such flights of fancy have to serious scholarly issues of interpretation and analysis? We can begin to answer this question by contextualizing Llull's own design (though it is an answer best embodied in the design and production of new tools rather than simply explicated historically).

Llull's algorithmic and combinatorial device emerged not from mysticism or playful experimentation, but rather from a crisis in communication and interpretation. The Ars Magna was meant to serve as an aid to hermeneutic thought and cross-cultural understanding in light of seemingly insurmountable (and unassailably rigorous) problems of textual criticism and rescension. That they seem playful in use is a mere fringe benefit of the serious interpretive burden Llull meant his spinning wheels to bear.

Llull was born on Majorca, only a few years after the king of Aragon and Catalonia had retaken the island from its Islamic conquerors. In Llull's time, Majorca was a melting pot: at least one-third of the population was Muslim, there was a strong and influential Jewish minority in the economic and political center, and the rest of the island's inhabitants were Catholic. Künzel calls the Mediterranean of Llull's day "a kind of interface for three expanded cultural streams."[52] Llull recognized many elementary commonalities among the three combative monotheistic religions represented on Majorca, but despite the sharing of basic concepts and notions of divinity, cultural tensions grew and Llull became deeply committed to the cause of resolution and appeasement. We find it therefore "necessary to regard his invention as embedded within a special situation, i.e. embedded in a deep crisis of communication."[53] Admittedly, Llull saw himself as a Christian missionary and his tools as enabling devices for the conversion of the infidels—not by the sword, as the failed Crusades had attempted, but by logical reasoning facilitated through the innovative combination of familiar, shared ideas.

Earlier attempts at peacefully convincing unbelievers, Llull recognized, had failed because of problems of bibliographical analysis and textual criticism: theologians from the various camps had "based their arguments on sacred texts" (trying to point out errors in the Koran, the Talmud, or the Bible)—a practice that "invariably became bogged down in arguments as to which texts were acceptable to whom and how to interpret them."[54] A passage from Llull's *Book of the Gentile and the Three Wise Men*—written ca. 1275 as a popular companion to the Ars Magna, in which the complex operands of that method are softened through presentation as the flowers and leaves of a tree—demonstrates the author's consciousness of the text-critical nature of religious problems of his day:

> "I am quite satisfied," said the Gentile to the Jew, "with what you have told me; but please tell me the truth: do Christians and Saracens both believe in the Law you mention?" The Jew replied: "We and the Christians agree on the text of the Law, but we disagree in interpretation and commentaries, where we reach contrary conclusions. Therefore we cannot reach agreement based on authorities and must seek necessary arguments by which we can agree. The Saracens agree with us partly over the text, and partly not; this is why they say we have changed the text of the Law, and we say they use a text contrary to ours."[55]

The innovation of the Ars Magna was to abstract philosophical concepts in play from their textual condition, by identifying notions common to the documentary sources of all three major religions and offering a combinatorial method for fusing them together and analyzing their relations. Llull's hope was that Christian arguments inspired by the Ars Magna would be satisfactory to Muslims and Jews, stemming as they did from logical combinations of their own basic beliefs. There is, however, no quality or assumption inherent in the Llullian method to enforce a certain interpretive slant. It is just as easy to use Llull's wheels to formulate arguments that favor Judaism or Islam. All the interpretive impetus is placed on the *artista*, the human user of the Ars Magna.[56]

Dynamic Diagrams

Llull's method was not only notable for being clearly delineated; it was also self-testing, in the sense that the execution of iterative combinatorial motions was only carried out until contradictions or obvious untruths emerged. These untruths, naturally, would not appear as a parsing error or blue-screen breakdown in any material system at hand (the wheels, the diagrams), but rather in the conceptual system taking shape over the course of interaction with the Ars Magna in the mind of its user. At that point, the wheels themselves (and therefore all the marked primitives and practiced algorithms in play) could be examined and reconfigured. In this way, Llull's Great Art was both a generative and autopoietic mechanism, through which new posited truths and refined combinatorial and analytic methods could emerge.

Emergence, rather than derivation, is in fact the hallmark of Llullian method. The diagrams generated by Llull's wheels operate on principles of equivalency, not cause and effect, generating statements "*per aequiparantium,* or by means of equivalent relations," in which ideas are not chained causally (the primary method for deriving logical and predictive relations), but are instead traced "back to a common origin."[57] In the same way, Llull's idea of an *ars combinatoria* is not flatly combinatoric, but also fundamentally relational in structure and scope, in the manner of proof-theoretical semantic tableaux.[58] Even better, for Llull's uses, is that inherent value placed on human associations and the interpretive interplay of concepts ensures Laputian "wisdom" or random nonsense can be rejected. We must, in looking at Llull's diagrams, appreciate his attitude toward their primary elements, the "constants" represented by an alphabetic notation.[59] In Llull's estimation, nothing in the world is inactive. Nothing simply is; rather, everything performs whatever its nature dictates. So Llull's emergent definitions (for example, the wheels may be spun to generate the simple statement "Goodness is great"), which "to some commentators have seemed simply tautological, in fact imply a dynamic reality articulated in a large web of interactions."[60] Llull's definitions for alphabetic ciphers are "purely functional," after the style of "modern mathematicians, who do not say what a thing is, but only what it does."[61] This dynamism provokes computer scientists like Ton Sales to argue that Llull invented the graph.

It is clear that "concept-structuring or taxonomic" graphical designs—such as tree structures—predate Llull.[62] Llull's typical graph was not built on a static, taxonomic model, however, but "conceived rather as a present-day's 'semantic network' and intended to be 'followed,' i.e. dynamically executed as though it were truly a fact-finding 'program' or a 'decision tree' as used in AI decision procedures."[63] Such an image was not a chart or illustration, but instead an "actual net of links that allowed the user to explore in a combinatorial fashion the relations that existed among the currently manipulated concepts."[64] In this way, Llull's designs resembled or prefigured modern conceptual graphs and semantic networks, as they "presupposed a dynamic interpretation" in which to know the concepts at hand meant to follow and explore their consequences and associations, to participate actively in the manufacture and representation of knowledge.[65]

Dark, Satanic Millstones?

Perhaps the finest quality of Llull's now-neglected system is that it assumes activity at all its levels. It works at once mechanically and graphically, and it offers a method by which its users may respond interpretively, interactively, and iteratively to its combinatoric output. Here, we are not asked to feed data into a closed system (the algorithms of which were perhaps fashioned by others, necessarily for other purposes and materials than our own) and wait passively for a visualization or tabular report. We are instead meant to create, mark, and manipulate a wheel; to record its statements diagrammatically; and to follow and explore those resultant diagrams as a means of formulating, testing, and refining both ideas and rules, or algorithmic and combinatorial systems of interpretive constraint. No satanic mill, Llull's open-ended mechanical model instead follows William Blake's imperative: "I must create my own System, or be enslaved by another Man's." For no matter how benign and even profitable the typical enslavement to after-the-fact "aesthetic provocation" in humanities computing tools may be, algorithmic instruments that do not work on Llull's principle can only deliver us "answers" that are either pre-known or inaccessibly random—that is, either derivative from algorithms and content models that express deep-seated, framing preconceptions about our field of study (as in typical, last-stage "aesthetic provocation"), or derivative of deformative and aleatory automations that too often do not open themselves adequately to the participation of a subjective agent during their operation.[66]

Janet Zweig, in her overview of ancient and modern *ars combinatoria*, asks a fundamental question, relevant to appreciating Ramon Llull and his Great Art in the context of digital scholarship and computer-assisted hermeneutics: "What is the qualitative difference between permutational systems that are intentionally driven and those systems that are manipulated with chance operations?"[67] It is important to understand—as Llull's critics and the slow forces that have driven him into obscurity did not—that the Ars Magna is not a game of highfalutin, theological *Twister*: a governing, user-manipulating system of chance operations and random (or worse—insidiously circular) output.

Zweig's question about the qualitative difference between aleatory and intentionally driven mechanisms implies its own answer: the differences are qualitative, embedded in, and emergent from our familiar world of humanistic interpretation. We are not meant merely to get output from Llull's wheels. They are designed to generate insight into their own semi-mechanical processes and into our rhetorical and hermeneutic methodologies of use. Like so many (often misunderstood) humanities computing projects, Llull's wheels assert that interpretation is merely aided by mechanism, not produced mathematically or mechanically. That this assertion is sometimes lost on the general academic community is not simply a failure of the devices scholar-technologists produce (although, as this chapter has sought to suggest, we can do a better job of anticipating and incorporating patently interpretive forms of interaction on the part of our users into the systems we create for them). Instead, it displays our failure to articulate the humanistic and hermeneutic basis of our algorithmic work to a lay audience. Further, it reveals the rampant underappreciation among scholars of the algorithmic nature of an overfamiliar machine on which all our work is predicated: the book.

When I began to examine Ramon Llull, I anticipated closing a description of the Ars Magna with some examples of how computing humanists or digital historians and literary scholars might use his wheels to analyze and reconfigure combinatorially the hidden rules and assumptions that drive our own practice. Instead, I am inclined to argue that the best new use for Llull's old machines might be as defamiliarizing devices, modeling—for a larger and often skeptical or indifferent academic community—the application of mechanical or algorithmic systems to problems of interpretation with which scholars engage on a day-to-day basis. A dearth of clear and compelling demonstrations of this applicability to the interests of the academy is the central problem facing the digital humanities today. It is the reason our work, like the allegedly "precritical" activity of bibliographers and textual critics before us, remains insular.[68]

Llull tells us that he chose a graphical and mechanical art partly through inspiration (the Ars Magna was revealed in fiery letters on the manipulable and discrete leaves of the lentiscus plants on Majorca's highest peak)—and partly out of a recognition that the elements of interpretation should be finite in number, explicit in definition and methodological use, and visually memorable. Seen in this (divine?) light, interpretation lends itself easily to algorithm and apparatus. Why should any of us feel fettered? Let us build enabling devices for scholars—digital environments that marry methodological openness and mechanical clarity to the practice of humanities interpretation.

NOTES

1. Jonathan Swift, *Gulliver's Travels*, ed. A. J. Rivero (New York: W. W. Norton, 2001), part III, chapter 5.

2. Swift, part III, chapter 5.

3. See John Unsworth, "'Scholarly Primitives': What Methods Do Humanities Researchers Have in Common, and How Might Our Tools Reflect This?" paper presented at "Humanities Computing: Formal Methods, Experimental Practice," King's College, London, 2000, accessed July 31, 2012, http://bit.ly/p8O0i.

4. Ton Sales, "Llull as Computer Scientist, or Why Llull Was One of Us," Instituto Brasiliero de Filosofia e Ciencia Raimundo Lulio 2.3, *ARTS '97 Proceedings of the 4th International AMAST Workshop on Real-Time Systems and Concurrent and Distributed Software: Transformation-Based Reactive Systems Development.*

5. Some seventy medieval manuscripts of the Ars Brevis alone (a shortened expression of Llull's tools and methods) survive, and Anthony Bonner records twenty-four Renaissance editions of this popular work. For a succinct reception history, see Bonner's introductions to "Llull's Thought" and "Llull's Influence," in *Selected Works of Ramon Llull (1232–1316),* trans. Anthony Bonner (Princeton, N.J.: Princeton University Press, 1985), 577.

6. François Rabelais, *Gargantua and Pantagruel,* trans. Sir Thomas Urquhart and Peter Antony Motteux (London: David Nutt, 1900), 231.

7. Francis Bacon, *De Augmentis Scientiarum. Of the Advancement and Proficience of Learning; or, The Partitions of Sciences,* trans. Gilbert Wats (Oxford: Litchfield, 1640), VI.2.

8. Martin Gardner, "The Ars Magna of Ramon Lull," in *Logic Machines and Diagrams* (Chicago: University of Chicago Press, 1982), 19.

9. Gardner, 18.

10. Peter Bexte and Werner Künzel, *Allwissen und Absturz: der Ursprung des Computers* (Frankfurt am Main: Insel Verlag, 1993), introduction.

11. Werner Künzel, *The Birth of the Machine: Raymundus Lullus and His Invention,* accessed July 31, 2012, http://www.c3.hu/scca/butterfly/Kunzel/synopsis.html.

12. Künzel.

13. All thumbnail images of Llull's figures and mechanisms presented here are taken from Bonner's reproduction of the Ars Brevis (Escorial, MS f-IV-12, folios 3, 4, 6, and 7) in the *Selected Works.*

14. Anthony Bonner, "What Was Llull Up To?" Instituto Brasiliero de Filosofia e Ciencia Raimundo Lulio, accessed July 31, 2012, http://bit.ly/i4wocZ.

15. Stephen J. Ramsay, *Algorithmic Criticism* (Ph.D. dissertation, University of Virginia, 2003), 15ff.

16. Anthony Bonner, *Doctor Illuminatus: A Ramon Llull Reader* (Princeton, N.J.: Princeton University Press, 1993), 294.

17. Gardner, 1.

18. Gardner, 14–15.

19. Quoted in Janet Zweig, "Ars Combinatoria: Mystical Systems, Procedural Art, and the Computer," *Art Journal* 56, no. 3 (1997): 22.

20. Sales, 2.3.

21. Frances Yates, *The Art of Memory* (London: Routledge, 1999), 306.

22. Sales, 2.1.

23. Sales, 3.

24. Countess of Lovelace, "Sketch of the Analytical Engine Invented by Charles Babbage, Esq. By L. F. MENABREA, of Turin, Officer of the Military Engineers," trans. Augusta Ada Byron King, *Scientific Memoirs* 3 (1843): 666–731. See "Note G."

25. Gardner, 18.

26. Lovelace, "Note G."

27. Johanna Drucker and Bethany Nowviskie, "Speculative Computing: Aesthetic Provocations in Humanities Computing," in *A Companion to Digital Humanities*, ed. John Unsworth, Ray Siemens, and Susan Schreibman (Oxford: Blackwell, 2004).

28. Alan Turing, "Computing Machines and Intelligence," *MIND, A Quarterly Review of Psychology and Philosophy* 59, no. 236 (October 1950): 433–60.

29. Algorithmic text analysis tools such as those designed by Stephan Sinclair in an OuLiPian mode have been aggregated (among less consciously ludic applications) at TAPoR, the Canadian Text Analysis Portal for Research, directed by Geoffrey Rockwell. See TAPoR, accessed July 31, 2012, http://portal.tapor.ca/. Ben Fry's work at the MIT Media Lab and elsewhere is available, accessed July 31, 2012, at http://benfry.com/. See especially his genomic cartography, "Favoured Traces," and organic information design projects, all of which have been applied to text analysis (but only in art installation contexts unhappily ignored by textual scholars).

30. See Colin Symes, "Writing by Numbers: Oulipo and the Creativity of Constraints," *Mosaic* 32, no. 3 (1999): 87. Interestingly, Florian Cramer points out that Friedrich Schlegel, in the 1790s, defined Romanticism in terms of recursion and formal self-reflexivity—the same terms under which contemporary algorithmic and combinatorial digital art (of which Cramer himself is a Lullian practitioner) takes shape. See Cramer's Tate Modern talk, "On Literature and Systems Theory," of April 2001, versions of which remain at the Internet Archive, accessed July 31, 2012, http://userpage.fu-berlin.de/~cantsin/homepage/#theory.

31. Jon Elster, "Conventions, Creativity, and Originality," in *Rules and Conventions: Literature, Philosophy, Social Theory*, ed. Mette Hjort (Baltimore: Johns Hopkins University Press, 1992). See discussion in chapter 1 of Alan M. MacEachren's 1994 *How Maps Work: Representation, Visualization, and Design*. And it is no new notion; see the discussion of constraint in the work of Dante Alighieri in Jerome McGann and Lisa Samuels's seminal essay, "Deformance and Interpretation," accessed July 31, 2012, http://www2.iath.virginia.edu/jjm2f/old/deform.html.

32. Symes, 88.

33. Symes, 88.

34. Symes, 90.

35. This idea is closely tied to the biology of autopoiesis as articulated by Francisco Varela and Humberto Maturana. See their *Autopoiesis and Cognition: The Realization of the Living* (Dordrecht: Reidel, 1980).

36. Symes, 89.

37. Elster, "Fullness and Parsimony," in *Explanation and Value in the Arts*, ed. Ivan Gaskell and Salim Kemal (New York: Cambridge University Press, 1993), 164.

38. Robert de Beaugrande, "Writing and Meaning: Contexts of Research," in *Writing in Real Time: Modelling Production Processes*, ed. A. Matsuhashi (Norwood, N.J.: Ablex, 1987).

39. The difficulties involved in rigorous analysis of this quality of poetic production have been framed as a "problem of overlapping hierarchies" by the humanities and linguistic computing communities. Trace the discussion to Michael Sperberg-McQueen's comments at the Extreme Markup Conference 2002 ("What Matters?" accessed July 31, 2012, http://www.w3.org/People/cmsmcq/2002/whatmatters.html) and debate by Alan Renear and Jerome McGann at the 1999 joint conference of the Association for Computers and the Humanities and Association for Literary and Linguistic Computing ("What is Text?").

40. On the relation between hermeneutics and design, a developing interest in the architectural community, see especially D. Schön, "Designing as a Reflective Conversation with the Materials of a Design Situation," *Research in Engineering Design* 3 (1992): 131–47; Adrian Snodgrass and Richard Coyne, "Is Designing Hermeneutical?" *Architectural Theory Review* 1, no. 1 (1997): 65–97; Richard Coyne, *Designing Information Technology in the Postmodern Age: From Method to Metaphor* (Cambridge, Mass.: MIT Press, 1995). See also Nigel Cross's "Designerly Ways of Knowing," *Design Studies* 3, no. 4 (1984): 221–27; and Terry Winograd and Carlos F. Flores, *Understanding Computers and Cognition: A New Foundation for Design. Language and Being* (Norwood, N.J.: Ablex, 1986), 12: "We also consider design in relation to systematic domains of human activity, where the objects of concern are formal structures and the rules for manipulating them. The challenge posed here for design is not simply to create tools that accurately reflect existing domains, but to provide for the creation of new domains. Design serves simultaneously to bring forth and to transform the objects, relations, and regularities of the world of our concerns."

41. Loosely, "rats who build the very maze they propose to quit." Quoted in Symes, 43.

42. See Turing, Section 6.

43. This is an enhancement I embodied in the design of the Temporal Modelling PlaySpace environment, ca. 2001–2, and described, with Johanna Drucker, in Blackwell's *Companion to Digital Humanities*, 2004.

44. See, most recently, Neatline, a National Endowment for the Humanities Start-Up and Library of Congress–funded project for "geospatial and temporal interpretation of archival collections," undertaken by the Scholars' Lab at the University of Virginia Library, accessed July 31, 2012, http://neatline.org/.

45. Chris Crawford, author of the first major handbook for computer game design, contends that all great designers must think algorithmically, concentrating on process over fact and on trend over instance. The antithesis of "algorithmic thinking," he writes, is "instantial thinking," which always leads to poor interactive designs. The instantial thinker "comes up with great cut scenes," the passive, movie-like animations

that close chapters or levels in many digital action games, "but lousy interactions," which are the heart of gameplay, and "when he designs an adventure game, [the instantial thinker] loves to cook up strange dilemmas in which to place the player, but the idea of a dilemma-generating algorithm is lost on him." See Crawford, *The Art of Computer Game Design* (New York: Macmillan-McGraw-Hill, 1984).

46. Martin Shubik, "On the Scope of Gaming," *Management Science* 18, no. 5 (1972): 34.

47. See, for instance, Peter Suber's "Nomic," and *Imaginary Solution #1: Dr. Kremlin's Disc*, a game described in my unpublished dissertation, executed as a hands-on activity at the 2010 "Playing with Technology in History" symposium, accessed July 31, 2012, http://www.playingwithhistory.com/wp-content/uploads/2010/02/nowviskie-game.pdf.

48. C. S. Peirce, *Collected Papers* (Cambridge, MA: Harvard University Press, 1933), 4.361.

49. Bexte and Künzel.

50. Bonner, *Selected Works*, 573.

51. Zweig, 23.

52. Künzel.

53. Künzel.

54. Bonner, "What Was Llull Up To?"

55. Llull, book II.3.6, trans. Bonner.

56. Bonner points out that the word "art" was the "usual scholastic translation" for the Greek τεχνη (*technē*). Llull's work is best understood as a "technique; it was not a body of doctrine, but a system. Or to put it in contemporary terms, it was a structure." *Selected Works*, 62.

57. Gardner, 13.

58. Sales, 2.4.

59. Anthony Bonner suggests that Llullian alphabetic ciphers are constants rather than variables ("What Was Llull Up To?"). Clearly, the wheels and their primitives open themselves to adjustment by a human user, or *artista*. I therefore take this assertion to mean that the letters, once placed in the practical matrix of Llull's wheels and charts, are best understood as having a one-to-one relationship with the objects or ideas they represent, the better to enable the sort of dynamic, performative interaction of an *artista* with a diagram Llull favored.

60. Bonner, "What Was Llull Up To?"

61. Bonner, *Selected Works*, 573.

62. Bonner, "What Was Llull Up To?"

63. Sales, 2.7.

64. Sales, 2.9.

65. Sales, 2.9.

66. It is for this reason that I prefer the terms "environment," "instrument," and "mechanism" to "tool" when designing mechanical or algorithmic aids to humanities interpretation. An "environment" is by definition an inhabitable space. An "instrument" is played as well as used, and a "mechanism" is a system that can be opened up for analysis and adjustment. "Tool," on the other hand, implies self-containment and inviolability.

67. Zweig, 20.

68. A notable exception to this older trend is the work of maverick analytical bibliographer Randall McLeod, who comfortably straddles empirical and interpretive genres in the same way that writers like Susan Howe blend poetic practice and criticism.

With Technology

EIGHT

Making and Playing with Models

Using Rapid Prototyping to Explore the History and Technology of Stage Magic

William J. Turkel and Devon Elliott

At sites around the world, self-identified makers, crafters, hackers, "edu-punks," and DIY (do-it-yourself) fabricators are forming a community that is in the process of taking on all of the hallmarks of a new social movement.[1] The campaign is probably best summed up by *MAKE* magazine: "we celebrate your right to tweak, hack, and bend any technology to your will." *MAKE* is published by O'Reilly Media, whose motto is "spreading the knowledge of technology innovators." In addition to *MAKE*, O'Reilly also publishes a popular series of books on hacking (e.g., Tom Igoe's *Making Things Talk*) and hosts blogs and forums.[2] Articles in *MAKE* profile prominent makers, crafters, and hackers and provide step-by-step instruction in building projects at a variety of skill levels. The magazine also editorializes against practices like the copy restriction of software and media and the confiscation of Swiss army knives and multi-tools in airports, and in favor of the open source ethos and of products that invite users "to look inside and see the moving parts . . . make repairs and improvements, and even harvest components once the product ceases to be useful."[3]

O'Reilly sponsors a national meeting (the Maker Faire) and provides publicity for local hacker-artist groups like Dorkbot, which meets in about eighty cities worldwide, including Vancouver, Toronto, Ottawa, and Montreal.[4] In addition to participating in real-world activities, community members are able to perform online in a variety of forums—including a do-it-yourself instruction website called *Instructables*—rehearsing core values of sharing and openness, resourcefulness, a can-do attitude, and a willingness to open the black box. If they wish, they can even buy T-shirts with slogans like "If you can't open it, you don't own it," "re-use, re-cycle, re-make," "hacking is not a crime!" and "Make: void your warranty, violate a user agreement, fry a circuit, blow a fuse, poke an eye out . . ." When President Barack Obama celebrated "the risk-takers, the doers, the makers of things" in his 2009 inaugural address, O'Reilly immediately emblazoned the phrase on a T-shirt.[5]

The maker community extends far outside the ambit of O'Reilly Media, of course, overlapping with many other interest groups. It includes a global network of hackerspaces, workshops operated by community members who wish to share ideas, tools, and techniques, and to work collaboratively on projects.[6] It includes efforts to crowdsource the production of everything from automobiles to prosthetics.[7] And, most relevant to the work we describe here, it includes groups of people dedicated to producing software (like the programming language Processing), hardware platforms (like Arduino), and computer-controlled machines that are able to print small 3D objects (like RepRap).[8] We discuss all three of these technologies below. In each case, the designers and makers profess an ethic of open source, making tutorials, plans, software, and construction details freely available online.[9]

The present conjuncture—of making as a new social movement, of easy-to-use and freely available platforms that invite modification, of detailed online instructions for doing just about anything—makes it almost costless for historians and other humanists to research, teach, learn, play, and experiment with new technologies. These include digital technologies, of course, the blogs, wikis, podcasts, games, immersive worlds, and social media described by other contributors to this volume.[10] We argue that the time is right for humanists to play and experiment with technologies of material production, too.

Humanistic Fabrication

Manufacturers have been at the center of innovation in material products for centuries, but the work of researchers such as Eric von Hippel suggests that the balance is shifting somewhat.[11] As the cost of computers and software has fallen, it has become possible for individuals to acquire the equipment necessary to design complicated artifacts and electronics using computer-aided design (CAD) software, and to program simulations and test and measurement routines for prototypes. Some people are motivated to do this, because, as von Hippel notes, the only group that benefits directly from innovation are the users of a good or service. "All others (here lumped under the term 'manufacturers') must sell innovation-related products or services to users, indirectly or directly, in order to profit from innovations."[12] There is thus a strong incentive for users to be able to innovate on their own behalf, and the result has been a gradual "democratization of innovation" as more and more users have become involved in improving the services and products that they rely on. Furthermore, von Hippel's work shows that communities of user-innovators are much more likely than manufacturers to give away information about their own developments, creating a public good.

In a number of fields of design, this transition has already occurred. The widespread availability of very inexpensive laser and photo printers, the incorporation of desktop publication features into word processing software, and the free availability of photographs, fonts, and clip art make it possible for just about anyone with a modicum of equipment to produce a pamphlet, newsletter, poster, or booklet that has the same high quality as the professional products of two decades ago. There are even online tutorials to teach the fundamentals of vector illustration, coloring, photographic manipulation, kerning, and so on. This is not to say that professional graphic design has disappeared, merely that professional designers must now distinguish themselves in a sea of amateurs. Digital cameras and sites like *Flickr* have changed the landscape of photography; digital video cameras, blogs, and *YouTube* have changed journalism; and so on.

Techniques of material fabrication are taught professionally through apprenticeship, trade schools, art and design schools, and university programs. But here we are not primarily concerned with the training and accreditation of a carpenter, welder, industrial designer, or mechanical engineer. There are a handful of people in the humanities who already have a deep professional background in one or more kinds of fabrication. There are far more humanists, however, who cook, sew, repair and restore furniture or automobiles, paint with acrylics, do home renovations, build dollhouses or rockets or model ships, design jewelry, or practice any of a thousand other kinds of making as hobby or avocation. But there is very little evidence for any of this creative activity in their scholarly output. One of the legacies of professionalization is the idea that we have particular areas of "competence" that are certified by the training or licensing that we have undergone, and that we are not permitted to stray outside these boundaries in our teaching or research. Ridiculous! Barring a tiny number of situations that involve public health or safety, national security, or something of the sort, we can and should experiment with whatever techniques we find most congenial for learning and teaching. Whenever possible, we should encourage our students to do the same.

In the past few decades, the cost of commercial computer-controlled rapid prototyping and fabrication devices dropped precipitously. News articles from the early 1990s put the price of an entry-level commercial setup close to the million-dollar mark. By the turn of the millennium, an equivalent system could be had for about a tenth as much. Within the decade, 3D printer kits for home-built fabricators like RepRap or Maker-Bot could be purchased for $5,000 or less.[13] Meanwhile, services like Shapeways provide low-cost on-demand 3D printing for individuals.[14] As with the earlier case of desktop publishing, this democratization of innovation will certainly not lead to the demise of professional industrial design and manufacturing, but it will open up the space of material fabrication and customization to the masses.[15]

Like some commercially available 3D printers, the RepRap works by precisely positioning a tiny bead of molten plastic. If you have never seen one in action, imagine a robot wielding a tiny hot-glue gun, building up a 3D object one layer at a time. An example can be seen in figure 8.1. Unlike the commercial alternatives, however, the creators of RepRap are on a mission. The ultimate goal of these do-it-yourself manufacturers is to create a science-fiction-inspired replicator: a device that can make anything, including all of its own component parts. Many of them imagine a world far beyond the limitations of present-day technology, when people will have "wealth without money." When an appliance breaks, its owner will be able to scan the broken part and print a replacement. Whenever anyone needs something, they will be able to download free plans and print out a copy. When they are done with it, they will recycle the components to be used for something new. This imagined future is one of cradle-to-cradle manufacturing,[16] mass customization[17] and democratized innovation.[18] Some of the claims made on behalf of personal fabrication are extreme; that the practice will, for example, "bring down global capitalism, start a second industrial revolution and save the environment."[19]

Although we suspect that none of those things will actually come to pass, RepRaps are fun to play with and good to think with, and they beg to be understood in historical context. Two such contexts come to mind immediately: the industrial revolution and the birth of the personal computer in the 1970s. Both developments were stimulated by a rapidly changing landscape of costs and opportunities. During the industrial revolution, an unprecedented ability to harness and concentrate energy led to the growth of capital-intensive factories. The revolution in personal computing was stimulated, in part, by the availability of inexpensive electronic modules in the form of integrated circuits. In both cases, amateurs played a very important role in innovation.[20] The information costs associated with innovation have also been very different at different times, and a historically nuanced understanding of manufacturing and innovation in the present moment will

Fig 8.1: Photograph of MakerBot printing. Photo courtesy of Devon Elliott.

have to take these changes into account, particularly as humanists become makers themselves.[21]

We are interested in personal fabrication as historians, and we know that if we want to understand technical practices or material artifacts, we need to go beyond words to the things themselves.[22] This is imperative because there are good reasons for believing that much technical and scientific knowledge is tacit and embodied, and thus learned only with difficulty (and not by reading).[23] Peter Dear, writing about the technical tracts of the medieval and early modern periods, says:

> The historian William Eamon, in his studies of such literature, has characterized these "technical recipe books" as a means whereby the "veil of mystery" that had hitherto surrounded the practical crafts was lifted, so that ordinary people could see that the craftsman was not possessed of some arcane wisdom, but simply had knowledge of a set of techniques that, in principle, anyone could apply. This is not a notion that should be taken for granted, however. Studies in recent decades of the ways in which expert knowledge is constituted and passed on suggest that practitioners do indeed possess skills that are communicated only with difficulty. Their practical knowledge is

often unlearnable from the eviscerated accounts that appear in the pages of experimental papers (in the sciences) or technical manuals (in skilled craftwork in general). Thus, if Eamon is right, the growing sense that developed during the sixteenth century, as a consequence of printing and its uses, that practical craft knowledge ("know how") can be reduced to straightforward rules of procedure that can be acquired readily from books, was to a large degree an illusion. If this is so, it is an illusion that we have inherited.[24]

Historians, for the most part, have tended to ignore this problem of learning tacit knowledge, and continue to concentrate on the representational sources with which they are most comfortable, even at the cost of being excluded from a crucial understanding of their subject matter.[25]

Beyond understanding personal fabrication in historical context, we believe that it can play a central role in a new, experimental approach to the practice of history. In our work, we combine elements of traditional historical methodology with a reflexive pedagogical approach inspired by recent work in science and technology studies, and the hands-on, critical making that characterizes experimental archaeology. We follow Cyrus Mody and David Kaiser, who argue that pedagogy is a "central analytic category," not "merely as formalized classroom teaching techniques . . . but rather as the entire constellation of training exercises through which novices become working scientists and engineers." (From this perspective, pedagogy is central to our own development as humanists, too.) Participation in the reproduction of a community of practitioners holds out the hope of learning "broadly similar values, norms, and self understandings . . . not (or not only) in the abstract, but as enacted through daily interactions within specific settings."[26]

A related path to tacit knowledge is through the critical, reflexive practices of making that characterize experimental archaeology.[27] As John Coles noted in the early 1970s, many of the nineteenth-century founders of archaeology experimented with stone tools, reproducing artifacts as a way of understanding the conditions of their manufacture and use. Over time, the experimental method has become more widely used in the discipline, as researchers attempt to replicate earlier methods of growing crops; storing and preparing food; building houses; working with stone, wood, bone, antler, metals and other materials; and making paper, pottery, and musical instruments. We might ask, where is the experimental history to match this practice in archaeology?

There have been precedents, of course, in both research and teaching. Generations of intro physics students have followed in Galileo's footsteps by attempting to determine the law of motion using an inclined plane.

Historians of science have not always believed that Galileo performed the experiment that he reported, however. In the 1950s, Alexander Koyré described Galileo's experiments as "completely worthless," due to the "amazing and pitiful poverty of [his] experimental means." This view was subsequently challenged by Thomas Settle, who rebuilt the apparatus "essentially as Galileo described it," and recorded results in accordance with Galileo's. A further refinement was later provided by Stillman Drake. The historian of physics Robert Crease writes:

> By carefully studying a page of Galileo's notebook, Drake concluded that Galileo actually had arrived at the law using the inclined-plane method, but by marking out the time in a way that seems to have taken advantage of his strong musical training. As a competent lute player, Galileo could keep a beat precisely; a good musician could easily tap out a rhythm more accurately than any water timer could measure. Drake determined that Galileo had set frets into the track of the inclined plane—moveable gut strings of the kind used on early string instruments. When a ball was rolled down the track and passed over a fret, he would hear a slight clicking noise. Galileo, in Drake's speculative reconstruction, then adjusted the frets so that a ball released at the top struck the frets in a regular tempo—which for the typical song of the day was just over half a second per beat. Once Galileo had marked out fairly exact time intervals, thanks to his musical ear, all he would have to do would be to measure the distances between frets.[28]

Contemporary researchers like H. Otto Sibum, Mel Usselman, and Peter Heering have greatly extended the use of reconstruction, experiment, and reenactment in writing the history of science.[29] Their work provides new ways of understanding laboratory practices and the development of instrumentation, and directs attention to the importance of sensation and perception, material culture, and performance. Bruno Latour famously argued that scientific knowledge becomes encapsulated in "black boxes"; remaking experimental apparatus provides one way of temporarily reversing that process.[30] This kind of practice can also be brought into the classroom.[31] At MIT, Jed Buchwald and Louis Bucciarelli offered a "historic experimentation" course where students did a close reading of primary sources from the history of physics, then attempted to reconstruct the apparatus described and to replicate the reported results.[32] For a number of years, Anne McCants has been working with various colleagues to offer hands-on courses on subjects like ancient and medieval cooking, and spinning and weaving fabrics.[33] Outside the academy, crafters and reenactors make chain mail,[34] fire matchlock muskets,[35] grow heirloom vegetables,[36] take daguerreotypes,[37] and engage with the material past in an almost unimaginable variety of other ways.[38]

Barbie and Ken Play Penn and Teller

As an example of the utility of rapid prototyping and the experimental method, we present an extended case study related to Devon Elliott's doctoral work on the history and technology of stage magic.[39] Working together, we have created a number of historical illusions at model scale. These models serve as demonstration devices; have a playful, toy-like quality; and are pedagogically comparable to various kinds of other model-scale teaching tools, like scale mechanisms or crime scene dioramas.[40] By re-creating magical apparatus on dollhouse scale we are able to address a number of research questions: What design decisions were due to the constraints of particular media? How can we use the material culture perspective to read the production of various artifacts, including antique originals, modern replicas, and cheap plastic knockoffs? What new variations can we devise? How do these variations relate to the modern practices of stage magic? How does the possibility of mass customization change the art of illusion? What does the repeatability of a particular illusion or effect tell us about the history of sensation or perception? How does our own engagement with fabrication change our experience of what is methodologically possible?

There are a number of different types of magical effects but here we concentrate on two icons of performance: levitation and vanishing.[41] In the early nineteenth century, Jean-Eugène Robert-Houdin popularized an illusion known as *la suspension éthéréenne* (ethereal suspension) at his Soireés Fantastiques. The performer's son was suspended under his arms by two braces and apparently given a dose of ether. After succumbing to the effects of the drug, one of the supports was removed, and yet the boy remained stationary on the other. His legs were then lifted and his body tilted horizontally to the floor, where it remained suspended unnaturally on a single support.[42] Although Robert-Houdin's performance appeared to defy the laws of nature, the fact that it required one visible support under his son's arm was considered to be a technological weakness, especially when the method was published by Hoffmann in the popular press in the latter half of the nineteenth century. (In magicians' terms, a suspension differs from a levitation by showing some means of visible support.)

Suspensions were not only a popular form of magical performance, but had been a part of English literary culture from the eighteenth century onward. Accounts of magical feats from India—and one in particular, which became known as the Indian Rope Trick—often took the form of suspensions. In that trick, a rope was cast into the air, where it remained as if attached to some invisible support. A boy climbed the rope and disappeared at the top. There was a commotion, and his dismembered limbs fell to the ground. Put into a basket, the remains of the boy were often restored, completing a death and resurrection performance. Although the trick was recounted in travelogues and other writings, the historian Peter Lamont has shown that such a performance likely never occurred, but was rather a literary construction, a legend.[43] Even the Indian Rope Trick maintained a connection to the ground, however. Were it to be performed, attention would likely be drawn to the rope, and tracing the form of the rope would lead spectators to potential methods for accomplishing the feat. As a matter of practice, magicians and illusion designers strive to eliminate such weaknesses when designing effects. A stunt that appeared more magical would eliminate any visible means of support, and thus would appear to be a true levitation.

The first route to the performance of levitation came from suspension. The person to be levitated wore a harness hidden by clothing. The harness was attached at a single point to a rigid support hidden from the view of the audience by the bodies of the magician and the person levitated.[44] Over time, magicians refined the performance to mask the support mechanism and draw attention away from it. The support was better fitted to the magician's body. Even with refinements, the magician's movements were limited by the need to hide the apparatus, and a stationary, physical prop on the stage was also often employed to hide the support. It was still a weakness of sorts. If a spectator accepted the idea that levitation required a hidden support, he or she only needed to study the form of the performance to deduce where the support must be.

Two of the premiere magicians of the late nineteenth and early twentieth centuries, John Nevil Maskelyne in England and Harry Kellar in America, both worked to improve the technology of levitation.[45] Maskelyne was fortunate enough to have his own performance laboratory in the form of the Egyptian Hall stage.[46] Continuously performing there, he could create and test new illusions that were improved iteratively and tailored to his venue. One of Maskelyne's innovations was to introduce a "gooseneck," an S-shaped bended form between body and support that allowed solid hoops to be passed over the levitated body, creating a more convincing impression of floating. Maskelyne's other discovery was that thin threads on the stage were invisible to spectators. Each could support a small amount of weight, and when united, could lift a substantial load. Combining the gooseneck with a network of threads, Maskelyne revolutionized levitation, albeit in a form that was difficult to balance and tune and could not be easily moved from one venue to another.[47]

In re-creating scale models of Maskelyne's levitation, we wanted to work from a detailed description of the methods that he used to achieve his particular effect. Bruce Armstrong's *Encyclopedia of Suspensions and Levitations*, published for magicians in 1976, is a good resource. Numerous methods are described along with drawings from earlier plans, and stage movements and performance details are given where available. We found that material characteristics such as rigidity and elasticity played a significant role in the believability of the levitation illusion at model scale. When Elliott printed a small gooseneck out of ABS on one of our MakerBots, it flexed when weighted, and the downward deflection of the levitating body was enough to spoil the illusion of floating. The original plans called for iron rod, one inch in diameter. To achieve a believable effect, we replaced the plastic support with a more rigid one made from a coat hanger. One of these levitation models can be seen in figure 8.2. The process of photographing our models also underlined the importance of stage lighting. An intense light from the wrong direction can cause the hidden support to cast telltale shadows.

Nineteenth- and early twentieth-century stage magic drew on both technoscience—especially the class of effects that were previously known as "natural magic"—and spiritualism. The study of stage magic offers researchers one advantage that the study of spiritualistic phenomena does not: magicians often explained the secrets of their illusions somewhere.[48] Methods were kept from audiences, of course, but shared among magicians in the form of books, journals, and plans that explained how to build the necessary apparatus. These directions guided a magician in constructing his (or much less frequently her) own device, but important details such as dimensions or materials were often unspecified, thus keeping part of the performance a secret. Only by making a device and experimenting with it could one eventually re-create the feat. Thus by building and performing illusions based on these incomplete plans, we are able to partially re-create the pedagogical context of stage magicians in this period. Later, a commercial manufacturing system allowed aspiring magicians to purchase apparatus for accomplishing illusions, and this appealed to an increasing number of amateurs, domestic performers who entertained family members in the home. These amateurs also had access to a growing DIY magic literature. As magical devices became commercialized, the hands-on, constructive element of magical practice was eliminated. The widespread availability of magical apparatus allowed a new breed of magicians to gain a prominent position in venues, like vaudeville, which drew a mass audience.[49]

The other performer who worked to improve the technology of levitation was the American star Harry Kellar. Kellar visited London annually,

Fig 8.2: Photograph of Maskelyne-style levitation model. Photo courtesy of William J. Turkel.

often accompanied by his chief mechanic, in order to study the new illusions that his rival Maskelyne was showing at Egyptian Hall. Kellar viewed Maskelyne's levitation from the audience a number of times, but he was unable to discern its method. Finally he simply walked on stage during a performance, viewed the apparatus up close, then coerced one of Maskelyne's assistants into explaining to him what he had just seen. Returning to the United States, he is rumored to have employed the Otis Elevator Company to help refine the idea and to make it work.[50] The illusion went on to become a significant feature of Kellar's show, featuring prominently on his playbills and advertising lithographs.[51]

Maskelyne's version of the levitation was precise and delicate, well-suited to a single venue but impractical for touring. Kellar refined the levitation so that it could be set up and dismantled readily at each venue that he played. (A poster advertising Kellar's levitation appears in figure 8.3.) Since each stage had different dimensions and resources, Kellar's version of levitation needed

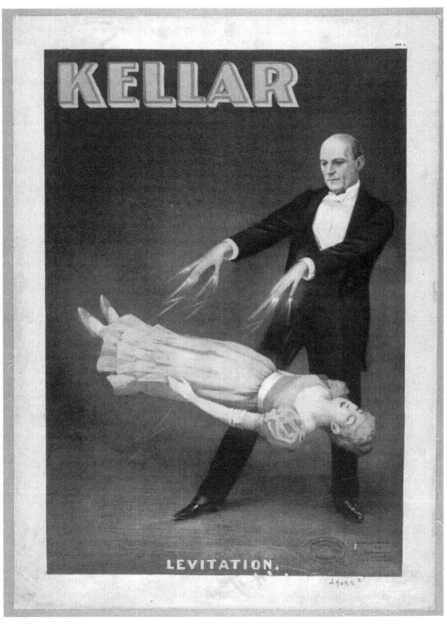

Fig 8.3: Kellar lithograph. "Levitation" Kellar poster. Strobridge Lith. Co., ca. 1894.

to be adaptable and robust. When Kellar retired, he named Howard Thurston as his successor and passed a levitation apparatus on to him. Thurston continued to perform the levitation, created lengthier presentations for it, and eventually, to Kellar's horror, invited witnesses from the audience on stage to view the levitation.[52] The illusion that Thurston was showing to audience members was not Kellar's final version of the levitation. He had continued to improve it for touring, eliminating the need to cut holes in the stage floor if none were already available or it was impossible to make such alterations. Dismayed by the direction that Thurston was taking, Kellar sold the improved levitation to Harry Blackstone.[53] Other magicians imitated Kellar's gall as well as his illusions. Carter the Great hired one of Thurston's stagehands in order to learn the secret, and then wrote to Kellar to ask how to treat the lines in order to camouflage them on stage. Incensed, Kellar did not respond.[54] Kellar's secrets appeared in print in *The Life and Mysteries of the Celebrated Dr. "Q"* and a magic company in California advertised plans for the illusion, ensuring that it would continue to be performed as long as magic was popular on the stage.[55] Installing, tuning, and using the apparatus was finicky, however, and the method went out of fashion. It is rarely seen today.[56]

In re-creating models of the more elaborate levitations, we started with commercially available toys and used their measurements to determine the scale of other components. A levitation model scaled to a pair of commercial toys is shown in figure 8.4. The bodies of performers were particularly important in stage magic because the apparatus was often fitted to a particular person, limiting the number of other people who could use it. If a performer stopped working with a particular magician, her (or much less frequently his) replacement would have to have similar measurements and range of flexibility. The illusion designer Guy Jarrett used the dimensions of his own body as a basis for designing his apparatus, and discovered that hiding spaces could be made much smaller than previously thought. Audiences tended to assume that certain spaces were much too small to hold a person, which made illusions more convincing.

Our choice of toys also raised questions about the role of contemporary models in understanding historical events. Strict accuracy would suggest using a male magician with a female assistant, dressed in period costumes. The heyday of stage magic was also associated with stereotypical, exoticized, and frankly racist depictions of Asian peoples and culture: for example, the "Marvelous Chinese Conjurer Chung Ling Soo" was actually discovered upon his death in 1918 to be a New Yorker named William Ellsworth Robinson.[57] We did not want to reproduce the gender roles or Orientalism of our historical actors unthinkingly, however, but rather to problematize them. So one of our model magicians looks roughly Mephistophelean, but will

Fig 8.4: Photograph of floating levitation model. Photo courtesy of Devon Elliott.

be recognizable to some as a character of twenty-first-century fiction, and rather than working with a female model assistant, he levitates a block of wood and disappears a gender-indeterminate mummy inspired by cheesy horror movies. For other model magicians and assistants we used posable stick figures, anthropomorphic but lacking most other detail. Each choice is intended to provide entry points into further reflective discussion. What if we made Barbie the magician and Ken the assistant? What if a giant rabbit pulled a magician from a hat? And so on.

The process of building more elaborate models also foregrounded the importance of the stage itself as a venue for creating illusions. How did space, seating, lines of sight, viewing distance, or the prestige of the venue affect the perceptions of the audience? Stages were not entirely fixed: magicians might cut holes or traps to facilitate their methods. When Harry Blackstone toured, his stagehands were happy to use stages that Thurston had once performed on because Thurston's people had already cut holes in the stage for the levitation wires.[58] Stages also provided spaces to hide assistants and apparatus behind, below, and above the visible section. As we build more complicated models, we are drawn into the need to model the surrounding context of the stage, too.[59] We substitute black thread for wires. In place of hydraulic lifts we use commercially available hobby gear-motors and servos. In place of human assistance, we use the open source microcontroller Arduino. Arduino has roughly the functionality of an early 1980s-era computer, but costs less than $50, fits into the space about the size of a deck of cards, and can be easily hooked up to sensors and actuators. We use Arduinos extensively in building interactive exhibits of all sorts. We can program an Arduino to turn on and off lights, draw and close curtains, play sound effects, raise and lower pieces of apparatus, and do just about anything else that we need to do to further an illusion. In addition to printing out custom plastic parts on a RepRap, we fabricate stage and apparatus from foamcore, peg board, masonite, lightweight woods like basswood and balsa, metal construction kits (e.g., VEX robotics), and other modeling materials. After building a prototype by hand, we have the option of laser scanning pieces to create a 3D model, and then milling out further versions with small CNC (computer numerator control) mills and lathes. Rapid prototyping allows us to iteratively improve stage and effects, in much the same way that Maskelyne was able to continually improve his own equipment and performances. In keeping with the open source ethos of the community, we also share ideas and improvements in blogs and forums and on sites like *Thingiverse* and *Instructables*.[60]

A second type of illusion that we have re-created at model scale is the vanish. For centuries, magicians have vanished small objects such as coins and cork balls using sleight-of-hand.[61] In the nineteenth century, magicians directed their attention toward vanishing the human body. Illusions such as Pepper's Ghost used optics to make spectral images appear, transform, and disappear; other effects relied on carefully placed mirrors.[62] In 1886, Buatier de Kolta performed L'escamotage d'une dame en personne vivante (the vanishing lady). A newspaper was unfolded on the stage and a chair placed on the newspaper. A woman sat down and was covered with a sheet. Her form could be seen through the sheet right up to the moment the magician pulled it away, when she apparently vanished. The trick was front-page news in London for a full month. Karen Beckman writes that "this spectacle of vanishing both reflects and refutes Victorian anxieties about female surplus, offering us important insights about Britain's relationship not only with the early feminist movement but with domestic political issues of unemployment and the care of the poor."[63]

While rebuilding a simple vanishing cabinet, we encountered many familiar questions in somewhat altered form: choice of actors, staging, lighting, materials, mechanisms; directing attention and controlling lines of sight; hiding the gimmick; and so on. A photo sequence of the vanishing cabinet model appears in figure 8.5. Vanishing also raises epistemological questions. How do you communicate the idea that something is no longer present, especially when it really does remain but is unseen? An object (or person) is introduced

Fig 8.5: Four photographs of vanishing cabinet. Photo courtesy of William J. Turkel.

and made familiar. When it disappears, its absence has to be emphasized by what remains. As one builds and works with the models, one takes on roles of apparatus builder, magician, assistant, and audience member.

Spaces for Making and Playing

It is a sad fact that, in North America at least, most of the spaces available for graduate teaching and learning in the humanities are less suitable for hands-on making and experimenting than just about any kindergarten classroom in the country. We know that this kind of activity is crucial for child development, but is there any evidence that it is less crucial for people in other age groups? For at least a century, scholars like John Dewey, Jane Addams, and the members of the Bauhaus and the Foxfire projects have argued (in different ways, of course) that useful making and doing are an essential part of learning. This is not something new, it is something we seem condemned to repeat. Teachers or students who want to introduce hands-on work into the humanities often face an initial problem of finding suitable spaces to make things; to store tools, supplies, and work-in-progress; and to demonstrate final projects. Part of the challenge of playful learning is getting out of—and getting rid of—carpeted beige cubbyholes designed for office labor.

Making and playing with models is one part of our wider practice as researchers, teachers, and (perpetual) students. In classrooms and workshops we ask people to consider how history would be different if it were presented in the form of an appliance: we turn on a tap and water comes out; what if we could turn on a device and it "dispensed" history? How does our historical consciousness change when ideas are presented in the form of a toy, game, gadget, device, situation, or environment? How does our imaginative engagement with material culture allow us to communicate tacit knowledge or more sensuous understandings of the past? Allowed to brainstorm, students come up with delightful projects, some realizable and some pure fantasy. Public history graduate students at Western University in Ontario, for example, imagined

- *Heritage knitting needles.* Passed down within a family, they remember every pattern that they have been used to create. You might use them to knit a copy of the same blanket that your grandmother made for your mother when she was a baby.
- *Reverse "babel fish."* Put this device in your ear, and everyone around you will appear to be speaking Old English. Rather than a translating device, this helps to communicate the idea that "the past is a foreign country."
- *Yelling documents.* A bad-tempered microfilm reader that can correct you when you make an untenable interpretation of a source.
- *Tangible spray.* An aerosol that creates a cloud of mist. Reach into the cloud to feel the past. When it dissolves, you are left grasping thin air.

In our interactive exhibit design course, graduate students learn to create 3D representations by drafting with *SketchUp* and by scanning with laser or touch probe. They can then go on to materialize their designs in paper using a CNC cutter like the Craft Robo, in plastic with MakerBots, in wood or acrylic with a laser cutter, or in various media through subtractive machining. They can then combine these digital and physical objects with laptop computers and electronic components like Arduino to create museum exhibits that have interactive, tangible, or ambient components. In recent classes, students have created a working model of Sputnik, a simple robot that re-creates historic plays on a tabletop hockey game, and a wearable museum exhibit, among many other projects.[64]

In the context of a public history graduate program, we have been fortunate to work with librarians, curators, K–12 teachers, and educational technology specialists who have access to different spaces and different mindsets. We have also found a lot of enthusiasm in local communities of artists, crafters, and hackers. If you want to do something similar and are drawing blank stares in your own department, try working from the outside in: join a hackerspace or crafting group and start there. Or invite like-minded individuals to work with you in your garage, your basement, or your uncle's barn.[65] When you have something to share, put it online, blog or tweet about it, and show it to your colleagues, students, or classmates. Everyone is welcome in the DIY movement, and the most important thing that we tweak, hack, and bend to our will may be the process of learning itself. Remember, "if you can't open it, you don't own it."[66]

NOTES

Generous support for this work was provided in part by SSHRC (Research Development Initiatives grants, 2005–7, 2009–11); by Image, Text, Sounds and Technology grants (2007–9, 2009–11); and by Western University (Fellowship in Teaching Innovation, 2005; Research Western, 2007–12).

1. Charles Tilly, *Social Movements, 1768–2004* (Boulder, Colo.: Paradigm, 2004). According to Tilly, a new social movement is characterized by the innovative synthesis of three things: a campaign; a repertoire of performances; and displays of worthiness, unity, numbers, and commitment. Each of these is evident in the community of makers, widely construed. Makers also constitute a "recursive public" in the sense of Christopher M. Kelty, *Two Bits: The Cultural Significance of Free Software* (Durham, N.C.: Duke University Press, 2008).

2. Tom Igoe, *Making Things Talk* (Sebastopol: O'Reilly, 2007). O'Reilly also published a companion magazine called *CRAFT*, now defunct, and regularly updates a site on craft projects, http://craftzine.com.

3. Dale Dougherty, "Maker Friendly," *MAKE: Technology on Your Time* 3 (2005): 7.

4. See the Dorkbot website, accessed July 31, 2012, http://dorkbot.org. Dorkbot also meets in Second Life.

5. Barack Obama, "President Barack Obama's Inaugural Address," *The White House Blog* (January 21, 2009), accessed July 31, 2012, http://www.whitehouse.gov/blog /inaugural-address/. For the t-shirt, see http://blog.makezine.com/archive/2009/01 /winner_make_the_risktakers_the_doer.html, accessed April 16, 2010.

6. See http://hackerspaces.org/wiki/, accessed April 16, 2010. Hackerspaces have already sprung up in many Canadian cities. See, for example, VHS in Vancouver, accessed July 31, 2012, http://vancouver.hackspace.ca/doku.php; THINK|HAUS in Hamilton, accessed July 31, 2012, http://www.thinkhaus.org/; Kwartzlab in Kitchener-Waterloo,

accessed July 31, 2012, http://kwartzlab.ca/; unLab in London, accessed July 31, 2012, http://unlondon.ca; or hacklab.to in Toronto, accessed July 22, 2010, http://hacklab .to/. Elliott is a member of the London unLab.

7. For automobiles, see Local Motors, http://www.local-motors.com, accessed April 16, 2010; Chris Anderson, "In the Next Industrial Revolution, Atoms are the New Bits," *Wired* 18, no. 2 (February 2010), accessed July 31, 2012, http://www.wired .com/magazine/2010/01/ff_newrevolution/; Joel Johnson, "Atoms are Not Bits; Wired is Not a Business Magazine," *Gizmodo* (January 26, 2010), accessed July 31, 2012, http://gizmodo.com/5457461/atoms-are-not-bits-wired-is-not-a-business-magazine. For prosthetics, see The Open Prosthetics Project, http://openprosthetics.org, accessed April 16, 2010.

8. See Processing, accessed July 31, 2012, http://processing.org; Arduino, accessed July 31, 2012, http://arduino.cc; RepRap, accessed July 31, 2012, http://reprap.org.

9. Steven Weber, *The Success of Open Source* (Cambridge, Mass.: Harvard University Press, 2005); Phillip Torrone, "Open Source Hardware, What is It? Here's a Start . . . ," *MAKE: Blog* (April 23, 2007).

10. For games, see chapters in this volume by Gouglas et al. (chapter 6), Graham (chapter 10), Kee and Graham (chapter 13), McCall (chapter 11), and Compeau and MacDougall (chapter 4); Levy and Dawson (chapter 3) and Dunae and Lutz (chapter 14) describe immersive worlds; the other contributors invoke a wide variety of other online and digital media.

11. Eric von Hippel, *Democratizing Innovation* (Cambridge, Mass.: MIT Press, 2005); idem, *The Sources of Innovation* (Oxford: Oxford University Press, 1988); idem, "The Dominant Role of Users in the Scientific Instrument Innovation Process," *Research Policy* 5, no. 3 (1976): 212–39.

12. von Hippel, *Democratizing Innovation,* 3. Of course, the same logic suggests that humanists will be best served by software that they create for themselves. Ramsay's chapter in this volume provides a particularly striking example.

13. By comparison, the first widely available laser printer, the Apple LaserWriter, had a starting price around $7,000 in 1985. A MakerBot, a RepRap derivative kit, could be purchased in 2010 for U.S. $750 at http://makerbot.com, accessed April 16, 2010. Between the two of us, we have already built a RepRap and four MakerBots, have helped to build three or four other MakerBots, and have two more RepRaps under construction.

14. See Shapeways, accessed April 16, 2010, http://www.shapeways.com.

15. Cf. the exchange between Anderson and Johnson.

16. William McDonough and Michael Braungart, *Cradle to Cradle: Remaking the Way We Make Things* (New York: North Point, 2002).

17. Stephen Kieran and James Timberlake, *Refabricating Architecture: How Manufacturing Methodologies are Poised to Transform Building Construction* (New York: McGraw-Hill, 2004).

18. Neil Gershenfeld, *FAB: The Coming Revolution on Your Desktop—From Personal Computers to Personal Fabrication* (New York: Basic, 2005); *When Things Start to Think* (New York: Henry Holt, 2000).

19. James Randerson, "Put Your Feet Up, Santa, the Christmas Machine Has Arrived," *The Guardian* (November 25, 2006).

20. For the industrial revolution, see, for example, Anthony F. C. Wallace, *Rockdale: The Growth of an American Village in the Early Industrial Revolution* (New York:

Knopf, 1978); Jenny Uglow, *The Lunar Men: Five Friends Whose Curiosity Changed the World* (New York: Farrar, Straus and Giroux, 2002); Margaret C. Jacob and Larry Stewart, *Practical Matter: Newton's Science in the Service of Industry and Empire 1687–1851* (Cambridge, Mass.: Harvard University Press, 2004); for personal computers, see Martin Campbell-Kelly and William Aspray, *Computer: A History of the Information Age* (New York: Basic, 1996); Paul E. Ceruzzi, *A History of Modern Computing*, 2nd ed. (Cambridge, Mass.: MIT Press, 2003); Fred Turner, *From Counterculture to Cyberculture: Stewart Brand, the Whole Earth Network, and the Rise of Digital Utopianism* (Chicago: University of Chicago Press, 2006).

21. Pamela O. Long, *Openness, Secrecy, Authorship: Technical Arts and the Culture of Knowledge from Antiquity to the Renaissance* (Baltimore: Johns Hopkins University Press, 2001).

22. Michael S. Mahoney, "Reading a Machine," Ms., Princeton University, 1996, accessed April 18, 2010, http://www.princeton.edu/~hos/h398/readmach/modeltfr.html.

23. Michael Polanyi, *Personal Knowledge: Towards a Post-Critical Philosophy* (Chicago: University of Chicago Press, 1974).

24. Peter Dear, *Revolutionizing the Sciences: European Knowledge and Its Ambitions, 1500–1700* (Princeton, N.J.: Princeton University Press, 2001), 26–27.

25. For a related discussion, see Nowviskie's chapter in this volume about the relationship between procedural work and interpretive work (chapter 7), and the important role of the agent that interprets and performs a given procedure. Nowviskie herself is an active member of a crafting community.

26. Cyrus Mody and David Kaiser, "Scientific Training and the Creation of Scientific Knowledge," in *The Handbook of Science and Technology Studies*, 3rd ed., ed. Edward J. Hackett, Olga Amsterdamska, Michael Lynch, and Judy Wajcman (Cambridge, Mass.: MIT Press, 2008), 378.

27. John Coles, *Archaeology by Experiment* (New York: Charles Scribner's Sons, 1973); Daniel Ingersoll, John E. Yellen, and William Macdonald, eds., *Experimental Archeology* (New York: Columbia University Press, 1977); Heather Margaret-Louise Miller, *Archaeological Approaches to Technology* (Amsterdam: Academic, 2007); Penny Cunningham, Julia Heeb, and Roeland Paardekooper, eds., *Experiencing Archaeology by Experiment* (Oxford: Oxbow, 2008). Some of our colleagues in archaeology practice experimental methods; some do not and have suggested to us that the subdiscipline is in decline. We do not know if that is the case, but if it is we observe that the fortunes of any particular method often have more to do with social factors than effectiveness. We would not be surprised to see the rise of a new generation of experimentalists.

28. Robert P. Crease, *The Prism and the Pendulum: The Ten Most Beautiful Experiments in Science* (New York: Random House, 2004), 50–51.

29. H. Otto Sibum, "Experimental History of Science," in *Museums of Modern Science: Nobel Symposium 112*, ed. Svante Lindqvist (Canton, Mass.: Science History Publications, 1999), 77–86; Melvyn C. Usselman, Alan J. Rocke, Christina Reinhart, and Kelly Foulser, "Restaging Liebig: A Study in the Replication of Experiments," *Annals of Science* 62 (2005): 1–55; Peter Heering, "Regular Twists: Replicating Coulomb's Wire-Torsion Experiments," *Physics in Perspective* 8, no. 1 (March 2006): 52–63.

30. Bruno Latour, *Science in Action: How to Follow Scientists and Engineers through Society* (Cambridge, Mass.: Harvard University Press, 1987).

31. We have recently been in touch with Glen Bull, who is leading a project entitled *Fab@School: A Digital Fabrication Laboratory for the Classroom,* funded in 2010 for K–12 education. See http://www.digitalfabrication.org/ accessed July 25, 2010.

32. Jed Z. Buchwald and Louis Bucciarelli, "Historic Experimentation" (syllabus, Massachusetts Institute of Technology, 1999), accessed April 16, 2010, http://www.aip.org/history/syllabi/experiments.htm.

33. See, for example, Anne McCants and Margo Collett, "Old Food: Ancient and Medieval Cooking" (syllabus, Massachusetts Institute of Technology, 2010); Anne McCants, Margo Collett, and Miranda Knutson, "The Distaff Arts: Medieval Clothing Technology" (syllabus, Massachusetts Institute of Technology, 2010); Lynda Morgenroth and Emily Hiestand, "Medieval Tech: The Vibrant 'Old Ways' of Historian Anne McCants," in *Soundings* (Cambridge, Mass.: MIT School of Humanities, Arts, and Social Sciences, Spring 2010).

34. "Make Chainmail," accessed April 18, 2010, http://www.wikihow.com/Make-Chainmail.

35. *YouTube,* accessed April 18, 2010, http://www.youtube.com/watch?v=2KTS8 PQ06Qo.

36. Seed Savers, accessed April 18, 2010, http://www.seedsavers.org/.

37. Daguerrre, accessed April 18, 2010, http://www.daguerre.org/.

38. Jerome de Groot, *Consuming History: Historians and Heritage in Contemporary Popular Culture* (New York: Routledge, 2009).

39. Elliott is also a practicing magician and a card-carrying member of the International Brotherhood of Magicians. He started performing as a child and has worked at a variety of venues, from birthday parties and street festivals to fairs and exhibitions.

40. For mechanical scale models, see the Kinematic Models for Design Digital Library, accessed April 19, 2010, http://kmoddl.library.cornell.edu/; for crime scene dioramas, see Corinne May Botz, *The Nutshell Studies of Unexplained Death* (New York: Monacelli, 2004); Thomas Mauriello with Ann Darby, *The Dollhouse Murders: A Forensic Expert Investigates 6 Little Crimes* (Upper Saddle River, N.J.: Pi, 2004).

41. For classification, see S. H. Sharpe and Todd Karr, *Neo-Magic Artistry* (Los Angeles: The Miracle Factory, 2000), which includes a reprint of Sharpe's 1932 *Neo Magic,* 43–52; Dariel Fitzkee, *The Trick Brain* (San Rafael: San Rafael House, 1944), 21–31; Peter Lamont and Richard Wiseman, *Magic in Theory: An Introduction to the Theoretical and Psychological Elements of Conjuring* (England, Hatfield: University of Hertfordshire, 1999).

42. Jean-Eugène Robert-Houdin, *Memoirs of Robert-Houdin, Ambassador, Author and Conjurer,* Lascelles Wraxall translation of *Confidences d'un prestidigitateur* (London: Chapman and Hall, 1860), accessed July 30, 2012, http://www.archive.org/details/memoirsofroberth00roberich; Angelo John Lewis Hoffmann, *Modern Magic: A Practical Treatise on the Art of Conjuring* (London: George Routledge and Sons, 1877), accessed July 30, 2010, http://www.archive.org/details/modernmagic00hoffgoog. Simon During, *Modern Enchantments: The Cultural Power of Secular Magic* (Cambridge, Mass.: Harvard University Press, 2002), 129, describes this as "an illusion which provoked angry letters accusing Robert-Houdin of child abuse."

43. Peter Lamont, *The Rise of the Indian Rope Trick: The Biography of a Legend* (London: Little, Brown, 2004). For a discussion of the cruelty apparent in many magical illusions, see During.

44. Bruce Armstrong, ed., *Encyclopedia of Suspensions and Levitations* (Calgary: M. Hades International, 1976); Albert A. Hopkins, ed., and Henry Ridgely Evans, *Magic: Stage Illusions and Scientific Diversions, Including Trick Photography* (New York: Arno, 1977 [1897]), 31–34; Jim Steinmeyer, *Hiding the Elephant: How Magicians Invented the Impossible and Learned to Disappear* (New York: Carroll and Graf, 2003), 164. The illusion shown in figure 8.2 uses a variant of Maskelyne's gooseneck.

45. Magicians themselves tend to think of the period from the 1880s to the 1930s as the golden age of stage magic—for example, see Milbourne Christopher and Maurine Christopher, *The Illustrated History of Magic*, updated ed. (New York: Carroll and Graf, 2006). A much wider perspective is provided by Noel Daniel, Mike Caveney, and Jim Steinmeyer, *Magic, 1400s–1950s* (Köln: Taschen, 2009).

46. Although Maskelyne did not found the stage, he was able to gain control of it and turn it into a venue known for magic. Egyptian Hall was originally established as a museum and exhibit hall, featuring an Egyptian collection.

47. Steinmeyer, *Hiding the Elephant*. Among Maskelyne's other inventions was a public pay toilet that was used a great deal in England.

48. Although spiritualists did describe how to hold séances, query spirits, attempt automatic writing and table rapping, and so on, they explained apparently magical phenomena by reference to spirits, with whom they claimed to be in contact. Spiritualists of the period, like Daniel Douglas Home, used levitation during séances. Peter Lamont, *The First Psychic: The Peculiar Mystery of a Notorious Victorian Wizard* (London: Little, Brown, 2005).

49. Cf. Robert W. Snyder, "The Vaudeville Circuit: A Prehistory of the Mass Audience," in *Audiencemaking: How the Media Create the Audience*, ed. James S. Ettema and D. Charles Whitney (Thousand Oaks, Calif.: Sage, 1994), 215–31; Hoffmann's was one early book that widely exposed the methods and diagrams of magical apparatus.

50. This episode is covered well in Steinmeyer, *Hiding the Elephant*.

51. Marian Hannah Winter, *The Theatre of Marvels*, trans. Charles Meldon (New York: B. Blom, 1964). There are copies of the posters at the Harry Ransom Center of the University of Texas and at the Library of Congress. The image shown here is from the Library of Congress, accessed July 31, 2012, http://www.loc.gov/pictures/resource/var.0259/. It measures 46 cm x 34 cm and was published by the Strobridge Lithography Company of New York around 1894. For other digital copies, see http://www.loc.gov/pictures/resource/var.0258/ and http://www.loc.gov/pictures/resource/var.1896/, accessed July 31 2012.

52. Guy E. Jarrett and Jim Steinmeyer, *The Complete Jarrett* (Burbank: Hahne, 2001 [1936]); Armstrong; Steinmeyer, *Hiding the Elephant*. Armstrong includes a number of other performance details for the levitation: one of Howard Thurston's scripts, music used by different performers during the act, comments from assistants who worked with the illusions, and so on.

53. Armstrong.

54. Steinmeyer, *Hiding the Elephant*.

55. Conlin Alexander, *The Life and Mysteries of the Celebrated Dr. "Q"* (Los Angeles: Alexander, 1921). Republished in Darryl Beckmann, *The Life and Times of Alexander, The Man Who Knows, A Personal Scrapbook* (Rolling Bay, WA: Rolling Bay Press, 1994).

56. It was revived in the 1990s by John Gaughan and Jim Steinmeyer, illusion builders and magic historians, and performed at an invitation-only gathering of elite magicians and magic historians in Los Angeles.

57. Jim Steinmeyer, *The Glorious Deception: The Double Life of William Robinson, aka Chung Ling Soo, the Marvelous Chinese Conjurer* (New York: Carroll and Graf, 2005).

58. Armstrong. This was recounted by one of Blackstone's people.

59. We note in passing that houses, spaceships, secret forts, and a variety of other kinds of environment may be purchased for many commercially available dolls and action figures. This situatedness of play with toys forms an important resource for us, and a direction for further research.

60. See http://thingiverse.com and http://instructables.com, respectively, accessed August 2010.

61. See, for example, Hieronymus Bosch's painting of a magician with a cup and balls set, ca. 1475–80, or Reginald Scot's *Discoverie of Witchcraft*, ca. 1585.

62. Hopkins; Steinmeyer, *Hiding the Elephant.*

63. Karen Redrobe Beckman, *Vanishing Women: Magic, Film, and Feminism* (Durham, N.C.: Duke University Press, 2003), 20.

64. These projects were created by Devon Elliott (Sputnik Model), Jordan Goldstein (Hockey Game), and Dana Johnson (Wearable Exhibit).

65. Hey, it worked for Mickey Rooney and Judy Garland.

66. "The Maker's Bill of Rights," *Make Magazine*, accessed July 31, 2012, http://makezine.com/04/ownyourown/.

NINE

Contests for Meaning

Playing King Philip's War in the Twenty-First Century

Matthew Kirschenbaum

> In a sense, King Philip's War never ended. In other times, in other places, its painful wounds would be reopened, its vicious words spoken again.
>
> —Jill Lepore, *The Name of War*

The historian Jill Lepore's summation of King Philip's War (1675–76)—a conflict many white Americans have never heard of—was again proven prescient in March 2010 when the *Providence Journal* in Rhode Island ran a seemingly improbable story about the plans of a small, Maryland-based board game publisher specializing in historical simulations to release a product based on this oft-overlooked episode in colonial New England history.[1] King Philip was in fact Metacom, the Wampanoag sachem responsible for rallying the northeastern tribes in an ultimately failed attempt to resist increasingly aggressive colonial expansion; the widespread fighting that ensued, featuring scorched-earth tactics reminiscent of the European religious wars, engulfed four separate colonies and led to hundreds of Puritan and as many as five thousand Native American deaths, including that of Metacom himself. (So ferocious was the enmity that his severed hands were brought to the colonial seat of Plymouth for public display.)

The subsequent narration of the conflict was to be no less totalizing. None other than Increase Mather set the terms for how the war would be characterized in print: "That the Heathen people amongst whom we live, and whose Land the Lord God of our Fathers hath given to us for a rightfull Possession, have at sundry times been plotting mischievous devices against that part of the English Israel which is seated in these goings down of the

Sun, no man that is an Inhabitant of any considerable standing can be ignorant."[2] These "mischievous devices" consisted in an unprecedented degree of coordination and common purpose among the native New England tribes, united by the charismatic person of Metacom. The two years of bitter warfare that resulted became instrumental in the construction of a nascent American identity, argues Lepore: "Not all colonists agreed about the causes of the war, or about how it should be waged, but most agreed about what was at stake: their lives, their land, and their sense of themselves."[3]

The war thus defined relations between colonists and natives for generations to come, not only in its immediate political, military, and economic ramifications, but also culturally and indeed textually, through histories like Mather's and the outpouring of other writings that followed (Mary Rowlandson's captivity narrative is perhaps the most famous). The controversy I describe below will therefore be familiar to anyone who pays attention to ongoing projects of cultural identity formation and negotiation. Still, it is clear that the specific status of the artifact in question as a *game* was a major part of what was at issue, a new and (for some) needlessly cruel twist in the oft-contested histories of King Philip's War (the name itself betrays the representational frames that quickly fell into place). Reaction to the *Providence Journal* story, which the vast majority of readers viewed online, was almost instantaneous. Native American groups were outraged, finding the notion of what was initially perceived to be a fun-for-the-whole-family treatment of the topic as gruesome as it was exploitative. John Poniske, the game's designer (and a middle-school history teacher), and his publisher, Multi-Man Publishing, Inc., meanwhile maintained that they were simply interested in presenting the story of the conflict to a wider audience, and that the design was a fair and accurate portrayal of historical events based on appropriately studious research.

King Philip's War (*KPW*) was published later in 2010 with some degree of reconciliation, Poniske with newfound sensitivities and the objectors acknowledging some of its educational potential (see figure 9.1). Its reception in the hobbyist community that was its target audience has ironically been lackluster, the consensus apparently being that it is a good but not great entry in the niche market for tabletop conflict simulations. (The average user rating on *BoardGameGeek*, the widely used hobbyist portal, is 7.01 out of 10 at the time of this writing, placing *KPW* well into the mid-list of the site's rankings of thousands of published war games.) But why did the game arouse such passions in the first place? Does playing the past create expectations different from merely consuming it through books and film? What does the game as published actually teach us about King Philip's War? And did it make a difference that it was a board game (with a paper map,

Fig 9.1: Components of *King Philip's War*, Multi-Man Publishing, 2010. Courtesy of the author.

dice, and cardboard unit tokens) that was causing all of the fuss, instead of a high-end computer game with sophisticated graphics and sound effects?

The Controversy

The public controversy began on March 15, 2010, when the *Providence Journal* published a brief item by a staff writer titled "King Philip's War No Game to Native Americans."[4] It described a title currently up for "pre-order" with Multi-Man Publishing (MMP), which operates via a subscription model, meaning one of its board games is printed only when it accrues a certain number of pledges. While short on details, the piece limned the contours of the debate that would follow. "Colonial players win by gathering points or eliminating King Philip and other Indian leaders. Indian players win by accumulating points or seizing the settlements of Boston and Plymouth," the article explained. Statements from tribal historians from the Narragansett and Nipmuc were included, invoking racism and race war: "The message seems to be, it's still OK to kill Indians." Paula Peters of the Mashpee Wampanoag tribe was quoted as saying that the game "seems to trivialize a very tragic event in our history." Predictably perhaps, the terms of the discussion rapidly polarized: "Would we play a game called The Holocaust?" she added. Several statements are also included from the game's designer, John Poniske, chief among them that he "immediately saw the gaming potential in the historical situation." MMP's Brian Youse is quoted to the effect that the game "tells a story that many people outside of New England don't know." By the end of the piece it also emerged that MMP is co-owned by former Boston Red Sox pitcher Curt Schilling.

Several factors that shaped subsequent discussion are worth pointing out here. The brief description of the game itself, with its emphasis on collecting "points," seemed to lend credence to the charge that it was trivializing or exploiting a troubled and tragic history. Poniske, meanwhile, comes across as more opportunistic than scholarly, seeing mainly good "gaming potential" in the material. Even the improbable detail regarding Schilling seemed calculated to reinforce the binary between hegemonic American mass culture and Native American traditions routinely relegated to the regalia of mascotry.

The article was quickly noticed in the gamer community, where it spawned a lively discussion on Internet forums such as *BoardGameGeek* and *ConSimWorld*. Reaction in these venues was predictable. "I don't see any harm in drawing attention to history, especially one in this time period where more people should be made aware these events even happened" is representative of the more measured strain that, like MMP itself, simply saw the game as a vehicle for historical education packaged in a recreational format.[5] Other responses immediately dialed the rhetoric to an extreme, with foaming accusations of "political correctness" run amok and defiant claims that the best response was to double-down and place an extra order to get the game printed all the sooner (the preorder cost was around $30). Poniske, who remained levelheaded throughout, took the opportunity to offer a more extended statement:

> As a teacher I know that people have different styles of learning. I take advantage of all styles and I firmly believe that simulation-gaming (recreating conflict via cardboard and paper) can turn players into learners. King Philip's War is a case in point. I did not intend to sensationalize anyone's suffering—the exact opposite. I designed the game to present to the world OUTSIDE of New England a tremendous conflict between American natives and the Puritan colonists who encroached on their tribal lands. . . . I love gaming and I love learning. I combined the two so that I could inform and educate, AND perhaps entice players into digging further into details of the conflict. I would submit that the term "game" in and of itself assumes that the

topic is trivialized. On the contrary. There is a world of simulation gaming that allows players insight into the past that they might never otherwise obtain.[6]

The notion that conflict simulation gaming has the potential to offer worthwhile historical insights is one that is finding increasing traction in the literature. Philip Sabin, for example, professor in the War Studies Department at King's College London, regularly uses games designed by himself and his students in his courses on military history. Ironically, as Sabin has argued, it is often the low-tech cardboard and paper-based games that provide a more nuanced experience. The computer games market is dominated by big-budget blockbuster productions: one does not play *Call of Duty* for any real insight into the Normandy landings, but students might very well turn to one of the many dozens of tabletop board games on the subject to help answer the question of why the Allies landed on the Cotentin peninsula and not somewhere else along the coast of France. Playing a game illustrates geography, distances, and variables related to such considerations as supply and the positioning of enemy forces more dynamically than a book or film. Playing a tabletop game in particular allows students to inspect the systems and processes that constitute the rules of the game, and thus its interpretation of the historical record. As Sabin notes, "Since I believe that designing simulations for oneself is a far better way of gaining insight into the dynamics of a real conflict than is simply playing someone else's computer game on that subject, I see the much greater design accessibility of manual simulations as a major reason for their continued production and relevance."[7] Poniske and MMP's claim that *KPW* offered a unique mode of engagement for illuminating this dark corner of New England history is therefore quite defensible, and Poniske has made a point of describing the game as a starting place rather than the final word on the topic.

Some objectors insisted that the game was nothing but an attempt to cash in. But while *KPW* was not going to make anyone rich (profit margins in this niche marketplace are generally slim), there were undeniably other motives at work. For instance, we can return to Poniske's earlier comment that he saw "gaming potential" in the historical narrative. What can this mean? From the standpoint of military history and conflict simulation, the situation is indeed an interesting one, a classic case of asymmetrical warfare where an indigenous population confronts a militarily more powerful invader. This translates into different roles for each player and a richer range of decisions and strategies to explore. There was also a significant political layer to the conflict, with uneasy alliances between the New England colonies and the loyalty of various Native American tribes uncertain (the Mohawks,

Fig 9.2: Participants in the March 20, 2010, protest in Providence, Rhode Island. Photo by LeeLee Phillips. Used by permission.

for example, have the potential to join either side—historically they were hostile to Philip). Moreover, the topic had never before been "gamed"; in a hobby that still manages to publish more than one hundred new titles every year for its enthusiasts, the search for novelty amid the reservoir of actual historical events is a factor that cannot be underestimated. (It is not unusual for a long-time war gamer, or "grognard," to have a couple of dozen Bulge, Waterloo, or Gettysburg games on his shelves.) To stumble across a conflict of such scope and import as King Philip's War without other treatments of it already in gamers' hands was thus indeed a coup.

Following the publication of the *Providence Journal* article, events began to unfold quickly. The key figure to emerge at this point was Julianne Jennings, who is a member of the Nottoway Tribal Community in Virginia and, at the time of the controversy, held an adjunct appointment in cultural anthropology at Rhode Island College. She became a leading spokesperson on behalf of the protest effort. On March 20 she organized a street protest in Providence, drawing around seventy-five attendees as well as additional media coverage in the local papers (see figure 9.2). Signs carried by the protesters read "Stop Playing the Genocide Game" and "Would a Holocaust Game Be OK?"

A *Facebook* group entitled "Stop the release of King Philip's War game" also went online, and quickly garnered several hundred members. The description read: "Stopping the production of this game is our focus, but the broader goals are raising awareness of Indians' continued existence. And the multiracial and multicultural nature of this existence, especially on the East Coast."[8] By this point it was clear that there was a communications gap. Keeping in mind that the game was not yet in print, the objectors were acting at most on the advertising samples posted on the MMP website (which, amid previews of the artwork and map, enticed prospective players with "a momentous example of New England frontier savagery"). Clearly, the vexed connotations of "savage" in this context were not uppermost in the mind of whoever wrote the advertising copy. Still, as one forum poster put it, "When most people hear the word 'board game' they think Monopoly, Risk, Clue, or disposable games based on movie franchises."[9] This point is worth underscoring: as others in this volume have addressed,[10] the term "game" in the popular imagining is generally synonymous with exactly these sorts of trivial pursuits. Concepts such as "serious games" and "meaningful play" were not part of the discourse as conducted in the streets of Providence. (One could productively answer the rhetorical question about playing a Holocaust game with Brenda Brathwaite's *Train*, for example.)[11] Other gamers' reactions ranged from a kind of earnest piety (insisting they played games merely out of a love of history) which, while no doubt sincere as far as it went, generally failed to acknowledge that at the end of the day one also played games about warfare and violence for, well, for want of a better word . . . fun. The piety was also inevitably coupled with a seemingly contradictory outrage, with numerous posters insisting that *KPW* was "just a game" and that the protestors should find a more urgent cause to which to devote themselves. Regardless, preorders saw a sharp uptick following the publicity, and *KPW* was quickly slotted into the MMP production queue. By August it was in gamers' hands. So, what does it actually mean to play *King Philip's War*?

Playing the Game

While doubtless appearing formidable to the uninitiated, *KPW* is a game of only low to middling complexity by the standards of the conflict simulation hobby. There are about a dozen pages of rules to absorb before beginning, and the game takes around three hours to play to completion. It is set on a map of historical New England featuring colonial settlements and native villages, as well as relevant geographical features such as rivers that affect the course of play. Each player has a number of 5/8-inch square cardboard tokens, called "counters," representing companies of colonial soldiery and "war bands" of Native Americans. Counters are also included for prominent leaders on each side such as Metacom and Benjamin Church; other counters represent assets such as muskets or the presence of scouts or a lurking spy.

The game is structured by turns, each denoting a calendar season between 1675 and 1676, nine total. Each turn consists of a strict sequence of steps ("phases") that must be completed in order. Since many readers will be unfamiliar with conflict simulations, it is worth reproducing the sequence of a turn in full in order to give a sense of the conduct of the game. I have added brief glosses to each.

> *Church/Allied Indian Roll.* To add interest, the key personage of Benjamin Church enters the game randomly, determined by a die roll. Once he does small groups of Native American fighters may join the settlers, also determined by a die roll. Church's presence significantly boosts the military capacity of the colonial side, but no player knows exactly when he will come into play.
>
> *English Reinforcements.* New companies of soldiers appear to replace losses. Each colony contributes soldiers in accordance with its population, with Massachusetts having the most to field.
>
> *Indian Diplomacy.* Philip may attempt to convince additional tribes to join the war on his side. The outcome of these efforts is determined by his success in the game to that point, with a winning campaign spurring additional tribes to action. The powerful Mohawk nation is a special case whose allegiance is determined by a die roll; Philip may attempt to entice them to intervene on his behalf only to have them instead join with the colonists (as happened historically).
>
> *Indian Reinforcements.* Similar to phase 2 above; the Native American player places new groups of "warriors" on the map.
>
> *Indian Movement.* The settlements and villages on the map are connected by a network of trails and watercourses. Unlike a game such as chess, players may generally move as many of the units on their own side as they like each and every turn. Restrictions on the range and extent of movement are imposed by the terrain and by the presence of enemy forces.
>
> *Indian Combat.* Warfare in the game consists of both attacks against enemy combatants and attacks against villages or settlements. The process is described in more detail below. In order to reflect the operational tempo of a preindustrial military campaign waged in the wilderness, there are arbitrary limitations on the number of combats that can take place each turn.
>
> *English Movement.* Similar to above. Until Benjamin Church enters the game, the English are forbidden from moving along the waterways.

English Combat. Similar to above. Note that the sequence of play dictates that the English player will usually occupy a reactive posture, responding to movement and combat on the part of the Native American player earlier in the turn.

Winter Attrition. In the winter turn only, units are removed from play as a function of how many settlements or villages that player has lost to enemy activity.

Check Victory Conditions. The game can end either upon conclusion of the final (ninth) turn, or by fulfilling certain specified criteria sooner, as described below. If neither player has won the game in the course of the turn and if there are still remaining turns to play, then the sequence is reset and the next turn begins.

It should be obvious that playing a game like *KPW* is a highly structured and regimented activity, the rigid sequence of play belying the chaos and uncertainty that attends any military conflict. But while the game does ensure that actions will occur in predictable patterns, chance and randomness are introduced through the vagaries of die rolls, which influence key events ranging from combat to the arrival of reinforcements. As with most conflict simulations, these die rolls are rarely straight heads or tails win or lose propositions. Instead, most tabletop conflict simulation is an exercise in Monte Carlo modeling, a Cold War technique in which the probabilities of complex events are distributed along a randomized spectrum influenced by relevant variables and inputs. While in chess a pawn can always take a queen in the correct circumstance, in a typical war game a smaller force attacking a larger one that is also ensconced on good defensive terrain (like a hilltop) may have only one chance in six of success. In this way a player can make reasonable judgments as to likely outcomes while still preserving the elements of fate and chance that are ineluctably an element of any military action (perhaps that small force has discovered a hidden trail around the back of the hill . . . etc.).

As a war game, armed conflict is obviously at the center of *KPW* and so it is worth a closer look at exactly how the game represents the fighting. Generally, combat is a function of the presence of opposing forces in adjoining spaces on the map. Each side performs a calculus of "strength points," which are accumulated through the presence of soldiers or warriors, as well as leaders, fortifications, and muskets (for the Native Americans). Each side then rolls its own six-sided die simultaneously, and consults a "Combat Results Table" that cross-indexes the result of the die roll with its total number of strength points; the numerical result indicates the number of losses inflicted on the enemy and, depending on the proportion, the attacker either advances to claim the space or is rebuffed. If the die rolls from both sides happen to come out equal, however, then a special third die is consulted: a custom so-called Battle Die included with the game, whose six faces are occupied by pictographs with results like Ambush, Spy, Reinforcements, Massacre, Panic, and Guide. The effects vary: Ambush, for example, means that the combat is resolved sequentially rather than simultaneously, so one player may eliminate the other without loss. Spy and Guide both confer special abilities to that group of units, potentially aiding them in further actions. Massacre, oddly, has only the effect of providing one of the players with an additional unit of reinforcements, presumably an abstract representation of the response to an atrocity somewhere in the vicinity.

In addition to battles between rival units, both players may also utilize the combat procedure to attack unguarded English settlements and Native American villages with the objective of razing them. This is a key element of the game, as the number of settlements and villages destroyed is a variable in turn impacting the rate at which reinforcements are acquired, which tribes join Philip in his campaign (or drop out of it), how much each side suffers during the winter months, and finally, the determination of victory. (Historically, hundreds of settlements and villages were attacked by both sides during the war, with numerous unarmed inhabitants slaughtered.) While players can also win by razing the two major colonial settlements of Boston and Plymouth or capturing Philip and a second sachem, Canonchet, such outcomes are rare given competent play. Much of the game therefore consists of players waging a campaign of destruction against opposing settlements and villages, with the major strategic questions being how much effort to expend defending one's own territory versus attacking the enemy's, and to what extent to engage the military forces being fielded by the opposing side in an open battle (see figure 9.3).

So where (a reader might be forgiven for wondering) is the fun in all this? For all of the emphasis on violence, it is a very different kind of pleasure or satisfaction than one derives from a first-person shooter, where the real-time pace keeps the gamer on a constant stimulus-response treadmill, adrenalin and dopamine flooding bloodstream and brain stem. Playing *KPW* is a much more sedate experience; players are not going to shout or flinch or pump their fists in the air. Gameplay becomes about resource management and risk taking, features characteristic of a great many games of all types. But if the appeal to such classic ludic traits is to serve to remediate the game in the eyes of the skeptical, then it must also expose the potential downside of conflict simulation: for many players, I suspect, the semiotic particulars of the Puritan soldiery and Native American warriors, and the burning villages and settlements collectively recede as the physical components of the game become

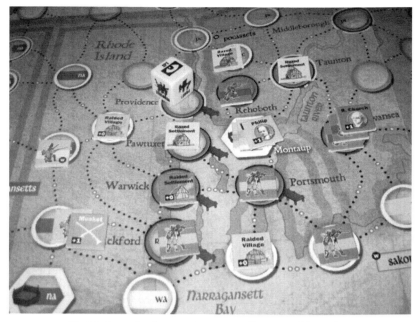

Fig 9.3: Example of a game in progress. Courtesy of the author.

absorbed through familiarity. Players, it is true, are not deriving much vicarious pleasure from razing a village, an action operationalized in the game by nothing more visceral than a die roll, a chart look-up, and the placement of a marker counter. By the same token, however, the acceptance and inevitable absorption of the game's semiotic field means that the historical particulars are to some extent supplanted by the more abstract strategy and decision making that comes to characterize the immersive experience of the game.

As a brief example to make the point, consider the role of muskets. Both the English and the Native American troop counters are illustrated with figures carrying firearms, implying their relative ubiquity, but the Native Americans also have the opportunity to acquire additional Musket counters as part of their reinforcements. During certain specified turns of the game these counters may be placed with any war band that is currently occupying a riverine or coastal space on the map, lending it an additional strength point in any combat situation in which it becomes embroiled. In gaming parlance this is "chrome," a small detail meant to solidify the theme or atmosphere of the game. Here the muskets reflect the technology transfer that typically characterizes what would today be dubbed a "counterinsurgency operation" by the modern military. In fact, however, the Native American firearms trade was symptomatic of the extent to which the indigenous population had become imbricated in colonial economic systems, a reality reflected in the game by the mandate that the recipients of the muskets be in a waterside space conducive to commerce. By virtue of their +1 strength point bonus they confer, the Musket counters then function as a commodity token in the probabilistic economy of the game's predominant subsystem, its combat procedures. Meanwhile, though, the awkward semiotic doubling that comes from placing the additional Musket marker on top of figures already depicted as carrying firearms perhaps serves to reveal the manner in which whole systems of economic relations are subsumed by the simple physical representations of the game—in this instance a cardboard token that (rather inelegantly) must either sit on top of the unit and thereby obscure it or else be placed underneath, where it may be overlooked in the heat of gameplay.

Airwaves and Wires

On March 27, less than two weeks after the onset of the public controversy, designer John Poniske and Julianne Jennings appeared together on air at the invitation of *Spooky Southcoast*, a paranormal-themed AM radio talk show hosted out of Fairhaven, Massachusetts.[12] (The "spooky" connection was apparently the plethora of New England ghost stories spawned by the events of King Philip's War.) This event was the culmination of what had by all accounts become a rather remarkable back-channel conversation among Poniske, the principals at MMP, and Jennings and others within the protest movement. Despite much of the public vitriol (whether aggrieved gamers going to the mat against political correctness or objectors insisting that the game was merely a pretense for race war) a genuine dialogue had begun between the two sides, with an honest exchange of communication and grudging respect for one another's positions. One key point focused around the usage of the word "eliminated" in the description of the forthcoming game to describe the fate of Metacom and the Wampanoag. The concern was the implication that the native peoples were completely eradicated, with surviving tribal culture and communities rendered invisible by this textual representation. The language was revised by MMP as a result of that back-channel conversation. In the discussion that ensued on *Spooky Southcoast*, Jennings and Poniske engaged in a thoughtful, mutually respectful dialogue for nearly an hour. The concern over the effacement of present-day tribal community emerged as quite real: in the course of the discussion, Poniske himself freely acknowledged it never occurred to him to contact descendants of the original native population. "Many people think of history as static, [as] there being one history; there's no such thing," he concluded.[13]

Despite this seemingly amicable outcome, the controversy had not yet run its course. On April 15 the Associated Press picked up the events with a story that was distributed globally.[14] "Schilling pitches bloody board game," read one headline, seemingly unperturbed by the fact that despite his nominal stake in MMP the major leaguer's involvement with the design and production of the game was nil. More helpfully, the AP story noted that "the pushback to the game reflects a broader, continuing effort by Native American tribes to challenge images in society, whether they're school logos bearing the likeness of scowling warriors or names of professional sports teams that they deem as offensive or connoting hostility." Unlike the initial spate of reporting, it also manages to convey the genuine interest in history and simulation that motivated the game, as well as a conciliatory if somewhat resigned statement from Jennings: "We're not going to stop this game from coming. . . . If we can't stop it, why not try to contribute to the content?"

In the designer's notes included in the rulebook to the published game, Poniske acknowledges the controversy, but adds that subsequent to the AP wire story attempts were made to contact tribal councils to arrange a demonstration of the game but to no avail: "It would appear that media hype has poisoned the opportunity for any possibility of further discussion," he writes, but adds: "In publicizing King Philip's War, perhaps we, MMP, native protesters and myself, will raise awareness and understanding of the continuing and vital native cultures in our country."[15] He also furnishes a bibliography for further reading, which includes Lepore's book alongside others, as well as the PBS documentary *We Shall Remain*. But as statements from Jennings and other tribal authorities repeatedly made clear, the issue for them was as much the game itself as its contribution to the ongoing cascade of Westernized Native American representations. While *King Philip's War* is an earnest effort to responsibly represent military and political aspects of the conflict and perhaps spur those who play it to further study, it ultimately fails to fully reconcile itself to the complexities of its own status as a representational artifact in a semiotic environment still charged nearly three and a half centuries after Increase Mather first put quill to parchment.

Contests and Meanings

If war games are to be taken seriously as educational as well as purely recreational pursuits, something that Poniske, Sabin, and others (including myself) advocate, then designers and publishers must become more attuned to the semiotics of their promotion and production.[16] As the historians Ronald Smelser and Edward J. Davies have shown, even a topic as seemingly remote in Western contexts as the Eastern Front in World War II can function as a semiotically replete conduit for mythos, the heroic (read white and Westernized) Wehrmacht facing off against the anonymous hordes of the Red Menace. They convincingly argue that this particular narrative of the Eastern Front has become engrained in the popular imagination through a range of media, including memoirs by the German generals, pulp novels, comics, films, and, finally, tabletop war games.[17] War gamers, themselves overwhelmingly white and male, tend to be impatient with such critiques: the debates quickly become polarized, or in Internet parlance "Godwinized." There is a vociferous resistance to any suggestion that "history" is being sanitized or whitewashed out of deference to anything perceived as "political correctness."[18]

As Smelser and Davies acknowledge, selecting a certain sort of cover imagery for a war game or a book or a film poster does not make one a Nazi sympathizer; but it does indicate that one has unconsciously accepted a particular ideological construct of a historical event and, by dint of naturalizing it as "just an image" or "just a game," allowed the representation to become a relay station for that ideology's ongoing propagation. In the case of King Philip's War, Lepore makes the point that narrativizations, images, and commemorations of the war have all fed the cultural economy of its ongoing representation, one that is dependent on technologies of inscription and representation that underwrite the dominant white frameworks for interpreting the past. The response on the part of some gamers to defiantly order an extra copy has everything to do with asserting authority over the means of cultural production (and having the disposable income at hand by which to do so). As Lepore writes, "If war is, at least in part, a contest for meaning, can it ever be a fair fight when only one side has access to those perfect instruments of empire, pens, paper, and printing press?"[19]

Adding the D6 (the six-sided die) to this litany is perhaps a bit much, but that the game operates within Westernized frameworks of cultural production and consumption is undeniable. The artwork on the box depicts colonial soldiers but no Native American fighters. More tellingly perhaps, it inadvertently underscores the authority of textualized narratives of the conflict through the faded manuscript page presented as a backdrop to the cover art and, especially, the depiction of a quill pen and inkwell on the back cover beside a sheet of parchment with the words "King Philip's War" (see figure 9.4). The history the game seeks to deliver is thus underwritten via exactly the instruments of empire Lepore enumerates. That the "natural" semiotic choice for lending a historical veneer to the game's artwork turns out to be originally European contrivances for the transmission and codification of narrative merely reinforces the concerns of Native American spokespeople like Jennings that, regardless of intentions, the game cannot help but operate within Western frameworks of representation, truth, and authenticity. (By

Fig 9.4: "Contests for meaning": front and back of the box cover. Whose history is thereby inscribed? Courtesy of the author.

contrast, the Battle die described in the previous section, with its clip-art pictographs [see figure 9.3], is perhaps an absent-minded attempt at inclusion of an alternative sign system, tellingly as the harbinger of "chance" and "fate.")

Conflict simulation gamers tend to be well educated, curious, and serious about their devotion to history. They buy books, compare notes, argue over interpretations, show up at lectures to wrestle academic historians to the mat, and sometimes even conduct original archival research on topics that interest them. There is no doubt that the publication of *King Philip's War* succeeded in bringing attention to the conflict, and that it led some of those who bought the game to read further. Even without any additional study players of the game will have understood that at some point in the colonial New England past there was a bitter ethnic war characterized by the killing of noncombatant natives and settlers alike, the large-scale destruction of homes and property as a matter of organized military policy, and massacre and atrocity throughout the region. They will have understood that allegiances on both sides were fragile, that nationalized identities we now take for granted were still in their formative stages. And they will have doubtless grasped, even if unaware of the 2010 controversy, that they are skimming the surface of events vastly more nuanced and complex than ludic systems and procedures can represent. All of that is to the good. But history, as the saying goes, is written by the victors. In this case it is also undeniably being played by the victors. And that makes it a very delicate game indeed.[20]

NOTES

1. *King Philip's War*, Board Game, Designed by John Poniske (Millersville, Md.: Multi-Man Publishing, 2010).

2. Increase Mather, *A Brief History of the Warr with the Indians in New-England* (Boston, John Foster, 1676), 9, Online Electronic Text Edition, http://digitalcommons .unl.edu/cgi/viewcontent.cgi?article=1008&context=zeaamericanstudies.

3. Jill Lepore, *The Name of War: King Philip's War and the Origins of American Identity* (New York: Knopf, 1998), xiii.

4. Paul Davis, "Philip's War No Game to Native Americans," *Providence Journal*, March 15, 2010, A1.

5. Comment available at *BoardGameGeek*, accessed July 31, 2012, http://board gamegeek.com/article/4777506#4777506.

6. "King Philip's War," accessed July 31, 2012, http://boardgamegeek.com/article /4778339#4778339.

7. Phillip Sabin, "The Benefits and Limitations of Computerization in Conflict Simulation," *LLC* 26, no. 3 (September 2011): 326.

8. As of this writing the *Facebook* group is inactive and slated for archiving, accessed July 31, 2012, http://www.facebook.com/#!/group.php?gid=111132838897207.

9. Comment available online, accessed July 31, 2012, at http://boardgamegeek .com/article/4796597#4796597.

10. See especially chapter 6.

11. See http://playthisthing.com/train (accessed November 19, 2012) for commentary on *Train*, a brilliant and emotionally shattering game that asks players to route railroad cars filled with prisoners to concentration camps.

12. *Spooky Southcoast*, radio broadcast, March 27, 2010.

13. A recording of the show is available at the *Spooky Southcast* archives, accessed July 31, 2012, http://www.spookysouthcoast.com/Archive/Archive2010.html.

14. E. Tucker, "Settlers-vs.-Indian Board Game Rankles Tribes," Associated Press, April 15, 2010.

15. Poniske, 16.

16. See my blog essay "War, What is it Good For?" accessed July 31, 2012, http:// www.playthepast.org/?p=1819.

17. Ronald Smelser and E. J. Davies, *The Myth of the Eastern Front: The Nazi-Soviet War in American Popular Culture* (Cambridge: Cambridge University Press, 2008).

18. See David Hughes, "Sleeping with the Enemy: Pro German Bias in WW2 Wargaming," *Battles* 5 (December 2010): 53–55.

19. Lepore, xxi.

20. This note is to acknowledge that I am credited as a playtester in the *King Philip's War* rulebook. At a convention in January 2010, prior to the advent of the public controversy, I played the game a single time under Poniske's supervision. I subsequently offered some brief feedback via email. This is the extent of my personal involvement with the design and production of *KPW*. For comments on drafts of this essay, I am grateful to Jennifer Guiliano and David Hughes.

TEN

Rolling Your Own

On Modding Commercial Games for Educational Goals

Shawn Graham

Members of online communities dedicated to the modification of commercial games debate and develop scenarios with fine attention to authenticity and realism, practices that we seek to cultivate in the students taking our history courses. While self-organized modding communities succeed at creating and playing history, the same activities, approached by educators, have not shown the same degree of success. In this chapter I explore why enthusiasts experience a high degree of success in their modifications, while formal classrooms do not—in this case, set in the context of an online, undergraduate, distance-education classroom.

The communities that make modifications to existing commercial games have created strong and vibrant subcultures in modern video gaming. Strictly speaking, "modding" refers to a change in the rules by which a game operates, but in a less rigorous definition can involve scenario building and the staging of pieces on the game board. Many game publishers, recognizing the importance of modding, now provide modification tools with the release of a game as part of their marketing strategy. They have also reaped the benefits: publishers have recruited talented individuals from these communities and given them jobs as game developers, hoping to make use of the creative ingenuity that the modders have shown. Jon Shafer, the lead designer of *Civilization V*, is one notable example of a former fan, now paid developer, of a popular game franchise.

Some academic studies of *Civilization* have critically addressed its narrative of technological progress and American exceptionalism, while others have concentrated on its anachronisms, its theoretical presentation of history, and its potential for implementation in classroom settings.[1] I wish to focus attention on a different aspect of the *Civilization* franchise: on fan sites as loci for learning, which can inform the use of modifications in an online classroom.

In my pedagogical approach with my first-year undergraduate online classroom, I hoped to draw from a growing movement in which *Civilization* modifications are implemented to expand the possibilities for experience with history.[2] Using the modification, I sought to enhance the engagement of my online distance learners with the material, and cultivate an improvement of their critical historical thinking skills. With the help of participants on *Civfanatics*, I created a scenario with one change in the rules of the original *Civilization* (making it a mod) to address a problem I was having in my fully online, first-year Introduction to Roman History class concerning causality and contingency in Roman politics. The carefully crafted scenario reflected the events of 69 C.E., the Year of the Four Emperors; I devised an assignment to accompany it, and delivered it to my students. Unfortunately, their response was less than ideal. Its lack of success is due partly to the "creepy treehouse" phenomenon,[3] an urban legend in which treehouses are built with no other purpose but to lure children by appealing to their adolescent culture. In online learning, the "creepy treehouse" metaphor can be defined as the use of some aspect of social media, or of a "nontraditional" approach, that does not emerge naturally from the class dynamic but is imposed from the top and feels artificial to the participants. For instance, an instructor who "friends" students on a social network and requires every student to post three times a week to the class blog is transgressing into "their" space. This transgression imposes an unnatural behavior on the students, despite their familiarity and affinity for social networking and blogs.

In this chapter I explore why my experiment with modding and scenario building in an online classroom was unsuccessful and how it became a form of "creepy treehouse." That experience compelled me to focus my attention on the fan sites themselves and the participants who helped me build my scenario. Like the game publishers who seek out expertise in fan communities, educators must utilize the natural environment of online fan communities as spaces in which historically motivated modifications can have a desirable level of involvement. When we create modifications of a commercial game, or "roll our own," it is the aspect of creating it in public that might have the greatest educational impact. The nature of the fan sites promotes the kind of learning we labor to facilitate in our online classrooms; it is spontaneous and builds from the bottom up. It is also, notably, teaching without teachers.

The Year of the Four Emperors

The death of Nero in 68 C.E. launched the Roman Empire into a period of turmoil and civil war, as four emperors were declared in various parts of the empire in quick succession. The brief but brutal civil war lasted from April 68 to December 69. The students in my Introduction to Roman History class, an online distance-education course with approximately eighteen students, study Rome's evolution from monarchy to republic to high empire, and so roughly one thousand years of history, compressed into twelve weeks of readings and discussion board conversations. When we got to the early empire (the period covering the Julio-Claudian and Flavian Dynasties, of which the Year of the Four Emperors represents the pivot point), the students struggled to engage with the period and to understand the complexity of the political changes. Vespasian, whose bid for power was backed by his troops, was the last of the four contenders to be declared emperor. In their attempt to understand the period, my students began to explain Vespasian's success in pacifying the empire and consolidating his hold on Rome in terms of his later role as emperor: "Of course Vespasian would win the civil war because Vespasian was the emperor." Unfortunately, the students were reversing the order of cause and effect in order to make sense of a confusing historical situation. As I discussed the period with them, I realized that part of the problem, aside from confusion of cause and effect, was a poor understanding of the realities of Mediterranean geography and the difficulties of communication in a preindustrial world, which requires factoring in the time it took for news to travel and how that time lag influenced the political dynamic.

I wanted my students to understand that due to the contingency of history, Vespasian's eventual triumph was not foreordained, and that physical and political geography played a role in his success. In order to address the issue, I created a scenario using *Civilization IV*. The game contains software for setting up scenarios—what it calls the "world builder"—but I quickly became frustrated with this editing software. Though it is designed to allow the player to place all of the different pieces on the map, and to set up the starting positions for the game, many of its features are disabled by default, and cannot be unlocked until the player adds a line of code to the *Civilization* initialization file.[4] The code information is not provided by the publisher in any of the game documentation, which prompted me to seek out a solution on *Civilization* fan sites. My search led me to the online modding community, and my post detailing the unlock code and its function is consistently the most visited post on my research blog.[5]

As I became more excited about the possibilities of scenario building, I came to rely on fan sites for help, primarily *Civfanatics. Civilization IV* was built using XML to describe nearly every object in the game. By adjusting the information in the XML, the creator of a mod can change the names of leaders, cultures, and the like, or even create additional elements. Using similar code changes, the game calendar can be adjusted so that each turn represents a single day, week, or month. Ancillary information can be added to set the stage for the scenario when it opens, or prevent certain kinds of technology from ever being "discovered," allowing a world without gunpowder, for instance. I was only able to find this information, and change it, with the help of participants in the online community.

Eventually, with the help of a user with the screen name "Carloquillo," I created a working scenario of the Roman Empire of 69 c.e. In my mod, the player's ultimate goal was to outmaneuver the other claimants to the throne, whether through political or military machinations. The Roman "Senate" would periodically examine the balance of power in Italy, and declare the most influential competitor "emperor"—thus simulating the ineffectualness of the Senate during this period. The scenario was not perfect—if put under the control of artificial intelligence, Vespasian would always convert to Judaism.[6] I devised an assessment exercise for my online students, in which they would play through the scenario rather than write a final essay. At set intervals during gameplay, they would take a screenshot of the world map, and record a narrative of what was going on in their counterfactual history, taking on the role of historians. To conclude, they would identify and address the similarities and differences between the versions of "history" presented in the game with the available facts about the past. My hope was that in playing the scenario the students would begin to appreciate the difficulty of Vespasian's initial position, his inability to act, and the magnitude of his accomplishment in managing and controlling such an enormous, heterogeneous territory, and by identifying anachronisms and oddities, better understand the important concepts of the period.

Fail

To this point, the students had been receptive of the modification, but my experiment broke down when I introduced the option of using the game as an alternative to the traditional history essay. A number of my online students had copies of *Civilization IV*, so I had offered the scenario to these students as an alternative, confirmed that some of them were playing it, and waited to see what would happen. While feedback on the scenario was positive—"this was a fun scenario, sir"—none took up the offer to play the game for credit; all chose to write standard essays. I should note that it was not mandatory for any of the students to play this scenario, nor did I try to teach students new to the game how to play it, or how to install the scenario. There were no technological impediments or learning curves related to gameplay to overcome.

I asked my students why they chose the essay over the game response assignment; each answer was evasive. I initially attributed this to the conservatism of students: they understood how essays function and how they are marked, but the unknown territory of playing a game and responding to it made them hesitant. My course was an "affinity space"[7] for learning about Roman culture, a space where students had self-selected to come together in a group meant to explore Rome. That is, they had a displayed affinity for studying Roman culture, not one for playing a video game in order to learn from it. It is worth noting that my course description had not explicitly stated that game-based evaluations would be a component. If it had, perhaps I might have attracted students interested in playing a mod or game culture in general, or open to alternative assessment structures. More importantly, on reflection, I have realized that the fundamental conflict was that I sprung it on my students without any kind of preparation. Had I adequately prepared them, I might have overcome that conservatism. I might have carved out a new affinity space for this alternative assessment exercise. As it was, students were hesitant to fully commit to the game component because it was a kind of "creepy treehouse." I selected the period to model, and chose a technology with which many students are familiar, but tried to impose a specific method of interaction that was unnatural. Another factor may be one of intimidation: I invited my students to play the scenario with myself as an opponent; none of the students accepted the offer. The strangeness of the assignment, when combined with the unnatural imposition of technology, created a barrier that the students did not try to, or could not, overcome.

All was not lost, however. My experiment may have failed with my students, but it exceeded beyond my expectations with the Civfanatics community. The thread I started on Civfanatics, asking for help, attracted the attention of fourteen other players (almost the same number of community members as students in my class). They helped me to build the scenario, asked questions about the period, and suggested ways of implementing the model that I hoped to achieve. The scenario that I uploaded was tested by them, and has since been downloaded nearly one thousand times. On the *Civfanatics* site, my role as a university instructor did not put me in any privileged position vis-à-vis the other participants; I was just one of many people who enjoyed the game. Though learning did occur as a result of my experiment in scenario building, it was in the context of an online community rather than in my classroom.

Assessing the Educational Value of Online Discussion Forums

The major learning management systems used by colleges and universities rely on "bulletin boards" and "discussion forums." Students make posts and leave messages to comment on some topic. Posts are organized into threads that follow the conversation. Similarly, the *Civfanatics* community relies on posts and threads. Significantly, online courses rely on the instructor to keep the discussion flowing, to push it into the interesting areas, and to assess the students' learning in the forums. While *Civfanatics* has "moderators" who monitor the discussions, their role is solely to make sure that topics are in the right place—to ensure that you do not post your wish list of features for *Civilization IV* in the area marked for scenario swapping, for instance. There is no authority within any discussion on *Civfanatics*. The order and authority present within a given thread is largely self-organized.

The literature of formal online learning can be informed through an exploration of these sites, and specifically through an assessment of the kinds of learning taking place in these self-organized forums. In the thread that I started, other contributors were extremely helpful in the creation of the modification of *Civilization*. There remains the question of the ability to learn history through such an interaction, however. What of history?

In the classes that I teach, when I assess a discussion forum, I am looking for posts that demonstrate an understanding of the material, that engage with others' thoughts and comments, and that push the conversation forward. In truth, my rubric is not overly elaborate. A more rigorous rubric and approach is proposed by Sedef Uzuner in an article on discussion forums for online learning.[8]

Uzuner makes a distinction between "educationally valuable talk" (EVT) and "educationally less valuable talk" (ELVT). He situates this distinction in the traditions of Lev Vygotsky's 1934 insights concerning language, and how "knowledge building is created between/among people in their collaborative meaning-making through dialogue."[9] Uzuner's approach therefore is firmly rooted in a constructivist approach to education. Uzuner suggests that EVT, in the context of discussion threads, is

> a particular interactional pattern in online discussion threads characterized as dialogic exchanges whereby participants collaboratively display constructive, and at times, critical engagement with the ideas or key concepts that make up the topic of an online discussion, and build knowledge through reasoning, articulation, creativity, and reflection.[10]

Uzuner illustrates EVT in a table, which I have reproduced below (table 10.1).

TABLE 10.1.   Uzuner's illustration of EVT

Indicator	Acronym	Defined	Examples
Exploratory	EPL	Recognition of some confusion/ curiosity or perplexity as a result of a problem/issue arising out of an experience/course readings; posing a problem and enticing others to take a step deeper into it	"I wonder . . ." "I am not sure if what the author suggests . . ." "In the article X, the author said . . . This brought up a few questions in my mind."
Invitational	INVT	Inviting others to think together, to ponder, to engage by asking questions, requiring information, opinion, or approval	"Jane says . . . What do you think?" "Do you think . . . ?" "The authors suggest . . . , no?"
Argumentational	ARG	Expressing reasoning (with analogies, causal, inductive, and/or deductive reasoning, etc.) to trigger discussion	"If teachers . . . , then . . ." "Teaching is like . . ." "X is important because . . ."
Critical	CRT	Challenging or counter-challenging statements/ideas proposed by others OR playing devil's advocate	"I agree that . . . However, . . ."
Heuristic	HE	Expressing discovery (similar to "Aha!" moments or expressions like "I found it!"); directing others' attention to a newly discovered idea	"I did not know that there is a name for XXX. I think XXX is . . . Has anyone experienced that too?"
Reflective	REF	Examination of past events, practices (why/how they happened), or understandings in relation to formal content	"I've noticed that I had a tendency to . . . After reading X's article, I've learned not to . . ."
Interpretive	INTP	Interpretation of formal content through opinions that are supported by relevant examples, facts, or evidence	"In my opinion X is . . . Y is a good example of why . . ."
Analytical	ANL	Interpretation of content through the analysis, synthesis, and evaluation of others' understanding	"The original question was . . . Joe said . . . Mary said . . . As for me . . ."
Informative	INF	Providing information from literature and relating it to course content/ topic of discussion	"I read an article about X once and the author said . . . You can find more information about this in . . ."
Explanatory	EXPL	Chain of connected messages intended to explain/make clear OR statements serving to elaborate on the ideas suggested in previous posts	"I want to build on your comment that . . ."
Implicative	IMP	Assertions that call for action OR statements whereby participants formulate a proposal/decision about how to achieve a certain end based on the insights they gained from the course readings/ discussions	"Teachers should/should not . . ." "X must not be forced . . ."

In contrast, ELVT is talk "that lacks substance in regards to critical and meaningful engagement with the formal content or ideas that are discussed in the posts of others in an online discussion."[11] Uzuner then provides examples of different kinds of EVT and ELVT, with eleven kinds of EVT and five kinds of ELVT. Uzuner's second table is reproduced below (table 10.2).

What does Uzuner's schema reveal when we use it to assess the learning taking place in the discussion forums on *Civfanatics*? I decided to assess the posts in the most-viewed scenario in the Civfanatics.com *Civilization IV—Scenarios* forum, which was created by then-fan, now Civ-employee, John Shafer, on a World War I scenario.[12] Shafer's scenario was first posted on May 6, 2006; at the time of the writing of this chapter, it had been viewed more than 94,000 times; the most recent post was on January 19, 2009. There are 311 posts in this thread. I read each post, and tallied the kinds of educationally valuable or less valuable talk that was occurring, as in tables 10.3 and 10.4.

A simple tally would suggest that the less educationally valuable talk carries the day, with 315 posts to the 137 of educationally valuable talk. But this

TABLE 10.2. Uzuner's examples of EVT and ELVT

Indicator	Acronym	Defined	Examples
Affective	AF AA ASP	Short posts that ONLY contain a statement of personal feelings (likes and dislikes) Short posts that ONLY contain appraisal (praising and thanking someone) Questions or comments that add social presence to the discussion but do not contribute new information	"I never liked math either" "Thank you for offering your insights into . . ." "I have been to your country once and I visited X, Y, Z when I was there"
Judgmental	JA JDA	Short posts that ONLY contain brief statements of agreement without elaboration Short posts that ONLY contain brief statements of disagreement without elaboration	"Yes, I agree with you . . ." "I do not think so"
Experiential	EXP	Posts that only contain personal experiences, narratives, descriptions that are not followed by reflection	"I did the same thing when I was teaching X." "I did A, B, C. It was fun"
Reproductional	REP	Repeating/reproducing the ideas mentioned/proposed in the previous posts without elaboration	"You are right, X is . . ." (followed by a sentence)
Miscellaneous	MIS	Opinions that seem to be off topic OR statements regarding technical problems/course logistics	"I am unable to open Jay's file . . ."

TABLE 10.3. Educationally valuable talk in Shafer's World War I scenario thread

Kinds of Valuable Talk	# of Instances
EPL	10
INVT	31
ARG	28
CRT	22
HE	3
REF	13
INTP	2
ANL	8
INF	18
EXPL	0
IMP	2

TABLE 10.4. Educationally less valuable talk in Shafer's World War I scenario thread

Kinds of Less Valuable Talk	# of Instances
AF	2
AA	0
ASP	79
JA	11
JDA	11
EXP	14
REP	14
MIS	184

misses some important dynamics. The "miscellaneous" category captures two distinct kinds of posts—"how do I install this scenario / it didn't work" queries, and more complex play-throughs of the scenario that report what exactly took place. These latter posts are actually quite valuable; because the scenario is a kind of simulation, each play-through records a different trajectory through all of the possible outcomes of the scenario. It is a kind of sweeping of the scenario-as-simulation's "behavior space,"[13] that is, the whole range of possible outcomes given these starting conditions (all of the possible behaviors for every combination of the simulation's variables), and so provides important fodder for other kinds of educationally valuable talk. (Given the beneficial nature of these discussions, we could shuffle "miscellaneous" into educationally valuable talk, and dramatically tilt the balance of educationally less valuable to educationally valuable.)

The development of the forum follows a distinct trajectory. Shafer introduces it on May 6. A flurry of appreciative posts and "how do I . . ." technical queries ensues for about fifty posts, followed by a second phase of play testing and reporting of bugs. Educationally valuable talk increases in this second phase as various individuals pick up on items in the play-throughs. By post 79, the conversation has turned to how to best represent the carnage as well as the social and strategic impact of trench warfare given the procedural rhetorics of the game.[14] This phase continues for about another one hundred posts, and includes discussions of the real-world impact of the Russian Revolution on the war, and how this should best be simulated. There is a strong concern throughout these posts for verisimilitude and authenticity—but what constitutes authenticity is debated. A flame war, the online equivalent of a shouting match, erupts in post 92 on this very question, and is eventually quelled by Shafer, who notes in essence that this is just a game[15] and is meant to be engaging. In post 103, another individual suggests modifications to the scenario, and actually begins another thread elsewhere on *Civfanatics* to improve and expand on Shafer's work. In post 171, the author uses the scenario to leap into counterfactual history, and proposes quite a complex counterfactual based on his play-throughs of the scenario. By September 2006 most of the heat has gone out of the thread, and subsequent posts are again of the "how do I make this work" or the play-through variety. This continues until the thread goes dormant in January 2009.

Online Learning Is Social Learning: Who Talks to Whom?

The other aspect that needs to be considered besides the **content** of the posts, to give fullness to Uzuner's approach and Vygotsky's insight, is the social aspect. Who is talking to whom? From the perspective of an online instructor, it is important to be able to identify and foster the "catalysts" in any discussion forum.[16] I mapped out the pattern of social interactions in the forum as a kind of network. If "DoctorG" addressed "JLocke," then I connected the two individuals. If "Koba the Dread" posted a note recounting a play-through, I mapped that as a response to Shafer's original post. If Shafer responded to "Koba the Dread" quoting "JLocke," I connected all three together. The resulting network is more-or-less star shaped, with Shafer in the middle and everyone else radiating off as spokes. There are clumps of highly interconnected individuals, however, representing subconversations and discussions that developed in the forum (see figure 10.1). These clumps are important.

Using the Keyplayer program from Analytech[17] I assessed the most central individuals in this network, that is, the individuals whose removal from the forum would result in a disrupted graph, or would "break" the conversation. Keyplayer reported that the removal of Shafer, "JLocke," "Dom

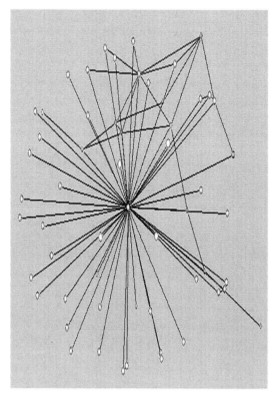

Fig 10.1: Conversation in the World War I scenario thread as a social network. Shafer is in the exact center. There are fifty-nine individuals. Courtesy of the author.

Pedro," "Kitten of Chaos," and "Koba the Dread" would cause this network to fragment almost completely. These individuals account for a majority of the educationally valuable posts made in the forum. This is quite interesting from the standpoint of an online educator, in that it suggests that we can determine from structure alone the individuals who are making the greatest contribution to the learning going on in a forum.

This was a forum without an official leader, or anyone acting in the role of "teacher." The contrast with my own Year of the Four Emperors thread is striking.[18] My thread began on May 16, 2006, and went stagnant by September. Fourteen individuals contributed, and noticeably, aside from my own initial post, there is (ironically) a large absence of EVT, unless you count the technical "how-to" posts I made and the play-through reports. As a social network, the graph is entirely centered on me with radial spokes (figure 10.2); no one is talking to each other, there are no clumps on the graph, just

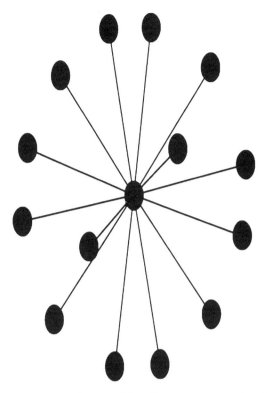

Fig 10.2: Conversation in The Year of Four Emperors scenario thread as a social network. Courtesy of the author.

responses to me and me alone. Why the difference? I think I once again created a "creepy treehouse." It was all about me. I was also very up front about my identity and the use I wished to put the scenario, which made it more of a curiosity than a scenario that got people excited.

Rolling Your Own: Lessons Learned?

The most important lesson learned is that we, the instructors, should not be building and directing mods for history education; it should be the students.[19] We should show them how the game works. Direct their attention to the procedural rhetorics of the game rules. Make them think about what "to simulate" actually means. Give them, or have them decide on, a historical scenario to model, and ask them to implement it in the game mechanics. Have them debate how to do this: What rules need to be changed? How do the rules impose a particular kind of expression of history? Build, and play-test, the resulting scenarios. What elements of the playing of the game behave as the students expected, and what elements surprise (like Vespasian's conversion to Judaism in my own scenario)?

If, however, we undertake to "roll our own" scenarios, or otherwise use commercial video games like *Civilization* in our teaching, we need to approach the task more from the point of view of a fan, and less from the perspective of a teacher. Do not do as I did. Otherwise, we create artifacts that do not support the kind of response that we wish. Learning is obviously going on in the fan forums, and using tools like Uzuner's typology is one way of assessing the kinds of learning taking place. The pattern of social interaction in fan forums, and their application to educational contexts, is equally intriguing. My conclusions here are, of course, preliminary; one would need to study a much greater number of the threads to see a fuller picture, and this is an area where text mining might be usefully employed.

Rather than fretting about how we can better reproduce real-world classroom interactions online, I am suggesting that we consider how we can reproduce the vitality of online fan forum discussions in our real-world and online settings, and more usefully employ game-based learning in fan forums in regular and online classrooms. And as we move forward with the integration of different kinds of analytical tools to support our assessment of class tools, we should give consideration to the way that the structure of these patterns of interaction correlate (or not!) with educational impact.

NOTES

1. See, for instance, the discussion in William Uricchio, "Simulation, History, and Computer Games," in *Handbook of Computer Game Studies*, ed. Joost Raessens and Jeffrey Goldstein (Cambridge, Mass.: MIT Press, 2005), 327–38.
2. See, for instance, Ethan Watrall, "Project Diary: Red Land/Black Land," accessed July 31, 2012, http://www.playthepast.org/?p=403.
3. Jared Stein, "Defining the Creepy Treehouse," 2008, accessed August 1, 2012, http://flexknowlogy.learningfield.org/2008/04/09/defining-creepy-tree-house/.
4. Open the ini file with MS Notepad. Find the line "CheatCode=0." Change this to "CheatCode=chipotle." Save the file but take care not to change the file extension. For more help on the world builder, see http://www.civfanatics.net/downloads/civ4/guides/WorldBuilderManual.zip.
5. See "Civilization IV World Builder Manual and Other Needful Things," Electric Archaeology, accessed July 31, 2012, http://electricarchaeology.ca/2008/01/08/civilization-iv-world-builder-manual-other-needful-things/.
6. Which points to an underlying procedural rhetoric of the game, and how the game envisions the role of religion in society. This mechanic has largely been expunged from the fifth iteration of the game.

7. James Gee, "Semiotic Social Spaces and Affinity Spaces: From *Age of Mythology* to Today's Schools," in *Beyond Communities of Practice: Language, Power and Social Context*, ed. D. Barton and K. Tusting (Cambridge: Cambridge University Press, 2005), 214–32.

8. Sedef Uzuner, "Educationally Valuable Talk: A New Concept for Determining the Quality of Online Conversations," *Journal of Online Learning and Teaching* 3, no. 4 (2007).

9. Lev S. Vygotsky, *Thought and Language* (Cambridge, Mass.: MIT Press, 1962 [1934]).

10. Uzuner.

11. Uzuner.

12. "Scenario World War I," accessed July 31, 2012, http://forums.civfanatics.com /showthread.php?t=170090.

13. Shawn Graham, "Behaviour Space: Simulating Roman Social Life and Civil Violence," *Digital Studies / Le Champ Numérique* 1, no. 2, (2009), accessed January 25, 2011, http://www.digitalstudies.org/ojs/index.php/digital_studies/article/view/172 /214; idem, "Vespasian, Civ IV, and Intro to Roman Culture" (2007), accessed February 24, 2011, http://planetcivilization.gamespy.com/View.php?view=Articles.Detail &id=33; idem, "Re-Playing History: The Year of the Four Emperors and Civilization IV," accessed February 24, 2011, http://www.heacademy.ac.uk/hca/resources/detail/re _playing_history.

14. Ian Bogost, *Persuasive Games: The Expressive Power of Videogames* (Cambridge, Mass.: MIT Press, 2007).

15. In post 99 on the "Scenario World War I" thread, accessed July 31, 2012, http:// forums.civfanatics.com/showthread.php?t=170090&page=5, Shafer remarks that his goal is just so that people have fun playing the scenario. See also http://forums .civfanatics.com/showthread.php?t=111105 and http://forums.civfanatics.com/show thread.php?t=111488 from the same thread for a discussion by the modding community on the "Historiography of Civilization."

16. If one is using an LMS (learning management system) such as WebCT or Moodle, there is a plug-in that will provide these sorts of metrics automatically on discussion board posts. See "SNA Diagrams," *Social Networks in Action*, accessed July 31, 2012, http://research.uow.edu.au/learningnetworks/seeing/snapp/index.html.

17. Steven Borgatti, accessed July 31, 2012, http://www.analytictech.com.

18. *The Year of the Four Emperors*, accessed July 31, 2012, http://forums.civfanatics .com/showthread.php?t=171164.

19. See Kee and Graham in this volume, chapter 13.

ELEVEN

Simulation Games and the Study of the Past

Classroom Guidelines

Jeremiah McCall

What does an effective use of a simulation game in a history class look like? For too many interested in the games and learning field, it is not entirely clear. While the theory delineating the potential of games as learning tools is growing steadily,[1] discipline-specific practical applications are still too few and far between. Developing practical uses of games as learning tools requires two components: the formulation of discipline-specific theories and classroom-specific implementations. As an early offering in the area of practical uses for games, this chapter proposes a theory for effectively using simulation games in the history classroom, a theory developed through my training as a historian and experiences as a high school history teacher who uses simulation games. Subsequently, this theory is translated into practical guidelines for using simulations in a history class.

The Importance of Taking Risks

The practical guidelines offered here have emerged from a cyclical process over the last five years of designing, implementing, refining, and even sometimes wholly rejecting lessons involving simulation games. While simulation games offer compelling learning opportunities, they come with significant challenges. Success using simulation-based learning in these early stages of the medium progresses equally as much from learning what not to do as what to do. Philosophically, teachers learning to use simulation games as learning tools need to be willing to engage in play. We must take risks, wading into the chaos, navigating the mess, and implementing a sense of order and meaning that helps students learn how to study the past. We must be willing to make mistakes and accept failures, for learning from mistakes enables us to design ever more compelling and effective lessons about the study of the past.

How does this work in practice? Accepting several important principles can help empower teachers to experiment, take risks, and make mistakes. First, teachers must come to see themselves as the expert guides rather than the sources of all worthwhile information and arbiters of what is true or false. Second, history must be approached as a discipline that embodies a set of core skills, not solely or even primarily a set of content. Among these skills are the ability to analyze and evaluate evidence, sequence ideas, and form compelling written and oral arguments. Third, a main goal of history teachers is to create learning environments where students can engage interesting source materials, analyze them, and construct formal responses to them in written, oral, and digital media. In this context, so long as students are engaged and tasked to hone these skills, a simulation-based lesson will not truly be a failure even when there is room for improvement.

The Advantages of Simulation Games

There is good reason to take risks where simulations are involved. Simulation games provide educators powerful tools that offer particular strengths for teaching the authentic skills of a historian, not to mention familiarity with twenty-first-century media. Quite simply, the advantages of simulation games for promoting meaningful study of the past demand concrete and effective classroom applications. The first step to developing this argument is to ground the key terms. At its broadest, a simulation is a dynamic and, to some necessary extent, simplified representation of one or more real-world processes or systems. Into this category fall a great number of analog and digital models of biological, physical, and chemical processes and systems. There are also interactive trainers, whose primary function is to prepare participants to function effectively in real-world tasks: flight simulations, air traffic control simulations, and business simulations are some of the best known examples in this category.[2] A game, on the other hand, to paraphrase the definition of Katie Salen and Eric Zimmerman, is a rule-based system in which players undergo a conflict or competition in an attempt to achieve a quantifiable goal, such as winning or losing.[3] So, a simulation game is a game that functions as a dynamic model of one or more aspects of the real world. A number of commercial and nonprofit computer games fall into this category, strategy games that place the player in historical roles, ranging from traders and subsistence farmers, to rulers and generals. The commercial game *Civilization*, for example, tasks players with exploring and colonizing a digitally rendered landscape, while the free, browser-based *Ayiti* challenges players to manage a family's economy in an impoverished country. These games, indeed all simulation games, invite players to explore and manipulate digital worlds defined by representations of real-world geography, structures, institutions, and inhabitants.

The educational advantages historical simulation games can offer may best be thought of as advantages of immersion and provocation. When playing a simulation, as opposed to using other forms of instruction, a learner can become immersed in a virtual representation of the past and, in doing so, be provoked to consider how and why humans lived, made choices, and acted the way they did in the past. These are insights about the systemic contexts in which people lived, which is really just another way of saying the networks of obligations, necessities, and desires that link individuals to the environment and to the rest of human society. It is all too easy for students and teachers to forget the fundamental realities of the past that shaped decisions and actions. People of the past acted in physical and spatial contexts, securing food, walking places, and working to obtain their basic needs and, ideally, gain some comforts. To look at it another way, they lived and acted, as do we all, as parts of systems. These past people were both influenced by and influenced the systems in which they lived and operated. When the study of the past is treated as simply a set of established facts and interpretations to be learned, it becomes far too easy to divorce the people of the past from their physical, spatial, and social systems and from reasonable considerations of cause and effect.

Simulation games can help bridge this conceptual divide between humans and their systemic contexts because the games themselves are interactive systems. The principle is straightforward: to analyze a system, use a roughly analogous, but simplified, model of the system, which is just what a simulation game is. The moving parts, as it were, of the game bear a closer analogy to the moving parts of the past than other representations of the past, whether speech, text, videos, images, or discussion. These simulations place student-players into dynamic models of the past where problems must be solved and challenges overcome.[4] The players must make choices based on limited information and experience the effect of those choices on the game world and their assumed persona in it. Such simulation games provide a virtual systemic context, a source of experience that provides learners a rich frame of reference when considering the motives and actions of people in the past. They provide students with visual, interactive models and experiences, however vicarious, of how their own decisions influenced, for example, the success of a trade, the development of a culture, the creation of an empire, or the outcome of a battle.

Perhaps because simulations provide the opportunity to study systems from the inside as an active participant, they are also able to provoke students to raise deep and meaningful historical questions. Though no firm conclusions can be drawn without formal research, important considerations suggest simulation games may actually inspire more students to ask a variety of deep historical questions better than other forms of media. Why might this be the case? Consider that research clearly suggests students all too easily accept what they read in texts at face value. This is especially true when reading from a textbook. At the high school level, even the best student readers often have a tendency to read without offering the level of challenge and criticism required for a historian. To put it another way, they read for information rather than to discern a point of view.[5] This habit can continue to be a problem with college readers. Without a high level of commitment to analyzing the information received and its source, it is exceedingly difficult to raise substantial questions about a text and its implications. If it is quite normal for students to accept most texts they read at face value, will they actively critique the ideas presented by their teachers in class? A simulation, on the other hand, may simply not be perceived as quite as authoritative a source of information. At the very least it is harder to treat a simulation as a text that must simply be read for facts. It may also be the case that, because simulation games provide immersive, rich audiovisual and tactile experiences with numerous opportunities for students to play and process at their own pace—including sidetracks—there may simply be more going on, for lack of a better phrase, to provoke questions in the time spent playing a simulation game than during a comparable amount of time reading a text or listening to a lecture. Perhaps, too, being put in the role of a decision maker causes a player to be more aware and more engaged in the historical environment presented by the game, and this leads to the formation of deep questions. Again, it will require substantial research to test these implications, but they are worth noting. At the very least, it can be said that simulations can be harnessed to inspire deep historical questioning.

It is worth noting that nowhere in this chapter is the use of simulation games advocated because they are fun. This is quite purposeful, but deserves an explanation. Certainly, simulations can be incredibly engaging, it is a good feeling when students are enjoying a lesson, and creating an educational atmosphere where students want to come to class is a worthy goal. Nevertheless, there are serious flaws with using the idea of fun as a criterion for effective lessons, particularly lessons involving simulation games. First, fun is both relative and broad in scope. Suppose a student was asked if her sessions playing, observing, and intensively critiquing a simulation game were fun. What should the student use for comparison when answering? Spending time with friends outside of school? Riding a roller coaster? Watching a movie? These all can be considered fun and arguably more fun than having to critique a game. Really, by the standards of fun playing a game without being required to take notes and present a critique is generally superior. The second problem is that fun is not equivalent to educationally valuable. Teachers know this. Exercises for developing effective analytical writing skills, for example, or researching arguments and advancing them in a logically compelling order, are highly valuable, yet no teacher—at least none I know of—asks their students if they would enjoy writing a paper, or whether they found the experience of writing a paper to be fun; it is simply beside the point. Finally, and this is a particularly important point, by no means does every student look forward to the idea of playing and critiquing a simulation game. Some find it highly intimidating; others prefer the lecture where they can more easily "check out" than in a simulation exercise. Certainly, simulation games can engage. They can hold attention, create intriguing and interesting situations, and provoke interesting questions and ideas. Where engagement is a desirable feature of a successful lesson, however, fun is not. Teachers who choose to use simulation games primarily because they are fun and expect to find all their students enthralled are both setting themselves up for disappointment and missing the point. Simulation games have compelling features as educational tools; whether they are fun is not at issue.

The Qualities of Effective Simulation Games

Despite the great potential of simulation games in history education, there is a significant caveat teachers must remember. Many of the most viable simulation games are commercial products designed to entertain, not teach, and this shapes their presentation of the past.[6] Those that are not designed primarily for commercial purposes, on the other hand, may be particularly polemical in promoting their point of view. The teacher considering a game for classroom use needs to consider the characteristics that qualify a historically themed game as a simulation before using a game in class. Ultimately, though, the teacher must table the thornier theoretical issues of what features constitute a simulation and consider not whether a certain game is a simulation game, but *how effective a simulation game* it is.

By their very nature, simulation games will yield different outcomes each time they are played. Consequently, they should not be employed as static descriptors of factual details about the past. Valid simulation games need not, and indeed cannot, represent each and every detail of the past accurately. There are better tools available for such a task. Text or image, for example, is often better suited to illustrating, say, how a specific Roman city looked at one specific moment in time. The simulation game offers, on the other hand, a more-or-less broad model of how that Roman city functioned. Choose the learning tool based on the desired learning outcome. One cannot expect a simulation of a war to yield the same outcome as the war itself or a city builder to limit urban plans only to those found in the past. Broadly speaking, for the outcome to be the same as that in the past, the causes, including the decisions made, must be the same. If a simulation game is to allow players choice at all, there must be the possibility for outcomes that did not occur in the past.

So if it is not an exact digital reconstruction of the past, which incidentally is a physical and philosophical impossibility, what exactly makes a video game valid for classroom use as a simulation? Primarily this: *its core gameplay must offer defensible explanations of historical causes and systems.* The idea of a defensible explanation is important when handling simulations. Arguments accepted by one historian or generation of historians are often rejected by the next. When it comes to the critical elements of history, why and how things happen, there are no facts, only conventions. Conventions, in turn, are nothing more than arguments that have held up to criticism due to the strength of their explanatory power and the strength of the supporting evidence. There is always room for a historical convention to be undermined; indeed it is a time-honored tradition in history to challenge conventions. If this is true of the best arguments of historians, it is equally true of the interpretations of the past embedded in video games. To be considered a historical simulation, then, a game does not need to offer an interpretation that is perfect, whatever that might mean, but one that is reasonably based on the available evidence. Focusing on defensible arguments rather than correct arguments promotes the idea so critical for training flexible, creative thinkers, that when it comes to humans interpreting and making meaning of the past, there are far more shades of gray and maybes than certainties. Students need to be encouraged, therefore, to consider which models in a simulation can and cannot be sustained by historical evidence. So long as a game has enough historical merit in its core explanations that students will be challenged to critique its validity, it is worth consideration for classroom use. Indeed, inaccuracies in the game serve a useful function: they give students an opportunity to challenge, just as the accuracies give them a chance to support.

Once a game is selected for class that has the core defensible models, the next step is to begin considering the historical problems posed by the game in order to anticipate the types of resources and support students will need to analyze the game. These fall into two categories. The first category encompasses the historical issues modeled by gameplay itself. These are the problems agents in the past faced that are part of the simulation's core play. They correspond to the content of a history course. The most important of these is generally how to assess and make trade-offs. A trade-off exists whenever there are multiple decisions the player can make, the decisions cannot all be satisfied simultaneously, and there is no clear-cut correct priority, but rather a variety of priorities that can shift depending on the goals of the player. Simulation games tend to revolve around this mechanic.

The second kind of problem is one of interpretation. These are the meta-level problems that must be considered when using simulation games effectively. If students are not asked to reflect on the accuracy of the models in the simulations they play, the teacher has simply replaced one authoritarian source of truth, whether a textbook, film, primary source, or the teacher, with another: the game. This will not do. The great strength of a foundation in history is that it imparts the skills to critique and question claims to the truth, not to accept others' claims without substantiation. Hence, teachers should encourage students to consider the problems of interpretation in a game, not just the problems of content.

Identifying a game's interpretation of the past is no more a natural exercise for most students than unearthing the bias of a primary source or the underlying assumptions of a modern author. Concrete guidelines, therefore, are needed to scaffold students as they examine a simulation's interpretation. The following questions are at the core of uncovering any simulation's point of view:

- What is the role of the player in the game world and what are the challenges the game world presents to the player?
- What actions can the player take or not take to overcome the challenges? What resources does the player have with which to overcome challenges?
- What are the trade-offs in the game when it comes to actions and the spending of resources?
- What strategies or actions lead to success or failure and how are success and failure measured in the game?

A game reveals its designer's vision of the past by expressing success and failure in certain terms—a number of votes, an amount of money, a certain population size—and dictating the types of actions the player's historical persona can take.

From Theory to Practice: A Classroom Case Study

Now that the theoretical value of simulation games as interpretations has been surveyed, it is time to demonstrate the theory by illustrating the practical steps needed to design and implement simulation-based lessons. In particular, the essential steps can be reduced to six:

1. Select a game with defensible core gameplay.
2. Select resources and design supplemental lessons that correspond to the historical problems posed by the game.
3. Allocate time to train students to play.
4. Arrange students and structure time to allow for observation notes.
5. Provide opportunities for analytical exercises involving the game.
6. Cap the experience with opportunities for reflection and for critique of the simulation.

The success of these steps requires that the teacher serves as an expert guide, actively monitoring students' progress, posing questions, and offering assistance as needed.[7]

The steps outlined above will be illustrated through reference to current practice in a 2010 unit on Roman history studied by two ninth-grade classes from Cincinnati Country Day School. As noted at the beginning of this chapter, the practices currently employed in these classes have emerged from several years of design, implementation, a mixture of successes and failures, and refinement. The steps are reasonably well tested and provide an effective starting structure for lessons involving simulations. The particular games will change, but the basic structure will remain serviceable for some time. Still, these steps are by no means the last word on the subject; more effective strategies will emerge in response to further classroom practice.

The year 2010 marked the fifth year implementing simulation-based lessons for the ninth-grade Roman history unit. The goal of this iteration was to build on smaller-scale past simulation game experiences and develop a more substantial implementation. Previous simulation game exercises in the class had served as supplemental critical thinking exercises. The students played the Battle of the Trebia in the game *Rome: Total War*, for example, read the accounts of the battle passed on by the ancient historians Polybius and Livy, and wrote critiques of the accuracy of the game based on these sources. By 2009 this had developed to the point where students could choose to play either *Rome: Total War* or *CivCity: Rome* and research and write a critical essay. While these were worthwhile exercises in historical methodology, they seemed to be only loosely connected to the rest of the unit on Roman history. The Hannibalic Wars were referenced in the class but, due to time constraints, not studied in any depth; the same could be said for Roman warfare and Roman city life. Essentially, students were exercising their skills as historians but not focusing on a topic that was in any way integral to this particular unit on Roman history. The goal of the 2010 implementation, then, was to integrate the simulations more completely into the unit. In other words, the unit was redesigned so that the topics in the simulation games were made central. This way the advantages of simulations to teach systems would be integral to the unit of study. There are many games available on Roman history, but not a great breadth of topics. Essentially, there are games that focus on Roman warfare and imperialism, and games that focus on Roman cities and the economy. Out of these, two games in particular were selected to serve as the core classroom simulations: *Rome: Total War* and *CivCity: Rome*.

Were these legitimate to use as classroom simulations? To determine this requires considering the core gameplay of each, the first step in designing any lesson based on simulation games. The Creative Assembly's *Rome: Total War* is a hybrid turn-based and real-time strategy game that runs on Windows-based PCs.[8] In the turn-based campaign mode, the player assumes leadership over one of three aristocratic Roman factions: the Brutii, Julii, or Scipii—it is possible to play non-Roman factions, but this option was not extended to students for the class exercise. Each faction starts in control of two Italian cities. The player must manage the cities under her control, constructing buildings that add to the economy, happiness, and growth of the settlement. Additional buildings determine the types of military units that can be levied in the city. Using these cities as bases, the player conducts diplomacy with, and campaigns against, any number of ancient powers as she chooses. Campaigns are carried out on a stylized topographical map of the ancient Mediterranean world, where armies, spies, and diplomats are each represented as individual figures. The Senate of Rome, a faction controlled by the computer, also issues missions to the player; these missions consist of military actions, ranging from blockading ports to sacking enemy cities. When the player successfully completes missions in the time allotted, her family's reputation within the Senate increases and family members can win key political offices. If the player ignores or fails to complete the Senate's missions, she may be branded a rebel and forced into civil war against the Roman Senate.

When an army attempts to enter a space occupied by an enemy army or city, a battle ensues. These are conducted in real-time mode. In a pitched battle, the player begins by deploying his troops on one side of a battlefield with terrain ranging from deserts to trees and mountains. In a siege the deployment takes place around a settlement. Either way, the player knows nothing about the placements of the enemy army except that they will be deployed somewhere on the opposite side of the map. After deployment, the positions of the units in both armies are revealed, and the battle begins. Using his mouse, the player issues orders to individual units of infantry, cavalry, missile troops, and skirmishers. Units may march, wheel, change the depth and facing of their formations, attack, and retreat. Orders are not carried out instantaneously; for a unit to change formation, for example, the individual soldier models in the unit (ranging from 40 to 240 models per unit) must shuffle from their current positions into the new positions. Individual units will fight so long as their level of morale remains high enough. If subjected to enough casualties, harassment, or danger—real or perceived—a unit will rout and flee the field. Once all of the player's or computer's units are destroyed or in flight, the battle is over and the army with units remaining on the field is the winner.

There are certainly problems with the game's accuracy, but this is true of all simulation games: being too simplistic in places, incorporating inaccurate details, and allowing the player an extreme level of control that a real Roman general would have traded his favorite warhorse to possess.[9] Yet many of the core mechanics in the game, while not flawless, are historically defensible. The campaign mode illustrates in broad brushstrokes the historical constraints on Roman imperialism. Communication and travel are slow, too slow given the length of game time encompassed in each turn. The important part is that travel clearly takes time in the game as it should in the preindustrial world, particularly when the terrain is rough. Diplomats must journey to the cities of the player's rivals to negotiate deals, or vice versa, reinforcing the idea that, in the ancient world, communication took place at the speed a human or animal walked. Playing the campaign mode, one gets the sense that a fair amount of financial management and planning was necessary to support Roman military campaigns—complementary to the historical reality that armies were expensive and required the flow of tax money.

The game also has a solid model of ancient battle. The unit types available are generally historically accurate, consisting of various forms of infantry, cavalry, and missile troops. The formations of light infantry and heavy infantry differ, as do those of light and heavy cavalry. As an added touch of realism, units move as groups of individuals, and it takes a fair amount of shuffling for a unit, once commanded, to change formation. The inclusion of morale as a critical factor on the battlefield is an especially nice touch. Each unit has a morale level and is rendered inoperative when that level dips too low. The idea that morale, not casualties, was the most critical factor in the outcome of ancient battles is an important component of understanding ancient war.

CivCity: Rome complements the military and imperial focus of *Rome: Total War* by concentrating on managing and supporting the lives of Roman city-dwellers. *CivCity: Rome* is a game of systems.[10] As governor and city planner, the player manages and develops a Roman city. Food production, trade, water supplies, entertainment, defense, taxation, and a number of other aspects of urban life must be carefully managed to build a profitable, growing city. Essentially, the key task is to create a net revenue stream through trade and property taxes. Both require a sizeable and happy population, which in turn requires desirable housing within walking distance of a variety of goods and services. Houses begin as shacks and can evolve into villas when their inhabitants have nearby access to necessities and luxuries ranging from water and meat, to clothing, education, and entertainment. Access to water is provided by constructing a nearby well or cistern. All other products are provided by shops, each selling one type of good. As a house evolves it provides greater tax revenues.

The underlying economy of the game functions using what is sometimes called a daisy chain model: two or more buildings work in conjunction to produce a finished food product or item from raw materials. So, for example, wheat is grown on a wheat farm, ground into flour by a mill, and baked into bread. The digital inhabitants of houses within walking distance of the bakery will get their food there; access to the bakery, in turn, is one of the lower-level requirements for desirable housing. Surplus bread is stored in the city's granaries and becomes part of the general food supply for the city. Trees from forests, to give a second example, are turned into lumber by lumber camps. Bed makers and cabinet makers construct their respective products from the lumber and sell them to the populace. Surplus goods of this sort are stored in the city's warehouses. Trade occurs when the player constructs the necessary building chains to create, store, and trade goods abroad through a trade center or dockyard.

None of these endeavors will succeed, however, if the general population is not kept happy, a separate issue from catering to the desires of individual property dwellers. Measured on a scale from -100 to 100, the happiness of the population increases when enough inhabitants have access to sufficient food, housing, jobs, services, and amenities. Conversely, a lack of these lowers happiness. When the level of happiness is positive, the city will attract immigrants; negative happiness causes citizens to abandon the city.

CivCity has its share of flaws.[11] The most egregious of these is the command economy. As one might expect from a city-building game, the player has the ultimate decisions about what is constructed, what is produced, and what is sold. Certainly, emperors and governors worked to secure grain supplies, provide entertainment, and maintain infrastructures for urban populations, but there was a sizeable market element at work in the economics of ancient cities. A second problem, though one more easily overlooked, is that buildings are constructed instantaneously without labor or supplies, though they do cost money. On a more general level, though, the core models are defensible. The idea, for example, that Roman cities were filled with consumers whose needs had to be satisfied to a certain level in order for the city to thrive is reasonable.

The general supply models are also reasonable. The principle that inhabitants in a city walked or used animals to transport goods is well reflected. Resources must be provided within walking distance of a house for the house's inhabitants to benefit from it. Roads speed travel, making it easier for traders and consumers to obtain more goods more quickly. Furthermore, the principle that all products undergo a set of steps from raw material to finished good is also well represented. Overall, the illustration that the needs and wants of Roman urbanites had to be met for a city to be peaceful and prosperous is sound.

Both of these games contain some defensible explanations of human activity and, thus, were essentially suitable for the ninth-grade class. This all sounds very good on paper, but some educators examining these games might reasonably object that the criteria applied here are too forgiving. In a sense, one might concede, *CivCity: Rome* has a defensible economic model in that consumers' needs are met by businesses that gain their products from manufacturers who extract raw materials from the environment, but only in a sense. This is a general model at best, some will say, and outweighed by the sense of a command economy presented by the game. Or, one might object, *Rome: Total War* has a reasonable battlefield model, but the fact that players can create hodgepodge armies composed of troop types from the republic fighting alongside troop types of the empire and players can personally govern cities as a family faction leader, not an agent of the government, is taking too many liberties.

Two considerations are critical in the rationale for using games such as these. First, history itself is not a static, perfected representation of the past. It is a set of meaningful and defensible interpretations. History students, therefore, are taught best when they are taught the skills and methods of the historian, not saturated with a list of events, causes, and effects already established by the authorities. The flaws in a game cannot be overlooked. Quite the contrary: large-scale flaws in a game provide excellent opportunities for students to practice their skills of criticism. If the only flaws in a game are subtle minutiae, students will not have any reasonable opportunity to offer critiques, the core of the historian's practice. Better still, one person's flaw is another person's accurate portrayal. So, for example, while one student analyzing the game concluded that the command economy in *CivCity: Rome* is a fundamentally flawed model for the early empire, another focusing on the late third century noted that Diocletian fixed prices and even mandated that sons follow their fathers in the same professions. Second, the teacher must serve as the core resource and facilitator to make sure that the necessary kinds of criticism take place. If students do not, on their own, notice the command economy in the game or the unhistorical units, the teacher must pose questions and provide opportunities for students to engage in the necessary critiques.

Having established that these simulation games were suitable for classroom use, the next step was to determine the sorts of problems they pose. This would dictate the kinds of documentary evidence, support materials, and related learning activities that needed to be arranged. Problems of content in *Rome: Total War* include:

- how to overcome challenges posed by geography, limited resources, and personnel to develop a lasting empire;
- how to weigh economic, political, and military alternatives in the development of an empire and choose between competing goals;
- how to deploy and employ different troop types in battle to take advantage of terrain, maximize morale, and achieve military victories.

CivCity: Rome presents its own set of historical problems, including:

- how to organize city development so that city inhabitants receive the necessary supplies and materials to carry out their lives and professions;
- how to satisfy the subsistence needs, and higher-level desires of city inhabitants in economically effective ways;
- how to foster an effective manufacturing, trade, and supply network using preindustrial forms of production, transport, and communication.

As far as the problems of interpretation, they are nearly limitless. Any element of the games can be subjected to scrutiny.

To support the study of these content problems, a set of supplemental lectures, core readings, and other supporting media should be prepared corresponding to the key content areas in the simulations. In the case of these two simulations the lecture topics selected were an overview of Roman history, the constitution of the republic, the alliance system, aristocratic competition, urban planning, and daily life in cities. Excerpts of modern secondary source readings provided additional detail on each of these topics. In addition, a set of relevant ancient primary and secondary source excerpts was collected: the writings of Polybius and Livy, the letters of the governor Pliny, epitaphs for working women in cities, and the like. It is beyond the scope of this chapter to go into the details of gathering these resources, but it is worth noting that the Internet contains many if not all the original source materials needed for anything short of a professional-level analysis of these topics. Above all, students need to engage a variety of rich sources of evidence as they play. Although a chapter like this understandably focuses on the games, the time that should be spent studying these sources of evidence is a critical part of any simulation lesson.

With the content problems and supporting resources relatively set, the remaining learning objectives needed to be determined and the appropriate lessons designed to achieve those objectives. In the case of the Roman history unit, these learning objectives focused on several core skills critical to the discipline of history and, in some cases, future professional success in the world:

- practicing collaboration to solve problems;
- developing writing fluency through regular practice of written expression;
- forming meaningful historical questions about Roman history; thinking about the world of the Romans and how they behaved in it;
- conducting research based on the historical questions posed;
- composing a formal essay evaluating the accuracy of the interpretations in the simulations; checking the information in multiple sources against each other.

These are far from the only things of value students can learn while studying historical simulations, but they are a core set of highly important skills.

Learning objectives established, the next step was to plan for productive play and observation sessions that would lay the foundation for later research exercises. There are several basic steps in planning effective simulation experiences. The first, already mentioned, is selecting rich sources of evidence and supplemental resources. The others are:

- training students to play the game;
- forming play and observation teams;
- promoting and facilitating observation;
- fostering reflection and analysis.

It is important to trace the progression of experiments and reasoning that led to these steps, particularly the imperative to begin by training students well to play the game. Since the ultimate goal of history teachers is to get students to analyze, synthesize, and evaluate, it can be very tempting to rush students learning a game and move them quickly into analysis. While I assumed, in my first uses of simulation games in the classroom, that students would need some time to become familiar with the game, I greatly underestimated the actual amount of time needed and tried to jump quickly into analysis—say, after forty-five minutes of exposure to the game. Time has demonstrated that rushing students through this training can undermine the effectiveness of the whole lesson. Resisting the temptation to hurry on to the analysis is critical. Students must be taught to play the game and given sufficient opportunity to do so before they are asked to analyze and evaluate the game's models. The overall quality of the learning experience can be diminished greatly by shortchanging the time spent learning to play the simulation. It is all too often assumed that students under the age of, say, 25 are naturally disposed to playing video games. This is a suspect assumption at best, but certainly not the case with historical strategy games, the core genre for simulations. Some students simply do not play video games, and skill manipulating a cell phone, navigating a webpage, or communicating through *Facebook* is not the same thing. Many do play video games, but they are console games like *Left 4 Dead* and *Modern Warfare*, which emphasize fast reflexes, superior hand-eye coordination, and quick tactics rather than the slower-paced, managerial and strategic skills required by a historical strategy game.

Perhaps most importantly, it is decidedly not the case that students will be categorically so overjoyed to play a simulation game that they will throw themselves wholeheartedly into the task of learning to play. This will be true of some students at least. Some students would simply rather not play a simulation—though the same could be said about writing a paper. They find the experience offers unsettling challenges, requiring them to exercise a level of independence and problem solving to which they are unaccustomed, all the while concerned about how this activity translates into the grades they will earn in class. This is most often the case with the strongest traditional learners. Many, though hardly all, would rather sit through a traditional lecture because they know how to score well on tests and papers in that environment; conversely, a simulation game would challenge them to think in different ways. This is a major reason why they should play simulation games: to learn to think flexibly. Indeed, one of the values of a history education is to learn to challenge assumptions—others' and one's own; that includes assumptions about what forms of media can be subjected to historical analysis. Expect, however, that not all students will be enthusiastic. Under ordinary circumstances, though, how regularly does or even should a teacher ask for the consensus of the class on every single topic of study and assessment? Simulation games are well worth including in the classroom. If they are incorporated primarily for entertainment reasons, however, rather than for their relevant strengths as learning tools, the teacher is in for a disappointment.

Since the potential appeal of simulations does not guarantee students will wholeheartedly and easily learn to play, like any other skill in a class, playing a particular game must be taught. Although some video games have excellent built-in tutorials, it is sometimes more effective to bypass the tutorials and devote one or two classes to training students how to play directly. The scope of the tutorial relative to the gameplay the teacher wants to emphasize, the available class time, and the motivation of students to learn are the key factors when deciding whether to go with a game's preexisting tutorials or to create a more tailored training experience. The tutorial in *Rome: Total War*, for example, spends a great deal of time focusing on the particulars of commanding armies in battles. If the emphasis in class will be on the higher strategic level of play, the tutorial may effectively be replaced by the teacher's instruction. If the focus is on battlefield dynamics, on the other hand, the tutorial is a great tool to help learn the game. The basic principles of *CivCity: Rome*, on the other hand, can probably be relayed more efficiently by a teacher than by the game's own tutorial. The bottom line, though, is that students need to learn the game fairly well to be able to critique it.

This principle has developed from the experiences of numerous classroom implementations, including the most recent lessons using *Rome: Total War* and *CivCity: Rome*. For various reasons—as I recall, the last-minute disappearance of a projector that would allow me to lead students by example through the early stages of the game—the students learned to play *Rome: Total War* through the tutorial. A number became bogged down by the battlefield component. Since they were not able to save their progress in the middle of the battle tutorial, these students effectively had to spend more than one class completing what ideally might have been a forty-five-minute tutorial. Ultimately, I had to provide a fair amount of additional support to help students become comfortable with playing the game, support that might well have been unnecessary had I directly trained students. In contrast, students received direct training in *CivCity: Rome* and were clearly far more comfortable with that game. There were assuredly other factors at work—there always are—but erring on the side of providing formal training, while not always essential, will tend to produce the most consistent results.

What does formal training look like in practice? The number of students, their ages, their abilities, and their levels of motivation will determine the feel of the classroom. It is best, however, to err on the side of creating a highly structured training environment; this will help keep more rambunctious students on task while also providing extra support for those who need reassurance. First, run the game on a computer that has a projected display. Start the game on the easiest setting and provide explicit instructions for playing the game. While it can be helpful to have students observe the game and take notes before playing along, most will not begin to learn how to play until they actually have to do so themselves. This can be accomplished in a structured fashion by having students follow along on their own computers and carry out the instructions executed by the teacher.

These instructions will vary from game to game and class to class, but there are some common elements. First, introduce students to the basic goals of the game. In *Rome: Total War*, the general goal is to complete the missions assigned by the Senate and, in general, expand one's empire by capturing enemy territories. In *CivCity: Rome*, on the other hand, the general mission is to build a city that generates a positive revenue stream. It is not always immediately apparent to students what they should be doing in a game. Providing general goals keeps students focused on gameplay and enables them to play more independently. Second, instruct students in basic game mechanics and provide simple strategies for a successful start to the game. In *Rome: Total War* this means surveying the basics of building up cities, recruiting soldiers, maneuvering armies, and conducting sieges. In *CivCity: Rome* this means training students to identify and create the various daisy chains that support the economy and provide necessities to developing residential areas. Third, provide students with general problem-solving strategies and resources. These include their peers, web forums devoted to the game, and the game manual. If available, it can be particularly helpful to set up an online discussion forum using Moodle or some other online content management system so that students can ask and answer questions in a format that the whole class can see. Depending on the motivation of students, it does not hurt to incentivize or explicitly require posting questions and answers on the forum. The amount of time devoted to training will vary. With games of moderate complexity like *Rome: Total War* and *CivCity: Rome*, plan for about two hours of training. This can be portioned in different amounts of class and out-of-class time, as time and resources allow.

After students learn the basics of the game, they should shift into the observation phase. The goal of this phase is to create a lab-like environment in which students can observe how the simulation works and make notes accordingly. To this end, it is often a good idea to form teams of three for the observation phase rather than have students play the game individually, at least when play takes place during class time. In this kind of grouping one student plays the game while the other two take observation notes; after a certain amount of playtime, the team members exchange tasks. This kind of setup encourages the taking of effective notes and prevents an individual from getting too engrossed in the play to reflect; it is the method that was used most often in the Roman history unit. With most students, it is a good idea to stop classroom gameplay every twenty to thirty minutes and spend five minutes catching up on notes. Children and adults alike can easily get too engrossed in a game to stop and make notes without prompting. The point of the whole simulation exercise, however, is not for students to be entertained; it is for them to learn.

Providing guidelines can enhance the quality of observations. Sometimes this is just a matter of introducing the leading topics students should use to focus their notes. Some general examples suited for most simulation games include:

- the role of the player in the game world and the challenges the game world presents;
- the actions the player takes to overcome the challenges;
- the trade-offs in the game between competing actions and the spending of finite resources;
- the strategies and actions that lead to success or failure and the measurement of success and failure in the game.

Certain games, especially short web-based games, lend themselves to a system where the player records the choices she makes every turn, rationales for each choice, and the results of the choices. *Rome: Total War* and *CivCity: Rome* are complex enough, however, to justify taking regular pauses from the game even though students were generally arranged in trios of one player and two note takers. These pauses emphasize the need to observe and record the play experience.

After logging sufficient observations, more analytical tasks can be introduced. These can include problem-based learning style exercises inspired by student questions, explicit teacher instructions, or both. When analyzing *Rome: Total War*, for example, some students attempted to determine how far Roman armies could travel in a six-month game turn. They needed to develop problem-solving strategies to do so. With a bit of Socratic questioning on the teacher's part, students began looking at online maps, making rough calculations of distances and times, and comparing them to historical data on troop marches. Other students were concerned with how winter affected the Roman army. They engaged in a series of experiments, looking at the supply costs for the armies in spring and in winter. These experiments all arose from students' primary research questions and so only the students researching travel, for example, ran travel experiments in the game.

Encouraged by the sight of students conducting experiments with *Rome: Total War*, however, inspired me to assign to the whole class some explicit analytical tasks concerning the game models in *CivCity: Rome*. For example:

- Diagram three food supply systems and product supply systems. Include each step in the chain.
- During play, you receive the message, "Sir, your granary is empty." What does this mean? What steps must you take to thoroughly diagnose the problem? Draw a flow chart to indicate the potential problems and solutions.

The ability of simulation games to serve as foundations for problem-based learning (PBL) exercises is one of the more promising areas in need of development. Excellent PBL sessions can be created by posing inquiry tasks that require students to develop problem-solving plans. In future uses of these games, for example, students could be charged to:

- determine the scale of the city map in *CivCity: Rome* and based on this scale compare and evaluate the amount of farmland compared to the amount of civic space;
- determine the ratio of farms to people in the game and compare this to historical evidence for peasant societies;
- determine the scale of armies in RTW and, based on this scale, determine the accuracy of the map and the speed at which armies can travel in the game.

Exercises like these can hone problem-solving skills, increase students' familiarity with game models, and generate some insights into the past at the same time.

Throughout the observation and analysis phases, students should study historical evidence and reflect regularly on their experiences in the game. The Country Day students used a blog to record observation notes, enter reflections on their gaming experiences, and pose questions about the interpretations of the games. The advantage of the blog system is it promoted the idea that the students are a learning community and that they can share and learn from one another.[12]

Once the observation, analysis, and reflection components are completed, the historical resources studied, and lectures heard, it was time to undertake some form of formal research and written critique. In accordance with the great importance of developing students' critical writing skills, my ninth-graders were tasked to research and write a formal critical essay about some aspect of the game. This was an exercise in forming meaningful questions, understanding how the game answers the questions, studying evidence, and constructing a formal analysis. First, students posted two or three historical questions raised by the game and discussed these in class. The questions ran an impressive gamut. For *Rome: Total War*:

- How did the Romans treat captured cities?
- What were the strengths and weaknesses of the Roman alliance system in Italy?
- How did distance and geography affect communications between the Senate and armies in the field? How did these factors affect diplomacy with other peoples?
- Did the Romans acquire an empire in self-defense or through active aggression?
- How were sieges conducted?
- What was the role of morale in battlefield victories and how did the Romans raise and maintain morale?

CivCity: Rome evoked these questions:

- How extensive was trade between private citizens in the Empire as opposed to government-sponsored trade?
- To what extent was the economy of the city controlled by the government?
- How important were public gardens, fountains, and other amenities to the happiness of an ancient city's inhabitants?
- To what extent was the happiness of Roman citizens really a high priority for government officials?
- Where and how did Romans obtain their supplies for constructing cities, especially when suitable resources were not nearby?
- How critical a problem was fire in ancient cities and how did the Romans deal with firefighting?

Interestingly enough, one of the most common sources of frustration and most common historical questions raised by the game concerned the distances the inhabitants of *CivCity: Rome* were willing to walk to satisfy their needs. Many felt the radius the digital inhabitants were willing to travel was simply too limited and raised the question: how far could or would inhabitants of a Roman city have to travel to obtain the goods and services they wanted and needed?

The significance of these questions should not be underestimated. The students essentially came up with their own meaningful, high-level historical questions. Perhaps most striking, all of these questions have been the subjects of research and writing by professional historians; when presented with a game, these students were able to pose the kinds of questions that experts in the field do. [13] Rather than be assigned a research question, every student was able to formulate a meaningful question for research.

The students then presented the questions in class that they wanted to investigate for their papers. I offered suggestions, as necessary, for avenues of investigation and sources of evidence. To promote the legitimacy of their authentic historical questions and encourage a spirit of collaboration, students were able to switch questions and pursue different lines of inquiry if a classmate presented a question they found more intriguing. Subsequently, they researched and wrote persuasive, evidence-based essays arguing how accurately the simulation portrayed the issues they chose to investigate. *Google Books* was the assigned research tool, though students were also encouraged to use primary and secondary source excerpts from their class readings. *Google Books* offers considerable advantages as a tool for teaching basic research. While the system does reduce the need to pore through library stacks, arguably that is not the core of research anyway. With large numbers of book excerpts available, students can pursue virtually any topic raised by the simulation. Nor are the students' obligations to read and consider the evidence negated by the search tool. Any search can return large numbers of texts. This means students must practice scanning works to find those that are actually useful for the argument they are making—a core research skill. This also requires them to make sure they understand enough of the context surrounding the evidence, to avoid misrepresenting evidence.

These papers served as the primary form of assessment for the simulation units. The effectiveness of the exercise can only be demonstrated anecdotally, but several aspects of the papers the students wrote stood out from the typical ninth-grade persuasive essay assignments I have assigned over the decade. First, as noted earlier, the great variety of high-quality topics that the students pursued was impressive. This was both a function of the simulations' ability to raise a variety of questions and the flexibility of the available research tools. For most of us, getting students to explore authentic, high-quality questions and construct formal answers based on historical research is a difficult task, indeed. One common solution is to get students to form their own questions. Asking students to form their own questions without sufficient grounding in the possibilities, however, can sometimes lead to the writing of reports rather than arguments, or the tackling of questions too large or too general to be appropriate for a class paper. Assigning a single question to the whole class, on the other hand, can ensure that the task students undertake is viable. But this kind of standardization has its costs; it removes the opportunity for students to form their own questions and pursue their own lines of inquiry. This has certainly been my experience over the years. These simulation papers were something different from the norm. They were varied and original. Indeed, some students chose to pursue the same question, but conducted their research and argumentation in strikingly different ways. In short, these papers were excellent models of the kind of work historians and history teachers should value.

At no point should it be understood that the use of simulation games in the classroom has reached anything approaching a pinnacle of effectiveness. There are many areas where further experimentation, in addition to formal research, is needed. The goal of using simulation games as a tool for studying, researching, and critiquing historical models was generally successful in this most recent implementation. Still there are important areas to expand on in the future. Two in particular stand out. First, exercises should be developed that require students to explore and learn the general content of the games more closely. It is critical to the use of historical simulation games to take them as interpretations and thus in need of corroboration from historical sources. For practical purposes, however, there are areas of well-established historical convention within these and other simulation games that the teacher can identify for students to learn while still maintaining the standard that the games are interpretations, not sources of truth. For example, it is reasonable for students to review, record, and be assessed on elements of content contained in the games such as, for example:

- What were the key components of a Roman army and their equipment?
- What were the different types of housing in a Roman city and how can each be accurately characterized?
- What are the geographic locations of the Romans, Greeks, Macedonians, Gauls, Carthaginians, and the like? What are the main topographical features of the regions each culture occupied?
- What were primary forms of entertainment in a Roman city?

Obtaining purely factual knowledge by itself, as opposed to honing higher-order analysis and evaluation skills, is an insufficient reason to justify the time and potential expense of a simulation. It does not follow, however, that teachers should pass up obvious opportunities to get students to learn core information as they engage in the simulation. Of course, care must be taken by the teacher to make sure that students are guided through the more and less accurate aspects of game content.

The second area for expansion is to discuss in more quantifiable terms with students the core mechanics that are at work in the games themselves.

Theorists on the role of games in learning and popular culture increasingly stress the importance of procedural literacy: that those who wish to treat simulation games critically must be aware of the procedures—the algorithms and routines—that underlie them.[14] The implementation outlined above treated the games as texts, which they certainly are, and focused on discussing the interpretations of these texts. The discussions, however, did not really address the fact that the games have quite precise, although sometimes simplistic, mathematical models underlying them and those models themselves are inherently subject to human bias, let alone miscalculation. Introducing the idea that these games contain quantifiable models that are, despite their quantification, far from perfectly accurate, is an important step along the way to learning to treat technology as a tool, not a deity. Topics like this could readily be addressed through general discussions of variables and their relations at a level reasonable for those with a basic knowledge of algebra. So, for example, students could outline what the main variables likely are in the battlefield model of *Rome: Total War* and how those variables likely interrelate, or something similar for the determination of property values in *CivCity: Rome*.

In closing, it is worth considering once again why many teachers, even those who have kept reading up to this point, still feel uncomfortable or outright skeptical of the idea of experimenting with simulations. This is probably particularly the case for those who teach public school curricula dictated by school boards, state standards, and high-stakes tests. Educators in these situations—and there are many—may rightly feel that they have little room to improvise, innovate, and experiment, little room to deviate in any significant way from traditional methods of instruction and the prescribed curriculum. To be fair, teaching in an independent school has provided me, like so many independent school teachers, with greater discretion in setting classroom curricula and pedagogical approaches than teachers have in many schools. Still, there are ways for teachers with less flexible curricula to incorporate simulation games effectively in the classroom. The options for simulations extend far beyond *Rome: Total War* and *CivCity: Rome*. There are simulations addressing a wide variety of topics and periods. There are also a host of freely available web-based simulations that address contemporary issues and require no more than a half hour to play. Those who cannot spend days away from a mandated curriculum can use these smaller-scale games to engage in more economically chunked critical-thinking exercises.

With so many options, large and small, let's turn this primary objection on its head. The real question is, what are we teaching our students if we never improvise, innovate, and experiment; never deviate in any significant way from traditional methods of instruction and the prescribed curriculum?

How can history teachers effectively prepare their students for the twenty-first century by suggesting that teachers are the sole source of authority; that learning is something that is received through oral and written texts alone; that historical interpretations can only be captured in letters, never in image and code? Simulation games can play an integral role in teaching history as a twenty-first-century discipline, when they are treated as some of the many forms of interpretation of the past, with special properties for representing the world, but no particular claim to truth. In practice this requires allowing simulations to pose problems and inspire authentic questions about the past that students can tackle.

A final thought: certainly, adopting this stance and pedagogy does require teachers with some confidence and skill in the methodologies of a historian. When a class shifts from the transmission of information to open-ended problem solving, there will be many times when the teacher simply does not have an answer on hand. This is the point; students need to learn, over time of course, to function as independent historians, not simply to rely on the closest source of authority for answers. Adopting this principle has the potential to open up a teacher's history classes to engage in something far closer to the true inquiry of the professionals. There is much to be gained. In a world with so many competing claims to the truth, where vocal figures in politics, the media, entertainment, and religion offer versions of reality that are often in conflict and in need of critique, an educated person must be able to judge the validity not only of discrete facts, but of competing claims to historical truth. Students who are taught more than the chronology, or even the story of history, and learn to do history have the opportunity to acquire crucial skills of critique, analysis, and interpretation of human events. Students who learn that interpretations are not only ensconced in writing, but are embedded in videos, podcasts, mash-ups, and, yes, video games, can gain valuable tools for negotiating the modern world.

NOTES

1. The seminal work in the field comes from James Paul Gee, and readers interested in learning about general games and learning theory should start with his books, *What Video Games Have to Teach Us about Learning and Literacy* (New York: Palgrave Macmillan, 2003) and *Good Video Games and Good Learning* (New York: Peter Lang, 2007). See also David Williamson Shaffer, *How Computer Games Help Children Learn* (New York: Palgrave Macmillan, 2006). Important work has been done in the journals, and the following articles offer good points of introduction to the field: Rosemary Garris, Robert Ahlers, and James E. Driskell, "Games, Motivation, and Learning: A Research and Practice Model," *Simulation & Gaming* 33 (2002): 441–67; Harold F. O'Neil, Richard Wainess, and Eva L. Baker, "Classification of Learning

Outcomes: Evidence from the Computer Games Literature," *The Curriculum Journal* 16 (2005): 455–74; Kurt Squire et al., "Design Principles of Next-Generation Digital Gaming for Education," *Educational Technology* 43 (2003): 17–23; Susan McLester, "Game Plan," *Technology and Learning* 26 (2005): 18–26; S. Tobias and J. Fletcher, "What Research Has to Say about Designing Computer Games for Learning," *Educational Technology* 47 (2007): 20–29. For a counterpoint to these studies, see R. Clark, "Learning from Serious Games? Arguments, Evidence, and Research Suggestions," *Educational Technology* 47 (2007): 56–59. Be sure to read Squire's response to Clark in K. Squire, "Games, Learning, and Society: Building a Field," *Educational Technology* 47 (2007): 51–55.

2. For some definitions, see S. Tobias and J. Fletcher, "What Research Has to Say about Designing Computer Games for Learning," *Educational Technology* 47 (2007): 20–29; Christian Elverdam and Espen Aarseth, "Game Classification and Game Design: Construction through Critical Analysis," *Games and Culture* 2 (2007): 3–22, accessed October 12, 2010, http://gac.sagepub.com/cgi/reprint/2/1/3; Katie Salen and Eric Zimmerman, *Rules of Play: Game Design Fundamentals* (Cambridge, Mass.: MIT Press, 2003), 422–58.

3. Salen and Zimmerman, 80.

4. This can be compared to the established use of micro-worlds in science and mathematics education. On micro-worlds, see John Bransford et al., eds., *How People Learn* (Washington D.C.: National Academy Press, 1999); Shaffer, 67–71; James M. Monaghan and John Clement, "Algorithms, Visualization, and Mental Models: High School Students' Interactions with a Relative Motion Simulation," *Journal of Science Education and Technology* 9 (2006): 311–25; Barbara White and John R. Frederiksen, "Inquiry, Modeling, and Metacognition: Making Science Accessible to All Students," *Cognition and Instruction* 16 (1998): 3–118; Leslie P. Steffe and Heide G. Wiegel, "Cognitive Play and Mathematical Learning in Computer Microworlds," *Educational Studies in Mathematics* 26 (1994): 111–34; Roxana Moreno et al., "The Case for Social Agency in Computer-Based Teaching: Do Students Learn More Deeply When They Interact with Animated Pedagogical Agents?" *Cognition and Instruction* 19 (2001): 177–213; Maria Kordaki, "The Effect of Tools of a Computer Microworld on Students' Strategies Regarding the Concept of Conservation of Area," *Educational Studies in Mathematics* 52 (2003): 177–209.

5. Samuel S. Wineburg, *Historical Thinking and Other Unnatural Acts* (Philadelphia: Temple University Press, 2001), 63–88, details a seminal experiment in the difference between how students and professional historians read texts.

6. As recently as his interview for Kotaku Talk Radio on May 5, 2010, mp3 interview file, accessed July 31, 2012, http://kotaku.com/5531995/an-hour-of-sid-meier-brilliance-including-his-surprise-guitar-hero-regret. Sid Meier, the creator of the *Civilization* series, noted once again that he and his design teams focused on making an entertaining and engaging game first and added the historical research after the fact.

7. Richard E. Mayer, "Should There Be a Three-Strikes Rule against Pure Discovery Learning?" *American Psychologist* 59 (2004): 14–19, is an excellent study suggesting that inquiry learning is most effective when the teacher remains an active presence in the activity.

8. Currently available through the online services *Steam* (store.steampowered .com), and *Direct2Drive*, accessed July 31, 2012, www.Direct2Drive.com; Amazon.com is an excellent source for hard copies.

9. These are not particularly controversial points in the field, but for some support of the general outlines here, one could examine John Rich and Graham Shipley, *War and Society in the Roman World* (London: Routledge, 1993); William V. Harris, *War and Imperialism in Republican Rome 327–70 B.C.* (New York: Oxford University Press, 1979); Jeremiah McCall, *The Cavalry of the Roman Republic* (New York: Routledge, 2001); Adrian K. Goldsworthy, *The Roman Army at War, 100 BC–AD 200* (Oxford: Clarendon, 1996).

10. Also available through the online services *Steam* (store.steampowered.com) and *Direct2Drive* (www.Direct2Drive.com); Amazon.com is an excellent source for hard copies.

11. The reader might turn to the following books to start when considering the issues involving Roman cities: John E. Stambaugh, *The Ancient Roman City* (Baltimore: Johns Hopkins University Press, 1988); Pierre Grimal, *Roman Cities*, trans. G. Michael Woloch (Madison: University of Wisconsin Press, 1983); Patricia Crone, *Pre-Industrial Societies* (Oxford: Basil Blackwell, 1989).

12. We used *Ning*, which has recently ended its free hosting of social networks. Interested teachers will need to do some online research to find acceptable substitutes.

13. Entries in Rich and Shipley cover most of these subjects. The groundbreaking works on communications between the Senate and field commanders and the motives for imperialism, respectively, are Arthur M. Eckstein, *Senate and General: Individual Decision Making and Roman Foreign Relations 264–194 B.C.* (Berkeley: University of California Press, 1987), and Harris.

14. See, for example, Ian Bogost, *Persuasive Games: The Expressive Power of Videogames* (Cambridge, Mass.: MIT Press, 2007).

By Building

TWELVE

Playing into the Past

Reconsidering the Educational Promise
of Public History Exhibits

Brenda Trofanenko

Throughout its history, the public museum has been a powerful educational institution. As one of the most prestigious of public spaces where valued material objects serve as essential forms of evidence of art, culture, history, and science, the public museum mediates the knowledge produced by its exhibitions and displays with the various attending publics, as a means to define, educate, and impress its citizens.[1] In public history museums, various objects, images, and narratives of the past are marshaled in the name of the nation, which collectively contribute directly to the construction and presentation of a specific history.[2] Public history museums remain one of the most popular and trustworthy places from which our youth gain an understanding of the past, and as a result, they hold much influence.[3]

Recently, public history museums are moving beyond the traditional museum displays to entertain new ways of displaying objects and information. The advent of digital technologies (notably the world wide web) has prompted public history museums to reexamine their specific knowledge paradigms. The opportunities offered by *Google*, *YouTube*, and *Flickr*, for example, have transformed the collections and information about the collections into a more open flow. Visitors may now attend museums that link their collection searches to *Google*, placing them in a wider flow of interconnected cultural, political, economic, and technological ideas and resources. Through these public spaces, visitors are able to garner knowledge within wider cultural and social contexts.

The last several years have witnessed the emergence of an increasingly robust collection of research and scholarship on museums and digital technologies.[4]

Several issues have emerged. The first, initially raised by Michelle Henning[5] is whether history museums (like other disciplinary museums) are placing an increasing emphasis on their experiential and performative aspects in exhibitions, resulting in decreasing opportunities for public engagement with historical inquiry through identifying information from the objects, comparing and corroborating information, and analyzing information in order to understand issues associated with historical events. The second, as noted by Fiona Cameron, addresses the current mandates and authority of many museums, which continue to posit the bricks-and-mortar museum as a privileged symbol of the past, of culture, and of national identity, and simplify the information each object provides the public, when various available technologies could contextualize that information and support knowledge creation.[6] Museums are presently deciding whether, and to what extent, to adopt web 2.0 platforms and practices. Adoption of these technologies could promote the public's engagement with museum collections, and support feedback and relationships with those who have attended museums and those who share a common interest. At the same time, adoption of these technologies may mean that the museum no longer controls what knowledge is created, and is instead contributing to a more collaborative production and sharing of knowledge.[7]

There is a moment when visiting history museums when the full measure of the intersection between the past and the present reveals itself. This relation occurs through displayed objects entwined with narratives that inform the visitor of what has passed. Images, objects, and narratives are selected to authenticate history and to represent interconnected and divergent past events. While this complexity comes across in a simplified and objective manner through which knowledge is to be gained directly from the object, history is considered something "taken in and taken home."[8] This didactic notion ignores the contemporary debates about how knowledge is interactively produced, consumed, and distributed in a museum. History museums grapple with contemporary debates about issues, including their public relevance and usefulness and knowledge production.[9] The increased utilization of technologies raises questions for museums about how best to use social media in pedagogically sound ways that support their mandates, personnel expertise, and public expectations.[10] It is not enough for museums to focus specifically on the idea of "if we build it they will come" but instead, to consider how to meld their various mandates with the increasingly prolific technologies.

When considering the playful nature of history by way of historical inquiry, as noted in chapters 6 and 7 in this volume by Sean Gouglas and Bethany Nowviskie et al., the digital media and computer technologies that may support such inquiry are often mismatched. Certainly, the increasing commitment by scholars and cultural heritage institutions (including museums, archives, and libraries) to democratizing history by encouraging people to participate in preserving and presenting the past has opened up increasing access to resources. What is often missing, though, is providing opportunities for youth to work with tools in order to gain meaningfully from these resources. I am often at a loss in understanding why displays and exhibitions revert back to a didactic transmission of knowledge even when the institution itself is utilizing various technologies and the youth attending are engaged with these technologies beyond the museum. Why do museums limit the playful engagement in understanding the past when history is a dynamic and playful discipline? There are two reasons. The first is that museums attempt to advance and achieve their broad educational mission with an obvious end goal of presenting factual knowledge about the past. The second answer is related to how history is defined in history museums: the traditional presentation of history in museums relies on objects and text panels. The objects serve as evidence that a past did indeed exist, while the text panels attempt to provide the narrative context of the historical event. The history presented in a museum is often one framed as the commodity to be taken from the museum. The knowledge gained from any object is often thought to be singular and truthful instead of multiple and open to interpretation. The public history museum's role as a communicator of messages and the public as the recipients of those messages depend on the objects as "utterances"—instances of "speech" organized into a "grammar" through practices of collection and display.[11] This dependence on an object-based epistemology, where "the focus is on what knowledge is gained directly from the object itself," ignores what information can be attained within and beyond the museum through the utilization of technologies.[12] The availability of additional information that contextualizes what is placed on display can extend the knowledge drawn from the exhibition itself. It seems as though the opportunities to engage in playfulness within the museum are limited in exhibits, where the materiality within the museum carries authority as evidence and knowledge. By utilizing various technologies that provide additional text, images, maps, and the like, museums can provide students with increased sources from which to understand what is on display, what relevance it may hold to historical understanding, as well as transforming the museum from an authority to a facilitator.

I have argued elsewhere that youth have the capacity to develop a historical consciousness and to question what historical narratives are proffered in public history exhibits and for what purposes.[13] I have also argued that museums need to allow for, and invite, opportunities for our youth to critique the exhibit itself in order to advance the museum's educational mandate.[14] Can the knowledge gained from a history museum go beyond the didactic knowledge deemed essential? Can public history museums move away from being the sole authority of knowledge in order to advance their historical democratic sensibilities? In this chapter, I offer insight on how a group of students engaged the National Museum of American History (NMAH) in Washington, D.C., as they worked to understand the museum as an educational source. This research will serve as a call to educators to reconceptualize the museum as a pedagogical site, to invite our youth to advance their own learning about the past through the interchange between the museum and technology, and to utilize the technologies beyond the museum to return to the playfulness of learning. Here I present a brief explanation of a research project involving students developing a digital mash-up, a media project mixing various texts, graphics, audio, and video, to advance their own historical knowledge about war and its role in U.S. identity formation.

Research Context

In the fall of 2005, I began a multiyear research project that involved working with a group of grade 8 students at a charter school in Washington, D.C. The large-scale project focused on how students came to understand identity formation, how identity is defined and by whom, and how individual and collective identities are advanced through specific public institutions (including schools, museums, archives, and memorials) and particular school subjects (including history, literature, and biology). This particular study also provided an opportunity to examine how various technologies were utilized to aid classroom instruction and student learning, which served to satisfy one of the charter school's main mandates. A second feature of this study was the weekly off-site activities, also a school mandate, which included (in this case) a regularly scheduled day-long experience in several of the museums within the Smithsonian Institute organization.

During the three months I spent in the classroom, I observed the teacher working with the students to understand the association between history and identity, and the relevance of museums in defining both personal and collective identities through history. Each day I witnessed various teacher and student activities: the teacher providing directed lectures about working with source materials, the students attempting to understand what information the selected source material provided to their overarching focus, and both the teacher and the students engaging in discussions and debates about who defines what history is, when displayed in the public realm of a museum. As well, I observed how the students utilized various social media and web-based technologies in their own classroom learning opportunities, and how the teacher explained the ways in which technology served various pedagogical purposes.

The teacher's own educational background as a historian and as an educator ensured that the students received instruction about history's disciplinary elements (notably: close reading of the source, textual analysis, identifying corroborative information, and narrative structure and argument). She also provided learning activities she believed were pedagogically sound, which allowed the students to understand the art of history instead of solely learning historical fact (specifically the identification, analysis, and comparison of source materials to formulate an argument). This commitment was evident in various ways: in the classroom activities undertaken prior to the museum visits; the weekly museum visits that extended throughout the school day; and the post-visit classroom activities (which resulted in the production of a five-minute mash-up video that incorporated digital archival documents, music, altered photographs, and exhibition objects that highlighted the students' representation of a collective U.S. identity). These mash-ups provided the students with an opportunity to present their own meta-narratives of the museum's representation of a collective identity vis-à-vis war and military engagement. The students visited the National Museum of American History to understand its role in defining both personal and collective identities, with weekly dedicated time spent in *The Price of Freedom: Americans at War* exhibit.[15]

Prior to attending the exhibit, the students debated the relationship between history and identity and the purpose museums serve to both. Several open and frank discussions about the learning that occurred (or not) within a museum also took place prior to and throughout the unit. The teaching directed the students to examine selected objects and "read" the information easily obtained from the label, consider how this information contributed to the larger exhibition narrative, and argue its broader application to identity formation. The teacher-student interactions also focused on how the students could use various technologies (*Google*, *YouTube*, *Flickr*, digital collections from the Smithsonian Institute, the Library of Congress, the National Archives and Records, for example) to gain information that would inform their mash-up videos.

Students were evaluated on their understanding of history at several stages during the study, including student engagement with digital technologies (as directed by the school's charter-mandate), informal conversations between the teacher and students about their works in progress, written justification of selected topic and suitable sources, and the final mash-up.

The students were assessed on basic historic information obtained from the exhibit, how their selected exhibition element (an object, theme, or narrative) aligned with their mash-up theme, and the support of their argument of the museum's role in identity formation. The evaluation included classroom-based examinations and grading of the final project. While the teacher did not assume all students could engage with technologies to an equal skill and complexity level, she knew individual student abilities (and organized the student groups to ensure various abilities).

Research Results

The NMAH, like other museums, is a "guardian of important things," of objects and material goods displayed in order to advance their educational purpose of providing experiences from which the attending public can learn about the past.[16] The objects assume an object-based epistemology; each is readily conceptualized and offers, as Henrietta Riegel noted, "a lesson at a glance, a confirmation of actual life as documented and preserved."[17] The physical objects serve as the evidence on which history depends for verification, and their presence in the museum provides the authority for museums to tell a their selected story of a past. Andreas Huyssen, for example, argues that "one reason for the new found strength of the museum in the public sphere may have something to do with the fact that it offers the material quality of the object."[18]

This point was not lost on the students. When asked about the museum's educational role, a student named Stuart replied that this exhibit was "more than a collection of guns." But he quickly followed up by saying that "you can learn more about guns, if you really, really want to." He listed, and then showed, the various sites where he and his group obtained information and noted the ease of a *Google* search and the amount of sources from which he may draw. He acknowledged openly the necessity of objects as the basis of learning within the museum, but also noted the limited information provided by each object within the exhibit. His group used guns as a point of reference for their mash-up. He also spoke about how his group, when bringing in computers to the exhibit, would access sites to present immediate additional information, which would then have to be analyzed as to their relevance and dependability.

Stuart and his fellow group members (Lisa, Luci, and Paulo) spoke at length about the limits of the exhibit and the information gained from the objects. Lisa stated that the obvious knowledge gained from the object "depends on the label," while Paulo noted that people bring their own knowledge to the exhibit. The exchange among the group members moved to how they used various technologies through their assignment. They included videos they completed of the exhibit itself, photos of the material objects displayed, pictures of the text panels and tags, and clips from movies that featured guns (specifically war movies and westerns). Their mash-up, which they called *How the West Was One*, centered on the idea of guns as a metaphor for bringing together and dispersing people.

Perhaps the most cogent point in the student discussions concerned how history is presented in the NMAH through the displayed objects found within a temporal 3D space organized around a time line. The students collectively highlighted how objects considered relevant to an exhibition were arranged near key dates to illustrate the points on the time line and to fit neatly into the chronology of events. Lisa pointedly argued, following Alun Munslow's claim, that history is "assembled as a string of selected and linked events and recounted in the shape of a narrative."[19] The NMAH follows Munslow's claim that the traditional exhibition standard is to "turn the displayed objects into something else [a narrative]—that which we call history."[20] Lisa echoed this point when she stated how "boring" she found the display of objects. She extended this point by noting how each object forms an "incomplete sentence in a historical narrative" and served to contribute to "an otherwise really, really boring exhibit."

This expression of boredom about the exhibit is akin to the commonly held belief that history is a subject that is uninviting and dull. When pressed further about this detail, the four students spoke openly about their own knowledge of the playfulness of history, noting specifically how history "can serve as a game where you can learn without thinking that you are learning." Paulo further explained, when pressed, that the element of play within history is "finding knowledge you never knew, is like going through a maze. . . . You know, when you hit a wall you have to rethink everything. You bring in more information to understand and get past the block . . . and then you have to decide if the knowledge is necessary or useful." The students collectively suggested such playfulness was absent in the exhibit, even in those sections that had a technological base (such as the expansive television monitors featuring broadcasts of the Vietnam War). It was the mash-up assignment that provided the students with the challenge of engaging in the art of history through a commonly utilized media.

While many would consider the student mash-up videos to be a playful example of how students could advance their technological skills, I argue that it allowed the students to rethink how they learn about the past. Their interaction with various technologies worked to build an expression of their knowledge about the relationship between history and identity. The mash-up itself, while clearly an activity to engage the students, was effective because much of the content presented works through a combination of knowing something new (in the case of Stuart's group, how the identity of American men is one of strength and hardiness) with a more interesting way of presenting the information. The mash-up presented a combination of aesthetic appreciation (including a sepia tone along with computer-created graphics of blood) and the cultural memories of the West as a nostalgic time and place. The mash-up included a sound track containing Western background music (from, no less, *The Magnificent Seven* and *How the West Was Won*), photographs of the students themselves inserted into the archival documents and exhibit, and the students' physical presence in the museum exhibit. Accompanying the mash-up were images of guns displayed in the museum, transposed pictures of massive U.S. casualties from the Vietnam War, and a film clip of a confrontation between natives and non-natives. Will these students ever attend another museum and know that they can gain more information about what they see in front of them through the digital realm? I suspect so. And I also suspect that they have some sense that learning the past can be fun, and that museums do have a particular purpose. As one of them stated: "I know they [the museum] has all of these objects. I just don't know what they want us to learn about the objects."

Discussion

Commentators have lately expressed concern about the apparent lack of historical knowledge held by our youth. In their arguments about the short-comings of public education in the United States, education policy makers frequently use standardized test results (specifically the National Assessment of Educational Progress results) to show the limited knowledge students possess. The response to this lack of knowledge was a movement toward widespread utilization of primary source materials and the dependence on document-based questioning as the basis for history education. By using primary and secondary sources, it continues to be argued, students can develop historical knowledge by engaging in the act of history.[21] The focus on the development of content knowledge (the "what" of history) and procedural skills (the "how" of history) can be included in the larger issues of asking why particular representations are presented within the museum. These students came to understand how knowledge is constructed in the museum, as well as how knowledge can be reconstructed using digital technologies. Their goal was to create a mash-up that included a narrative about history and national identity. They learned many new technological skills. They not only gained a rudimentary skill set related to the use of iMovie, but they also acquired and presented a mature understanding of where other information may be found. To formulate their arguments about history and museums, they identified and located additional information necessary for their argument. Although some students in this study saw the formation of identity through history in fairly narrow terms—that history itself was a static element without opportunity to change—most were engaged in a more critical process consistent with the concept of historical consciousness, that is, the ability to understand through critique how a particular historical representation serves specific purposes.

The use of technology within the public history museum appears to aid museums in achieving their educational mandates. Researchers within the museum studies discipline over the last five to six years have investigated how museums are utilizing web 2.0 technologies, including social media such as *Twitter* and *Flickr*.[22] From the development of digital collections, to accessing information through museum dashboards, through specifically developed smartphone apps (to name only a few), museum personnel are identifying technology that may serve a useful purpose for the museum. But the students whom I studied expressed a critique of the technology used within the exhibit, which we should take as a warning about the educational potential of technology. The students gathered information additional to that presented by the exhibition labels and text panels by producing digital media files creating their own narratives about the exhibit. The additional information gathered allowed for a more open and flexible collection of knowledge specific to the interests of the students. When questioned by the museum personnel about their lack of engagement with the various technologies incorporated into the exhibit itself, the students cogently argued that the digital media within the exhibit reflected the museum's current technological focus (which assumed such technologies would be a draw for youth to learning from the exhibit). Yet, the students also thought that the technology within the exhibits (limited to looped films and still photographs displayed on walls) did not specifically contribute to furthering their knowledge. The students realized that the History Channel and a local independent media company produced many of the media elements within the museum (individuals within the videos were actors and *not* "real" Medal of Honor recipients), and they spoke critically about the use of a perceived authentic award to gain an emotional tie to the exhibits' larger message (of connecting the necessity of conflict to that of freedom). Although the museum did claim to engage with technology primarily in the form of media, such technologies were as didactic and directed as any of the objects, text panels, and labels. The students used other sources available online and drawn from other sites beyond the museum while wondering about the museum's parallel online exhibit. The students considered the online exhibit a missed opportunity in accessing additional information about the exhibit, the wars included in the exhibit, and the objects constituting each display. Instead, the students' awareness of the site was apparent during the research when they discovered it through an online search.

Conclusions

The public history museum continues to grapple with ensuring that its educational relevance continues as it addresses the challenges of incorporating various technologies into its public mandates. Not only are museums dealing with making information about their objects and exhibits open and accessible, they are also dealing with a public who comes to expect opportunity to find such technologies available within exhibits. This change challenges educators and museums to rethink how historical inquiry in public history museums can be supported through the use of technology. How can museums provide opportunities within their exhibition spaces (and on dedicated websites) to engage in historical inquiry that moves beyond text labels and objects? How can museums come to support exhibits that actively engage students to critique what is presented and develop an understanding about the importance of such a presentation? The challenge facing public history museums is working toward changing their own (and the public's) conception of the museum as a knowledge authority. Instead, I suggest, there is a need for museums to consider themselves as brokers of knowledge and that such knowledge can come through engagement with technology within and beyond the museum.

Although previous research has demonstrated that our youth may be actively involved in appropriating or resisting particular historical narratives, many of those involved in this study were engaged in a more complex process. The four students I interviewed and observed clearly pointed out the limitations within the museum that inhibited their understanding about the past. The knowledge they developed in the classroom led them to seek additional information when in the museum, and they struggled to integrate new ideas they encountered in each. Although some of the students simply accepted the history narrative displayed in the museum, most were aware that the objects and the narratives were used for advancing a particular collective identity. By being aware that by utilizing various technologies, they came to appreciate the fact that their own education exposed them to the playfulness technology offered and appreciated the fact that technology could encourage a more critical historical perspective, particularly by exposing them to source materials beyond the museum. Even as they sought to expand their own historical viewpoints, however, they were willing to acknowledge the limited information presented by the museum. Both the highly contentious nature of historical representations in the United States and the factual emphasis of the school curriculum may contribute to students simply accepting or rejecting historical narratives based on personal experience, preferences, or prior knowledge. This points, then, to the value of historical study that focuses on students' utilization of technology to gain experience working with tools (which may well be computer based) in order to enrich their own historical understanding through digital media. I am not suggesting that every student attending a public museum ought to be engaged in a mash-up experience. What I am suggesting is that we need to harness the interest students do hold in history to activities that will fashion a set of skills and knowledge. By asking our youth to be critical of the history presented in public museums is not to ignore the importance each institution holds in providing such information. Can our youth problem solve, communicate, or be creative and innovative by attending a history museum? I cannot say for certain. But I can suggest the need for public history museums to provide opportunities for those youth who are interested in knowing and learning more about the past, something that can easily be done within museums with the open web access many provide their public. Those opportunities can be vehicles for bringing these youth into rich conversations about our past, about museums and education, and about how their skills and knowledge are developed outside of the traditional classroom.

NOTES

1. Didier Maleuvre, *Museum Memories: History, Technology, Art* (Palo Alto, Calif.: Stanford University Press, 1999), 10.

2. Gustavo Buntinx et al., eds., *Museum Frictions: Public Cultures/Global Transformations* (Durham, N.C.: Duke University Press, 2006), 1–31.

3. Roy Rosenzweig and David P. Thelen, *Presence of the Past: Popular Uses of History in American Life* (New York: Columbia University Press, 1998), 106.

4. See, for example, www.museumsandtheweb.com, www.mcn.edu, and www.hastac.org, accessed November 28, 2012. Each of these sites provides an archive of scholarship and research that traces the utilization of technology by museums.

5. Michelle Henning, "New Media," in *A Companion to Museum Studies*, ed. Sharon Macdonald (Oxford: Blackwell, 2006), 302–18.

6. Scholars have examined how technology impacts the ways in which museums represent information. See, for example, Paul Marty, "Information Representation: Representing Museum Knowledge," in *Museum Informatics*, ed. Paul F. Marty and Katherine Burton Jones (New York: Routledge, 2008), 29–34.

7. See Nancy Proctor, "Museum as Platform, Curator as Champion, in the Age of Social Media," *Curator* 53, no. 1 (2010): 36–42, for examples of institutions that have utilized web technologies for user-generated content, crowdsourcing, and collaborative initiatives. See also Nik Honeysett and Michael Edsen, "Philosophical Leadership Needed for the Future: Digital Humanities Scholars in Museums," *Journal of Digital Humanities* 1, no. 1 (April 2012), accessed November 28, 2012, http://journalofdigital humanities.org/1-1/philosophical-leadership-needed-for-the-future/.

8. Mieke Bal, "Telling, Showing, Showing Off," in *A Mieke Bal Reader* (Chicago: University of Chicago Press, 1991), 173.

9. Fiona Cameron, "Beyond the Cult of the Replicant—Museums and Historical Digital Objects: Traditional Concerns, New Discourses," in *Theorizing Digital Cultural Heritage: A Critical Discourse*, ed. Fiona Cameron and Sarah Kenderdine (Cambridge, Mass.: MIT Press, 2007), 49–76. As Simon Knell notes in *Museums and the Future of Collecting* (London: Ashgate, 2004), as museums have become knowledge institutions there has been a decline in the prominence of objects that were once feature attractions. See also Sharon Macdonald, "Collecting Practices," in her *A Companion to Museum Studies* (London: Routledge, 2006), on changes to collecting practices of museums.

10. See, for example, Ross Parry's *Recoding the Museum: Digital Heritage and Technologies of Change* (London: Routledge, 2007), and *Museums in the Digital Age* (Leicester: University of Leicester Press, 2010); Fiona Cameron and Sarah Kenderdine, eds., *Theorizing Digital Cultural Heritage: A Critical Discourse* (Cambridge, Mass.: MIT Press, 2010); and Loic Tallon and Kevin Walker, eds., *Digital Technologies and the Museum Experience* (Lanham, Md.: AltaMira, 2008).

11. Eilean Hooper-Greenhill, *The Educational Role of the Museum*, 2nd ed. (London: Routledge, 1999), 5–8.

12. Steven Conn, *Museums and American Intellectual Life, 1876–1927* (Chicago: University of Chicago Press, 1998), 100.

13. Brenda M. Trofanenko, "More Than a Single Best Narrative: Collective History and the Transformation of Historical Consciousness," *Curriculum Inquiry* 38, no. 5 (2008): 579–603.

14. Brenda M. Trofanenko, "The Educational Promise of Public History Museum Exhibits," *Theory and Research in Social Education* 38, no. 2 (2010): 270–88.

15. The exhibit sought to provide a "comprehensive and memorable overview of America's military experience and the central role it has played in our national life" (Smithsonian Institute, 2005). Although the exhibit closed on September 5, 2006, the online component remains a popular educational resource.

16. Susan M. Pearse, "Objects in the Contemporary Construction of Personal Culture: Perspectives Relating to Gender and Socio-Economic Class," *Museum Management and Curatorship* 17, no. 3 (1999): 223.

17. Henrietta Riegel, "Into the Heart of Irony: Ethnographic Exhibitions and the Politics of Difference," in *Theorizing Museums*, ed. Sharon Macdonald and Gordon Fyfe (Oxford: Blackwell, 1996), 87.

18. Andreas Huyssen, *Twilight Memories: Marking Time in a Culture of Amnesia* (London: Routledge, 1995), 255.

19. Alun Munslow, "Aesthetic Turn," in idem, *The Routledge Companion to Historical Studies*, 2nd ed. (London: Routledge, 2006), 22.

20. Munslow, 22.

21. Bruce Van Sledright, *The Challenge of Rethinking History Education: On Practices, Theories, and Policies* (New York: Routledge, 2011).

22. To see the extent of research utilizing various technologies, access the collection of online papers presented at the annual Museums and the Web conference, accessed July 31, 2012, www.archimuse.com.

THIRTEEN

Teaching History in an Age of Pervasive Computing

The Case for Games in the High School and Undergraduate Classroom

Kevin Kee and Shawn Graham

Historians have always been interactive with the content that we study, constantly challenging, reworking, and indeed, remixing information to "do history." And we have incorporated that interactivity into our teaching, analyzing primary and secondary sources with our students in seminars, and helping students draw on those sources to craft their own historical narratives. The arrival of computer technologies has provided new ways to support interactivity in our teaching.

Our students require it: there has always been a world wide web for the undergraduates in our classes. Personal computers were first introduced en masse into primary and secondary education in the 1980s, and those students have already graduated from university. Computers went, in the span of a few years, from being a rarity to a commonplace. We now live in an age of "pervasive computing,"[1] in which digital devices proliferate into every corner of our lives. Students interact with this technology less like a tool (something to get the job done) and more like a musical instrument (something with which to be creative). The key aesthetic of computing today is not keyboarding, or re-creating previous media in digital format, but rather, content creation, mash-ups, and remixes: in short, interactivity.[2] Several years ago a 2007 Demos Report surveyed primary- and secondary-level students and parents in the United Kingdom and created focus groups to study the digital impact of new media on their day-to-day lives and especially their learning environments. The key finding was that for young people (today's university students) the new media tools were used to strengthen existing social networks and to create expressive content.[3]

How do we teach history in an age of pervasive computing, where interactivity with (rather than consumption of) media in the context of social networks (rather than in isolation) is key? Not through "websites" or "bulletin board forum posts." These are interim technologies—what the historian John Sutton Lutz called the "horseless carriages" of the computer revolution. Instead, we need to progress to "the automobile." One phrase expressed the new invention in terms of existing technology; the other coined a completely new idea to describe the technology. Just as the arrival of "the automobile" coincided with mass production and mass access, the new way of interacting with digital media has started to create its own idioms and metaphors. Social apps. Facebooks and Machinima. MMORPGs (massively multiplayer online role-playing games).

These last two terms are connected to computer games, the most exciting, technically demanding, computing applications today. They are the digital media "automobiles" of the twenty-first century. Game technologies have driven the development and evolution of computer hardware, artificial intelligence, database management, and a host of allied technologies. Computer games are some of the most complicated and sophisticated simulations available, with design and development budgets that dwarf those of many movies, and certainly any Humanities Department's research budget. As a result, game studies are growing, but the nascent discipline is dominated by computer science and psychology research; the humanities have had relatively little to offer.

While the humanities have shown limited interest in games, games have shown great interest in the humanities, and especially in history. A recent survey showed that 26 of the 133 PC-based games that have sold at least 1 million units have been based on a historic theme, or have employed historical tropes.[4] Clearly, given that a fifth of the all-time best-selling computer games have historical themes, there is room for humanities- and history-based analyses of computer games, and consideration of how best to use this popularity to further the teaching and learning of history.

We intend to go further. We believe that the best way to teach history in an age of pervasive computing is through collaborative learning with computer games. This chapter is divided into four parts. We begin by suggesting that games should be used in our undergraduate courses in much the same way that we have used texts. History games are synthetic historical worlds, similar to the narratives on our class reading lists, except that these are expressed in computer code, not language. While the academic literature has championed games as a teaching "tool," we take a different view: that these are artifacts that should be deconstructed, in the manner of historiography. But how do we know which history games to use? The marketplace has made claims for history games that must be challenged, and we propose a specific typology by which to understand the place of history games in our undergraduate courses.

In the second part of the chapter, we show how students can build on their analysis of games by creating their own histories through game "mods" (modifications of commercial games). The process is similar to that which sees students build on their analysis of texts to write historiographical essays and benefit from peer review. Examples from web forums, and our own experience, highlight the potential for peer review. In the third part of the chapter, we draw on our own experience to show how students can move beyond analysis, and modding, to collaboratively developing their own games, in much the same way that they write research papers. Finally, we reflect on our use of games for history to suggest how we might best assess the work of our students. In these ways, we show how historians can tap the potential, while avoiding the pitfalls, of learning with games.

Narratives and Games as Synthetic Worlds

A conventional history course requires that a student engage in the literature related to the topic. In both lecture and seminar courses, students read in preparation for small-group discussions, guided by an instructor or teaching assistant. Historians who want to use technology in an age of pervasive computing can use computer games in the same way that we have previously used books and articles.

Those books and articles are worlds that we have created, drawing on evidence from the past that has been preserved in the archives. The past is disorganized, meaningless, and exists beyond the rules of language. History is organized, meaningful, and expressed with the rules of language.[5] Created by historians writing in the present moment and therefore occupied with present concerns,[6] and written in narrative form, our histories follow an artificially linear path, with a beginning, middle, and end. We ask our students to immerse themselves in these synthetic worlds, and draw from them insights that they can apply to their understanding of the topic at hand.

In a similar way, as the game theorist Edward Castranova has pointed out, a game is a synthetic world. But where historians' books and articles make a persuasive case through narrative, games are compelling because these practice "just-good-enough" virtual reality. As Castranova notes: "a game perspective focuses all thought and research on the user's subjectivity and well-being. It insists on immediate usability. It thrives on widened access and multiple users. And it generates a willing suspension of disbelief, without which genuine immersion cannot happen."[7] If a game is effective, it immerses a player, so that she projects her mind—her sense of self—into it. From these experiences, as the linguist and game theorist James Paul Gee has pointed out, gamers learn a great deal. Indeed, according to Gee, games are one of the most effective teaching tools yet devised.

The challenge for historians is that, with a few notable exceptions, history games are not created by researchers focused on learning; they are built by gamers obsessed with fun. But that does not make them a waste of time. Just as we ask our students to assess "popular history," so too can we use popular games for the purposes of learning. Indeed, our task in the age of pervasive computing is to reconcile these two kinds of synthetic worlds. But how do we assess the suitability of a game for history? How do we know which games to put on our "gaming list"? Presently, the term "history game" is used to denote many different kinds of experiences with computer media. If we are going to be clear about how collaborative learning with computer games can teach history in a new era of pervasive computing, we need to clarify what we mean by "history games." Alas, the marketplace has only muddled the issue.

History Games in the Marketplace—The Genre Problem

The type of game (the way it is played, its structure) is how the vast majority of games are classified and marketed. Games are usually discussed via a comparison of one game to another or by reference to a genre.[8] Genre in games usually refers to the gameplay mechanics from the point of view of the player, such as first-person shooter or role-playing game. These categories are not overly useful for understanding how historically themed games could be employed by a professor or student since many of these kinds of categories are artifacts of the technology used to deliver the game. First-person shooters evolved from video arcade games to home consoles such as the Sony Playstation; role-playing games evolved from text adventure games to home PCs. As these technologies have developed, taking on qualities of one another, the genre categories have begun to overlap as well. Most of today's first-person shooters, for example, contain many of the attributes of role-playing games.

In a marketplace saturated with thousands of first-person shooters and role-playing games, game publishers have attempted to distinguish their products by covering the gameplay mechanics with a façade of content. As a result, we have first-person shooters set far in the future, such as the highly popular *Halo* series, and others based in the past, such as the equally successful *Call of Duty* franchise. Ask a 15-year-old if he plays history games, and he may catalogue the German soldiers he killed in his attempt to defend Chambois, ca. 1944. There is history learning here, but it is incidental. And any historian who attempts to use *Call of Duty* to teach history will quickly realize the limitations of the product. At the end of an hour, this history game is essentially about shooting people.

The frustration with history games that results from genre confusion is evident in discussions surrounding another popular franchise, and one that is marketed as specifically historical: *Civilization*. The first wave of research into history games for learning pointed to the potential of *Civilization* as a tool in the classroom.[9] Kurt Squire has expanded this focus, with an emphasis on its effectiveness with elementary students in concert with other tools, such as encyclopedias.[10] But other researchers have criticized the game's implicit narrative of technological progress as the prime mover of history, and questioned its appropriateness for history education.[11]

Civilization and other comparable games are, according to the conventional genres, turn-based strategy games, where each turn builds on the actions taken in previous turns. In the case of *Civilization*, the player guides a tribe of people from the Stone Age to the Space Age, conquering the world as she goes. It would be hard to imagine an alternative conception of historical process being built into a turn-based strategy game—the mechanics of the game are built for "progress." Historical contingency has been determined by the formal rule system, which has been created by the computer programming.[12]

The point, as other critics have noted, is that the game, or any computer game for that matter, is ultimately about mechanics, and not about content. The content is window dressing, and deep playing of a game such as *Civilization* teaches little about history, but everything about how to manipulate the complex algorithms that model the simulation. As Robert MacDougall points out,

> *Civilization*'s game play erases its own historical content. Learning to play means learning to ignore all the stuff that makes it a game about history and not about, say, fighting aliens. One could easily program a different game with a different set of ideological assumptions—Galloway imagines a "People's *Civilization*" game by Howard Zinn—and see precisely the same de-historicizing effect. Mastering the simulation game necessarily involves a journey away from reality towards abstraction, away from history towards code.[13]

History Games for Historians—A Typology of Time and Space

If a so-called history game primarily teaches a player how to win, why bother? The answer is that there is much to learn about history through an understanding of the history game's programming. As a result, those of us who are interested in using games for history learning need to focus on the computer code, rather than on the marketing hype or content façade. The code determines the rules of the game (the way it operates). And if the rules promote a particular way of looking at the world—if they make an argument in code for a particular worldview (what Ian Bogost calls "procedural rhetoric"[14])—then we need to understand which rules, which games, best embody the historical epistemologies we wish to teach. We also need to imagine the possibilities beyond *Civilization*, including modified games, or new games, which could manifest the epistemologies we want to express. Following William Urrichio, we need to "think of the rule systems that characterize various brands of history as constituting the potential rule systems for game play." Addressing the criticisms that have been leveled at *Civilization*, he points out that "by embedding various historiographic epistemologies as structuring agencies rather than relying implicitly on *Civilization*'s narratives of truth, progress, and the American way, a new dimension could be added to play, more coherently addressing history."[15]

The first step to "coherently addressing history" in play is to determine which epistemology to teach. The possibilities are numerous, the focus of a rich vein of literature, and outside the focus of this chapter. Presuming that the historian knows what it is that he wants to teach, we can move to the second step: understanding the power of different games for addressing or reinforcing different kinds of history. To accomplish this, we need to replace the marketing hype and content façades with a clear and unambiguous typology. One such typology organizes games according to their relationships to goals.[16]

On one side are games as goal-oriented challenges; the mental challenge provides the fun. Too easy, and the game is boring; too hard, and the game is frustrating; to be in the sweet spot between the two is to be in a state of "flow."[17] On the other side are goalless games such as *The Sims*, or heavy management simulations like *RailRoads!* For Jesper Juul, such "goalless" games, or games without set end-states, allow the player to push social norms (deviant behavior in *The Sims*) or express personal aesthetics (like making the most beautiful city in *Caesar IV*).[18] Goal and goalless is still too broad and nebulous a foundation on which to build a typology because a single game might have aspects of both, and an effective typology must create unambiguous categories. Alternatively, Espen Aarseth et al. have developed a typology of games (not just computer video games) that considers games according to spatial movement.[19] Broadly, this open-ended typology depends on classification of movement along five axes: space, time, player-structure, control, and rules. Each of those categories can be further broken down, but for our purposes we will concentrate only on the categories of space and time, as per table 13.1. By considering movement as the basis for the typology, Aarseth and his colleagues eliminate the possibility of overlaps, which is what a good typology must do. They also focus attention on how the game treats time and space. Historians are trained to move through time, if only in our minds. The narrative "synthetic worlds" that we produce out of our travels—books and articles—reflect those journeys. Historians who use games, these "synthetic worlds" supported by computers, which immerse the player in a "good enough reality" that mimics 3D space, must necessarily move through time and space as well.

How can this typology help us determine which games we might "assign" to our students to play, and later analyze in class? Let us compare two games that were released within months of each other, and that we have used with students: *Civilization IV* (published in November 2005) and *Caesar IV* (a rival game that was launched soon after). Both of these games take us into a "synthetic world" loosely based on antiquity. *Gamerankings*, a highly popular website that ranks computer games and classifies them according to "genre," treats these as essentially the same: *Caesar IV* is listed as "Strategy, City Building, Historic," while *Civilization IV* is categorized as "Strategy, Turn-Based, Historic." There is nothing mutually exclusive about these categories: a "City Builder" game could be "Turn-Based," and *Civilization IV* can be played in a concurrent, non-turn-based mode, in its multiplayer version. The genre classifications make these games appear similar, and tell us nothing about their underlying epistemologies or procedural rhetorics.

When we break them down according to Aarseth et al.'s movement typology, the differences become clear (table 13.2). *Caesar IV* is a city-management simulation based in ancient Rome. In terms of space, the view is "Omnipresent"; no part of the game environment is unknown to the player. In

TABLE 13.1.   Aarseth et al.'s game typology

Space	Perspective	Omni-Present / Vagrant
	Topography	Geometrical / Topological
	Environment	Dynamic / Static
Time	Pace	Real-Time / Turn-Based
	Representation	Mimetic / Arbitrary
	Teleology	Finite / Infinite

TABLE 13.2. *Caesar IV* and *Civilization IV* according to Aarseth et al.'s game typology

		Caesar IV	*Civilization IV*
Space	Perspective	Omni-Present	Vagrant
	Topography	Topological	Geometrical
	Environment	Dynamic	Dynamic
Time	Pace	Real-Time	Turn-Based
	Representation	Arbitrary	Mimetic
	Teleology	Finite	Finite

Civilization IV, in contrast, much of the early gameplay is built on exploration and discovery, and actions by other "civilizations" that occur off-screen can affect the player; the "Perspective" is "Vagrant." In *Caesar IV*, the player interacts with the "Topography" by placing buildings or other structures in limited areas ("olive groves," for instance, can only be placed on "farm land"), and so the topography is "Topological," whereas in *Civilization IV* the player may move the game pieces almost anywhere, and so the topography is "Geometrical." The "Environment" of both games is dynamic; it changes according to, but sometimes regardless of, the player's actions.

Consider also what Aarseth and his colleagues call the "Pace" of time within both games: in *Caesar IV*, time moves forward regardless of the player's actions, so the game is played in "Real-Time." In *Civilization IV* time stops while the player moves his pieces around the board, so its time is "Turn-Based" (each player must wait for the other players to complete their turn, as in *Monopoly*). The "representation" of time, as Aarseth et al. frame it, differs in both games as well. In *Caesar IV*, if a player has the *denarii*, a brand-new Coliseum can instantly be placed within a city (time is "Arbitrary"), whereas in *Civilization IV* time is "Mimetic" (imitated), so it takes a number of turns, reflecting something of the actual cost in time, to build a Coliseum. Finally, addressing what Aarseth and his colleagues call the "Teleology" of time, *Caesar IV* is a finite game: it has a definite end point (when mission goals are reached). *Civilization IV* is also a finite game: famously, it ends when you launch a colonization mission to the stars (although other end-games are possible, including the annihilation by, or of, your foes).

An analysis of these axes can help us better understand when and how to use these games with our students. In the case of *Caesar IV* and *Civilization IV*, the different treatments of perspective and the representation of time suggest that *Caesar IV* would be helpful in addressing specific issues: exploring microeconomics of cities or the role of religious belief in urban life; rebuilding specific real-world cities, to contrast what the game suggests about how life was lived in the past versus current historical thinking, or the current understanding of the archaeological record. *Civilization IV*, on the other hand, would be better suited for exploration of large-scale issues: diffusionism as a theory in cultural evolution (and the historiography of diffusionism), the dynamics of Roman civil wars, or the emergence of city-states in different climatic conditions.

This kind of analysis, using a typology of movement, can also help students understand why and how a game forces them to think along certain paths. The game becomes, not a teaching tool, but a kind of artifact that must be studied to determine its procedural rhetoric, which can then be deconstructed in the tradition of historiography. In the same way that we teach our students to recognize an author's viewpoint, and to analyze a text, we can teach our students to recognize implicit points of view in a game, and to analyze the rules encoded in the programming.

Modding and the Meta-Game

But we need to go further; we must use these technologies to help our students create their own representations of history. In this section, and the one that follows, we discuss two approaches to using digital games to help students create history: first, creating new content in the context of an already existing game, and second, creating an entirely new game, ex novo. Both of these operate at the level of what we call the "meta-game," and it is here that we find the greatest opportunities for teaching history in an age of pervasive computing. Meta-gaming refers, in a limited sense, to game tactics that exploit bugs or features of a game in a way that was not originally intended by the game designers—like using a glitch in the game physics to scale walls that were meant to be impassable.[20] We employ the term in this way, but we also use it in a larger sense, to refer to an outside-looking-in awareness of the game mechanics. This is a "gaming of the game," in which students' engagement with history games moves beyond treating them as artifacts that must be analyzed, to modifying and even building them for themselves. The task is similar to that faced by students in a conventional history course, in which they go beyond analyzing texts to engaging them through the act of writing. In these "literature reviews" or "historiographical papers," students articulate a thesis, using the building blocks of professional researchers. The task is both creative—students are developing their own representation of history, and synthetic—they are drawing on the literature created by historians. In a sense, they are playing with the texts.

The most common application of meta-gaming to commercial games is to tweak, adapt, modify, or otherwise alter the original game. In the early days of computer gaming, this was often accomplished by exploiting bugs in the game's programming. Savvy game publishers soon realized that there were commercial benefits to this activity, and many now provide in-game editors to allow the players to tweak the gameplay easily. The commercial rationale is straightforward: the more that players talk about the game, and provide additional content, the greater the "buzz" and the number of copies of the game sold. Some of these modifications (mods) become so popular that they eclipse the original game. *Counterstrike*, to take the most notable example, was a mod that became more popular than its progenitor, *Half Life*.

Civilization IV, to return to our earlier example, is one such modifiable game. Previous versions of the game allowed players to customize the map and starting conditions. The most recent version lets players change the actual rules of play, and in this way contest the procedural rhetoric of the game. Only a minority of players have the requisite skills to rewrite the rules; most settle for more cosmetic changes. *Civilization IV* distinguishes between these as "mods" (rule changes) and "scenarios" (customized starting conditions). There are a number of sites that help the player achieve these customizations, with *CivFanatics* and *Apolyton* among the most popular. Indeed, *Apolyton* even operates Apolyton University website, where players can study tutorials to increase their skill in play and modding. An informal poll of 111 participants on *CivFanatics* conducted in April 2008[21] found that 18 percent considered themselves to be "professional historians," 25 percent considered themselves to be non-historians, while the majority saw themselves as "amateurs." These were "amateurs" in the most literal sense, "amators" or "lovers" of history, debating and discussing in a manner not out of place in a university seminar.

Like undergraduate students, "Civfanatics" present their work to their peers (game mods, rather than essays), which their colleagues play, rather than read (for review).[22] Feedback from the discussions that follows is used to guide further modifications and enhancements of the mod. For example, several "Civfanatics" in 2006 engaged in a meta-game of *Civilization IV* connected to a mod set during the Crusades.[23] A participant who went by the name of "Holyone" began the discussion with a post outlining the period that he had modeled, an indication of the depth of his mod (his scenario would require several hours of intense gameplay), and the downloadable file. The forum post, written with the distinctive spelling, syntax, and grammar of the Internet, read as follows: "Holyone" posted: "The Crusades (European Middle Ages Mod). . . . The scenario is set in the Middle East during the time of the Crusades. The time period is 1100–1300 AD at Marathon speed, which means 1 year per turn. Playable civs: Kingdom of Jerusalem (Baldwin I of Boulogne); Byzantiine Empire (Basil II); Egypt (Saladin); Rum Sultanate (Alp Arslan); Tatar Khaganate (Timur Lenk)."

Within days, other Civfanatics had downloaded the scenario, played it, and offered their feedback and suggestions—peer review: "Drtad" posted: "Nice work Holy One, but shouldn't you have the Armenian Kingdom of Cilicia in their, do a Wiki search as they were important during the Crusades by letting the Crusaders pass." "Holyone" replied: "Of course they were important! I also miss the Kingdom of Georgia, another important christian kingdom, but that part of the map is just way too crowded. Perhaps on a bigger one. I saw nice Middle East maps elsewhere, so maybe I will use one of them. But if anybody knows one, link it here, pls!" The feedback was not concerned with gameplay—after all, "Holyone" had not modified the computer code—but rather with historical accuracy: "Ohcrapitsnico" posted: "Wasn't Salah al-din the king of the abbasids not just egypt? Secondly, are you planning for this just to be a scenario or like a mod?" "Holyone" pointed out that, given the limitations of the map (the game board, with its computer code) he could not include every "civilization" that had occupied the real-world territory. Like a student writing an essay with a predetermined page limit, he had to make choices: "Holyone" posted: "Yes he was, but it's easier to have only one civ and leader for the different time period. Even in this short(?) 200 years there was a different Egypt when the Crusaders arrived in 1097–99, another one that is Saladin's and when the mameluks took over is yet another story." He justified his choice of Saladin by noting that "he is a rather emblematic figure of the Crusades (along with Richard I). But if you ask his territorial rule, in the scenario Egypt starts with the Nile valley and Mesopotamia (Baghdad, Damascus) under her rule. And also Mecca as it is the Islam holy city."

The concern with historical accuracy continued, but with an additional focus on the need to change the game rules so that the period might be properly modeled: "Drtad" posted: "Nice work on the new map Holyone. But shouldn't Lesser Armenia and Georgia be Orthodox? They surely were not Catholic." "Holyone" replied: "I too thought about that, but there are sooo many branches of christianity especially that part of the world. Georgia for example is the first christian country, that time there was no orthodox or catholic christianity. Christianity in Syria, even today, is neither, but (you are right) more close to orthodoxy. The patriarch of Antioch and Alexandria had great dogmatic debate with the Patriarch of Constantinople, and they practically broke up. I did choose Catholicism because of the diplomatic relation bonus, but I can still change one of them (or both), if it suits you better." "Drtad" answered with an admonishment: "Georgia was definitely not the first Christian nation of the world. That title belongs to Armenia. 301 AD if I am not mistaken. King Drtad adopted Christianity after St. Gregory cured him of a didease just by touching his forehead."

"Holyone" responded by creating a new map and instituting several rule changes. *Civilization* models religious influence in a specific manner (civilizations with the same religion tend to be allies) so the debate concerning Orthodox or Catholic Christianity in Georgia was significant not just for historical accuracy, but also for gameplay. The debate over content forced a debate over the computer code, and a resulting alteration, which spurred further discussion. The act of creation and exchange was not unlike that which occurs in a university seminar. Instead of writing a historiographical paper using the publications of historians, "Holyone" created a mod drawing on the game *Civilization IV*. Instead of presenting it to a class, and engaging in a debate with his colleagues, he published it to the web, where his peers could respond, with passionate arguments, expressed in misspellings, emoticons, and other signifiers of the Internet age. "Drtad" was a significant player in this meta-game, and not just because he had taken the name of the king of the first country to adopt Christianity. As a result of his comments, and those of the rest of the community, "Holyone" modified and enhanced his scenario, resulting in a more persuasive product of historical play.

This kind of peer review is not unusual. In "The Rise and Fall of Rome," another Civfanatics discussion, amateur historians, not historians or classic students, developed a historically "authentic" simulation of Roman culture. They explored the conditions behind the emergence of the Social War (the war between Rome and its Italian allies, or *socii*, during the early first century b.c.e.), and devised a way to allow for the possibility of the war to emerge out of gameplay.

These examples from the meta-game surrounding *Civilization IV* demonstrate how we envision teaching through gaming. As we showed in the first part of the chapter, the game itself becomes not a teaching tool, but rather a kind of artifact that we study to determine its procedural rhetoric, which we then deconstruct in the tradition of historiography. Students can then build on this analysis, as we show immediately above, and through modding and the meta-game, create their own representations of history.

Building a Game ex novo, and the Meta-Game

If historians understand computer code as another language through which to express historical thinking, we can move beyond tweaking the algorithms of an established game such as *Civilization*. Taken to its logical conclusion, the ultimate meta-game is the construction of a game ex novo, in which code is used to develop an original artifact. In the same way that students write a research paper, investigating primary and secondary sources and then assembling an essay in an effort to persuade the reader of a thesis, students can develop games, engaging the sources and then building a system to argue for a specific explanation of history.

Educators have long pointed out the benefits of building knowledge and understanding in this manner. Led by Seymour Papert, theorists have advanced the notion of "constructionism" (a term coined by Papert and Idit Harel,[24] promoting the construction of knowledge in the mind of the learner). In the field of computing, Papert drew on the work of Jean Piaget to develop the Logo programming language for students, so that they could write and execute basic programming functions, including the programming of robots.

In the field of history, students can use computer code as a language to express historical thinking, through games. In a 2007/08 upper-level undergraduate course project taught by Kevin Kee at Brock University in St. Catharines, Ontario, students opted to use C++, a general-purpose programming language, with Open GL (Open Graphics Library), a set of procedures enabling a computer's operating system to produce 2D and 3D graphics. Programming in C++ is beyond the knowledge and abilities of the vast majority of humanities undergraduates, so the course project included upper-level undergraduate computing science students.

The history students split their time between conventional seminars, tutorials, and design sessions. The seminar required that they read and discuss the epistemology of history, the manner in which computers have provided new opportunities to express these epistemologies, the essential debates in the new field of games for learning, as well as project management and game design. The computing science students, for their part, split their time between traditional lectures, and joined the history students in the tutorials and design sessions. They focused on the challenges faced by computing scientists collaborating on software projects, including working as members of a team.

In groups of six to eight students, the history and computing science majors began by brainstorming a game concept, focused around the War of 1812 in Niagara. They next defined the goal of their game, and drafted a proposal that included the game description and an overview of the content. The proposal also incorporated documents relating to their work together as a team: a contract among the team members, a chart outlining the phases of their work, and a schedule of deliverables. A "Design Document" followed, specifying aspects of the game (such as its target audience and its technical requirements). Only after these steps were complete did they begin development. The final class saw them "launch" their games online, with family, friends, and colleagues in attendance.

Fig 13.1: *Brigade: A War of 1812 Saga.* Screenshot courtesy of the authors.

The results of their work paled in comparison to a *Civilization IV* mod. The graphics were simple, and the gameplay restricted. But what these lacked in complexity and depth, they made up for in originality. Some of the games, such as *Brigade: A War of 1812 Saga* (see figure 13.1 above) addressed key battles in the war, enabling players to re-fight the conflicts from the American or British side.[25] The results provided opportunities to examine counterfactuals, including how different battle strategies might have affected the outcome of the war. Other games addressed the economics of the war, including how merchants tried, and sometimes failed, to deal with a changing financial environment. *Tavern Keeper* (see figure 13.2 below), for instance, put the player in the apron of the proprietor of one English Canada's oldest inns, in Niagara-on-the-Lake.[26] Serving drinks from behind the bar brought the player into contact with battle-weary British soldiers, anxious merchants, and concerned farmers.

The students' goal, one of the developers noted afterward, was to combine political history, with its focus on geopolitical events (the War of 1812), with social history and its concern with the lives of "ordinary citizens" (the tavern keeper). The end result was a game that provided an omnipresent perspective, allowing the player to see everything, and gain confidence in this new environment. The player had relatively little freedom to move around the tavern, and none beyond it—the space was topological. The environment was static—while the player could influence the environment (cultivating a

Fig 13.2: *Tavern Keeper.* Screenshot courtesy of the authors.

relationship with a patron, for instance) the object of the changes was altered in number only; the environment itself remained essentially unchanged. In terms of time, the game was turn-based: the player made a decision (for example, to reinvest profits into the tavern, or to use them to diversify the business and purchase land), and then awaited the consequences of her actions. The representation of time was mimetic; events occurring in the game mimicked the corresponding time in the real world—cultivating a relationship with an influential patron might yield valuable, insider information later in the game. Finally, *Tavern Keeper* was teleologically finite— the player eventually reached a final win or lose state.

The omnipresent, topological, static space of the tavern limited the movement of the player, and concentrated her attention on a specific place. The turn-based, mimetic, finite timeframe rooted the player in the war period, while providing her with time to consider carefully her choices and grasp the complexity of her changing economic environment. In this way, the student leader noted, "the game showed a single individual merchant's experience on a cultural and personal level and then put it into a large context by linking it to the War of 1812, showing why it is important. With a game we were able to show a nuanced, specific micro-history and make it relevant by incorporating a larger important historical event."27

The students accomplished this not by creating a narrative, as they would if they were writing a research paper, but by developing, and then programming, a specific rule set. By focusing on games as systems with rule sets, students can develop what this student leader called "a module to process preexisting historical data," according to the choices of the player. The resulting gameplay experience provides new opportunities for students to express their own representations of history, in all of its complexity. As these students knew, distant geopolitical forces could turn what appeared to be a good decision into a bad one; in this case, a tavern keeper's (player's) attempt to diversify his business by investing in nearby farmland could result in bankruptcy if the British farmers (no longer able to sell their produce to their American customers) defaulted on their loans. These students had programmed caution into the computer code, and in this way rendered their judgment on the reasons behind the economic havoc of the war period. By expressing these historical events in computer language that was appropriate to the content, the students were able not only to capture these events, but also to provide opportunities to imagine how this story, and many others like it, might have turned out differently.

Assessment

The developers of *Brigade* and *Tavern Keeper* responded to the challenge of creating a history game with enthusiasm. For young people who have grown up using digital technologies to create content and connect with one another, the opportunity to develop a game with a group of their colleagues is strikingly refreshing. But the excitement of the project's initial phase was quickly replaced by anxiety. Students recognized that this assignment did not fit the conventions of a typical undergraduate humanities course, in which they separately write texts addressed to their professors. How could a team of students develop a game to be played by their peers?

These kinds of concerns are shared by students learning through games, whether they are playing, modding, or building ex novo; how, they ask, will this project be marked? The students in our courses have three main concerns: (1) How will they receive regular feedback on their progress? (2) How will they know what is being marked? (3) In the case of group projects, how will the instructors ensure that students' grades reflect their participation in the group project? We shared our students' first concern about feedback, but from a different perspective: how will we manage, and mark, the mass of material that is produced as a by-product? In the end, we have developed a marking scheme that ensured that the students received regular responses to their game development. In Kevin Kee's third-year course, for instance, where the game counts for 30 percent of the student's final grade in the course, each step of development is graded: the Draft Proposal, due at the end of November, out of 5; the Design Document, due at the end of February, out of 5; the report from the first round of testing, at the beginning of March, out of 5; the report from the second round of testing, near the end of March, out of 5; the final product, due in April, out of 10. In this way, students are given opportunities to work with the professors and teaching assistants to correct errors as they emerge.

Our students are also concerned with how their performance is being measured. In a first-year course taught by Shawn Graham, in which students played a scenario that had been built in *Civilization IV*, the assessment structure included a "game diary" that asked specific questions of the students at particular points in the game, forcing them to reflect on the anachronisms and other artifacts of the gameplay that corresponded or conflicted with their previous readings of history. The game diary was intended to replace one of the assigned essays, but in the end, every student opted to hand in a traditional essay. The reluctance to "play for marks" was partly one of academic culture, but also one of explication: the students did not know what was to be marked when they played the scenario.

The solution we propose is familiar to many teachers of technical courses: rubrics. These have the advantage of distilling the marking to a checklist of criteria. Students can see at a glance what the professor expects them to do to achieve a superior grade (see table 13.3).

For a project in which a student is developing a scenario in *Civilization IV*, the rubric defines expectations according to choice of subject, research, preparation for development, appropriateness of the subject to the medium, collaboration, recognition of the limits of the medium, and facility with the technology. The first criterion addresses the question: has the student selected a good problem to try to render in a scenario? (As noted above, *Civilization IV* has built-in assumptions about how history unfolds. Does the proposed scenario play to those assumptions, or does it challenge them?) The second criterion assesses whether the student has assembled the appropriate primary and secondary sources to ensure the authenticity of the scenario that she intends to develop (and a very good student will explore what makes for an authentic scenario). The next two criteria are aimed at the student's preparation: Has the student addressed the key issues inherent to the content to be modded? Has she chosen, for instance, an appropriate place to map, with an appropriate geographical and time scale? The following criteria assesses whether the student recognizes the problems inherent to developing a historical mod. The "uses forum/wiki" criterion highlights the

TABLE 13.3. Rubric for assessing the development of a scenario in *Civilization*

Criterion	Level 4	Level 3	Level 2	Level 1
Analyze Given Scenario	Analysis of given scenario provides thorough insight	Provides considerable insight	Some insight	Limited or superficial insight
Assess Research Information	Assessment of research information demonstrates thorough use of criteria	Considerable	Some	Limited
Communicate Design Ideas	Communicates these with a high degree of clarity	Considerable	Some	Limited
Create a Design Plan	Creates a design plan with excellent organization	Considerable	Some	Limited
Demonstrate Understanding of the Topic	Demonstrates a thorough understanding	Considerable	Some	Limited
Use Forum/Wiki to Communicate Information to Members of the Group, Teacher	Uses these tools with excellent success	Considerable	Some	Limited
Identify Design Issues	Thoroughly identifies design issues	Substantially identifies design issues	Adequately identifies design issues	Briefly identifies design issues
Manipulate Game Engine	Is able to use (or write) more complex programs or the worldbuilder to manipulate scenario with facility	With good success	With some success	With limited success
Use Appropriate Software to Document a Complete Project	Chooses appropriate software and uses special features to thoroughly document all parts of the project	Well documented	Is able to use a word processor to complete most of the documentation	Is able to use a word processor to complete parts of the documentation

expectation that students will collaborate in the forum or wiki developed for them, and offer help to one another as they design their scenarios. The "identify design issues" criterion forces the student to demonstrate that she is aware of the constraints of the *Civilization IV* environment. And the last two criteria focus on the tool. Just as a student who is incapable of writing will be judged for his grammar and syntax, a student modding a game will be evaluated for the manner in which he uses the computer language that he, in this course, has been trained in.

The final criteria highlight the challenge for students who are not literate with the software, and the computer languages that make them operate. How do we incorporate traditional humanities students into these projects? From the other side of the academic spectrum, how do we include in these projects a student who has a strong grasp of C++, xml, or scenario building, but is weak in history? In Kee's course, the solution was to assemble teams of students who together possessed the requisite knowledge and skills to develop a game. But this solution raised another problem: how, to highlight the students' third concern, would the development of their project be assessed in a manner that was fair to each student, some of whom might take on a high degree of responsibility, and others of whom might decide to let their peers do all of the work? The solution, in this case, was for the instructor to acknowledge that the students were best fit to determine the participation of their peers, and thus to award a mark to the assignment—for example, 25/30, and then let the students divide that mark according to their assessment of one another. If there were 10 students in a group, they would be apportioned a total of 250 marks for this stage (10 students × 25 marks), which they could then award to each of the members of their team. A student who decided to opt out of the last two months of development might be relegated to a mark of 15/25, which would allow for a student who had devoted 40 hours a week to the project to be awarded 35/25 (an unlikely, but possible outcome). Each student's total mark was then averaged (divided by 10) to determine the final mark (out of 25). The distribution of marks occurred anonymously, and anomalies (for example, involving two students who disliked each other, and awarded each other zeros) were easy to recognize, and if necessary, address.

Conclusion

New approaches to teaching history in an age of pervasive computing will necessitate inventive forms of assessment. And an innovative frame of mind will be needed as technology becomes more pervasive, and the manner in which we teach history changes further. For instance, the constant creep of computing into our daily lives is presently in the process of liberating gaming from the confines of computer monitors and tabletops, as augmented reality games bring together game-worlds and everyday life.

For instance, Kevin Kee's *Niagara 1812: Return of the Fenian Shadow* and *Queenston 1812: The Bomber's Plot* depend on smart-phone enabled GPS to provide clues to guide the player, via iPhone, around the historic core of the villages of Niagara-on-the-Lake and Queenston. In these environments, fictitious events occurring in the virtual world intersect with real-world space to create the game.

The challenge for teachers is that these games require students to be on-site in Niagara-on-the-Lake or Queenston, outside the safe boundaries of the school proper. More accessible to students in school are a new genre of games that treat the web like a physical space. *The Nethernet* (formerly *PMOG*) is a game that is played by clicking from website to website, following the prompts of a guide. While *The Nethernet* itself uses the metaphor of a "mission" to describe what is going on in the game (the idea being that other players will try to disrupt or enhance your movement through the Internet by laying mines that "blow up" your browser window, or portals that take you to unrelated websites), the players themselves often use the metaphor of a "tour" (with disruption kept to a minimum). Often, missions are really guided tours of specialty websites.[28]

Unlike standard games, the environments that *The Nethernet* or *Niagara 1812* are played in can themselves change the experience of the game. Websites are taken down, links become broken, it may rain in Niagara-on-the-Lake, or a street may be closed for repair. The game environments are outside the control of the game maker. Even so-called persistent world games like *World of Warcraft* have underlying structures controlled by the game maker. This means that for augmented reality games, the experience of the player, and the player's response, can never be fully accounted for and so "gaming the game" is part of the main gameplay: the meta-game and the game intersect. Finally, there is never a point where you have won a game of *The Nethernet*. You may complete the mission, the tour, but you are rewarded with points toward gaining another experience level (which are in practice infinite). In *Niagara 1812*, the game ends once and for all when you have finished the story.

The act of playing these games in this manner causes the player to engage with the material in a way she had not before: she is looking at a series of related sites from the perspective of the creator of the mission. One could imagine a student of Roman archaeology creating a *Nethernet* mission on curse-tablets. The mission might begin as a simple show and tell. Other students could then play the mission, leaving mines on pages they think are "bad" (poor information, bad research, whatever) or portals to "good" sites: the environment of the gameplay changes as the players play (like the rink in a hockey game gets chewed up by the skaters, influencing the way the puck bounces or skips across the ice). Inserting puzzles into the mission would force a deeper engagement still, and completing a puzzle mission would constitute a formative assessment exercise. Afterward, since the game records the play, another part of the meta-game would come in classroom discussions.

In this way, students play the meta-game. Educators have long been concerned that students do not adequately analyze information they find on a website. *The Nethernet* asks the student to treat web pages not as tools, but as artifacts to be analyzed. We began this chapter by contending that students may benefit from analyzing games, in the same way that they decode texts, and that students must recognize implicit viewpoints in games, just as they do in essays and books. And we showed that students can learn to build their own theses, as they do in the writing of historiographical and research papers, through the act of modding and building a game. Given that the creation of expressive content is among the primary forms of digital engagement by our students, it is an appropriate way to engage technology in an age of pervasive computing.

NOTES

1. "Pervasive computing" can also refer to the distribution of computing power across multiple platforms or devices (as in the *SETI@home* project, which divides up enormous computing problems into micro-chunks, and uses unused computing cycles in idle computers to perform calculations). We use the term to capture both ideas: that "pervasive computing" is distributed computing power across multiple devices and platforms, and into every corner of our lives.

2. *Open Knowledge and the Public Interest* (University of California at Berkeley, n.d.), accessed July 31, 2012, http://okapi.wordpress.com/2008.

3. Hannah Green and Celia Hannon, *Their Space: Education for a Digital Generation* (London: Demos, 2007), 9–10.

4. "List of Best-Selling Video Games," accessed November 15, 2012, http://en .wikipedia.org/wiki/List_of_best-selling_video_games#PC.

5. Keith Jenkins and Alun Munslow, *Re-thinking History* (London: Routledge, 2003).

6. David Lowenthal, *The Heritage Crusade and the Spoils of History* (Cambridge: Cambridge University Press, 1998).

7. Edward Castronova, *Synthetic Worlds: The Business and Culture of Online Games* (Chicago: University of Chicago Press, 2005), 3, 291–92.

8. Christian Elverdam and Espen Aarseth, "Game Classification and Game Design," *Games and Culture* 2, no. 1 (January 1, 2007): 3–4.

9. Tom Taylor, "Historical Simulations and the Future of the Historical Narrative," *Journal of the Association for History and Computing* 6, no. 2 (2003).

10. Kurt Squire, "Replaying History: Learning World History through Playing Civilization III" (Ph.D. dissertation, Indiana University, 2004).

11. Kevin Schut, "Strategic Simulations and Our Past," *Games and Culture* 2, no. 3 (July 1, 2007): 213–35; William Uricchio, "Simulation, History, and Computer

Games," in *Handbook of Computer Game Studies*, ed. Joost Raessens and Jeffrey Gold-stein (Cambridge, Mass.: MIT Press, 2005), 327–38; Esther McCallum-Stewart and Justin Parsler, "Controversies: Historicising the Computer Game," in *Situated Play: Proceedings of DiGRA 2007 Conference* (Tokyo: Digital Games Research Association, 2007), 203–10.

12. Martin Ryle, "Humanist mailing list 2: 592," n.d.; David Kushner, "In Histori-cal Games, Truth Gives Way to Entertainment," *The New York Times*, September 6, 2001, sec. Technology, accessed July 31, 2012, http://www.nytimes.com/2001/09/06/technology/in-historical-games-truth-gives-way-to-entertainment.html; Kacper Pob-locki, "Becoming-State: The bio-Cultural Imperialism of Sid Meier's Civilization," *Focaal—European Journal of Anthropology* 2009, no. 39 (2002): 163–77; Uricchio.

13. Robert MacDougall, "Madness and Civilization III," *Old is the New New*, n.d., accessed July 31, 2012, http://www.robmacdougall.org/index.php/2007/07/madness-and-civilization-iii/.

14. Ian Bogost, *Persuasive Games: The Expressive Power of Videogames* (Cambridge, Mass.: MIT Press, 2007), 28–44.

15. Uricchio, 336.

16. Jesper Juul, "Without a Goal," in *Videogame, Player, Text*, ed. Barry Atkins and Tanya Krzywinska (Manchester: Manchester University Press, 2008), accessed July 31, 2012, http://www.jesperjuul.net/text/withoutagoal/.

17. Juul; Mihaly Csikszentmihalyi, *Flow: The Psychology of Optimal Experience* (New York: HarperPerennial, 1991), 49–50.

18. In a previous article (Kevin Kee, "Computerized History Games: Options for Narratives," *Simulation & Gaming* 42, no. 4 (August 2011), Kee contended that history can be represented in different ways using this typology: with historical epistemolo-gies that focus on history as the mastery of a singular narrative matching well with goal-oriented games, and historical epistemologies that focus on history as the act of discovery about the past matching well with goalless games. In this chapter we go fur-ther, focusing beyond the goals within games to how we learn not just within games, but with and beyond games, in an age of pervasive computing.

19. Espen Aarseth, Solveig M. Smedstad, and Lise Sunnana, "A Multi-Dimensional Typology of Games," *Proceedings of the Level Up Games Conference* (Utrecht, Nether-lands Digital Games Research Association, 2003), 48–53.

20. "Meta-gaming," accessed August 1, 2012, http://en.wikipedia.org/wiki/Metagaming.

21. The poll was conducted by a user of the *CivFanatics* forums who went by the name of "wooter."

22. A notable example of blog-based peer review comes from Noah Wardrip-Fruin, accessed July 31, 2012, http://grandtextauto.org/2008/04/03/blog-based-peer-review-some-preliminary-conclusions-part-1/.

23. *CivFanatics,* accessed July 31, 2012, http://forums.civfanatics.com/showthread.php?t=187436.

24. Idit Harel and Seymour Papert, *Constructionism* (New York: Ablex, 1991).

25. The project website has been taken down, though the Interactive Arts and Sci-ence program's page was available as of July 31, 2012, http://www.brocku.ca/humanities/departments-and-centres/interactive-arts-and-science.

26. Interactive Arts and Science, accessed August 1, 2012, http://www.brocku.ca/humanities/departments-and-centres/interactive-arts-and-science.

27. Tom Mitrovic, reflection paper (unpublished student essay, Brock University, n.d.).

28. Alas, at the time of publication, *The Nethernet* was no longer online.

FOURTEEN

Victorian SimCities

Playful Technology on Google Earth

Patrick Dunae and John Sutton Lutz

The best vantage point for viewing a landscape is from above. That is the premise of *Google Earth*, which opens from a vantage point high in space, and then zooms down through the atmosphere to a point on the earth. Nineteenth-century visual image makers also knew that high places offered the best perspectives on the landscape. In a pre-airplane era, they imagined how landscapes would appear if they were seen from the perspective of a bird, flying high in the sky, or from a balloon floating over the land. They developed their imagined perspectives in panoramic lithographic views, which are commonly called bird's-eye views. When advances in photographic technology permitted, Victorian image makers perched on high buildings, whence they created a sequence of images that created panoramic photographs. These images—bird's-eye views and panoramic photographs—offer a remarkable picture of urban landscapes of the past, and a fascinating perspective for historians. The images also provide an engaging platform where students can play with the past. When these images are deployed with interactive digital technologies, our muse Clio is more playful than ever before.

We are using panoramic views in conjunction with *Google SketchUp*, the popular 3D modeling program, and *Google Earth* technology to engage secondary school students and undergraduate history students and draw them into the work of history by literally asking them to draw history. We are focusing on the city of Victoria, British Columbia, ca. 1890, for our prototype, but as we will explain, the historical resources that we have deployed can be utilized in other cities. Students are invited to become historical detectives and by building up documentation and inferences, re-create part of the lost landscape of Victorian Victoria. The more they play, creating buildings with *Google SketchUp* and uploading them to *Google Earth*, the more we expand our *SimCity—Virtual Victoria.*

Our method is to present history as a mystery, and the recovery of past landscapes as a particular mystery that students can help solve. Our objective is to introduce students to broad topics in historical geography and urban history, and our premise is that students learn best when they can see and experience the urban places. We cannot transport students back to Victoria, ca. 1890, via a Holodeck, but we can facilitate a process whereby they deploy historical records in a way that will enable them to see a world that is now gone and engage closely with this past.[1] Consider the process of a biographer, who reads extensively on his subject and manages to get "under the skin" or "inside the mind" of his subject. Or consider the words G. Kitson Clark, the distinguished Cambridge historian of Victorian England, used to exhort his students to read voraciously in order to connect to the historical period they were studying: "Read, read, read—until you can hear them [Victorians] speak."[2] Our students follow a similar regimen as they study and re-create buildings and streetscapes. At the end of the day, using playful technologies, we hope they will be able to experience the sights, sounds, and possibly the smells of a Victorian city.

We developed the project with encouragement of the new literature, which shows that students like digital technologies and are adept at acquiring and utilizing knowledge and skills in an electronic environment. A growing body of literature suggests that history students relate easily with primary documents in digital formats, and that students engage readily in self-directed learning activities when these opportunities are presented within a web environment.[3] The literature also suggests that critical reasoning skills increase when students understand how different kinds of primary records are related and can be used to better understand historical questions or events. In such cases, students learn to "think like a historian."[4] The challenge of teaching undergraduate students to think like historians was a catalyst in the creation of The History Education Network, a consortium of some of Canada's leading history education researchers.[5] Studies completed by these and other scholars confirm our view that teaching is enlivened if we can turn students into researchers and learning is enhanced if we enable students to answer historical questions themselves.[6] This pedagogy is sometimes called inquiry-based learning. Its growth parallels the exponential growth of primary sources that are available in digital formats online.[7]

In our own work we have observed that students find the past intriguing, are motivated to solve puzzles, and given a choice prefer to work on assignments that have real-world applications. They also put more effort into projects where they will be seen by a wide audience and for which they can claim some credit for the creation. We have designed our Victorian *SimCity* project to capitalize on all these motivating factors. While providing a background to the project we want to introduce four elements that link *homo discens* (the learner) to *homo ludens* (the playful). These elements involve detecting spatial perspectives, researching biographies of historical structures, re-creating lost urban environments, and repopulating historical landscapes.

Detecting Perspective

The projects described in this chapter began a few years ago with a project called *Virtual Victoria: View from the Steeple*. We had discovered a collection of photographs in the British Columbia Archives offering a panoramic view of Victoria. The photographer was unknown and the images were not dated. After some detective work and close analysis of the photographs we determined that Richard Maynard, a well-known photographer, had created them in 1891. By studying foliage, shadows, and other details in the photographs, we were able to pinpoint the date to May 1891 (see figure 14.1).

But this was only part of our *CSI: Urban History* (!) exercise. We needed to determine the photographer's vantage point. After further research, we realized that Maynard had taken the pictures from the top of the nearly complete

Fig 14.1: A panoramic photograph of Victoria, British Columbia, 1891. Image A-03380 courtesy Royal BC Museum, British Columbia, Archives.

Roman Catholic cathedral on Blanshard Street. Since the pitch of the cathedral roof was very steep, we concluded that Maynard had taken the pictures when the nave had been completed and covered but before the roof was installed. Building records indicate that this would have been around May 1891, thus confirming our earlier deduction about the date of the photographs. Later, we were able to determine where the photographer stood on the roof. We could do so because the cathedral caretaker allowed us to climb up to the cathedral bell tower. The top platform of the bell tower was level with the top of the roof and so offered nearly the same vista as Maynard experienced back in 1891.

While we do not advise students to engage in this form of extreme history, this kind of detective work is easily replicated by providing students with panoramas or even single images and asking them to identify the approximate year (which they can do by looking at other dated photos), the time of year (leaves, shadows), and the time of day (shadows), and then having them locate the perspective of the photographer.

Biographies of Lost Buildings

Comparing a photograph taken today with a photo or an artist's rendering of a city a century ago reveals that many buildings have gone missing and have been replaced in the ensuing years. What have we lost? In this stage of our project, we get students to solve that mystery one building at a time. There are two often overlooked wake-up resources that allow groups of students to work on collective projects, with the intention of publishing their work to the web: panoramic photos and panoramic lithographic views.

Panoramic lithographic views, commonly known as bird's-eye views, occupy a kind of middle space between maps and photographs. They were very popular in the United States and Canada from the mid-nineteenth century to the early years of the twentieth century. They were often commissioned by chambers of commerce and newspapers, which sold them to local subscribers. They depicted a community as it might appear from above.

Itinerant artists usually created these images. The artist would systematically walk every street, making sketches of all the buildings and distinctive landscape features he or she encountered. The artist then determined an imaginary vantage point and rendered all of the sketches into a perspective panoramic image. The images were printed as lithographs and sold to the public, usually in the community they represented. Since local residents knew exactly what their community looked like, at least from the ground, the images had to be accurate. And, for the most part, they were. True, they often exaggerated local commercial or industrial activities. In bird's-eye

Fig 14.2: Detail of 1889 bird's-eye view of Victoria, British Columbia. Courtesy of Library of Congress Geography and Map Division, catalog number 75696734; digital ID g3514v pm010770.

views, harbors are always crowded with vessels and railway yards are always bustling with freight trains taking locally manufactured goods to distant markets.[8] But they are accurate in showing the layout of streets and the location of major buildings, including schools and churches. Although the bird's-eye views usually focused on city centers, they frequently depicted residential homes in the suburbs. We have checked details on a bird's-eye view of Victoria published in 1889 with contemporary photographs and have been favorably impressed with the high degree of accuracy (see figure 14.2).

Archivists and map librarians have long appreciated the informational value of panoramic maps.[9] Curiously, though, urban historians and historical geographers have devoted very little attention to these records. But as the Cornell University historian and urban planner John W. Reps has noted, there are "a number of ways scholars can use images of North American cities produced during the era of urban lithographic viewing." Reps suggested several lines of inquiry in his magisterial survey, *Views and Viewmakers of Urban America*: "An individual city can be examined in detail to show many aspects of its land use and development. A view can also provide many helpful clues to the architectural character of a community. Views from two or more cities can be compared for a variety of purposes or as sources for images depicting such things as works of municipal engineering or maritime activities."[10] Moreover, as Reps remarked in *Panoramas of Promise*, a study of urban views of the Pacific Northwest, nineteenth-century lithographs are compelling and emotionally appealing. Even a casual observer can connect readily to the images. "Whether scholar or not, we can with the aid of these views take ourselves back in time to the early years of the towns and cities in the Pacific Northwest and in our imagination approach their outskirts, walk their streets, admire their buildings, and appreciate the richness and variety of the urban scene in this region a century or more ago."[11]

Although we could have used the 1889 bird's-eye view of Victoria, we started with the 1891 Maynard panoramic photos described above and were able to "stitch" them together to re-create the photographer's panorama. We afterward created a website—entitled *Virtual Victoria, 1891: View from the Steeple*—where we tried and tested some simple, but playful, digital technologies.[12] History students were assigned to write biographies of the more prominent structures in the photographs. To complete such an assignment, students conduct research using nineteenth-century city directories. These publications, which were compiled for every major city in the country, offer a wealth of information on urban landscapes. The directories were usually organized in two sections, comprising an alphabetical directory and a street directory. The former was a list of adult residents and householders, with information about the person's occupation, place of work, and residence. Street directories provided information about commercial, industrial, and residential places; they identified buildings according to their geographic location and placed them in relation to neighboring buildings and intersecting streets. Theodore Hershberg, the American historian and sociologist, utilized city directories to create his innovative "interdisciplinary history" of Philadelphia, and Sherry Olson, the eminent urban geographer and historian at McGill University, has used directories to create a social ecology of late nineteenth-century Montreal. We are building on their work in this project.[13] Directories for towns and cities in British Columbia, including Victoria, have been scanned and posted online by the Vancouver Public Library.[14] We have made information for Victoria even more accessible on our Vancouver Island digital archives, *viHistory*. Resources on this website include a searchable database of the 1892 alphabetical directory of Victoria and Victoria City property tax assessment records. The *viHistory* website also provides links to contemporary newspapers and indexes that enable researchers to identify architects, contractors, and other information about Victoria City buildings.[15]

In our prototype we annotated the Maynard 1891 panoramic images by creating image maps, with "hot spots" and pop-up windows (see figure 14.3). Admittedly, this was a "low-tech" exercise, but it was also very gratifying, as students enthusiastically engaged with the assignment. By consulting city directories, newspapers, and other contemporary records, students were able to chronicle the buildings in great detail. At this point we appreciated the value of creating building biographies.

Fig 14.3: A screen shot from the *Virtual Victoria*, view from the steeple website. Screen shot courtesy of the authors.

The next step in this exercise was to use the sequence of panoramic photographs to create the illusion of motion and a sense of virtual reality. We accomplished this by using Apple *QuickTime*. With this application, the sequence of historical photographs is presented as a video. Using their mouse buttons and the Control and Shift keys, viewers can make a full 360-degree flight around the city, and they can zoom in to buildings or streets at any time to have a closer look at the environment.

Rebuilding the Past

The faux-video flyover that we created was rewarding; students and members of the general public continue to access it on our *View from the Steeple* website in large numbers. But while our vantage point on top of the cathedral gave us a remarkably clear view of Victoria in 1891, our perspective was nevertheless limited. We could only see what the photographer saw. We could see the façades and roofs of downtown buildings, but we could not see the sides of the buildings or façades of buildings that were obscured by other structures. To mitigate these limitations, we determined to create a digital model of the buildings in one of the panoramic photographs. For this exercise, we selected a photograph that depicts a downtown city block bounded by Yates Street, Douglas Street, Johnson Street, and Blanshard Street. From the photograph, we could see the façades of buildings on Yates Street and the backs of buildings on Johnson Street. We could see portions of the buildings on Douglas Street and Blanshard Street. We wanted to see them entirely. We wanted to create an application that would allow us to walk around this downtown city block and inspect each of the structures. We wanted to explore the backyards of the buildings and fly over them. With these objectives in mind, we began to plan our 3D Virtual Victoria to see if we could get students to build the city with us. In this respect, we are following the work of John Bonnett, the Brock University historian and communications theorist who has created a 3D model of Sparks Street in Ottawa.[16] He built his digital model with Vectorworks, the robust computer-aided design (CAD) software program. But professional programs like Vectorworks can be rather daunting to students and require a relatively steep learning curve. After discussing our objectives with heritage architectural designers and educators, we decided to use *Google SketchUp*. We are very pleased with our decision because *SketchUp* is readily accessible, free, easily extensible, and already structured for *Google Earth*.

We searched the photographic collections of the provincial and city archives to locate photographs of the streetscapes and buildings we wanted to re-create. We used fire insurance plans to position the buildings precisely. Fire insurance plans or maps were produced by fire underwriting firms to assist in assessing fire risk. The plans were drawn to a scale of one inch to fifty feet and so are very detailed. They provide information about the size, shape, and structure of buildings. Fire insurance plans for Victoria, published by Charles E. Goad & Company in 1891, were particularly helpful in creating our 3D building models.[17]

The next task was to find a research assistant who had some expertise with *SketchUp*. Fortunately, a senior student at the University of Victoria, James Strickland, was available. He had a background in computing science and an interest in nineteenth-century architecture. He was ideal to help us embark on this project. Using historical photographs and fire insurance plans, James created a foundation and framework for several buildings. In one of his progress reports, he explained his methodology as follows:

I grab a portion of the [1891] fire [insurance] map, rotate it as necessary to account for the non-perfect scanning (and original drawing),
then import it into *SketchUp* as a 2D base, scaled to the correct size.
The determination of the "correct" size could probably be improved,
but the street dimensions I've calculated from the fire maps match the
street dimensions shown on the [present-day] Victoria CRD [Capital
Regional District] maps and *Google Earth* to within 1% or 2%. I then
trace the 2D outlines, converting them to 3D according to the best
sources I can find. Sources include: a) current photographs, modified as necessary to account for changes over the years; b) archival
photographs (including photos from the *Virtual Victoria, 1891: View
from the Steeple* website); c) the 1889 bird's-eye view of Victoria on the
viHistory website; d) the number of floors indicated on the 1891 fire
insurance plan—using approximate heights and roof shape according
to the plan.[18]

He exported one of the models to *Google Earth* and the results were very
encouraging (see figure 14.4). But the project proved to be very labor-
intensive and more time-consuming than we anticipated. Still, thanks to his
work, we had a better idea of the magnitude of the task.[19]

Fig 14.4: A *SketchUp* model and 1891 fire insurance plan geo-referenced to
Google Earth. Image courtesy of the authors.

The project resumed in the autumn of 2008 at Vancouver Island University with a new research assistant who had the technical skills and creative vision that we wanted to bring to the project. Andre Serin specializes in computer-designed floor plans for building contractors and interior designers. Andre built on the foundations that James had created and used a similar methodology. He developed the designs in more detail and ultimately modeled an entire city block in downtown Victoria, ca. 1891. He created the streetscape using archival images and fire insurance plans, and with the measurements he made of the 1891-era buildings that are still standing. Having the actual specifications of certain buildings, he said, enabled him to estimate the specifications of buildings no longer extant. In this way, he was able to create a very accurate representation of this particular "lost landscape" of Victoria (see figure 14.5). With his *SketchUp* model, viewers can fly over and navigate between the buildings. They can maneuver around the block and see the distinctive corner entrances of structures that faced street intersections. They can see the diverse styles and relative scales of the buildings. Altogether, we are delighted with what we have achieved. Eventually, we intend to "landscape" the block by re-creating some of the trees and bushes that occupied the space in 1891.

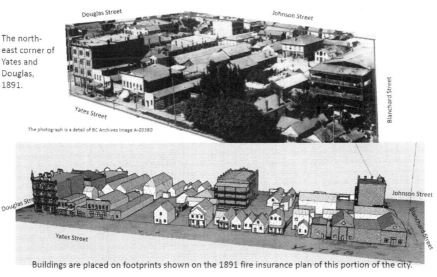

3-D models of a group of buildings in Victoria, BC, 1891

Fig 14.5: A panoramic photograph and *SketchUp* model of Victoria, British Columbia, 1891. Image courtesy of the authors.

With this experience the next step is to have students actually conjure up the buildings they have studied out of thin air and *Google SketchUp*,[20] borrowing from playful technologies and digital games, particularly from *Sim-City*. This popular computer game was first released in 1989. In the game, players create and manage a city, which becomes increasingly complex as the game proceeds. In the first version of the game, now called *SimCity Classic*, the urban environment is shown as a flat, top-down map. In the next version, *SimCity 2000* (1994) developers used an isometric model for the city and added a rotation feature that enabled users to view their city from different perspectives. The visual landscape was enhanced in *SimCity 3000* (1999), which also used an isometric model for the city and 2D sprites to simulate 3D buildings. *SimCity4*, a more recent version of the game, uses 3D modeling and animation. In their own way, the nineteenth-century artists who drew the lithographic views used 2D sprites to suggest a 3D environment. We are using a *SimCity* approach with our bird's-eye view of late nineteenth-century Victoria. We have started to create 3D models of a few buildings and a few city blocks as prototypes, but eventually we hope to expand the digital landscape to as much of the city as possible with student-built structures. Basically, we identify historical buildings on panoramic photos and bird's-eye views and invite students to create *SketchUp* models of the buildings. We have commenced with modest residential bungalows built pattern-book designs in Victoria neighborhoods like James Bay. Having modeled one of the bungalows, we can readily re-create neighboring structures in this part of the city (see figure 14.6). Similarly, many

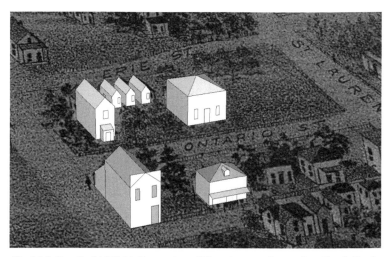

Fig 14.6: Detail of 1889 bird's-eye view of Victoria geo-referenced to *Google Earth* with *SketchUp* sprites by Nick Ward. Image courtesy of the authors.

warehouses and office blocks in late nineteenth-century Victoria were built to standard and relatively simple designs and can be modeled quite easily. And as our *SketchUp* skills increase, we will tackle more challenging structures, such as the city's architecturally ornate churches and cathedrals. Models of the structures can then be examined in desk-top viewers or uploaded to *Google Earth*. As more structures are modeled and placed online, our Virtual Victoria will expand, in the same manner as a SimCity expands and develops in the course of the game.[21]

Repopulating Historical Landscapes

As part of a next phase we want to link the *SketchUp* models to a geographical information system (GIS). Essentially, GIS is a method of representing and analyzing geographically referenced information. In its simplest form, GIS is a way to link attribute data (information about people and events) to spatial data and points on the earth. Our attribute data are derived from city directories and nominal census records. We have detailed census records for the entire population of Victoria in 1891 and with this information we can repopulate the historical landscape of the city.[22] When we associate the census data to our 3D models of historical buildings, viewers will not only be able to zoom over and walk around the buildings. They will be able to virtually knock on the building doors and, through the census information, meet the occupants! Ultimately, we can see a time in which an avatar of the researcher will meet and interact with avatars of Victoria's 1891 population. In this respect, we are developing an application that William G. Thomas anticipated in his essay on digital humanities and the historical imagination. He encouraged historians in the field of digital humanities to use GIS and other technologies in order to achieve "highly interpretative and imaginative digital creations." By extending historical GIS, he suggested, historians "might attempt to recreate 'lost landscapes' in ways that fully allow readers to move and navigate through them." The goal of our Virtual Victoria project is to re-create the downtown core of Victoria in 1891 in 3D and to link each building to all the census, directory, tax assessment, cartographic, photographic, and anecdotal evidence that exits of it. Researchers will be able to query the spatial organization of the city and armchair time-travelers will be able to wander the streets and meet occupants.[23]

The prototype of much of what we are developing might readily be adopted and developed in other communities because many cities in Canada were documented in bird's-eye views. To offer a few examples, exquisite lithographic views were created for Brantford, Ontario, in 1875, Halifax (1879

Fig 14.7: Detail of a panoramic photograph of Toronto, 1856, suitable for a 3D model. City of Toronto Archives, Fonds 1498, Item 14.

and 1890), Sherbrooke (1881), Winnipeg (1884), Montreal (1889), Ottawa (1895), St. Thomas, Ontario (1896), Vancouver (1898), and Dawson City (1903). The images are freely available on Library and Archives Canada's *Living Memory* website and the U.S. Library of Congress's *American Memory* website.[24]

As far as photographic panoramas, Toronto is documented in a remarkable set of photographs created in 1856. The photographs, thirteen in all, provide a 360-degree view of the city. They were taken from the top of the newly opened Rossin House Hotel (later called the Prince George Hotel) on the corner of King Street and York Street (see figure 14.7). The panoramic photographs of Toronto could be treated in the same way as the Maynard images of Victoria. They could be annotated as image maps and presented in a *QuickTime* faux-video application. That would be a very useful, and fun, exercise.[25]

Conclusion

A recent study on heritage and social media considered the proliferation of computer-generated visualizations of historical landscapes and raised questions about the "seductive misuse of digital technologies." The authors were worried that "virtual" historical landscapes, which sometimes appeared to be "realer than real" on fixed video screens, could mute rather than stimulate, critical reflections about the past. "For a public increasingly accustomed to the passive consumption of historical content," they wrote, "there is a dangerous illusory aspect of which digital archaeologists, humanists and heritage professionals need to be aware."[26] Digital historians will appreciate their concerns. But the digital applications described in this chapter involve creation, not consumption; they call for critical scrutiny, not a passive gaze. If the past is indeed "a foreign country," as L. P. Hartley and David Lowenthal have famously suggested, we are going to travel there as building contractors and detectives, not tourists![27] And as we observed in a recent forum on pedagogy, since the past is not boring, the discipline of history can only appear to be dull if we, history teachers and practitioners, present it in a boring way to our students. "History becomes dull when we take the mystery out of it and deprive students of the real work of the historian: finding clues and solving puzzles."[28]

By challenging students to solve the mystery of the missing buildings, to identify and do a life history on the buildings when found; and then, using fire insurance plans, old photographs, and lithographic views to reconstruct them, we are asking students to deploy a wide range of historical skills and learn a new one, the use of *Google SketchUp*.

With the mystery of the photographer's perspective, the challenge to identify landscape features, and the quest to bring them back into being, we have presented three ways of playing with visual representations of the past that exploit the puzzle-solving element that is the essential element of game-based learning. But unlike games, these playful historical strategies have real-world outcomes of interest to both the student-creators and a much larger audience on the world wide web. They offer us a new perspective on the past—the view from outer space as we zoom into 1890s Victoria on *Google Earth*.

NOTES

1. Our reference is to the virtual reality facility featured in the popular television series, *Star Trek: The Next Generation* (1987–94). In the series, officers aboard the twenty-fourth-century starship *Enterprise* used the Holodeck as a portal to the past and a vehicle for exploring, among other places, Victorian London, the frontier American West, and 1940s Hollywood. Holodeck historical episodes are described in Denise Okuda and Debbie Mirek, *The Star Trek Encyclopedia* (New York: Pocket, 1994).

2. G. Kitson Clark, *Portrait of an Age: Victorian England* (London: Oxford University Press, 1977), 179.

3. Robert A. Scheider, "Improving Student Achievement by Infusing a Web-Based Curriculum in Global History," *Journal of Research on Technology in Education* 36, no. 1 (2003): 77–93; David Hicks, Peter Doolittle, and John K. Lee, "Social Studies Teachers' Use of Classroom-Based and Web-Based Historical Primary Sources," *Theory and Research in Social Education* 32, no. 2 (2004): 213–47; Cynthia Hynd-Shanahan, Jodi Patrick Holschuh, and Betty P. Hubbard, "Thinking Like a Historian: College Students' Reading of Multiple Historical Documents," *Journal of Literary Research* 36,

no. 2 (2004): 141–71; Richard Van Eck, "Digital Game-Based Learning: It's Not Just the Digital Natives Who Are Restless," *Educause* (March–April 2006): 16–30.

4. John W. Saye and Thomas Brush, "Scaffolding Critical Reasoning about History and Social Issues in Multimedia-Supported Learning Environments," *Educational Technology Research and Development* 50, no. 3 (2002): 77–96; and A. M. Shapiro and D. Niederhauser, "Learning from Hypertext: Research Issues and Findings," in *Handbook of Research on Educational Communications and Technology*, ed. David H. Jonassen, 2nd ed. (Mahwah, N.J.: Lawrence Erlbaum Associates, 2004), 605–20.

5. The History Education Network is "a collaborative network across the diverse fields of history, history education and school history teaching in Canada. It brings together people from across Canada and internationally to inform, carry out, critique, and implement research into history education." Like many scholarly organizations in Canada, it is a bilingual body, known in French as Histoire et Éducation en Réseau. Its acronym is THEN/HiER and its website, accessed October 15, 2012, is http://www.thenhier.ca.

6. Peter Seixas, "A Modest Proposal for Change in Canadian History Education," *Teaching History* 137 (December 2009): 26–32; Ruth Sandwell, "Reflections on the Great Unsolved Mysteries in Canadian History Project: A Pedagogical Perspective," *Canadian Diversity / Diversité canadienne* 7, no. 1 (2009): 88–92; Peter Seixas, "What is Historical Consciousness?" in *To the Past: History Education, Public Memory and Citizenship Education in Canada*, ed. Ruth Sandwell (Toronto: University of Toronto Press, 2006), 11–22; Ken Osborne, "Teaching History in Schools: A Canadian Debate," *Journal of Curriculum Studies* 35, no. 5 (2003): 585–626. There is a large and growing literature on this, which is perhaps best summarized in Keith Barton and Linda Levstik's *Teaching History for the Common Good* (Mahwah, N.J.: Lawrence Erlbaum Associates, 2004).

7. John Sutton Lutz, "Riding the Horseless Carriage to the Computer Revolution: Teaching History in the Twenty-first Century," *Histoire Sociale / Social History* 34, no. 68 (November 2001): 427–36.

8. The imagery of urban lithographs is discussed in Richard H. Schein, "Representing Urban America: 19th-Century Views of Landscape, Space and Power," *Environment and Planning D: Society and Space* 11 (1993): 7–21. Schein discusses a shift in the perspective provided in these popular images and how the shift represents a late Victorian "industrialist-capitalist order." The images are also examined by Isabel Thompson Breskin in a Ph.D. dissertation on the history of art entitled "Visualizing the Nineteenth-Century American City: Lithographic Views of San Francisco, 1849–1905" (University of California, Berkley, 2002).

9. In 1976 the Public Archives of Canada organized a major exhibit of lithographic views and published an informative exhibit catalogue. See Canada Public Archives, *Bird's-Eye Views of Canadian Cites: An Exhibition of Panoramic Maps (1865–1905), July to November 1976* (Ottawa: Public Archives of Canada, 1976).

10. John W. Reps, *Views and Viewmakers of Urban America: Lithographs of Towns and Cities in the United States and Canada, Notes on the Artists and Publishers, and a Union Catalogue of Their Work, 1825–1925* (Columbia: University of Missouri Press, 1984), 78.

11. John W. Reps, *Panoramas of Promise: Pacific Northwest Cities and Towns on Nineteenth-Century Lithographs* (Pullman: Washington State University Press, 1984), 63. See also idem, *Cities on Stone: Nineteenth Century Lithographic Images of the Urban*

West (Fort Worth, Tex.: Among Carter Museum, 1978), and *Bird's-eye Views: Historic Lithographs of North American Cities* (Princeton, N.J.: Princeton University Press, 1998).

12. *Virtual Victoria, 1891: View from the steeple*, accessed October 15, 2012, http://cdhi.mala.bc.ca/steeple/index.htm.

13. Theodore Hershberg, ed., *Philadelphia: Work, Space, Family, and Group Experience in the Nineteenth Century. Essays Toward an Interdisciplinary History of the City* (New York: Oxford University Press, 1981); Sherry Olson, "Occupations and Residential Spaces in Nineteenth-Century Montréal," *Historical Methods* 22, no. 3 (1989): 81–96.

14. Vancouver Public Library, British Columbia City Directories 1865–1947, accessed October 15, 2012, http://www.vpl.ca/bccd/index.php.

15. Victoria city directories and an extensive array of other historical records are accessible at our *viHistory* website, accessed October 14, 2012, http://www.vihistory.ca. This website, launched in 2005, is a joint venture by the University of Victoria (UVic) and Vancouver Island University (VIU). A database of building permits, issued for the City of Victoria, 1877–1921, was added to the *viHistory* website recently. Historical material about Victoria, British Columbia, is also available at the *Victoria's Victoria* website, which features digital research projects, mainly by undergraduate history students at UVic. It was accessed on October 17, 2012, and is located at http://web.uvic.ca/vv/. *Victoria's Victoria* includes an index to the Victoria *Daily Colonist* newspaper. The online edition of this newspaper, 1858–1920, was accessed October 15, 2012, and is available at http://www.britishcolonist.ca.

16. See John Bonnett, "New Technologies, New Formalisms for Historians: The 3D Virtual Buildings," *Literary and Linguistic Computing* 19, no. 3 (2009): 273–87; idem, "Mediating the Past in 3D, and How Hieroglyphs Get in the Way: The 3D Virtual Buildings Project," in *Mind Technologies: Humanities Computing and the Canadian Academic Community*, ed. Raymond George Siemens and David Moorman (Calgary: University of Calgary Press, 2006).

17. On the function and value of these spatially related records, see Diane L. Oswald, *Fire Insurance Maps: Their History and Application* (College Station, Tex.: Lacewing, 1997). See also Jason A. Gilliland and Mathew Novak, "Positioning the Past with the Present: The Use of Fire Insurance Plans and GIS for Urban Environment History," *Environment History* 11, no. 1 (January 2006): 136–40.

18. The Victoria Capital Regional District (CRD) has posted geo-referenced maps for Victoria on its Regional Community Atlas, accessed October 16, 2012, at http://crdatlas.ca. The CRD Atlas features a wallpaper image of an 1878 bird's-eye view of Victoria.

19. This work was supported by two SSHRC Image, Text, Sound and Technology grants awarded to Kevin Kee (Brock University): "Simulating History: The Collaborative Development of Best Practices for History Simulations and Serious Games" (2006) and "The Poetics of History Simulations" (2007).

20. Students and faculty who have access to a site license for ESRI products might like to investigate their recently released (2012) CityEngine software, which allows the creation of highly detailed and generic 3D buildings.

21. We have benefited greatly from the expertise of Nick Ward, a digital design engineer and consultant based in Cumberland, British Columbia. He has provided guidance in transforming historical bird's-eye views into *SketchUp* models, which are

accessible on *Google Earth*. He is developing lesson plans suitable for secondary school courses in history, geography, and anthropology using *SketchUp* modeling software. His work is described on the *Rebuildcanada* website, accessed October 15, 2012, http://rebuildcanada.org/rebuild/tiki-index.php.

22. Nominal census records, created during the 1891 census of Canada, are preserved on microfilm and available from Library and Archives Canada. Records for the city of Victoria were transcribed in 1998 as part of the Canadian Families Project. We are grateful to the project directors, Peter Baskerville and Eric Sager (History Department, University of Victoria), for sharing portions of their database with us. Census data for Victoria and other Vancouver Island communities, ca. 1871–1911, are available on *viHistory*.

23. William G. Thomas III, "Computing and the Historical Imagination," in *A Companion to Digital Humanities*, ed. Susan Schreibman, Ray Siemens, and John Unsworth (Oxford: Blackwell, 2004), 56. Thomas, professor of history at the University of Kansas, was the director of the Virginia Center for Digital History and co-editor of the award-winning *Valley of the Shadow* website, accessed October 18, 2012, http://valley.vcdh.virginia.edu.

24. The Library and Archives Canada images are available at their website, accessed October 18, 2012, http://www.collectionscanada.gc.ca/website/index-e.html; the Library of Congress images are available at http://memory.loc.gov/ammem/pmhtml/panhome.html, accessed October 15, 2012.

25. The panoramic photographs of Toronto were discovered some years ago in the British Public Record Office in London. Apparently, they had been submitted to the Colonial Office by municipal officials in Toronto to bolster the city's bid to be selected as the permanent capital of the United Province of Canada. The images, accessed October 15, 2012, are posted at http://commons.wikimedia.org/wiki/Panorama_of_Toronto_in_1856.

26. Neil Silberman and Margaret Purser, "Collective Memory as Affirmation," in *Heritage and Social Media: Understanding Heritage in a Participatory Culture*, ed. Elisa Giaccadi (Abingdon: Routledge, 2012), 18.

27. The reference is to the frequently quoted opening lines in L. P. Hartley's novel, *The Go-Between* (London: Hamish Hamilton, 1953): "The past is a foreign country: they do things differently there," and to the influential study by British historical geographer David Lowenthal, *The Past is a Foreign Country* (New York: Cambridge University Press, 1985).

28. John Sutton Lutz, "Should History Be Fun? Putting Mystery Back Into History," *Canadian Issues / Thèmes Canadiens* (Fall 2006): 75.

FIFTEEN

True Facts or False Facts—Which Are More Authentic?

T. Mills Kelly

Q: What happens when you teach students how to lie?
A: They learn how to be historians.

It is a safe bet that every History Department in North America requires undergraduate history majors to take a course in what is most typically called "historical methods." In such a course students learn a variety of skills—how to distinguish between primary and secondary sources, how to do research in libraries and archives, how to analyze source material, and how to write analytical or narrative history. Many History Departments, mine included, also attempt to introduce students to historiography at the same time they are learning historical methods on the premise that one cannot write good history without knowledge of methods and of historiography.

I have taught our historical methods course several times over the past few years and have become increasingly dissatisfied with the results. My students do not seem to be *really learning* the lessons I have tried to impart. For this conclusion I have evidence both from my classes, but also from colleagues who taught my students in later semesters and report that some of my students still could not tell the difference between a primary and a secondary source. That feedback alone would have been enough to convince me that I needed to try a different approach to the course. Given how important it is that our students are well grounded in historical methods, even a few students who could not tell the difference between a primary and a secondary source was too many. But in addition to worrying about the results my colleagues were seeing from my teaching, I was also dissatisfied because of all the courses I teach, my methods course was the one where my students seemed the most disengaged despite what I thought were some very interesting readings and learning exercises, and despite the very strong end-of-semester ratings my students gave the course and my teaching. It was clear to me from their comments on the end-of-semester surveys that they had enjoyed the course, but my own observations of their level of engagement did not match what they told me in those comments. They just seemed less connected to the material than I wanted them to be. So, I did the worst kind of survey research—I asked a random group of colleagues at my institution and elsewhere how their methods course works and how it is received by students in their departments. The most common response I get is that the methods course is one of their least favorite courses to teach and, not surprisingly, that it is one of the least favorite courses among their students. At least I was not alone in feeling like a failure.

Given that historians care a great deal about historical methods and that history majors are presumably interested in the methods of their chosen discipline, how is it that the methods course could have become an apparent nexus for so much dissatisfaction from both faculty and students? After thinking about this problem for quite a while, I decided that there are two very likely answers to the problems I and others find with this course. The first possible answer is that when it comes to teaching historical methods, historians have lost their sense of fun, their sense of playfulness when it comes to our discipline (assuming we ever had such a sense of fun in the first place). The second possible answer is that in the increasingly intermediated world our students now live in, the traditional approaches to historical methods—in fact the traditional approaches to history itself—are increasingly disconnected from the lives our students live. Theirs is a world increasingly infused with mashed-up content—music, images, video, art, maps, text—blended together in new and different ways. And in that world new sensibilities about what is and is not authentic are emerging.

Take, for example, the recent interview in *The New York Times* with bestselling (and 17-year-old) German author Helene Hengemann. Her novel *Axolotl Roadkill* is a best seller, has been nominated for a major book prize, and is heavily plagiarized by almost any definition of the term one cares to use. Hengemann is unabashed by any criticism of her mixing in of content from other authors because, she says, this mixing and remixing is the point of the book, which is a meditation on youth culture in Berlin, especially the mash-up/remix culture she is a central player in. In a formal statement defending her approach to writing/remixing Hengemann argued: "There's no such thing as originality anyway, just authenticity."[1] One can imagine poor Leopold von Ranke spinning in his grave at such words, but just how different is Hengemann's position from Carl Becker's 1931 essay "Everyman His Own Historian," in which Becker said:

Mr. Everyman works with something of the freedom of a creative artist; the history which he imaginatively recreates as an artificial extension of his personal experience will inevitably be an engaging blend of fact and fancy, a mythical adaptation of that which actually happened. In part it will be true, in part false; as a whole perhaps neither true nor false, but only the most convenient form of error. Not that Mr. Everyman wishes or intends to deceive himself or others.[2]

Or, for that matter, how far removed is Hengemann's position from that of Thucydides, who explained his approach to recording the great speeches of his day thus:

With reference to the speeches in this history, some were delivered before the war began, others while it was going on; some I heard myself, others I got from various quarters; it was in all cases difficult to carry them word for word in one's memory, so my habit has been to make the speakers say what was in my opinion demanded of them by the various occasions, of course adhering as closely as possible to the general sense of what they really said.[3]

It does seem as though our students' increasing willingness to see history as more malleable than we might like has historical antecedents after all.

There are many ways one could approach a revision of the historical methods course to improve the degree to which students achieve the learning outcomes stated in the syllabus. Before revising the course I spent some time scanning other syllabi of other history faculty at my own institution and elsewhere and found that my version of the class was fairly typical. I had organized the class around group work, problem-based learning, and what I thought were some fairly innovative in and out of class exercises, and I thought the readings I had selected were fine. Given that I thought I was doing it right but still was not getting the results I wanted, I decided it was time to start over, from scratch. From the beginning I decided to challenge my students to have fun, to be playful, while they learned historical methods and, as we will see, did so in a way that is very atypical of historical methods courses. I offer the example of my revised course as *one way* that a full-scale reorientation of the course might be achieved, not as the *only* way. Others might include a course focused on conspiracy theories, or on foodways (with students making some of the food they study). I also recently taught another version of the course that uses local family cemeteries as the locus of the students' learning—a course I call Dead in Virginia. While we will not be creating what the students in my Lying About the Past course dubbed "false facts,"

I hope we will be having as much or perhaps even more fun as we learn. Creative historians can certainly come up with hundreds of possible options.

My decision to redesign the course around a playful approach to the past arose from two sources. Over the years I have become convinced that history as a discipline has become a bit too stodgy for its own good. It seems to me that we are taking ourselves a little too seriously of late (if there was ever a time when we did not). The second source for my decision to try to be more playful was an experience I had teaching a large group of fifth-grade students about historical research. While some might be tempted to argue that elementary students cannot do sophisticated historical research, I am in the Bruce Van Sledright camp and believe that fifth-graders can do some very sophisticated work when given the proper tools and context.[4] During the one and one-half hours I had with approximately seventy-five fifth-grade students, I not only found that they could work with such primary sources as military service records from the American Civil War and pages from the U.S. Census, I also noticed how much fun they had while doing it, fun I do not see my own students having when I give them sources to work with. For instance, when it was time for them to start writing, those fifth-graders threw themselves down on the floor, self-organized into groups, started drawing pictures to go with what they were writing. They laughed, they chatted, they made faces as they concentrated. In short, they were kinetic, engaged, and as focused as 11-year-olds get. And they produced some really good history from the sources I gave them.[5] What happens to young people, I wondered, between the fifth grade and university to convince them that historical research is not fun? Is it them? Or is it the course? Or is it me? I am almost never willing to blame the shortcomings of a course on the students taking the course, and am confident enough in my abilities as an instructor to not blame myself (too much), so I decided that it was a combination of the course and my approach to the course that was to blame.[6] Part of my goal in the revision of my methods course was to recapture the sense of fun that those 11-year-olds demonstrated when they were doing their historical research.

To respond to what I had seen during my day with that group of fifth-graders, I rewrote my historical methods course and taught the new version for the first time in the fall of 2008. The course title that fall was Lying About the Past, and the organizing focus was an exploration of historical hoaxes. In the first half of the semester the students did what students do in most history classes—they read books and articles, watched documentaries, discussed these materials both in small groups and as a class operating in seminar mode, and they wrote short papers analyzing information gleaned from the materials I assigned. The reading list, however, was fairly unconventional for an upper-level history course. The first article we read was "The Violence of the Lambs" by John Jeremiah Sullivan that appeared in the February 2008 issue of that stodgy academic journal *GQ*.[7] This article, a hoax that ends with a brief paragraph in which Sullivan admits to making up most of the story, an admission he says he did not want to make but that his editor insisted on, signaled to the students that mine was not your typical history course.

I also told them, on day one, just how I felt about history and fun in the context of the course they were signed up for. The syllabus says:

> I believe that the study of history ought to be fun and that too often historians (I include myself in this category) take an overly stuffy approach to the past. Maybe it's our conditioning in graduate school, or maybe we're afraid that if we get too playful with our field we won't be taken seriously as scholars. Whatever the reason, I think history has just gotten a bit too boring for its own good. This course is my attempt to lighten up a little and see where it gets us.[8]

Not surprisingly, the seventeen undergraduates in the course took to my approach to the course with gusto. There is not a single "serious" academic work on the syllabus—no Herodotus, no Thucydides, no von Ranke, no Foucault, no Nora. Instead we read works by popularizers you have probably never heard of, watched documentaries such as *Český sen* (*Czech Dream*) and faux documentaries like *The Old Negro Space Program*, and searched websites such as the *Museum of Hoaxes* and *Snopes* for useful information about historical hoaxes.[9] In eighteen years of college teaching I do not think I have ever had a group of students be as consistently prepared for class, or think so critically as a group about the fundamental principles of historical research and scholarship and what it means when the public engages with the results of historical scholarship. Those students worked *hard*.

Up to the mid-point of the semester nothing we did in Lying About the Past was particularly controversial. I am sure that plenty of colleagues around the country might look a bit askance at the "soft" readings I assigned, but at least my students were doing research and writing papers. These papers all included the kind of research skills that a methods course is intended to teach them, including identifying a topic, creating a thesis they can support with research, then finding an appropriate set of primary and secondary sources to support their argument. All of these assignments will be familiar to anyone who teaches historical methods. It is instead what happened in the second half of the course that was unusual, that was generative, and that turned out to be a bit controversial in the academic blogosphere.

After the seventh week of the semester my students began building their own historical hoax, a hoax they eventually launched into the digital world with great pride and satisfaction, not to mention a fair amount of glee. After half a semester researching the history of historical hoaxes, the class had to decide on a hoax that they could construct and publish as a group. Using a consensus model, I asked everyone to come up with ideas for a possible hoax and as a class we winnowed the choices down to two finalists. The students developed the standards for what the hoax should be, including that it would have to be historical, that it would have to be somewhat plausible, that there would be a sufficient evidentiary basis for that plausibility, and that there would be a "hoaxable community" out there, that is, a community of people liable to buy into the hoax because it appealed to them for personal or professional reasons. As will be shown below, the hoaxable community turned out to be one the students (and I) did not expect—academic historians and educational technologists. The proposal that did not make the final cut was focused on the now extinct town of Joplin, Virginia, that offered a rather unusual explanation for the town's extinction (involving economic crisis, mass hysteria, guns, and squirrels).[10]

The hoax the class finally settled on, *The Last American Pirate*, was organized around the senior research project of a fictitious student the class named Jane Browning (so she would have a very common name) who uncovered her Virginia pirate quite by accident. This man, Edward Owens, was a Confederate veteran who, during the Long Depression that began in 1873, found that he could no longer support his family by oyster fishing and so turned briefly to a life of crime. He and his crew of two robbed pleasure boaters in the lower Chesapeake until the economy recovered, at which point Owens went back to fishing and clean living. He left behind a legend and, as luck would have it, a last will and testament detailing both his exploits and his guilt over what he had done. There really was a man named Edward Owens who lived along the lower Chesapeake at the time and my students chose his name for two reasons—he really did exist, and they could find no evidence that any of the millions of genealogists out there knew anything about the real Edward Owens.[11] Also, the name Edward Owens was generic enough that a *Google* search would turn up too many possibilities to be sorted through in a timely manner. The platform the students chose for perpetrating their hoax was one they were very familiar with—a blog assigned by Jane's professor as part of a senior research seminar (Jane was a history major at an unnamed university).[12] Along the way Jane chronicled her search for a topic, her search for sources, her attempts to make sense of what she found, and finally her struggles with writing up the results of her work. In addition to the blog, she posted several *YouTube* videos, posted notices in social networking sites like *Stumbleon*, and created an entry on Edward Owens in *Wikipedia*.[13] Before deciding on a student blog as the best way to perpetrate their hoax, the students also discussed creating a website, but in the end decided it would be too much trouble. As we will see, the choice of a student blog had important implications for who ended up falling victim to the hoax.

At the beginning of the semester I told the students that their hoax could run until the last day of class, at which point we would expose it ourselves (if someone had not found us out already). I think it is fair to say that the majority of the students, if not all, would have preferred to let the hoax live on until it was exposed by someone in the wider world, but I insisted that we shut it down at the end of the term. Had the students not exposed their hoax, it is an open question how long Edward Owens might have survived online. For one thing, the question of who the "last" American pirate was is not one that attracts a great deal of attention. Even with the publicity that accrued from the post-exposure controversy, as of April 30, 2010, only 7,500 unique visitors have been to Jane's website. A primary reason why the students chose a pirate hoax was because they thought the pirate lovers of the world, especially those who enjoy "International Talk Like a Pirate Day," represented a hoaxable audience. When the fall of 2008 turned out to be a period of intense media interest in piracy because of the activities of real pirates off the coast of Somalia, my students thought they had stumbled on to the perfect topic for their hoax. Alas, those with "piratitude" failed to take notice of Edward Owens until after the hoax was exposed.[14]

Only a few days after the hoax appeared online, academic bloggers including history teachers and professors, instructional technologists, and librarians began writing about Jane's blog as an exemplar of how undergraduate students could use new media to represent their research and writing in digital form.[15] The hoax found its way into the academic blogosphere because two graduate students at my university's Roy Rosenzweig History and New Media tweeted about it on their personal feeds—not as a hoax, but as evidence of an interesting research result from an undergraduate student: "This is incredible: A history student has found the last American pirate."[16] These two tweets found their way through the twitterverse to several academic bloggers who then wrote about Jane's project on their own blogs. It is worth quoting one at length to provide a sense for how Jane and her project were embraced by academics enthusiastic for digital media:

> I found not only a really cool example of the power of these tools for an individual to track and frame their own educational experience, but some absolutely exciting research about a 19th century Pirate (possibly the last US pirate of his kind) no one's ever heard of: Edward Owens. This undergraduate took her research to the next level by framing the experience on her blog, full with images and details from

her Library of Congress research, video interviews with scholars and her visit to Owens house, her bibliography, along with a link to the Wikipedia page she created for this little known local pirate.

What is even cooler is the fact that she not only framed a digital space for her research by getting her own domain and setting up a blog there, but she understood that she could also protect her identity at the same time by keeping certain information private. It is such a perfect example of the importance of framing your identity as a student/scholar online, and it really buttresses beautifully with the ideas we've been thinking about recently in regards to digital identity at UMW. More than that though, is the fact that this project was hers and she was fired up about what she had accomplished, and she could actually share that fact with others through her blog.[17]

Academic victims also interacted with Jane directly, writing comments on her blog such as, "What you have done here in documenting your experience is an amazing example of the power of technology in aiding historical research. Well done."[18] That academics turned out to be the primary victims of the hoax generated some controversy in the academic blogosphere—a controversy discussed in more detail below. In the aftermath of the hoax's exposure, the class received some media exposure and then, like all small stories, this one died away.[19]

What then did my students learn from playing with the past in this way?

Historians are fond of saying that one of our main goals in teaching is that our students should learn to "think historically." Such claims are even more common in historical methods courses because teaching students to think historically is the point of the exercise in such courses. What then do we mean by "historical thinking"? A brief definition that I am partial to is by Stéphane Lévesque:

> Historical thinking is, indeed, far more sophisticated and demanding than mastering substantive (content) knowledge, in that it requires the acquisition of such knowledge to understand the procedures employed to investigate its aspects and conflicting meanings. . . . To think historically is thus to understand how knowledge has been constructed and what it means. Without such sophisticated insight into ideas, peoples, and actions, it becomes impossible to adjudicate between competing versions (and visions) of the past.[20]

In his work, Lévesque distinguishes between content knowledge and procedural knowledge and it was the latter that my course emphasized. To be sure, my students learned some things about nineteenth-century Virginia history and about maritime history in general, but this content was incidental to the larger lessons about methods. First and foremost my students had to understand how knowledge is constructed in the digital realm, but also in the analog world. Their goal was to create a narrative built on enough "true facts" that the "false facts" would go unnoticed. To do that, they had to acquire a fairly sophisticated understanding of how such historical knowledge is created online and the digital skills necessary to make that happen. But to acquire the "true facts" they needed to make the "false facts" plausible—they needed to know how to find the information they needed on such things as the maritime history of the lower Chesapeake. When we teach historical methods to our students, one of the goals we generally espouse is teaching our students to do research in places other than the web. Much of what my students used for their hoax—the "true facts"—came from libraries and archives rather than websites, in part because the sources they needed just are not online. For me this was a very positive result of the course, but one that was largely coincidental to the topic they selected.

More important to my learning goals was teaching my students to be much more critical consumers of online content. Too often these days students search for plausible information using the "type some keywords into Google and see what comes up" method. When a reasonable source appears through such a search, they often use that source with almost no critical analysis of the quality of that source.[21] In other words, they spend little or no time "adjudicat[ing] between competing versions (and visions) of the past." Instead, they seem to employ a rough and ready plausibility test: "Does it look good enough? Okay then, I'll use it." In contrast to this attitude about finding and using plausible information, one of the students in the class wrote a comment in my blog as a response to an earlier draft of this essay:

> I guess what I am trying to say in a very long winded and wordy sort of way is that we as historians, in this day and age of technology, should know better than to take anything anyone sends us at face value, I don't care if someone tweeted about it, or if they updated their status on facebook. Not because everyone is out there to deceive [sic] us, but because in a day and age of technology it is so easy to create a story or an idea and cover your tracks.[22]

The students who took this class will almost surely think twice before ever employing such a plausibility test with content they find online and, one hopes, historical content in any form given the amount of time we spent discussing the prevalence of what a colleague calls "zombie facts" in the historical literature. For instance, we devoted close to half a class period examining just how ubiquitous and tenacious H. L. Mencken's fabricated story about the first bathtub in the White House has turned out to be.[23] The profound skepticism my students acquired in this course will serve them well throughout the rest of their lives, not merely in their work as historians. That this skepticism has value beyond the history curriculum was highlighted in a comment on the course by Bill Smith of the University of Arkansas, who wrote that in a world where many believe that the moon landing was a fake, "A healthy skepticism is an important part of citizenship."[24]

One of the things historians tend to spend a lot of time on in historical methods courses is the nature of historical sources—which are primary sources, which are secondary sources, what sorts of tests should be applied to each category (primary, secondary) and each type within that category (text, image, film, artifact) and each subtype (text, novel, letter, government report, newspaper story, poem, sacred text, etc.). Because my students were going to create at least a few invented sources to set beside real sources from archives and libraries, they needed to think carefully and critically about the nature of each type of source, if only so we would know better how to fake them. One type of source that historians have devoted a lot of ink and many pixels to is photographic images. Students often like to think of photographs as being particularly authentic representations of reality at the moment the photographer snapped the picture. After all, the camera does not lie, does it?[25] In this age of PhotoShop and digital image manipulation, many students are at least a little skeptical about some images, and the obvious cases like the *Bert is Evil* website are easy for them to figure out. But what about more sophisticated fakery like the amazing disappearing Leon Trotsky, in which Soviet publicists were required to excise Trotsky from all publications in the Soviet Union after he and Joseph Stalin had their falling out?[26] The manipulation of images my students engaged in was not nearly up to Soviet standards. They merely made images too small to read so the reader of Jane's blog could not see them clearly enough, or clipped out passages from a nineteenth-century will to support a particular version of the story they wanted blog readers to see.[27] But they did learn how easy it is to lie with an image and so came away from the course as skeptical not only of text, but also of other sources.

In addition to skepticism about historical sources, what other historical methods did my students learn? Along the way they learned how to do archival research at the National Archives and the Library of Congress. They learned how to work with a variety of original sources, including naval records, census records, manuscript sources from the U.S. Cutter Service (now the Coast Guard), images, letters and diaries, maps, and historical newspapers. And they learned how to do something that von Ranke first insisted on—the use of multiple sources in order to check the consistency of accounts in each source. After all, if their "true facts" did not triangulate properly, then the hoax would be more easily exposed for what it was. They had to portray Edward Owens's world as it actually was, even if he did not exist in that world. And it turns out, they liked doing this sort of serious historical research:

> As one of the students that worked on the historical background of Edward (making sure there weren't any anachronisms), it was a lot of genuine research—going through census records, looking up specifics in the regions we were placing Edward, and the like. I feel very knowledgeable in the ways of Coastal Virginia after the Civil War now. It's not like we were filling our minds with information that was completely bogus. We were studying real time periods, real situations and real conditions in order to make this work. This was probably the most exciting part for me.[28]

In addition to learning to work with this variety of sources and to use them for the purposes of triangulation, the students also learned that the creation of history is a collaborative endeavor. They worked together in class, but they also learned the value of calling on the expertise of others. Once they decided on their hoax they contacted one of our graduate students who is an expert in underwater archaeology and another who wrote her MA thesis on law enforcement in Virginia during the nineteenth century. Being able to ask these historians questions moved the project along much more rapidly than would have been the case if the students tried to do all the work on their own—a valuable lesson indeed. They also learned many new skills in the production of historical knowledge in the digital world. In addition to Jane's blog (for which they all wrote drafts, but one student wrote in her own voice), they learned how to scan or download and then manipulate images, how to write and edit *Wikipedia* entries, basic video scripting and production, and how to find an audience, albeit a small one, for their work by visiting various websites and posting notices about Jane's project. They also played extensively in the sandbox they were most comfortable in—Jane had a *Facebook* page and a *YouTube* channel.

How many historical methods courses take their discussion of ethics beyond a unit on plagiarism of the small and large variety? In such units, students are generally treated to admonitory lectures on student plagiarism (especially copying and pasting from websites) and on such bigger stories as the plagiarism controversies swirling around the work of such popular historians as Stephen F. Ambrose and Doris Kearns Goodwin.[29] The message of such units is clear—plagiarism is bad, bad, bad, and should be avoided at all costs. Who could disagree?[30] But such units do not really get to the heart of ethics in historical inquiry because they touch on only one, admittedly important, aspect of those ethics. My students had to grapple with much more difficult ethical issues, not the least of which was what it meant to create a lie and purvey it on their own website but also on the websites of others such as *Wikipedia*. After all, is not one of the primary obligations of the historian to tell the truth about the past? Much of the work of historians is directed at "setting the record straight" in the face of fantasy versions of the past that correspond to the evidentiary record to some greater or lesser degree. Historians set themselves and their work against myth and imperfect memory in the hope that somehow histories we have written will convince our audiences of the truth of what we say in the face of outright lies, exaggerations, shadings, and other less accurate versions of what happened in the past.[31] If there is some sort of historians' Hippocratic Oath compelling us to always tell the truth (or at least the truth as we know it), then my students and I violated that oath.

But the nature of "historical truth" is one that can certainly be debated—and is debated almost constantly by historians. For instance, is it "true" that daily life in medieval Europe was dominated by religious observance, or is this "truth" one we accept because the greatest store of evidence available to us about that daily life comes to us from a small circle of elite chroniclers who had a vested interest in playing up the importance of religion in daily life? Which account of the past is more "true"—the one that focuses on the accomplishments of leaders of a state, or the one that focuses on the accomplishments of the masses? Historians debate such "truths" constantly and students, who want to know which account of the past is "best" or "most correct," struggle to understand how five historians can look at the same evidence and write five different books. Teaching them how to negotiate through this maze of competing truth claims is one of the goals of most methods and historiography courses, but many of the historians I have spoken with who try to teach introductions to historiography report that lessons about historiography are even more difficult to impart than lessons about types of evidence and how to work with them.

I decided to tackle the problem of helping students sort through competing truth claims by having my students create their own (false) version of historical truth. To do that, they had to embed their work in existing histories that the students assumed to be as accurate as the authors of those works could make them. In this way they saw just how difficult it is to determine which truth claims should hold sway over others. Intentional fabrication is certainly very different from asserting that our version of the past was more correct or accurate than yours. Therefore, I challenged my students to think about whether or not we were crossing an ethical Rubicon that we really should not be crossed. To have this conversation at all we had to discuss the whole business of historiography and competing truth claims, if only to decide how far removed our project was from the debates among historians. Engaging historiography from the space of intentional fabrication turned out to be surprisingly productive. Because my students knew they were on one end of a truth-falsehood continuum, they could then move along that continuum to decide where the dividing line between deliberate falsehood and something one of them called "just competing interpretations" could be found. To put it another way, they knew they were lying, and therefore had to figure out how to tell where deliberate lying about the past ended and legitimate argument about the past began—a useful distinction to be able to draw. We never found that exact point, but discussed examples such as the denial of the Holocaust as exemplars of the distinction we were trying to draw. Once we were satisfied that we understood something about that distinction, it was still up to the students to decide how far to go in their fabrication of the historical record. Admittedly, I did not give them a choice about whether or not to create a hoax, but this aspect of the course is clearly stated in the syllabus and so students uncomfortable with the entire project could have dropped the class at the outset of the semester. To the best of my knowledge, no student dropped the class. This is not to say that students were completely comfortable with intentional fabrication of the historical record—some were, some were not. The important thing is that we talked about it a lot. And I am not a believer in the idea that education is supposed to be completely comfortable for students at all times, so the fact that my students were uncomfortable at various points in the semester was not a bad result from where I sat. In fact, ethical concerns were a part of our discussions in class almost every session once work on the hoax began. In the end, the distinction that made it possible for several students to feel more comfortable with the hoax was thinking of it as humor or satire rather than "serious history." We never intended the hoax to last forever and knew we were going to expose our hoax as falsehood at the end of the semester, so it was not as though we were creating zombie facts and turning them loose forever. Knowing that the hoax would end made it easier to see the entire project as humor rather than a lie . . . more like what one might find in *The Onion* rather than what one would find in a book trying to convince readers of a deliberately false version of the past.

Once the class had debated the largest ethical issue—were we doing the right or wrong thing—then the students had to consider even thornier questions such as which subjects were out of bounds for their hoax, the specifics of copyright law, and responsible use of computing policies—subjects sure to elicit fluttering eyelids and perhaps even some drooling on the desk from the average student. I gave the students some specific limits about what they could *not* select for their hoax. For instance, one out-of-bounds topic my students readily agreed on was anything to do with medicine or health. Too many people rely on the Internet for information about health and health care and so there would be nothing funny about creating a hoax in this domain. In the end, our list of other topics unavailable for hoaxing included anything that might have caused someone to send us money (wire fraud under U.S. law), anything to do with national security (I had no desire to visit Guantanamo, Cuba), and anything to do with the American Civil War. Why the Civil War? This was a practical rather than ethical decision because the community of historians, professional and amateur, devoted to the study of the American Civil War is so large and their knowledge of the details of this conflict is so vast and precise, we decided that there was no chance of perpetrating a successful Civil War hoax. Anything the students tried to do would be exposed almost instantly. Finally, I insisted that any hoax created would not violate the university's responsible use of computing policy, because I had no desire to be censured or fired as a result of a student project. This latter stipulation ruled out, for instance, any hoax that had to do with pornography or gambling. With the boundaries of the hoax firmly established, my students were then free to create any hoax they might think up.

That my students learned to think critically about such ethical issues is evident in what one student wrote in her personal blog:

> Ethically, the only doubt I have regarding my own participation in this project is the e-mail I sent to the writer of [the *USAToday* blog] Pop Candy. I do not exactly regret that action, but I do question it every time I think of it. Though I did not personally know this woman, I purposefully set out to deceive her for my own gains, taking advantage of the trust she has in her readers. I apologize for taking advantage of her trust in such a way.[32]

In the aftermath of the hoax's exposure, another ethical issue arose that confirmed for me the importance of having cut the hoax off at the end of the semester so that we still had time to discuss the controversy that began to emerge as we dispersed for the winter break. Because ethical considerations were so much a part of what we discussed all semester, had we not had a little time to reflect on the response of those hoaxed once they found out they were victims, I think an important lesson of the semester would have been lost.

Finally, my students all learned that creating history, whether it is "real" history or a hoax, is *hard* and takes a lot of work. In the aftermath of the course the student just quoted wrote: "I would like to say that all the details fell into place, but they didn't. We all worked and pushed them into place step by step. It was hard. Most definitely the hardest project I've ever worked on. We were entirely self-motivated in our groups. We had to figure out what needed to be doing before we could do it, and had to figure out entirely how to approach each step."[33] But from my perspective, the most important lesson they learned was that history can be fun after all. This was a class in which the students showed up for class early and stayed late, remained engaged throughout the class sessions, worked in small groups outside of class, and laughed throughout the semester.

The major issue that arose after the exposure of the hoax is less a part of the main story of the class and the student learning results. But given that a number of historians, librarians, and others argued that the class design was inappropriate to a university setting, the question of whether or not the class was appropriate seems worth describing here.[34] The discussion of the course that arose in the academic blogosphere centered on what one author termed "academic trust networks," the web of social networks (blogs, twitters, discussion forums, etc.) that academics and others increasingly rely on to help us find and evaluate information. "Online information increasingly exists in a context that provides us with a wealth of information about how that information is positioned within a larger conversation. When I find something of interest online, I do not only evaluate it's face-value worth; I evaluate it in terms of who else I know is linking to it, talking about it, critiquing it."[35] Much of the criticism or support for the results of the course revolved around the issue of what my students' work had exposed about the reliance of academics (and others) on social networks as trusted sources of information. At one end of the continuum of this conversation was the argument that by encouraging my students to create a hoax and then purvey it in these trust networks, I had violated a basic tenet or two of my own professional community.[36] At the other end of the continuum was the argument that academics (especially academics) should know better than to accept what they find online at face value.[37] One simple test anyone looking at Jane's blog could have used was a *Whois* lookup of the domain registry for her blog, *The Last American Pirate*. Checking that registry would have turned up the interesting information that the domain did not belong to a student named Jane Browning, but to someone at George Mason University named Theodore Kelly, with the email tkelly7@gmu.edu and the telephone number 703-993-2152, in other words, me. A more careful reader of the *Whois* data would indicate that the domain was created on October 22, 2008. Given that Jane's first post in her blog was dated September 3, 2008, this more careful reader might have noticed something a little fishy. The question for those interested in the idea of academic trust networks is whether or not participants in those trust networks should be held to the same information literacy standards we expect from our students. Because the point of the class was to teach my students some things worth knowing about historical methods, I think I will let one of them have the last word on this particular issue:

> I don't regret the trust networks we violated only because those that we violated didn't do their jobs as historians, they didn't do their research, they didn't check their facts, they took what we presented them at face value because they wanted to believe in the project that we had created. (Which in my opinion is why so many hoaxes work, just look at the Hitler diaries, reputations and careers were ruined because people wanted to believe.) Some of them claimed that they did not look at our hoax closely because they were looking at it not for its value as a history project, but instead because it was a techonology based history project.[38]

In the spring 2012 semester I taught Lying About the Past for the second time. Because I had thirty students rather than seventeen, I broke the class into two groups and so there were two hoaxes. One hoax was the "Beer of 1812," in which the students created a fictitious beer-loving history buff whose neighbor gave him an old beer recipe that, it turned out, was from Brown's Brewery in Baltimore, Maryland, the site where the original Star Spangled Banner was sewn in 1812. Their beer buff then tried to promote his "find" to the craft brew community of Baltimore during the celebrations of the bicentennial of the War of 1812. Although the "Beer of 1812" hoax contained all the elements of a successful hoax, it never found much traction with the public and to the students' disappointment, died a quiet death.

The second hoax produced by the students in the 2012 class created more commotion. Their goal was to convince the world that a person (they created) had found evidence that linked her great uncle Joe to the murders of several prostitutes in New York City in 1897. These were real unsolved murders and, at the time, there was some speculation in the New York newspapers that Jack the Ripper might have turned up in New York after he apparently fled London. The venue the students chose to promote their hoax was *Reddit*, on the serial killer "sub-Reddit." For the first few minutes after their story appeared on *Reddit*, the participants in the "sub-Reddit" became very excited by the possibility of a new serial killer story. But less than thirty minutes into the hoax, one of the participants in the discussion noticed that the three Wikipedia entries created by my students about the prostitute murders (all 100 percent factually accurate) had been posted within minutes of one another from three different accounts. The timing of those postings raised the specter of "sock puppetry" in which one person creates multiple identities on Wikipedia to purvey false information. Almost instantly, the discussion on *Reddit* turned against the hoax and twenty-six minutes after it was launched, the hoax died.[39]

After the end of the semester, Yoni Applebaum, a writer for *The Atlantic*, published a story about my class and the two hoaxes my students had tried to purvey. His story exploded across the Internet, becoming the most viewed article on the website of *The Atlantic* that month (viewed several hundred thousand times), and appearing in different versions on various tech blogs such as *BoingBoing* and *TechCrunch*, and on various discussion forums such as *Mashable*. I received many emails and blog comments, ranging from very positive to extremely negative (even one veiled death threat). That so many people showed an interest in the failed hoaxes of my students demonstrates, I think, just how much people care about history and how it is taught. As with the first version of the course, the students in the 2012 class emerged from their work deeply skeptical about sources they find online and with a much keener sense of how careful they must be when doing their work in the digital space. They also laughed their way through the entire semester.

If the results of the not very scientific random survey of available colleagues I did back in 2007 is correct, and historical methods courses do need a new approach in this age of digital media, Lying About the Past offers one possible approach to the recasting of this course. As mentioned above, I am not suggesting that a hoax course, or even a course that centers on being playful, is the only possible solution. But I do come away from this experience with the belief that any recasting of the methods course needs to retain the elements of historical thinking we hold dear, but also needs to bring them to students in ways that are more in tune with the lives they live now and will live after graduation. My hope is that the lessons of this course offer some inspiration to others, and that we will soon see many new and interesting versions of a course our discipline cannot live without.

NOTES

1. Nicholas Kulish, "Author, 17, Says It's 'Mixing,' Not Plagiarism," accessed August 1, 2012, http://www.nytimes.com/2010/02/12/world/europe/12germany.html.

2. Carl Becker, "Everyman His Own Historian," December 29, 1931, accessed August 1, 2012, http://www.historians.org/info/AHA_history/clbecker.htm.

3. Thucydides, *The Peloponnesian War*, trans. Richard Crawley (New York: Dutton, 1914), 14–15.

4. Bruce A. Van Sledright, "Can Ten-Year-Olds Learn to Investigate History as Historians Do?" *OAH Newsletter*, accessed July 32, 2012, http://www.oah.org/pubs/nl/2000aug/vansledright.html. See also Stéphane Lévesque, *Thinking Historically: Educating Students for the Twenty-First Century* (Toronto: University of Toronto Press, 2008), 11. For a full description of what I did in that fifth-grade class, see "I'll Go First," accessed July 31, 2012, http://www.playingwithhistory.com/ill-go-first/.

5. For a more complete description of what happened with those fifth-graders, see T. Mills Kelly, "I'll Go First," *Playing With Technology in History*, accessed July 31, 2012, http://www.playingwithhistory.com/ill-go-first/.

6. On why blaming students is a bad idea, see Uri Treisman, "Studying Students Studying Calculus: A Look at the Lives of Minority Mathematics Students in College," *The College Mathematics Journal* 23, no. 5 (November 1992): 362–72; and Carl Wieman and Kathleen Perkins, "Transforming Physics Education," *Physics Today* 58, no. 11 (2005): 36–41.

7. John Jeremiah Sullivan, "Violence of the Lambs," *GQ* (February 2008): 118–21 and 187–91.

8. The syllabus is available via this PDF document, accessed July 31, 2012, http://chnm.gmu.edu/history/faculty/kelly/blogs/h389/f08syl.pdf. The class blog, which the students stopped using in mid-semester once they started work on their hoax, is at Lying About the Past, accessed July 31, 2012, http://chnm.gmu.edu/history/faculty/kelly/blogs/h389/.

9. The books assigned in the course were John Mitchinson and John Lloyd, *The Book of General Ignorance* (New York: Harmony, 2006); Robert Harris, *Selling Hitler: The Extraordinary Story of the Con Job of the Century* (New York: Random House, 1986); Robert Silverberg, *Scientists and Scoundrels: A Book of Hoaxes* (Lincoln, Neb.: Bison, 2007); and Michael Farquhar, *A Treasury of Deception: Liars, Misleaders, Hoodwinkers, and the Extraordinary True Stories of History's Greatest Hoaxes, Fakes and Frauds* (New York: Penguin, 2005). The video of *The Old Negro Space Program* can be found online, accessed July 31, 2012, at http://negrospaceprogram.com/blog/nsp-movie. For more on *Český sen,* see the Internet Movie Database, accessed August 1, 2012, http://www.imdb.com/title/tt0402906/.

10. "Joplin Virginia," accessed July 31, 2012, http://en.wikipedia.org/wiki/Joplin,_Virginia.

11. Finding out about the real Edward Owens taught my students how to use genealogical databases like Ancestry.com. According to the U.S. Census of 1910, the Edward Owens who lived in the region was 57 years old and so would have been 12 when the Civil War ended in 1865. If anyone interested in the project had bothered to check this fact, the entire house of cards would have collapsed, but the students assumed, correctly it turned out, that no one would go to that much trouble.

12. "Hello World," accessed July 31, 2012, http://lastamericanpirate.net/2008/09/03/hello-world/index.html.

13. The videos created by the class can be seen at "Jane Browning," accessed July 31, 2012, http://www.youtube.com/user/janebrowning; their version of the *Wikipedia* entry, accessed August 1, 2012, is at http://en.wikipedia.org/w/index.php?title=Edward_Owens&oldid=256742352.

14. See the official website of International Talk Like a Pirate Day, accessed July 31, 2012, http://www.talklikeapirate.com/.

15. See, for example, the blog of Jim Groom, accessed July 31, 2012, http://bava tuesdays.com/the-last-american-pirate/.

16. *Twitter*, accessed July 31, 2012, http://twitter.com/digitalhumanist/status /1036654663.

17. "The Last American Pirate," accessed August 1, 2012, http://bavatuesdays.com /the-last-american-pirate/.

18. "Videos Index," accessed July 31, 2012, http://lastamericanpirate.net/2008/12 /03/videos/index.html#comments.

19. See, for instance, Jennifer Howard, "Teaching by Lying: Professor Unveils 'Last Pirate' Hoax," *The Chronicle of Higher Education*, December 19, 2008, accessed July 31, 2012, http://chronicle.com/article/Teaching-by-Lying-Professor/1420, and Jerry Griffith, *Push/Pause*, "Pirates," accessed July 31, 2012, http://www.youtube.com/watch ?v=6RT9ZwlNLeY. For reactions to the hoax in the blogosphere, see the following posts in my blog, both accessed July 31, 2012, http://edwired.org/?p=418 and http:// edwired.org/?p=446. As a postscript to this particular controversy, had any of those taken in by the hoax bothered to look up the domain registry, they would have seen it belongs to me, not to Jane Browning. At Domain Tools, accessed July 31, 2012, http:// whois.domaintools.com/lastamericanpirate.net.

20. Lévesque, 27.

21. Thomas J. Scott and Michael K. O'Sullivan, "Analyzing Student Search Strategies: Making a Case for Integrating Information Literacy Skills into the Curriculum—Technology NewsredOrbit," *Teacher Librarian* 33, no. 1 (October 2005).

22. Comment by Kelly on "Was the Last American Pirate 'Authentic'?" *Edwired*, April 13, 2010.

23. Henry L. Mencken, "A Neglected Anniversary," New York *Evening Mail*, December 28, 1917.

24. "How Do You Know It's True?" accessed July 31, 2012, http://doctorbs.blogspot .com/2009/01/how-do-you-know-its-true.html.

25. Beverley C. Southgate, *History Meets Fiction* (Harlow: Pearson/Longman, 2009), 153.

26. Roy Rosenzweig, "Scarcity or Abundance? Preserving the Past in a Digital Era," *The American Historical Review* 108, no. 3 (June 2003): 735–37. The website now lives at http://www.bertisevil.tv. On the disappearing Trotsky, see "The Commissar Vanishes," accessed May 25, 2010, http://www.newseum.org/berlinwall/commissar_vanishes/index .htm.

27. "Last Will and Testament of Edward Owens," accessed July 31, 2012, http:// lastamericanpirate.net/2008/11/12/last-will-and-testament-of-edward-owens/index .html.

28. Comment by Kristin M. on "You Were Warned," *Edwired*, January 3, 2009.

29. On these two controversies, see "How the Ambrose Story Developed," *History News Network*, n.d.; "How the Goodwin Story Developed," *History News Network*, n.d., accessed May 25, 2010, http://hnn.us/articles/590.html.

30. On ethics in history education, see Lendol Glen Calder, "Not Dr. Laura," *Reviews in American History* 28, no. 2 (2000): 318–26.

31. Southgate, 23.

32. *Four Point Report*, January 4, 2009, accessed July 31, 2012, http://fourpoint report.com/blog/?p=117.

33. *Four Point Report.*

34. See, for instance, *Tech Therapy*, "Wikipedia's Co-Founder Calls for Better Information Literacy," June 9, 2010, accessed August 1, 2012, http://chronicle.com /article/Audio-Wikipedias-Co-Founder/65841/. In this podcast interview Jimmy Wales describes himself as "really, really, really" annoyed by projects such as those undertaken in this class. He does, however, admit to having been unfamiliar with the course until the podcast host posed a question about it.

35. *Edwired*, accessed August 1, 2012, http://edwired.org/?p=418#comment-28716.

36. "discovery and creation . . . and lies," info-fetishist.org, accessed July 31, 2012, http://info-fetishist.org/2009/01/03/discovery-and-creation-and-lies/, accessed May 26, 2010.

37. "Edward Owens, "Pirate and Hoax: Shiver Me Timbers!" Cathy Davidson (HASTAC), accessed May 26, 2010, http://www.hastac.org/node/1858.

38. Comment by Kelly on "Was the Last American Pirate Authentic?" accessed July 31, 2012, http://edwired.org/?p=608#comments.

39. For more on the hoaxes in the second iteration of the class, see Yoni Applebaum, "How the Professor Who Fooled Wikipedia Was Caught by Reddit," May 15, 2012, http://www.theatlantic.com/technology/archive/2012/05/how-the-professor-who -fooled-wikipedia-got-caught-by-reddit/257134/; and Brendan Fitzgerald, "Here There Be Monsters," September 14, 2012, http://www.themorningnews.org/article /here-there-be-monsters.

Afterword

Kevin Kee

In the introduction to this volume, we asked: "how might we playfully use technology to teach and learn history?" To explore possible answers was the goal of the small conference from which this book emerged. It brought together, as the preceding pages show, academic historians, public historians, digital humanists, undergraduate and graduate students, and teachers. Despite the diversity of our occupations and skills, everyone mixed freely. While the level of computational expertise at the conference was high, the gathering included people on a spectrum of proficiency, from dedicated hackers to those who rely on off-the-shelf tools.

Play was more than the subject because we also played with the conference format. No expert was called on to deliver a plenary address. In fact, the program was only roughly sketched out beforehand. Following an approach pioneered in "unconferences," and now well established in regular events such as THATCamps,[1] our first hour was occupied with identifying topics that we wanted to address, individuals with expertise on those subjects, and then a schedule that would support these various subgroup meetings. In addition, we set up a video camera "confessional" where we were asked to answer the question: "in the context of using technology in the teaching and learning of history, what would you do if you had no limitations?" We recorded the proceedings with photographs as much as text. In addition to a large meeting space, we set up a "toys room," where we could work with a variety of objects, instruments, and environments. During the first day of the symposium, we "played" in groups large and small with technologies from recipe cards to the 3D printers (on this book's cover). During the second day, we reviewed our articles about how to best play with the past. No presentations were allowed; authors were instead required to listen to the comments and discussion of their colleagues, and speak only in response.

Over the course of two days, and as this volume attests, a thesis emerged about how and why we should play with technology in history. What had started as a meeting of academics and teachers, tasked only with writing about that which most excited them, ended with a cogent argument. Why should we play with technology in history? Because doing so enables us to see the past in new ways, by helping us understand how history is created, honoring the roots of research, teaching, and technology development, requiring us to model our thoughts, and then enabling us to build our understanding.

Not incidentally, this approach to technology will also open up history to a wider audience. This was an unstated, though overarching goal of the meeting, and an aspiration for the book. What we hope to support, not just among a small group of dedicated enthusiasts, but across the discipline of history, and the humanities broadly, is "community, relationship, and play." As we reflect on the potential and challenges of incorporating technology into history, we look with expectation to the emergence of innovative, imaginative, engaging ways to communicate the past. Each day new projects are announced that help us to map the past, read and visualize its evidence, and hear its stories. Conversations about history, as demonstrated in this book, must be continual and dynamic. The pace of technology is relentless. The potential for new ideas and insights is unlimited. We do not worry about missing our audience, as I related in the opening pages of this book, because we are all in this sandbox together.

NOTES

1. Founded in 2008 by the Center for History and New Media (now the Roy Rosenzweig Center for History and New Media) at George Mason University, a THAT-Camp, according to the website, "is an open, inexpensive meeting where humanists and technologists of all skill levels learn and build together in sessions proposed on the spot." In the year 2013, THATCamps will be held across the United States and Canada as well as locations as disparate as Wellington, New Zealand; Panama; and Ho Chi Minh City, Vietnam. In 2013 THATCamps were held across the United States and Canada as well as locations as disparate as Buenos Aires, Argentina; Ghent, Belgium; and Wellington, New Zealand. Accessed November 4, 2013, http://thatcamp.org /camps/?region=all&date=2013&s=&groups_search_submit=Search.

Contributors

Timothy Compeau is a Ph.D. candidate at the University of Western Ontario. He studies honor culture and loyalism in Revolutionary North America; his work in public history has focused on how small museums and heritage sites can maximize their potential with digital media.

Dr. Peter Dawson is an Associate Professor of Archaeology in the Department of Archaeology, University of Calgary. He has conducted archaeological and ethnographic fieldwork in the Canadian Arctic for more than twenty years. His research interests include the visualization of archaeological data using 3D computer modeling (with Richard Levy) and using social networking sites to record traditional Inuit knowledge such as place names.

Dr. Patrick Dunae is a Research Associate at Vancouver Island University and Adjunct Associate Professor in the History Department at the University of Victoria. He has worked as a public historian at the BC Archives and the State Archives of Western Australia. He is the editor of the digital archive of Vancouver Island history, *vi.History*.

Devon Elliott is a Ph.D. candidate in history at the University of Western Ontario. His dissertation project focuses on magic tricks and illusions from the late nineteenth and early twentieth centuries. He uses digital fabrication and physical computing to explore the technology of illusions, as well as to create interactive exhibits. He also applies data mining and textual analysis to study the cultural history of magicians. His website is http://devonelliott.net.

Dr. Sean Gouglas is Senior Director of Interdisciplinary Studies in the Faculty of Arts and an Associate Professor in Humanities Computing at the University of Alberta. His research interests include the Canadian video game industry and the role of women in computer games as players, designers, and characters. He is also a Network Investigator and Research Management Committee member for the Graphics, Animation, and New Media (GRAND) Networks of Centres of Excellence.

Dr. Shawn Graham is Assistant Professor of Digital Humanities in the Department of History at Carleton University. Shawn is a Roman archaeologist who uses agent-based modeling and network analyses to explore ancient history. He has taught at all levels from high school to adult continuing education, which sparked his interest in public history and public archaeology. His publications have brought together digital media for teaching and learning, and research in history and archaeology.

Mihaela Ilovan has an MA in Classical Archaeology and is currently completing a joint master's degree in Humanities Computing and Library and Information Studies at the University of Alberta. Her thesis focuses on citation analysis, digital libraries, and humanities visualization.

Dr. Kevin Kee is Associate Vice-President, Research (Social Sciences and Humanities), and the Canada Research Chair in Digital Humanities at Brock University. He has been a Director and Project Director of History New Media at the National Film Board of Canada, and an Assistant Professor and Director of Undergraduate Programs in education at McGill University. He has developed several software projects, led numerous research programs, and published widely on the use of computer simulations and "serious games" for history. He is a recipient of the Journal of the Canadian Historical Association Prize, an Ontario Early Researcher Award, and a Brock University Faculty Teaching Award.

Dr. T. Mills Kelly is Professor of History and an Associate Director of the Roy Rosenzweig Center for History and New Media at George Mason University. He is the author of *Teaching History in the Digital Age* (2013), as well as numerous articles and book chapters about the intersection of historical pedagogy and digital media. His other historical work focuses on modern East Central Europe, especially Czech, Slovak, and Habsburg history. In 2005 he received the State Council of Higher Education in Virginia's Outstanding Faculty Award, the Commonwealth's highest recogniztion of faculty excellence. He was the inaugural winner in the category "Teaching with Technology."

Dr. Matthew Kirschenbaum is an Associate Professor in the Department of English at the University of Maryland and Associate Director of the Maryland Institute for Technology in the Humanities (MITH). A longtime "grognard" or conflict simulation gamer, he is a contributor to the *Play the Past* group blog and specializes in digital humanities, electronic literature, textual studies, and archives. His first book, *Mechanisms: New Media and the Forensic Imagination*, published by MIT Press (2008), won the 16th annual Prize for a First Book from the Modern Language Association (MLA), among other awards. He is currently completing work on a second book entitled *Track Changes: A Literary History of Word Processing*. Kirschenbaum is a 2011 Guggenheim Fellow.

Dr. Stéphane Lévesque is Associate Professor of History Education and Director of the Virtual History Lab at the University of Ottawa. His research focuses on students' historical thinking, Canadian history, and new media and technology in education. Author of *Thinking Historically: Educating Students for the 21st Century* (University of Toronto Press, 2008), Dr. Lévesque has also published numerous book chapters and articles in professional and scholarly journals. Very active in the national history community, he is a board member of Canada's History Society, the Virtual Museum of Canada, and the History Education Network/Histoire et education en réseau. He is the inventor of *The Virtual Historian©*, a computer program to teach Canadian history online. He served as educational expert for the advisory committee on the establishment of the Canadian Museum for Human Rights as well as curriculum expert for the Ontario Ministry of Education. In 2006, he was nominated by the Council of Ontario Universities for the Award for Excellence in Teaching with Technology.

Dr. Richard Levy is Professor of Urban Planning and Adjunct Professor, Department of Computer Science, at the University of Calgary. Dr. Levy is a founding member of the *Virtual Reality Lab* and is a co-director of the Computational Media Design Program at the University of Calgary. Dr. Levy's research focuses on urban planning, archaeology, GIS, virtual reality, serious games, education, and new media. His published work has appeared in journals including the *Journal of Archaeological Science, Internet Archaeology, Journal of Archaeological Science*, the *Journal of Visual Studies, Environment and Planning, Plan Canada, VSMM*, the *Canadian Games Association Journal*, and the *IEEE Journal*.

Shannon Lucky is currently completing a joint master's degree in Humanities Computing and Library and Information Studies at the University of Alberta. Her thesis focuses on real-world ludic spaces.

Dr. John Sutton Lutz is an Associate Professor in the Department of History at the University of Victoria. He is co-director, with Ruth Sandwell and Peter Gossage, of the award-winning *Great Unsolved Mysteries in Canadian History* project (www.canadianmysteries.ca), and Director/Curator of a number of scholarly websites including the *Colonial Despatches* (www.bcgenesis.uvic.ca), *The Governor's Letters* (www.govlet.ca), *Victoria's Victoria* (www.victoriasvictoria.ca), *Fort Victoria Journal* (fortvictoriajounral.ca), and *Auto(mobile) Biographies* (www.autobio.ca). He is the author of *Makuk: A New History of Aboriginal-White Relations*, which won the 2010 Harold Adam's Innis Prize, and the 2009 Clio Award for British Columbia.

Dr. Robert MacDougall is an Associate Professor in the Department of History at the University of Western Ontario and an Associate Director of Western's Centre for American Studies. He studies the history of information, communication, and technology; he is the author of *The People's Network: The Political Economy of the Telephone in the Gilded Age* (University of Pennsylvania Press, 2013). He is a longtime player and sometime designer of tabletop board and role-playing games, and is interested in all varieties of playful historical thinking.

Dr. Jeremiah McCall has taught high school history for more than a decade, mostly at Cincinnati Country Day School. His first professional love is high school teaching, especially designing instructional approaches that will guide students to think as experts in disciplines. He is also a researcher/designer of learning environments that incorporate simulation games to encourage critical inquiry, and recently published *Gaming the Past: Using Video Games to Teach Secondary History* (Routledge, 2011). He has an MA and PhD in ancient history from Ohio State University and has also published two books on Roman history, *The Cavalry of the Roman Republic* (Routledge, 2001) and *The Sword of the Republic: A Biography of Marcellus* (Pen and Sword, 2012).

Dr. Bethany Nowviskie is President of the Association for Computers and the Humanities, Director of the Scholars' Lab and Digital Research & Scholarship Services at the University of Virginia Library, and Associate Director of the Mellon Scholarly Communication Institute. Her research and development work rests at the intersection of algorithmic or procedural method with traditional humanities interpretation. Among her past digital projects and publications are NINES, the Networked Infrastructure for Nineteenth-Century Electronic Scholarship; Neatline, a tool for geo-temporal interpretation of archival collections; and #Alt-Academy, an open access collection of essays by scholar-practitioners in hybrid and nontraditional academic careers.

Dr. Stephen Ramsay is the Susan J. Rosowski Associate University Professor of English and a Fellow at the Center for Digital Research in the Humanities at the University of Lincoln–Nebraska. He splits his time between pontificating about digital humanities, teaching humanities majors to program, undertaking analysis and visualization of text corpora, and designing and building text technologies for humanist scholars. He is the author of *Reading Machines: Toward an Algorithmic Criticism* (University of Illinois Press, 2011).

Silvia Russell is currently completing a master's degree in Humanities Computing at the University of Alberta. Her thesis focuses on territoriality in cyberspace and cyber-warfare.

Dr. Ruth Sandwell is an Associate Professor in the Department of Curriculum, Teaching and Learning at the Ontario Institute for Studies in Education (OISE) at the University of Toronto. In addition to being a social historian of rural Canada, the family, and fossil fuels, she is interested in the intersection of history education and public memory in contemporary Canada. Her most recent book relating to history education is *To The Past: History Education, Public Memory and Citizenship in Canada* (University of Toronto Press, 2006). She is co-editor with Amy von Heyking of an edited collection forthcoming from University of Toronto Press, *Becoming a History Teacher in Canada: Sustaining Practices in Historical Thinking*. She is co-director, with John Sutton Lutz and Peter Gossage, and Educational Director of the history education website series, *Great Unsolved Mysteries in Canadian History*.

Dr. Brenda Trofanenko is the Canada Research Chair in Education, Culture and Community at Acadia University. Her research program spans the disciplines of education, museum studies, and critical pedagogy. She has established an international reputation as a scholar addressing issues of culture, identity formation, and disciplinary knowledge in order to develop a better understanding of the relationships, the intellectual processes, and the material practices and cultural associations that appear in public heritage institutions. She continues to commute between the cornfields of Illinois and the ocean beaches of Nova Scotia.

Dr. William J. Turkel is an Associate Professor of History at the University of Western Ontario and Director of Digital Infrastructure for NiCHE: Network in Canadian History & Environment. He is the author of *The Archive of Place* (University of British Columbia Press, 2007) and *Spark from the Deep* (Johns Hopkins University Press, 2013). His current research includes computational history; Big History; Science, Technology & Society; desktop fabrication; electronics, and physical computing—the design of computer-based systems that interact with people by sensing and controlling the physical world. His research website is http://williamjturkel.net.

Index

ethics, in history, 319–22
exhibits: historically, 67, 76–77; interactive, 189, 191–92, 257–67 passim

fabrication. *See* modeling
feedback: algorithmic, 160; technology, 129, 217, 258; teaching, 217, 285
flow, 9, 275
forums, online discussion, 219–225

game mechanics, 12, 92–93, 123, 126, 130, 162, 229–34, 249, 273–274, 278
game-based learning, 23, 32, 92–93, 121–32 passim, 216–18, 235–51 passim, 273
games: board, 198–213 passim; as artifacts, 12–13, 271–72, 278; learning through development of, 10, 14, 122, 132–34, 225–26, 271, 278–90; modifying, 12, 214; typology of, 276–77. *See also* augmented reality
gender, differences in gaming, 129
Great Unsolved Mysteries in Canadian History, 31–39

hacking culture, 175–76. *See also* modeling
historical models, critique of, in simulation games 234–50
Huizinga, Johan, *Homo Ludens*, 8, 121

immersive environments, 35, 77, 79, 105, 128–29, 131, 230, 272–73. *See also* flow
indigenous peoples, 7, 66–67, 103; dispossession of, 36, 38; heritage of, 77, 82–83, 103, 199, 209–11; racism toward, 36
interactive, 3, 16, 39, 57, 67, 76, 80, 81, 82, 94, 107, 128, 161, 170, 189, 191, 229, 230, 270, 292

Last American Pirate, The, hoax, 314–15
learning activities, 13, 48, 51, 62, 89, 93, 96–97, 99, 105, 240–42, 260–61, 267, 293
learning: with technology, 2, 43–46, 58, 83, 88, 121, 133, 190–91, 275; online,

219–26; playing as, 9–10; problem-based, 246; students', 14, 25, 37, 51–54, 58–62, 180, 229, 241, 260, 263, 270–71, 285–86, 323; *See also* game-based learning
Lee, Peter, 27–28, 58
Levstik, Linda, 27–28, 45, 59
libraries, research in, 114–17, 317–18
linguistics, 142, 155, 157, 158
literacy, historical, 25, 47, 53; test, Ontario, 49–50, 59

making. *See* modding; modeling; prototypes; reconstruction
mapping, 73, 97, 223–25
maps: fire insurance, 14, 299–300; panoramic, 296–97
mash-ups. *See* video mash-ups
material culture, 181–82, 191
micro-history, 31
modding communities. *See* forum, online discussion
modding, as learning experience, 12, 214–16, 272, 278–81; classroom case study of, 281–88
modeling: as learning experience, 11; in humanities scholarship, 176–82; light levels, 73; with technology, 128, 131, 182–90, 299–300
mods. *See* modding
museums, 14, 16, 67, 75–77, 80, 83, 102, 257–60; as pedagogical sites, 259–67

Osborne, Ken, 26, 59
Owens, Edward. *See The Last American Pirate*

participants, 49–50, 54, 59, 76, 87, 122, 127, 131, 215, 217–20, 237, 279
pedagogy, 36, 45, 60–62, 88–89, 258, 261, 293; games as, 93–94, 127–28, 132, 180, 251
performance, 150–155, 159–62
pervasive games, 7, 16, 17, 87–90, 96–102, 105, 106, 270–73, 288, 290–91
photography: as historical evidence, 318; in modelling, 184–84, 292, 294–305; panoramic, 298–300